Lecture Notes in Computer Science 2614

Edited by G. Goos, J. Hartmanis, and J. van Leeuwen

Springer

Berlin
Heidelberg
New York
Hong Kong
London
Milan
Paris
Tokyo

Robert Laddaga   Paul Robertson
Howie Shrobe (Eds.)

Self-Adaptive
Software: Applications

Second International Workshop, IWSAS 2001
Balatonfüred, Hungary, May 17-19, 2001
Revised Papers

Springer

Series Editors

Gerhard Goos, Karlsruhe University, Germany
Juris Hartmanis, Cornell University, NY, USA
Jan van Leeuwen, Utrecht University, The Netherlands

Volume Editors

Robert Laddaga
Howie Shrobe
Artificial Intelligence Laboratory
Massachusetts Institute of Technology
200 Technology Square
Cambridge, Massachusetts 02139, USA
E-mail: {rladdaga/hes}@ai.mit.edu

Paul Robertson
Dynamic Object Language Labs, Inc.
9 Bartelet St. 334, Andover, MA 01810, USA
E-mail: probertson@doll.com

Cataloging-in-Publication Data applied for

A catalog record for this book is available from the Library of Congress

Bibliographic information published by Die Deutsche Bibliothek
Die Deutsche Bibliothek lists this publication in the Deutsche Nationalbibliografie;
detailed bibliographic data is available in the Internet at <http://dnb.ddb.de>.

CR Subject Classification (1998): D.2, F.3, I.2.11, C.2.4, C.3

ISSN 0302-9743
ISBN 3-540-00731-8 Springer-Verlag Berlin Heidelberg New York

Springer-Verlag Berlin Heidelberg New York
a member of BertelsmannSpringer Science+Business Media GmbH

http://www.springer.de

© Springer-Verlag Berlin Heidelberg 2003
Printed in Germany

Typesetting: Camera-ready by author, data conversion by Olgun Computergrafik
Printed on acid-free paper   SPIN 10872899   06/3142   5 4 3 2 1 0

Preface

This volume emanated from a workshop on Self-Adaptive Software held in Balatonfured, Hungary in May 2001. The aim of the workshop was to follow up on the first workshop held in Oxford in April 2000 by bringing together researchers to assess the state of this rapidly developing field with an emphasis on the applications of self-adaptive software.

The papers presented at the workshop were in some cases revised after the workshop. Some of the papers in the collection were not presented at the workshop but were invited for inclusion here.

The first paper in the collection, "Introduction to Self-Adaptive Software: Applications," provides a brief overview of self-adaptive software and a description of the layout of the volume.

June 2002   Paul Robertson

Organizers

Gabor Peceli   (Technical University of Budapest)
Robert Laddaga   (MIT)

Program Committee

Gabor Peceli   (Technical University of Budapest)
Paul Robertson   (Oxford University)
Janos Sztipanovits   (Vanderbilt University)
Howie Shrobe   (MIT)
Robert Laddaga   (MIT)

Table of Contents

Introduction to Self-adaptive Software: Applications

Robert Laddaga, Paul Robertson, and Howie Shrobe

Massachusetts Institute of Technology
Artificial Intelligence Laboratory
{rladdaga,paulr,hes}@ai.mit.edu

Abstract. The second International Workshop on Self Adaptive Software was held on scenic Lake Balaton, in Hungary during May 17–19, 2001. The workshop was sponsored by the Technical University of Budapest, and organized by Gábor Péceli, Head of the Department of Measurement and Information Systems, assisted by Simon Gyula, Senior Lecturer in the department. This book presents the collection of papers delivered at this workshop, along with some related papers, and reports of the workshop activities.

Keywords: Self-adaptive Software, applications, information survivability, embedded software, machine perception, communication protocol

1 Introduction

This volume is the second in a series of proceedings of the International Workshops in Self Adpative Software (IWSAS). The second IWSAS was held in Baltonfured, on Lake Balaton in Hungary, in May of 2001. Self adaptive software is a new field of investigation in the areas of software engineering and cognitive systems.

By self adaptive software, we mean:

Self-adaptive software evaluates its own behavior and changes behavior when the evaluation indicates that it is not accomplishing what the software is intended to do, or when better functionality or performance is possible.

This implies that the software has multiple ways of accomplishing its purpose, and has enough knowledge of its construction to make effective changes at runtime. Such software should include functionality for evaluating its behavior and performance, as well as the ability to replan and reconfigure its operations in order to improve its operation. Self adaptive software should also include a set of components for each major function, along with descriptions of the components, so that components of systems can be selected and scheduled at runtime, in response to the evaluators. It also requires the ability to impedance match input/output of sequenced components, and the ability to generate some of this code from specifications. In addition, DARPA seek this new basis of adaptation to be applied at runtime, as opposed to development/design time, or as a maintenance activity [1].

R. Laddaga, P. Robertson, and H. Shrobe (Eds.): IWSAS 2001, LNCS 2614, pp. 1–5, 2003.
© Springer-Verlag Berlin Heidelberg 2003

A good introduction to the topic can be found in the proceedings of the first International workshop on Self Adaptive Software [2].

2 About the Papers

The papers from the first international workshop on self adaptive software were heavily weighted toward presentation of technologies for self adaptive software. While there is still considerable technology presentation in this second set of papers, they are more heavily weighted in the area of applications of self adaptive software. Accordingly, we have group the papers in the following categories: embedded applications, perceptual applications, communication protocol applications, information survivability, other applications and software technology.

2.1 Embedded Applications

Embedded systems are systems in which computer processors control physical, chemical, or biological processes or devices. Examples of such systems include cell phones, watches, CD players, cars, airplanes, nuclear reactors, and oil refineries. Many of these use several, hundreds, or even thousands of processors. The real-world processes controlled by embedded systems introduce numerous hard constraints that must be met when programming embedded processors. The necessity of monitoring and addressing real world changes (that affect and are affected by the real world constraints) makes the case for self monitoring and self optimizing software. This is the theme of the papers in this group, as well as the visual perception applications of the next group.

In the first paper: "Managing Online Self-Adaptation in Real-Time Environments", by Robert P. Goldman, David J. Musliner, and Kurt D. Krebsbach, the authors present a solution to the problem of how to schedule time for deliberation about changes to make during the operation of a real-time controller. They report on their work at Honeywell on the SA-CIRCA, self adaptive control architecture system.

The next three papers form a subgroup, dealing with the implementation and application of self adaptive software to embedded systems via hierarchical control systems.

The first paper in the subgroup: "An approach to self-adaptive software based on supervisory control", by Karsai, Ledeczi, Sztipanovits, Gyula, Pécelli, and Kovaschazy, presents the basic concepts of self adaptive software, and the hierarchical controller approach to implementation. Next, in: "Constraint-Guided Self-Adaptation" by Sandeep Neema and Akos Ledeczi, the authors utilize explicit, hierarchical models of the design space of an application, to implement self adaptivity. In the third paper: "Model-Based Adaptivity in Real-Time Scheduling", by Arpad Bakay, the author presents an approach to building soft real time controllers. His approach is based on reflective model based computing, and he argues that the cost of computing the on-line changes to the system are offset by the improved scheduling. He provides an example in the form of an autonomous network probe device.

2.2   Perceptual Applications

A second application area that can derive great benefit from a self adaptive approach is the area of perceptual applications. By perceptual applications, we mean those that derive symbolic information about the world from sensor data. Examples include visual data, voice, sound, or radar. Both of the papers in this group are concerned with interpretation of visual data, using probabilistic methods.

The paper: "Adaptive Agent Based System for State Estimation Using Dynamic Multidimensional Information Sources", by Alvaro Soto and Pradeep Khosla of CMU presents a self adaptive approach to dynamically combine multidimensional sensor sources. Individual agents responsible for individual sources combine their information probabilistically, and adaptively.

The second paper in this group: "A Self Adaptive Software Architecture for Image Interpretation" by Paul Robertson, describes a multiagent self adaptive software architecture (GRAVA) for interpreting aerial images. GRAVA utilzes description length as a uniform measure for evaluating agent performance.

2.3   Communication Protocol Applications

Communication protocols are clearly applications that can benefit from self adaptive software approaches. It is already understood that these systems must be extremely robust, and must adapt to severe environmental stresses.

The first paper in the group, "Self Adaptive Protocols", by Katalin Tarney, introduces the notion of a self adaptive protocol and related implementation concepts, and serves as an introduction to the two other papers in this group. The second paper, "FDTs in Self-Adaptive Protocol Specification", by Zsuzsanna Harangozó and Katalin Tarnay discusses Formal Definition Technologies, and their application to communication protocols. In this paper, they present a simple model of a communication protocol, and use two formal definition languages to analyze the protocol.

Finally, in the paper: "Frame-based Self-adaptive Test Case Selection" by Gusztáv Adamis and Katalin Tarnay, mechanisms for improving testing of communication protocols are discussed. In particular, the authors recommend a self adaptive approach to test selection, in order to maximize the benefit of the relatively limited time that can be spent testing protocols. They utilize the WTP (Wireless Transaction Protocol of WAP) as an example of their approach.

2.4   Information Survivability

With the passing of the "Maginot Line" mentality in designing systems to survive information attacks, as well as natural degradation, a more self monitoring, self repairing and self adaptive approach has come to the foreground. The two papers in this group report on this application area.

The first paper in the group: "Model-Based Diagnosis for Information Survivability", by Howard Shrobe, describes the application of self adaptive software to information survivability. In the paper Shrobe manipulates models of software operation, and diagnosis of software corruption.

The second paper: "Exercising Qualitative Control in Autonomous Adaptive Survivable Systems", by Jon Doyle and Michael McGeachie, describes the use of "active trust management" to build autonomous survivable systems. More specifically, it shows how to use qualitative preference specifications to exercise effective control over quantitative trust-based resource allocation.

2.5   Other Applications

The papers in this group all report on self adaptive software for diverse applications.

In the first paper: "Dynamic Change in Workflow-Based Coordination of Distributed Services", by Prasanta Bose and Mark G. Matthews, the authors propose a self adaptive workflow system to ensure that changes to workflow requirements are handled dynamically.

The second paper in the group: "A Smart Spell Checker System", by Deepak Seth and Mieczyslaw M. Kokar, describes a self adaptive approach to an automated spelling checker that learns how order suggested changes based on user feedback.

The third paper in the group: "Design Principles For Resource Management Systems For Intelligent Spaces", by Krzysztof Gajos, Luke Weisman and Howard Shrobe, describes self adaptive resource management technology for an intelligent room equipped with numerous sensors and effectors.

2.6   Self-adaptive Software Technology

Each of the papers in this group describes technologies that are useful for developing and implementing self adaptive software. These technologies form a diverse group from intention management, to probabilistic dispatch. Each of these papers also expresses some degree of philosophical discussion of appropriate methodologies for creating self adaptive software and systems.

The first paper: "Adaptivity in Agent-based Systems via Interplay between Action Selection and Norm Selection", by Henry Hexmoor, investigates the methods by which agents with explicit beliefs, desires and intentions select appropriate actions. It focuses on the creation of social norms, as a form of cooperative action selection in multiagent self adaptive systems.

The second paper in the group: "Probabilistic Dispatch, Dynamic Domain Architecture, and Self Adaptive Software", by Robert Laddaga and Paul Robertson, describes a general approach to self adaptive software called dynamic domain architectures, and focuses on techniques for improving the flexibility of dynamic binding of function calls to methods. Probability and expected value are used to dynamically determine the method to be called.

The third paper: "Self-Modeling Systems", by Christopher Landauer and Kirstie L. Bellman, is about using wrapping technology to build self modeling systems. They describe an ambitious project to build systems with complete models of themselves, as an essential step to creating computational intelligence.

The final paper in the group: "From Wetware to Software: A Cybernetic Perspective of Self-Adaptive Software", by A.G. Laws, A. Taleb-Bendiab, S.J. Wade and D. Reilly, discusses the relationship between the nacent field self adaptive software and the well established field of cybernetics. They also report on the practical application of cybernetic techniques for building self adaptive software in the context of their In-Vehicle Telematics System.

2.7 Concluding Paper

The final paper in the volume, by the editors, discusses the results of three workshop sessions, on:

1. Applications of self adaptive software;
2. Pressing research issues for self adaptive software, and
3. Design patterns for self adaptive software.

Acknowledgements

The editors would like to thank the other members of the program committee: Gábor Péceli, Technical University of Budapest and János Sztipanovits, Vanderbilt University. We would also like to thank Gábor Péceli and Simon Gyula for organizing an excellent workshop at an idealic location.

References

1. R. Laddaga. Self-adaptive software sol baa 98-12. 1998.
2. P. Robertson, R. Laddaga, and H. Shrobe. *Self-Adaptive Software, Volume 1936 Lecture Notes in Computer Science.* Springer-Verlag, 2000.

Managing Online Self-adaptation
in Real-Time Environments

Robert P. Goldman[1], David J. Musliner[2], and Kurt D. Krebsbach[3]

[1] Smart Information Flow Technologies (SIFT), LLC
2119 Oliver Avenue South
Minneapolis, MN 55405
rpgoldman@sift.info
[2] Honeywell Technology Center
MN65-2200
3660 Technology Drive
Minneapolis, MN 55418
musliner@htc.honeywell.com
[3] Lawrence College
Appleton, WI 54912
kurt.krebsbach@lawrence.edu

Abstract. This paper provides a solution to the deliberation scheduling problem for self-adaptive hard real time intelligent control using the
Self-Adaptive Cooperative Intelligent Real-Time Control Architecture
(SA-CIRCA). For self-adaptive software, deliberation scheduling is the
problem of deciding what aspects of the artifact should be improved,
what methods of improvement should be chosen, and how much time
should be devoted to each of these activities. The time spent in deliberation scheduling must be carefully controlled because it is time not
available for the primary self-adaptation task.
We provide a Markov Decision Process (MDP) model for deliberation
scheduling in SA-CIRCA. Directly solving this MDP is not feasible for
even relatively modest domains. We provide a polynomial time greedy
(myopic) approximation algorithm. We evaluate this approximation
against a "gold-standard" provided by the dynamic programming (value
iteration) algorithm for MDPs. Our experimental results show that the
approximation produces competitive solutions very quickly.

1 Introduction

Suppose we have an autonomous aircraft flying a complex mission broken into
several different phases such as takeoff, ingress, target surveillance, egress, and
landing. For each mission phase, the aircraft's control system will have prepared a plan (or controller) specifying particular actions and reactions during
the phase. Now suppose that the autonomous control system onboard this aircraft is self-adaptive: that is, it can modify its own behavior (plans) to improve
its performance. Why might it have to adapt? Perhaps because the mission is
changed in-flight, perhaps because some aircraft equipment fails or is damaged,

R. Laddaga, P. Robertson, and H. Shrobe (Eds.): IWSAS 2001, LNCS 2614, pp. 6–23, 2003.

perhaps because the weather does not cooperate, or perhaps because its original mission plans were formed quickly and were never optimized. In any case, the aircraft's self-adaptive control system is now facing a *deliberation scheduling* problem. It must decide which mission phase's plan to try to improve via self-adaptation, how to improve that plan, and how much time to spend on that self-adaptation process itself.

This deliberation scheduling problem has two strong real-time components. First, the deliberation scheduling process must take into account the time that self-adaptation will require: the value of the adaptation is affected by the time at which it can be produced, and its relationship to alternative uses for that computation time. Second, the deliberation scheduling process itself (i.e., deciding what to think about) consumes time, and hence affects the potential value of self-adaptation.

We are developing the Self-Adaptive Cooperative Intelligent Real-Time Control Architecture (SA-CIRCA) to address precisely this type of domain, including the deliberation scheduling problem [7, 8]. SA-CIRCA is a domain-independent architecture for intelligent, self-adaptive autonomous control systems that can be applied to hard real-time, mission-critical applications. SA-CIRCA includes a Controller Synthesis Module (CSM) that can automatically synthesize reactive controllers for environments that include timed discrete dynamics. This controller synthesis process can occur both offline, before the system begins operating in the environment, and online, during execution of phase plans. Online controller synthesis is used to adapt to changing circumstances and to continually improve the quality of controllers for current and future mission phases.

SA-CIRCA's Adaptive Mission Planner (AMP) is responsible for the highest-level control of an SA-CIRCA agent, decomposing the overall mission into phases while managing the agent's responsibilities (by negotiating with other agents) and its deliberation activity. We are currently developing the AMP's deliberation scheduling functions, emphasizing the real-time aspects of the problem. An experimental SA-CIRCA module uses stochastic models of the controller synthesis process to allocate computational effort to controller improvement across the mission phases. The synthesis process model addresses the first real-time aspect of deliberation scheduling: it attempts to predict how long the controller synthesis process will take for a particular type of improvement for a particular mission phase. This information can then be used in a decision-theoretic estimate of the expected utility for a proposed self-adaptation.

In this paper we address the second real-time aspect of deliberation scheduling, i.e., the time cost of the meta-level decision itself, by developing computationally feasible heuristics that make deliberation scheduling decisions "greedily" but quickly. To assess the performance of these greedy heuristics, we are building somewhat simplified Markov Decision Process (MDP) models of the AMP's deliberation scheduling problem and assessing both the optimal and greedy solution policies. Our preliminary results indicate that these greedy heuristics are able to make high-quality deliberation scheduling decisions in polynomial time, with expected utility measures quite close to the NP-complete optimal solutions.

```
;; to evade simple radar missiles, start the reliable temporal transition
;; and then, after it is done, resume normal path.
(make-instance 'action
               :name "begin_evasive"
               :preconds '((path normal))
               :postconds '((path evasive))
               :delay 10)

(make-instance 'reliable-temporal
               :name "evade_radar_missile"
               :preconds '((radar_missile_tracking T) (path evasive))
               :postconds '((radar_missile_tracking F))
               :delay (make-range 250 400))

(make-instance 'action
               :name "end_evasive"
               :preconds '((path evasive))
               :postconds '((path normal))
               :delay 10)

;; The radar threats can occur at any time.
(make-instance 'event
               :name "radar_threat"
               :preconds '((radar_missile_tracking F))
               :postconds '((radar_missile_tracking T)))

;; If you don't defeat a threat by N seconds, you're dead.
(make-instance 'temporal
               :name "radar_threat_kills_you"
               :preconds '((radar_missile_tracking T))
               :postconds '((failure T))
               :delay 1200)
```

Fig. 1. Example of the CIRCA description of a radar-launched SAM threat.

The SA-CIRCA agent was designed to control mission-critical systems, under time-pressure. In our current experiments, we are working with teams of SA-CIRCA agents controlling simulated Uninhabited Aerial Vehicles (UAVs), on combat missions. SA-CIRCA automatically and dynamically generates hard real-time control programs that are guaranteed to keep the platform safe while it executes the mission. The SA-CIRCA State-Space Planner (SSP) generates these controllers from models of the system's environment, and their guarantees are provided based on control and timing information in those models. For example, the SA-CIRCA UAV has a model of radar-guided SAM threats, containing information about how fast these threats operate (see Fig. 1). Among other things, the model specifies the minimum delay between the UAV's detecting that it has been "painted" by enemy radar, and its destruction by a missile of this type. SA-CIRCA uses this information to ensure that its controllers monitor enemy radar lock-ons frequently enough, and take countermeasures fast enough.

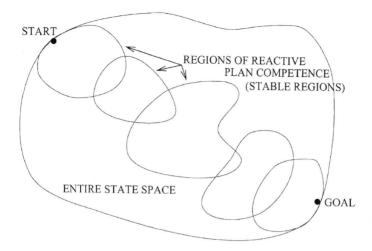

Fig. 2. Decomposition of a mission control problem into multiple single-phase control problems.

SA-CIRCA does not have unlimited resources at its disposal. In particular, it suffers from the problem of *bounded reactivity* [6]: it can only monitor and react to a limited number of threats concurrently. To overcome this problem, SA-CIRCA's Adaptive Mission Planner decomposes extended missions into multiple mission phases, each of which can have a different controller tailored to its particular needs (see Fig. 2). For example, an air mission with high and low altitude components would have different controllers for each. In the high altitude phase the UAV would monitor radar-guided SAM threats, whereas at low altitude these would not be relevant. At low altitudes, on the other hand, the aircraft would be relatively safe from radar-guided SAMs, but would have to guard against shoulder-launched, IR-guided SAMs.

In order to deal with dynamic situations about which we have only limited information, SA-CIRCA is able to tailor its mission phase controllers on line. For example, while in the process of traversing enemy airspace on the way to a target, the agent may be informed of a previously unknown SAM site on its exit path. The agent will generate a new controller for the egress phase of its mission that will be able to handle this threat.

Due to bounded resources, the opportunity of dynamic adaptation poses the corresponding problem of *deliberation scheduling* [1, 4]. The SA-CIRCA agent must determine how best to allocate its limited computational resources to improving controllers for various mission phases. For example, should the agent first improve the controller for the final phase, since it is perceived to be the worst, or should it allocate those resources to polishing the controller for an earlier phase, knowing that it can work on the final phase later? This paper describes our initial work on deliberation scheduling for the SA-CIRCA architecture.

2   The Adaptive Mission Planner (AMP)

The CIRCA Adaptive Mission Planner (AMP) is responsible for the highest-level control of a CIRCA agent [7, 8], determining and modifying the agent's responsibilities (threats to handle, mission goals to achieve), controlling the agent's reasoning (what plans to construct), and managing the agent's deliberation resources (i.e., how best to use computation time to improve the overall mission plan). More specifically, the AMP manages the agent's responsibilities by negotiating with other agents via contract bidding. It controls the agent's reasoning both by modifying problem configurations for the CSM, and by invoking (or halting) the CSM when appropriate. Finally, the AMP manages the agent's deliberation resources by scheduling the CSM to improve certain plans in a manner that yields the highest utility for the mission plan as a whole.

We are working on bringing the planning activity (deliberation) of the Controller Synthesis Module (CSM) under real-time control, so that the Adaptive Mission Planner (AMP) can manage and control that deliberation via a negotiation process. The AMP decomposes the problem into appropriate phases, for which the CSM generates safety-preserving real-time control plans. This planning process is performed prior to execution, and continues as the system is executing other portions of the high-level plan. Together, the AMP and CSM cooperate to effectively allocate this planning effort across the entire high-level plan while meeting intermediate deadlines imposed by execution-time constraints.

2.1   Problem Structure

The overall team mission is divided into *phases*, which correspond to modes or time intervals that share a fundamental set of common goals, threats, and dynamics. For example, our military Unmanned Aerial Vehicle (UAV) scenarios include missions that have phases such as ingress, attack, and egress. The ingress phase is distinguished from the attack phase both by the characteristics of the flight path (e.g., a nap-of-earth stealthy approach vs. a popup maneuver very near a target) and by the expected threats (e.g., the types of missile threats present at different altitudes) and goals (e.g., reaching the target zone vs. deploying a weapon).

2.2   Agent Responsibilities

The team of CIRCA agents must arrange to have different agents take responsibility for different goals and threats, depending on their available capabilities and resources (e.g., ECM equipment and weapons loadout). These goals and threats can vary from one phase to the next, and in fact, the mission is typically split into phases specifically to decompose the overall mission into manageable chunks aligned with a common set of threats, or a common goal which, when achieved, signals the end of that phase.

For each mission phase, the CIRCA agents must have plans, or controllers, that are custom-designed (either before or during mission execution) to execute the mission phase and make the best possible effort to achieve the goals and defeat the threats associated with the phase. The CSM, described elsewhere, is capable of automatically building these controllers, but this controller synthesis can be a complex and time-consuming process. The complexity (and hence duration) of the CSM process can be controlled by varying the *problem configuration* that is passed to the CSM to describe the characteristics of the desired controller for a particular mission phase [5]. The problem configuration contains information about the initial state of the world, goals to achieve, threats that are present, state transitions that can happen due to the world, and actions available to the agent to affect the world. By varying these details, the AMP can make a planning problem fall anywhere in a complexity spectrum from very simple to infeasible.

2.3 Predictive Deliberation Management

Given this, one of the primary responsibilities of the AMP is to determine which mission phase the CSM is trying to build a controller for at any moment, and how hard it should work to do so, by modifying the phase problem configurations. This is what we mean by the AMP's deliberation management function. Our current experiments center around allocating effort to maintain system safety by altering which of the phase's potential threats should be considered, and for how long. In each phase, the more threats that can be handled by improving the current plan for the phase, the better the agent's or the team's survival probability for that phase and for the mission. Thus, the problem can be cast as follows: Given a set of planning phases, quality measures of the current plan for each phase, a set of tradeoff methods (i.e., improvement operators) applicable in each phase, and some amount of time to try to improve one or more of the current plans, how should the AMP allocate the next segment of time to improve the overall expected utility of the mission plan as a whole?

To effectively decide what deliberation should happen now, the AMP must consider the potential deliberation schedule into the future. For example, the AMP might consider starting a lower-priority CSM task earlier if there is a shorter window of opportunity in which to execute that task, or the expected execution time is longer. In this case, the AMP would also need to consider whether it expects that this will still leave time to execute the higher-priority task later. As we will see, more efficient, but incomplete approaches to the problem can suffer from local maxima, and miss solutions that require this type of further lookahead and more complex analysis.

The second part of the problem is to select which of several improvement operators to apply to the phase it has selected. We assume that each improvement operator (deliberation action) takes an equal amount of time (one quanta), and that the same action can be taken in multiple quanta, if applicable to the phase. In general, action selection is only an interesting decision if there are tradeoffs between the various operators. In our current work, there is a tradeoff between the amount of expected improvement (if successful), and the action's probability of success.

3   A Simple MDP Model of the AMP

Our current experiments on deliberation scheduling are based on a Markov Decision Process (MDP) model of the deliberation scheduling problem. We have posed the problem as one of choosing, at any given time, what phase of the mission plan should be the focus of computation, and what plan improvement method should be used. This decision is made based on where the agent is in its mission and a probabilistic measure of the quality of the plan. In our current model, the quality of the plan is measured by how much reward it is expected to achieve, but the distribution of potential rewards among mission phases is fixed. The system improves its expected reward by reducing its likelihood of failure (which eliminates the possibility of future reward attainment).

In the most abstract form, we formulate the CIRCA deliberation scheduling problem as follows: The AMP has decomposed the overall mission into a sequence of **phases**:

$$\mathcal{B} = b_1, b_2, ..., b_n \ . \tag{1}$$

The CSM, under the direction of the AMP, has determined an initial **plan**, P^0 made up of individual state space plans, p_i^0, for each phase $b_i \in \mathcal{B}$:

$$P^0 = p_1^0, p_2^0, ..., p_n^0 \ . \tag{2}$$

P^0 is an element of the set of possible plans, $\mathcal{P}$. In general, it may not be possible to enumerate this set, and it certainly will not be possible to efficiently represent the set. However, we will see that we can usefully reason about classes of plans that are equivalent with respect to a measure of their quality. We refer to a $P^i \in \mathcal{P}$ as the overall **mission plan**. The state of the system, then, may be represented as an ordered triple of time index, the phase in which the agent is currently operating, and the current mission plan:

$$S = \langle t, b_i, P^t \rangle, t \in \mathbb{N}, b_i \in \mathcal{B}, P^t \in \mathcal{P} \ . \tag{3}$$

With some abuse of notation, we refer to the components of a state using operators $t(S), b(S)$ and $P(S)$ for $S \in \mathcal{S}$.

For simplicity's sake, we assume that the duration of each of the mission phases is known, and that the mission phases always occur in sequence. I.e., for each phase, b_i, there exists a known start(b_i), end(b_i) and dur(b_i). Therefore, for a given t we can determine the corresponding mission phase (phase(t)) as the b_i satisfying start(b_i) $\leq t \leq$ end(b_i).

The AMP has access to several **plan improvement methods**,

$$\mathcal{M} = m_1, m_2, ..., m_m \ . \tag{4}$$

At any point in time, t, the AMP can choose to apply a method, m_j, to a phase, b_i (written as $m_j(i)$). Application of this method *may* yield a new plan for mission phase b_i, producing a new P^{t+1} as follows: if

$$P^t = p_1^t, p_2^t, \ldots p_i^t, \ldots, p_n^t \ , \tag{5}$$

then
$$P^{t+1} = p_1^t, p_2^t, \ldots p_i^{t+1}, \ldots, p_n^t , \tag{6}$$

where
$$p_i^t \neq p_i^{t+1} . \tag{7}$$

Note that the application of this method may fail, yielding $P^{t+1} = P^t$. Application of a method never yields a new plan of lower measured quality than the original plan, since if we generate a worse phase plan, we simply discard it and keep the previous one.

Specifically, in CIRCA the available methods are implemented by code which generates a new problem configuration for the AMP to download to the CSM. The CSM will run for a fixed amount of time (a planning "quantum"), and then terminate with a new state space plan, or be interrupted when its quantum has been consumed.

To complete the formulation, we must have a utility (reward) function, U applying to the states. Again, to simplify, we assess the agent a reward, $U(i)$ on the completion of mission phase i. For example, if the aircraft completes its mission successfully and survives, it will receive some reward when completing the final phase. For some missions, it is also appropriate to add some reward to an intermediate phase whose successful completion corresponds to achieving some mission goal (e.g., overflying a reconnaissance target).

Different phases of the mission present different degrees of danger. We represent this by different probabilities of making a transition to a designated failure state. The probability of surviving a given phase is a function of both the hazards posed by that phase, and the quality of the state space plan for that phase. Accordingly, instead of representing the plans explicitly in the system state, S, we need only a vector of survival rates. With some abuse of notation, we will use p_i^t to represent not only the plan itself, but also the associated survival probability, the only aspect of the plan reflected in the MDP. Therefore, the chance of surviving phase i is:

$$\prod_{\text{start}(i) \leq t \leq \text{end}(i)} p_i^t , \tag{8}$$

and the expected reward in phase i is[1]:

$$U(i) \prod_{\text{start}(i) \leq t \leq \text{end}(i)} p_i^t . \tag{9}$$

Given the representation of plans as survival rates, the plan improvement operators are represented as actions that may take us to a state where the survival probability for a given phase is higher than in the current state. We are not yet considering plan improvement operators that increase the likelihood of achieving reward except by avoiding failure.

---

[1] Note that this is not the expected *utility*, which must also take into account the chance of the agent being destroyed in this phase.

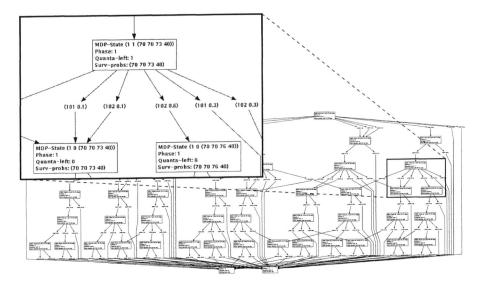

Fig. 3. A very simple AMP MDP for 3 phases with one quantum per phase and one deliberation action choice per phase.

Fig. 3 illustrates a very simple AMP MDP for 3 phases with one quantum per phase and one deliberation action choice per phase. Even this trivial problem forms a space of 43 states, which makes the diagram unreadable on a page. The zoomed area illustrates how the model works: the two edges labeled 102 leaving the uppermost state (1 1 (70 70 73 40)) correspond to the AMP deciding to perform deliberation action 1 on phase 2, which is 60% likely to succeed and result in improvement of the phase 2 survival probability (the right edge to state (1 0 (70 70 76 40))). Ten percent of the time that action is expected to fail, yielding no survival probability improvement (the left edge to state (1 0 (70 70 73 40)) and 30% of the time the system is expected to be destroyed during that deliberation quanta (the rightmost edge leading off the zoomed area, to the failure node.

With these simplifying assumptions, the problem of achieving reward is transformed into one of surviving to complete phases that provide reward. The problem of choosing a deliberation action for each state is limited to choosing which phase of the mission plan to try to improve, and which improvement operator to apply to improve it with. The conventional formulation of an MDP is:

$$\text{policy}^\star(s) = \arg\max_a \sum_{s'} P(s \xrightarrow{a} s')\overline{U}^\star(s') \qquad (10)$$

where a is an action, $P(s \xrightarrow{a} s')$ is the probability of reaching s' from s when the agent executes action a, and $\overline{U}^\star(s')$ is the expected utility of being in state s' while pursuing the optimal policy. With our model of deliberation schedule, we can reformulate the problem as:

$$\text{policy}^\star(s = \langle t, b_k, P^t \rangle) = \arg\max_{i,j} \left((1 - p^t_{b_k}) U(\text{destroyed}) + \right. \tag{11}$$

$$\left. p^t_{b_k} \sum_{s'} P(s \overset{m_j(i)}{\longrightarrow} s') \overline{U}^\star(s') \right)$$

where i corresponds to the choice of phase to be improved and j the choice of deliberation (planning) operator to use to improve that phase. In our state representation, s' will be constrained to be $\langle t+1, \text{phase}(t+1), P^{t+1} \rangle$ where P^{t+1} is identical to P^t everywhere except for (possibly) phase i. Eliminating constants in the above equation, we have:

$$\text{policy}^\star(s) = \arg\max_{i,j} \sum_{s'} P(s \overset{m_j(i)}{\longrightarrow} s') \overline{U}^\star(s') . \tag{12}$$

We have conducted several experiments using this formulation of the problem, directly evaluated using value iteration. We have used a Common Lisp version developed by Peter Norvig and Stuart Russell [9]. As one would expect, performance suffers with problem scale (experimental results are reported in the next section). Accordingly, we have been developing heuristic alternatives to exact evaluation, and comparing the results with optimal policies.

4 Optimal Deliberation Scheduling Agent

The Optimal MDP Agent determines the optimal decision to make in each possible state by employing an algorithm called *value iteration*. The basic idea of value iteration is to calculate the utility of each state by using the utilities of its successor states, and iterating over all states until the policy stabilizes. The Optimal MDP Agent constructs this optimal policy once, and then uses it repeatedly to take action, since the policy accounts for any possible state the agent might encounter.

Unfortunately, value iteration is only a feasible approach when the MDP model is very small. Fig. 4 illustrates how quickly the number of states makes the computation intractable even for very simple MDP representations. This graph show the number of unique states generated by the Optimal MDP Agent for a mission of three phases, where the number of quanta per phase and the number of actions per phase are allowed to vary from 1 to 4.

Fig. 5 similarly demonstrates how the computation time to generate the optimal policy for the set of states increases exponentially with small increases in problem size.

Note that the results shown here assume that the Optimal MDP Agent need only generate the optimal policy *once*. However, if the world dynamics cause the deliberation management problem to change dramatically, then the policy would need to be recomputed. This might occur, for example, if we were to discover a hitherto unknown threat in one of the later phases of the mission. Such recomputations would multiply the computational cost, making the optimal MDP policy

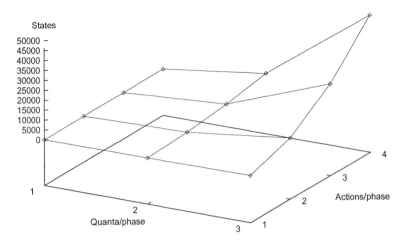

Fig. 4. Number of states generated for simple MDP models.

computation even more expensive than might initially be apparent. Such recomputations do *not* impose such a prohibitive cost on the greedy (myopic) approach we propose. We discuss this alternative approach in the following section.

5   Greedy Deliberation Management Agent

Because the optimal solution to our deliberation scheduling problem quickly becomes intractable, we have investigated a much simpler heuristic mechanism for making dynamic deliberation scheduling decisions. Rather than computing a policy that indicates what actions should be taken in any possible future state to maximize expected utility, the "greedy" agent myopically looks one state ahead along all of its immediate action choices and selects the action that results in the state (mission plan) with the highest expected utility. Since this expected utility computation is necessarily incomplete (because it does not project all future possible paths), the greedy agent is scalable but suboptimal.

Formally, we can say that the greedy policy is expressed in terms of a greedy utility measure $\overline{U}^{(1)}$:

$$\text{policy}^G(s) = \arg\max_{i,j} \sum_{s'} P(s \overset{m_j(i)}{\rightarrow} s')\overline{U}^{(1)}(s') . \tag{13}$$

The conventional utility measure used in the MDP formulation (see Sect. 3) must take an expectation over the future states, which have different plans. The myopic utility function, on the other hand, ignores all future planning, and assumes that the agent will complete the rest of the mission using the next-generated plan. That is, the greedy utility of state $s' = \langle t, b_i, P^t \rangle$ is defined as follows[2]:

---

[2] $\delta_{t=\text{end}(i)}$ is a Kronecker delta function, valued 1 if its argument meets the condition, i.e., when t is the last time point in phase i, and zero everywhere else.

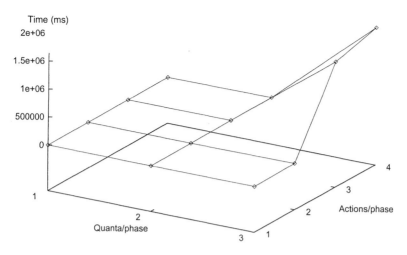

Fig. 5. Time for MDP solver to find optimal policy: note huge Y axis scale.

$$\overline{U}^{(1)}(t, b_i, P^t) = (1 - p_{b_i}^t)U(\text{destroyed}) + \tag{14}$$
$$p_{b_i}^t(\delta_{t=\text{end}(i)}(t)U(i) +$$
$$\overline{U}^{(1)}(t+1, \text{phase}(t+1), P^t) \ .$$

The greedy agent need not compute a complete policy; instead, it computes the policy lazily, determining the action choice for each state only when queried. Because the computation is local, its speed does not depend on the overall size of the MDP. In fact, it scales linearly with the branching factors of the MDP: the number of quanta per phase and the number of alternative operators per quantum. Fig. 6 illustrates the runtime difference between the optimal and greedy agents. The first time the optimal agent is called upon to make a decision, it computes a complete policy and from then on it simply looks up its answer in the resulting hash table. The greedy agent performs its policy^G computation each time it is asked for a decision for a state.

The price for this efficiency is lack of optimality: because the greedy agent is making decisions with limited lookahead, it has trouble assessing the relative merit of addressing near-term vs. far-term risks. For example, it is easy to construct MDP problems with non-monotonic reward profiles that fool the greedy policy into focusing attention on later phases, causing it to miss near-term opportunities for improvement that could be addressed without precluding the later-phase improvements. The "pothole" example illustrated in Fig. 7 illustrates a simple MDP survival probability distribution that dips early in the mission and then falls dramatically later. When assessing the possible actions at an early time in this mission, the simplest greedy policy will recognize the potential for large and important gains in survival probability in the last phase, and will choose to improve that phase first. The optimal policy, on the other hand, will recognize that it has plenty of time during the mission to improve

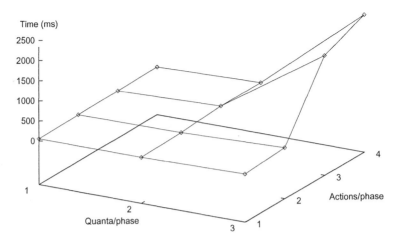

Fig. 6. The greedy agent's runtime performance scales linearly, while the optimal agent is exponential. Note the small Y axis scale, as compared to Fig. 5.

that phase, while the nearer-term dip in survival probability must be addressed quickly to have any effect. Indeed, for this scenario, the expected utility of the optimal policy computed by the MDP is approximately 0.85, while the expected utility of the greedy agent is only 0.63 (utility is normalized to a zero-one range).

To minimize the greedy agent's susceptibility to this effect, we can apply a discounting factor to future improvements. The discount factor captures the fact that there will be more opportunities in the future to perform plan improvements on mission phases that are farther in the future. Assuming that the discounting factor is α, a discounted myopic utility estimate $(\overline{U}_\alpha^{(1)})$ is as follows:

$$\overline{U}_\alpha^{(1)}(t, b_i, P^t) = (1 - p_{b_i}^t)U(\text{destroyed}) + \tag{15}$$
$$p_{b_i}^t(\delta_{t=\text{end}(i)}(t)U(i) +$$
$$\alpha\overline{U}_\alpha^{(1)}(t+1, \text{phase}(t+1), P^t) .$$

The addition of the discounting factor adds only minimally to the cost of computing the greedy action selection, yet improves the performance of the agent considerably. For the "pothole" scenario, with $\alpha = 0.99$, the time-discounted greedy agent's performance is as good as the optimal agent. We conducted a number of experiments on randomly-generated domains, with four mission phases, with initial plans whose survival probabilities for each phase were drawn from a uniform distribution ranging from 80-100%. A plot of the results is given in Fig. 8. The time-discounted greedy agent with $\alpha = 0.99$ performed better than the simple greedy agent in 175 of 287 experiments. Its average loss from the optimal policy was 11% and the average loss of the simple greedy agent was 15.2%.

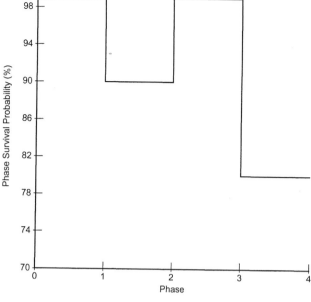

Fig. 7. A non-monotonic initial survival probability distribution that fools a simple greedy heuristic.

6 Related Work

6.1 Anytime Algorithms

To the best of our knowledge, the term *deliberation scheduling* was introduced by Boddy and Dean. There was a great deal of work in this area around the early 1990s by Boddy and Dean [1], Horvitz [4, 3], and Russell and Wefald [10]. These researchers (and others) investigated methods for using decision theory to address the problem of managing computation under bounded resources.

Boddy and Dean [1] categorize deliberation scheduling as being of two sorts: either discrete or anytime. In the discrete case, the agent must choose only *what* procedures to run, since the procedures are assumed to be uninterruptible and their run-times fixed. In the anytime case, procedures are assumed to be continuously-interruptible (anytime), and the agent must choose not only what procedure to run but also *when* and *for how long*.

Boddy and Dean and Horvitz' analyses and prescriptions are not *directly* applicable to the CIRCA deliberation scheduling problem, because they are particularly designed for controlling inference of suites of anytime algorithms. The CIRCA State-Space Planner is not well-suited to treatment as an anytime algorithm because it does not result in relatively continuous, smooth improvement in plans over time. Instead, the CSM acts more as a "batch mode" computation, taking in a particular problem configuration and, in general, returning either a successful plan (controller) or failure, after some amount of time.

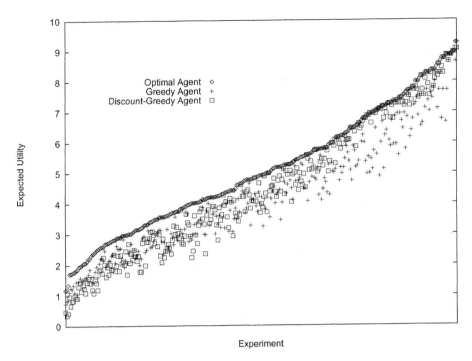

Fig. 8. Results of experiments comparing optimal, greedy and time-discounted greedy agents.

6.2   Rational Metareasoning

Thus our work more closely fits the model proposed by Russell and Wefald (R & W) [10], in being concerned with discrete units of computation, rather than anytime algorithms. Russell and Wefald provide a framework for what they call "Rational Metareasoning." This framework centers around the notion of an agent that is continually trading off between performing some (atomic) computation, and executing a "real" action that will affect its environment.

In this framework, when evaluating a computation, R & W treat it as having two effects on utility. First, it causes time to pass, and thus can incur an opportunity cost. Specifically, it will cause the agent to postpone taking its next "real" action for at least the duration of one computational step. Second, a computation will have some effect on the real actions chosen by the agent. That is, there are two possible outcomes of a computation. The simpler one is that it may change what the agent believes to be the best available action. The more difficult to analyze second case is where the computation does not actually cause a change in action choice, but adds some information to the agent's state. That additional information, in turn, would cause *later* computation to change action choice. We can call this the indirect utility of computation.

Our work fits R & W's framework for analyzing the benefits of atomic computation actions. Our work differs in three important ways. First, we draw on the structure of CIRCA domains to make a specific, survival-oriented utility function, which is relatively easy to compute. Second, our simplified problem does not involve the indirect utility of computation discussed above. In the current model, a quantum of computation will either provide a direct utility, in the form of a new state space plan for a particular phase, or it will produce nothing at all.

The third difference between our work and R & W's is that we are not faced with the problem of trading off deliberation versus action. Because CIRCA was designed to act in hard real-time environments, the CIRCA execution engine (the Real-Time Subsystem) was designed to execute in parallel with the AI subsystem and not to compete for computational resources [6]. So CIRCA deliberation scheduling involves only tradeoffs between alternative *planning* activities, not between planning and action.

The first two simplifications mean that it is trivial to estimate the value of a single quantum of computation in our model. The simplifications, however, impose a cost on the performance of our agents. In particular, it is never possible for our agents to gain the benefit of any computation that takes more than a single quantum of time. Future work will be aimed at relaxing this restriction. This relaxation will correspond to allowing the AMP to "resume" or "continue" controller synthesis tasks that it has already started in a prior deliberation quantum.

6.3   Design to Criteria

Another closely related stream of research includes the "design-to-time" (DTT) [2] and "design to criteria" (DTC) [11] efforts, which consider agent deliberation scheduling in the context of TAEMS task models. These task models capture some of the characteristics of our AMP problem (e.g., alternative atomic deliberation actions, success probabilities) and also can include more complex aspects such as task decomposition, interdependencies, and resource constraints. The DTT and DTC techniques use heuristics to build satisficing schedules for a full sequence of future activities; in contrast, our current approach to the AMP deliberation scheduling problem has emphasized bounded-time methods to return a single decision about the next deliberation action to take. In principle, we could model our problem in TAEMS and compare the current DTC system against our more myopic heuristics. If the software is available and compatible, this may prove a profitable avenue for future investigation.

6.4   Future Work

In this paper, we concentrate our attention on the AMP's management of the Controller Synthesis Module's deliberation. However, in general, we plan to endow the AMP with broad power and responsibility, requiring more extensive and sophisticated reasoning capabilities which intelligently consider more aspects of realistic problem domains. As examples, we plan to expand the set of techniques to adjust the CSM problem complexity by explicitly bringing goals under control, enable agents to negotiate to intelligently off-load burdens to other agents, and allow the AMP to add and remove control actions from the set available to each agent (for example, to make a plan feasible, or to force a plan to be more efficient).

Even within the scope of deliberation management, we plan to incorporate a much richer set of problem configuration modification operators with varying characteristics. For example:

Time Horizons: In many cases, the AMP can simplify a CSM planning problem by exploiting the observation that the resulting plan only needs to guarantee safety for a bounded time period (i.e., up to a *horizon*). For example, if the AMP knows that it already has (at least) a default plan to switch to after a certain length of time spent in the current plan, the CSM need not plan for any states that cannot possibly be reached within that horizon. We call the horizon *admissable* if the AMP can *guarantee* that it will swap in a new plan within the horizon (e.g., if an action to transition into the new plan will definitely be taken within some time bound). If the horizon is admissable, then imposing a time horizon on the CSM planning does not compromise safety, and the improvement is an optimization, rather than a tradeoff. The inadmissable case is a tradeoff with some likelihood of finding the agent in an unhandled state (beyond the horizon).

Timing Modifications on Temporal Transitions: CIRCA has traditionally always considered the worst-case time for temporal transitions to move the world from state to state. However, in overconstrained domains, this assumption can lead the CSM to conclude there is no safe plan. In situations where the likelihood of temporally transitioning at the earliest possible time is very low, a tradeoff can be made to modify (lengthen, in this case) the temporal transition time. Of course, if the transition occurs outside of the modified interval, safety is not guaranteed.

Minimal Regions of Competence: In the problem configuration, the AMP can specify how "goal-achieving" it wants the CSM to be as it generates a plan. Then, as the CSM is faced with decisions over which action to choose in each state, it can choose actions that increase the probability of goal achievement, or prefer to "bend back" into a state that has already been generated (and handled). The latter preference decreases the complexity of the planning problem by minimizing the set of states the CSM must plan for. In general, safety is not compromised with this method, but goal achievement might be.

Systematic Search for Feasible Problem: The AMP must know what to do when the CSM returns with no feasible controller, or does not return a controller in an acceptable amount of time. One solution is to have the AMP heuristically decide how to simplify the problem configuration in a systematic way, essentially searching for the highest-utility problem configuration for which the CSM can find a feasible plan.

Acknowledgments

The work described here was done at Honeywell Technology Center.

This material is based upon work supported by DARPA/ITO and the Air Force Research Laboratory under Contract No. F30602-00-C-0017. Any opinions, findings and conclusions, or recommendations expressed in this material are those of the authors and do not necessarily reflect the views of DARPA, the U.S. Government, or the Air Force Research Laboratory.

Thanks to Mark S. Boddy for guiding us gently into the literature on deliberation scheduling. Any misprision is entirely our own fault.

Thanks to Steven A. Harp for advice on experimental design and statistical hypothesis testing.

Thanks to Peter Norvig and Stuart Russell for the implementation of value iteration from their book, *Artificial Intelligence: A Modern Approach* [9].

References

1. M. Boddy and T. Dean, "Decision-Theoretic Deliberation Scheduling for Problem Solving in Time-Constrained Environments," *Artificial Intelligence*, 1994.
2. A. Garvey and V. Lesser, "Design-to-time Real-Time Scheduling," *IEEE Transactions on Systems, Man, and Cybernetics*, vol. 23, no. 6, pp. 1491–1502, 1993.
3. E. Horvitz, G. Cooper, and D. Heckerman, "Reflection and action under scarce resources: Theoretical principles and empirical study," in *Proceedings of the 11th International Joint Conference on Artificial Intelligence*, pp. 1121–1128. Morgan Kaufmann Publishers, Inc., 1989.
4. E. J. Horvitz, "Reasoning under varying and uncertain resource constraints," in *Proceedings of the Seventh National Conference on Artificial Intelligence*, pp. 111–116, Los Altos, CA, 1988, Morgan Kaufmann Publishers, Inc.
5. D. J. Musliner, "Imposing Real-Time Constraints on Self-Adaptive Controller Synthesis," in *Lecture Notes in Computer Science*, number 1936, Springer-Verlag, 2001.
6. D. J. Musliner, E. H. Durfee, and K. G. Shin, "CIRCA: A Cooperative Intelligent Real-Time Control Architecture," *IEEE Transactions on Systems, Man and Cybernetics*, vol. 23, no. 6, pp. 1561–1574, 1993.
7. D. J. Musliner, E. H. Durfee, and K. G. Shin, "World Modeling for the Dynamic Construction of Real-Time Control Plans," *Artificial Intelligence*, vol. 74, no. 1, pp. 83–127, March 1995.
8. D. J. Musliner, R. P. Goldman, M. J. Pelican, and K. D. Krebsbach, "SA-CIRCA: Self-adaptive software for hard real time environments," *IEEE Intelligent Systems*, vol. 14, no. 4, pp. 23–29, July/August 1999.
9. S. Russell and P. Norvig, *Artificial Intelligence: A Modern Approach*, Prentice Hall, 1995.
10. S. Russell and E. Wefald, "Principles of Metareasoning," in *First International Conference on Principles of Knowledge Representation and Reasoning*, pp. 400–411. Morgan Kaufmann Publishers, Inc., 1989.
11. T. Wagner, A. Garvey, and V. Lesser, "Criteria-Directed Task Scheduling," *International Journal of Approximate Reasoning*, vol. 19, no. 1–2, pp. 91–118, 1998.

An Approach to Self-adaptive Software Based on Supervisory Control

Gabor Karsai[1], Akos Ledeczi[1], Janos Sztipanovits[1], Gabor Peceli[2],
Gyula Simon[2], and Tamas Kovacshazy[2]

[1] Institute for Software-Integrated Systems
Vanderbilt University
Nashville, TN 37235, USA
{gabor,akos,sztipaj}@vuse.vanderbilt.edu
[2] Department of Measurement and Information Systems
Technical University of Budapest, H-1521 Budapest, Hungary
{peceli,simon,khazy}@mit.bme.hu

Abstract. Self-adaptive software systems use observations of their own behavior, and that of their environment, to select and enact adaptations in accordance with some objective(s). This adaptation is a higher-level system function that performs optimizations, manages faults, or otherwise supports achieving an objective via changes in the running system. In this paper, we show how this capability can be realized using techniques found in hierarchical control systems, and we discuss interrelated issues of stability, assurance, and implementation.

1   Introduction

Self-adaptive software seems to offer novel capabilities that are very hard to achieve using other methods. Software that adapts itself to momentary situations and requirements is envisioned as the vehicle for building complex applications that are robust and fault-tolerant, yet flexible and responsive. Robustness and fault-tolerance is typically achieved by software redundancy and exception management, although purely software-based fault tolerance is yet to be demonstrated in a practical situation. Flexibility and responsiveness is typically achieved by explicitly "designing in" all the alternatives in the system, and verifying that the system reacts properly in each situation. Unfortunately, the (somewhat) contradictory requirements of robustness and flexibility impose a big burden on the designer, as there is no established design approach and technique for self-adaptive software systems.

Self-adaptivity causes further problems. The complexity of today's systems makes it very difficult to explicitly enumerate (and verify) all states of a system, although we must do this for some applications [1]. If the system also exhibits self-adaptive behavior, the situation gets even worse as it is very hard to predict what a system will do if it can modify its own behavior and/or structure. To draw a parallel from control theory, it took about 20 years to prove a simple property: stability about adaptive controllers [2]. The point is that when a systems' behavior space is enriched by another dimension: adaptivity, it becomes extremely difficult to formally analyze that space.

We can recognize that unrestricted adaptivity may be just a new name for self-modifying code. However, restricted, well-designed, and engineered adaptivity is

R. Laddaga, P. Robertson, and H. Shrobe (Eds.): IWSAS 2001, LNCS 2614, pp. 24–38, 2003.

something worth considering, and it is a prime candidate for addressing the needs of robustness and flexibility mentioned above. According to our knowledge, the only engineering field that deals with engineered adaptivity is adaptive control theory [3]. In this paper, we show how techniques invented by control theorists and engineers can be applied to design and implement self-adaptive software, and what type of lessons control engineering teaches us.

2   Background

Control theory and engineering has been using adaptive techniques since the 1960s [3]. The prevailing principle for adaptive control is as follows. When a particular controller is designed for a system, the engineer makes certain assumptions about the dynamics of the plant. These assumptions may not hold over the lifetime of the deployed system, and the controller may not work optimally when circumstances change. Hence, an adaptation component is introduced that revises (re-tunes) the controller as the system operates by recalculating controller parameters. There are three major techniques for adaptive control [4]: gain scheduling, model-reference adaptive control, and self-tuning control. In each of these cases, adaptation is parametric (i.e. non-structural). In adaptive controllers, there are two, interlinked feedback loops: one is the usual feedback loop between the plant and the controller, while the other loop contains the adaptation component, which receives data from the plant, and configures the main controller by setting its parameters. Figure 1 illustrates the generic architecture of adaptive control: the adaptation mechanism can use measurements of the plant as well as the control signals generated by the regulators.

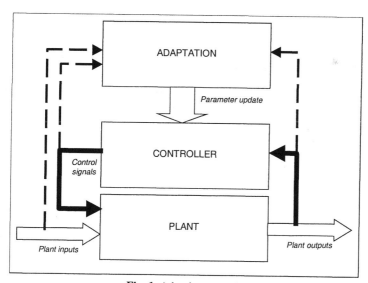

Fig. 1. Adaptive control

The typical technique for achieving stability and convergence in the adaptive system is to use much larger time constants in the outer loop than in the inner loop, i.e.

the adaptation process is much slower than the plant. Interestingly, it took a relatively long time to establish the mathematical framework for analyzing and proving the stability property of adaptive controllers. Adaptive control makes (at least) two important contributions to self-adaptive software: (1) the adaptation mechanism should be explicit and independent from the "main" processing taking place in the system, and (2) the overall system dynamics should be different for the adaptation mechanism and the main processing mechanism.

While adaptive control introduces a second layer in control, supervisory and hierarchical control techniques [5] bring this concept to full implementation. For the sake of brevity, we will consider only supervisory control here (which we view as a special case of hierarchical control). In systems that use supervisory control, the control function is implemented in two, interdependent layers. The lower layer implements the regulatory function, and it typically contains simple regulators that keep process variables under control. The higher level, supervisory control layer is responsible for maintaining overall operational control, and it implements higher-level, goal-oriented, often discrete control behavior. Figure 2 illustrates the architecture of systems using supervisory control.

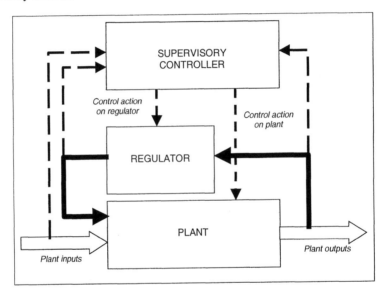

Fig. 2. Supervisory control

The supervisory controller can interact both with the regulatory controller layer and the plant. When interacting with the regulator, it may change setpoints and gains, as it may reconfigure the structure of the controllers. When interacting with the plant, it may perform reconfiguration and/or execute other discrete control actions. Note that the regulators must have their own thread of execution (as they are operating directly on the sampled data), while the supervisory logic must also have its own thread (as complex decision making can – and should – be rarely performed between two samples). The supervisory control approach contributes the following concept to self-adaptive software: higher-level, goal-oriented decision-making that leads to reconfiguration done in a separate layer and thread.

Note that both the adaptive and supervisory control approaches are clear examples of a powerful technique used in (software) engineering: the separation of concerns [6]. The technique simply states that one shall place different concerns into different components, address the concerns independently, and rely on some "generic interface" to combine the pieces. In the controllers above, that primary regulatory function happens on the lower level, while the higher level addresses the issues of optimization, discrete decision-making, and fault accommodation. This "componentization" of concerns will serve well in self-adaptive software as well.

Obviously, controllers using adaptation or supervisory layers are naturally suitable for implementing systems that exhibit adaptivity. However, in typical situations both the adaptive and supervisory mechanisms are designed to follow some principles and observe constraints. For adaptive control, the designer performs careful analysis and puts limits on the adaptation (e.g. limits on controller gains) to avoid undesired evolution in the adaptive system. For supervisory control, the designer "maps out" the entire discrete state-space of the supervisory controller. Furthermore, if the supervisory component is used to mitigate the effects of anticipated faults, all behaviors are (or must be) very carefully analyzed. This makes the design and implementation of these sophisticated controllers rather difficult. However, the potential advantages of a well-separated, higher-level layer in implementing controllers arguably outweigh the costs in most applications.

3   Supervisory Control for Self-adaptive Software

The principles and techniques invented in supervisory control offer a natural architecture for implementing self-adaptive software systems. Figure 3 below illustrates this canonical, generic architecture.

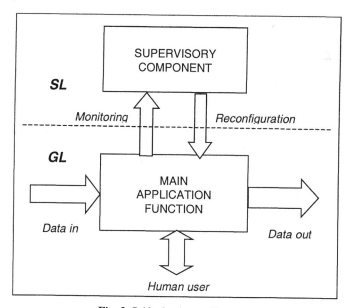

Fig. 3. Self-adaptive architecture

The obvious conclusion is that one can build a self-adaptive software system using "ground-level" (GL) layer that includes baseline processing and using a "supervisory-level" (SL) layer that is responsible for the adaptation and reconfiguration. The two layers address separate concerns: one is the tuned for baseline functionality and performance, while the other one is tuned for optimization, robustness, and flexibility. On the ground-level one can create components that are highly optimized for specific situations, while the supervisory-level will have to recognize what situation the system is in, and select the most optimal component.

The introduction of SL solves the simultaneous requirements of robustness and flexibility as follows. The designer can naturally prepare and encode a large degree of flexibility in the system by using architectural templates. By "architectural template", we mean a pattern, where alternative implementations are allowed for a particular function in the system. The designer may place all potential implementations into the GL, and select one of them for the initial state of the system. As the system's lifetime progresses, the SL may decide that another implementation is needed, and may chose to reconfigure to another implementation. Note that the alternative component is already present in the system: it is merely dormant. The reconfiguration is a form of adaptation, where the running system, the GL, is adapted to a new situation. When it is performed, the system is switched to a new component, and it continues operating. Note that a capability is needed for the very flexible configuration of components and systems. In fact, during run-time we need to replace entire component sub-trees, and silently switch over the functionality to the new implementation. Note also that by separating the concern of configuration from the concern of functionality we can actually build a simpler and more compact system than if these two concerns were addressed in one layer only.

To address the issue of robustness the designer can follow well-established engineering techniques by introducing explicit fault accommodation logic in the SL. In current software, exception handling is often an afterthought, if it is done at all. By making exception handling explicit in the SL, and forcing the designer to explicitly address exceptions in the logic, one can prepare the system for various fault scenarios. Fault accommodation logic means that the SL is made sensitive to exceptions generated by the GL, and the designer has the means of taking supervisory actions to mitigate the effects of those faults. The SL may also incorporate diagnostics functions if the exceptions do not easily map to failure modes of components in the system. The main goal of diagnosis is fault isolation based on detected discrepancies, down to specific components and their failure modes. Run-time diagnosis of software faults is a somewhat novel area, but if self-adaptation is to be used for achieving robustness in systems, it has to be addressed. The supervisory actions for the fault-tolerance are similar to the ones used in addressing flexibility: components (and sub-trees of components) may have to be replaced.

A common problem in reconfigurable systems is the size of the configuration space of components. It is easy to see that if one is using a hierarchical structure, where on each level of the component tree multiple implementations are allowed, the size of the space of configurations grows very rapidly. Figure 4 illustrates the problem: if the components in the middle layer allow multiple implementations (3, 2 and 3, respectively) the simple diagram has 18 different configurations. In real-life systems, it is not unusual to have 4-5000 components [7]. The configuration space spanned by these components is obviously astronomical. It is not obvious how we can manage, let alone build systems with configurations of this size.

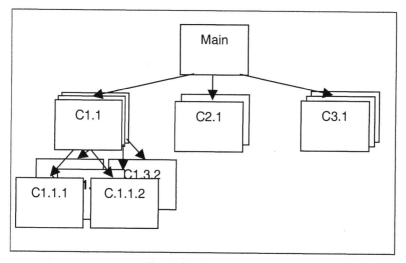

Fig. 4. Configuration space

Note that we don't have to store all the configurations in the system. We must store the components classes, such that we can quickly manufacture instances when needed, but only the active configuration is needed for functioning. The configuration space can be represented symbolically using a technique we describe later, such that when the SL decides on a new configuration it can quickly be instantiated.

4 Designing with the Supervisory Control Layer

Systems with a separate supervisory layer can be designed using well-established techniques, but the designer always have to consider the two-level nature of the architecture in these systems. For each class and component of the system, one has to answer the question: does this belong to the GL or to the SL? The purpose of GL is computation and functionality for the final application, so its capabilities and performance is the one that ultimately determines the success of the system. The purpose of SL is to provide flexibility and robustness, so its capabilities help ensuring the services provided by GL, but they alone will not directly implement application functionality. The designer also has to ask: is this a management function or is this an application function? The answer to this question will decide to what layer the function belongs.

When designing the SL, the designer has to anticipate "failures" in the GL. By "failure", we mean here both failures in the performance space and failures in the function space. Examples for failures in the performance space are: required accuracy in numerical computations was not achieved, or speed of computing results was not sufficient. Examples for failures in the function space are: the component has crashed, or the component has executed an illegal access. The SL has to have an ingredient: the "monitor" or "evaluator" that detects these failures and informs the supervisory logic about them. The monitor should have access to components in the GL, possibly all the data-streams connecting these components, and should be able to "tap into" the interaction patterns among components. Monitors may also be quite complex in order to detect performance degradation.

The GL/SL separation also imposes some design requirements on the components of the GL and run-time infrastructure. In order to monitor all interactions among components in the GL, all these interactions must happen through "channels" that can be accessed from the SL. Figure 5 illustrates the concept.

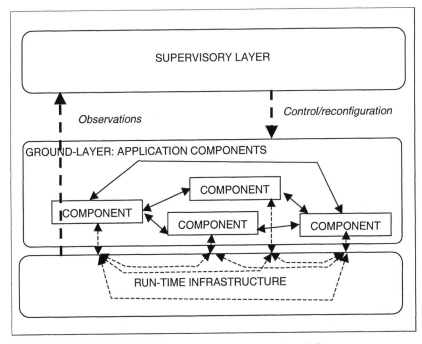

Fig. 5. Integration of SL and GL via the run-time infrastructure

The GL component interactions should be implemented via the services provided by the run-time infrastructure (RTI), and the infrastructure must provide access to these interactions from the SL. On the diagram, the solid lines among the components denote the logical interactions among the components. In reality, the components interact with each other via the run-time infrastructure, as shown with the dashed lines. The SL should be able to access these data streams in order to support the monitoring function. Furthermore, the run-time infrastructure must be able to catch exceptions generated by components and provide them for the SL.

In order to facilitate GL component interactions via the run-time infrastructure, the components have to be implemented in a way such that it is not physically dependent on other components it interacts with. Direct component interactions, like object method calls are to be replaced with communication via the infrastructure. Direct or indirect references, like pointers or CORBA [8] IOR-s to other components are to be replaced by logical links that are mapped via the RTI. This requirement also implies that all interactions will have to be precisely documented and modeled, in order to verify the correctness of component configurations.

The supervisory logic implements adaptation as follows. When the monitoring subsystem detects a need for change, the SL will change the parameters or the structure of the GL. When the structure is modified, a set of components of the running system is replaced with other components. This brings up some interesting questions about the verification of structurally adaptive systems. If the component configurations are encoded as hierarchies, with multiple alternatives on each level (like Figure 4), how can we ensure overall consistency of the system under all potential configurations? If we reconfigure in one part of the system, how will this be made consistent with configuration decisions in other regions? As it was discussed above, the configuration space is potentially huge, and the designer needs to have the capability to verify configurations, or, at least, specify undesirable configurations that the system must never reach. For high-confidence systems, it is desirable to have tool support for exploring the configuration space at design time to verify assurance.

5   Modeling and Analysis on the SVC Layer

The approach described above easily maps into the use of high-level models in the design process [9], and the use of model-based generation wherever feasible. The modeling must happen on two levels: on the GL, where components and component configurations are represented, and on the SL, where the supervisory control logic is captured.

The modeling on the GL has to offer capabilities similar to those usually available in modern CASE environments, like Rational Rose [10]. However, UML in itself is not sufficient. On the GL, one has to create architecture models that capture component instances, their properties and their interactions. UML supports modeling of software artifacts in the form of class diagrams, interaction diagrams, and others, but seems to lack sophisticated facilities for modeling architectures. Another issue is that modeling on the GL has to happen in conjunction with a component integration infrastructure. If, for instance, CORBA [8] is used as the run-time infrastructure, all component integration has to happen via the object broker, and the designer must explicitly be made aware of this fact. If components have internal structure, which they do not expose to the system level, intra-component communication does not need the services of the RTI. Obviously, this type of communication can be made very efficient. The two interaction types should be clearly distinguished in the design.

The modeling on the SL has to capture the supervisory logic of the self-adaptive application. One natural, well-known, and powerful way of capturing supervisory logic is to use the Statecharts notation [11]. Supervisory logic involves mostly discrete decision making, and the hierarchical parallel finite-state machine (HFSM) approach of Statecharts offers a natural way to capture this logic. Better still, a number of modeling tools are available. A supervisory layer can be implemented as shown on Figure 6.

The figure also shows an example HFSM. It has two, OR-states: A and B, A being the initial state. B is decomposed into two AND-states: B1 and B2. B1 contains two OR-states: C11 and C12, C11 being the initial state. B2 contains three states: C21, C22, and C23, with C22 as the initial state.

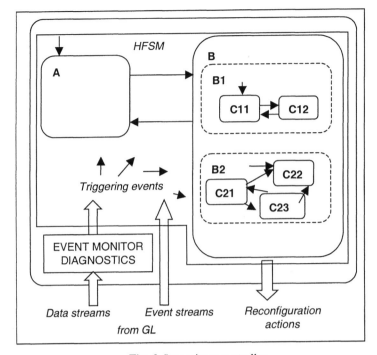

Fig. 6. Supervisory controller

In the modeling language of Statecharts, the basic building block is a state, which may contain other states, called sub-states. The sub-states of a state can be of type AND-state or OR-state. The sub-states of a parent state must be homogeneous: all of the sub-states must be of the same type. From among the OR-states precisely one can be active at any time (i.e. the FSM is "in" exactly *one* of those states). On the other hand, the FSM is "in" *all* of the AND type sub-states of the parent state, when the parent state is active. This latter situation is achieved by having multiple, concurrent FSM-s being active simultaneously.

A HFSM consist of states and transitions. Events trigger transitions among states, and the transitions can be enabled by conditions called *guards*. If a guard enables a transition, and a corresponding event is active, then the transition is taken. During the transition, the HFSM can execute an *action*. A triggering event is either generated by the event monitor, or it can be generated by a time-related function. Two examples for time-related functions are as follows:

- `after(Event,TimeValue)`
- `every(TimeValue)`

The first variant represents a triggering event, which goes active `TimeValue` units after the `Event` went active. The second variant represents a "clock": a triggering event with a fixed period: `TimeValue`. This time-triggered behavior allows initiating adaptation synchronized to time.

The supervisory layer can trigger reconfiguration actions, but it can also make parametric changes in the components of the GL. Both of these changes are facilitated through action expressions. In the HFSM, each state transition has three associated expressions: the guard, event, and action expression. The event expression is mandatory, while both the guard and the action expressions are optional.

A guard expression is a Boolean valued formula, which enables the transition to happen. A guard expression can refer to variable values that are calculated in the GL, or to states, etc., as specified in the Statechart documentation. Event expressions refer to specific events and follow the Statechart conventions with the addition mentioned above: event expressions can contain the `after(E,T)` and `every(T)` clauses as well.

There are two types of action expressions: (1) actions that influence the HFSM, and (2) actions that interact with the GL. The actions of the first type are similar to the ones available in Statecharts. Actions that modify the GL values can be, for instance:

- `set(Component, Attribute, Value)`
  Set the value of an attribute of a component in the GL.
- `send(Component, Message)`
  Send a message to a component in the GL.

The following actions are related to reconfiguration performed on the GL.

- `configure(Component, Configuration)`
  Select a configuration for a component. This action can be attached only to a state, and never to a transition. Strictly speaking, it is not an action, rather an assertion, which declares that when the state is active, a particular configuration of components is active.
- `select(Component, SelectorProcedure)`
  Select a configuration for a compound via a selector procedure. This action can be attached only to a state, and never to a transition. Strictly speaking, it is not an action, rather an assertion. It declares that when the state is entered, the selector procedure is invoked which will choose a particular configuration for the component.
- `construct(Component, ConstructorProcedure)`
  Generate a configuration for a GL component via a constructor procedure. This action can be attached only to a state, and never to a transition. Strictly speaking, it is not an action, rather an assertion. It declares that when the state is entered, the constructor procedure is invoked which will dynamically generate a particular configuration for the component.
- `strategy(Strategy)`
  Select a reconfiguration strategy. This action can be attached only to a transition, and never to a state. Strictly speaking, it is not an action, rather an assertion, which declares that when the transition is executed, a particular reconfiguration strategy is to be used.

The supervisory layer supports the reconfiguration on the component layer as follows. The reconfiguration is broken down into three phases: (1) determining the new component architecture, (2) calculating the parameters of the new architecture (if needed), and (3) switching from the currently active component architecture to the new architecture. There are three cases for determining the new component architecture.

1. The designer supplies component architecture alternatives for each situation and the supervisory logic simply selects from them based on input data. The input data may be data from the running components, measured performance data, fault information, etc.

2. The designer supplies controller alternatives and a *selector procedure*, which, possibly via complex calculations, determines which alternative to choose given input data.
3. The designer supplies a *construction procedure*, which, given input data, will dynamically calculate the topology of the new controller.

In the first two cases, the designer must supply component configurations, via architectural templates. An architectural template enumerates a set of structural alternatives.

The models for the supervisory layer capture these reconfiguration activities and options as follows. In each application that needs reconfiguration, the designer should build separate, parallel HFSM-s describing the reconfiguration logic. In the states of these HFSM-s, the designer can introduce `configure()` actions to declare what configuration is active in that state. Alternatively, the designer can use `select()` or `construct()` actions to facilitate the selection or dynamic construction of a configuration. The `strategy()` actions can be attached to state transitions, and they indicate that when switching from the current configuration into a new one, what kind of reconfiguration strategy is to be invoked. Figure 7 illustrates the technique for modeling reconfiguration with a (H)FSM. The example shows two states that use different alternatives (`alt1` and `alt2`) for a component (`c1`), and use two different strategies depending on the switching direction (`X` and `Y`).

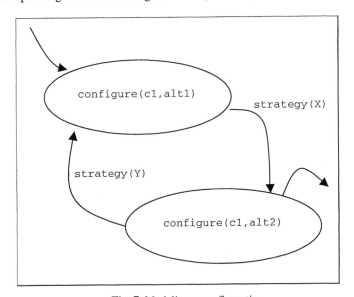

Fig. 7. Modeling reconfiguration

Naturally, using the approach of `configure()` is the simplest: the designer specifically selects the new architecture. The `select()` approach is somewhat more sophisticated: the designer can supply a complex decision making procedure that may perform some sophisticated reasoning to come up with the "best" new architectural alternative. The input to this reasoning process can be arbitrarily complex (e.g. performance data about the running system or fault data), but the selection is still made from a finite, pre-specified set of alternatives. The most sophisticated (and difficult) option is when the construct() action is applied: the designer has to supply a generative model [12] that, when executed, will synthesize the new architecture on the fly.

The supervisory layer can also be interfaced with a fault diagnostics system. A fault diagnostic system can be considered as a sophisticated event monitor that not only detects fault events in the GL, but also maps those events to specific components and their failure modes[1]. This interface is necessary for being able to model and implement *fault accommodation logic* with the supervisory layer. Imagine a scenario where the GL develops a fault, for example a component is generating bad data. The designer of the supervisory layer anticipates this situation, and wants to prepare the supervisory layer to manage the fault scenario by introducing changes in the GL. This portion of the supervisory control logic is called fault accommodation logic.

The interface between the fault diagnostics and supervisory layer is unidirectional: the fault diagnostics system supplies data and triggering events to the supervisory controller. The output of the diagnostic system is a *diagnostic event*. There are two types of diagnostic events:

- Fault detection events (that signal the presence of faults)
- Fault source identification events (that indicate the location of the fault)

Fault detection events (FDE) indicate a problem with a specific variable: for instance, a data stream in the GL. Usually, an FDE is triggered before the detailed diagnostics, and can be used as an early indicator of an incipient (or already existing) fault.

Fault source identification events (FSIE) indicate problems with specific components in the GL. They can be associated with requirement violations by components, or actual failure modes. An FSIE is activated after the diagnostics has reached the conclusion and identified the source of a fault. The source can be scoped to a component's failure mode or just to a component, or both. Thus, the FSIE activation is an indication of an existing fault.

The resulting events can be used in the HFSM to trigger transitions (thus initiate reconfiguration), but event information may also be passed into the decision-making procedures used in the select() and construct() actions. This gives rise to the opportunity to directly base the details of the reconfiguration decision on the circumstances that triggered the reconfiguration (i.e. the fault).

The strategy() action mentioned above has a very significant task: it provides a procedural description for the reconfiguration. It is very rare when software components can be simply removed and inserted into a running system. For instance, the procedure for reconfiguration may require the instantiation of the new architectural component, its initialization with data from the old component, gradually switching over to the new one, and garbage collecting the old one. The strategy() specification allows the designer to select the most appropriate script for reconfiguration.

Just like in adaptive control systems, the question of stability is of great importance for the designer of self-adaptive software. While there is no formal definition for "stability" for self-adaptive systems, as a working model one can use the following:

---

[1] We borrow here some terminology from the language of fault diagnostics of physical systems: by failure mode we mean a particular way a component fails and exhibits faulty behavior [13].

"a system is stable if the frequency of reconfiguration actions is significantly lower than the frequency of GL component interactions". This admittedly imprecise and vague definition tells us to avoid situations when the system spends most of its time in frequent switching between configurations. Further research is needed to precisely define what stability means for a structurally adaptive software system, and how to verify from the formal model of the supervisory controller.

Modeling both offers and necessitates the verification of supervisory controller for a self-adaptive system. Note that reconfiguration actions refer to specific components, and components may be nested hierarchically. Thus, if a reconfiguration action selects one configuration for a higher-level component, another, parallel FSM may select a completely inconsistent configuration for an embedded component. To avoid this situation, sophisticated model checking has to be performed on the HFSM to avoid contradictory actions on the GL.

In general, the verification and assurance of self-adaptive software is a complex problem. However, with the use of explicit models for the reconfiguration logic we can probably cast the problem in a model-checking framework, for which techniques are available.

6   Implementation

The approach presented above has relevant implications for the implementor who wants to build self-adaptive systems using it. Arguably, the following four issues need to be addressed by the implementation:

1. *Expectations for components:* Components should be developed with some degree of independence, i.e. they must not depend on the precise implementation features (only the interfaces) of other components. If the self-adaptive software is for embedded, resource-constrained applications, we need a way (e.g. a language) for characterizing the components. There is also a need for expressing alternative component architectures in the form of architectural templates.

2. *Expectations for the run-time infrastructure:* The RTI must provide services not only for component communication and coordination, but also for dynamic reconfiguration and probing of component interactions from another layer. Current middleware packages (CORBA and COM [14]) have some support for the first two, but do not have adequate support for the rest. We need an industry standard (perhaps a CORBA service) for supporting these activities.

3. *Expectations for the HFSM:* Experience shows that the HFSM model for the supervisory controller can be compiled into executable code in a straightforward manner. The procedures involved in the select(), construct() and strategy() actions may be formulated in a procedural language, but it would be interesting to investigate how to provide a modeling language for describing these procedures on a higher, more abstract level.

4. *Expectations for design space management:* As it was shown above (Figure 4), the configuration space for design hierarchies with alternatives can be potentially enormous. Efficient techniques are needed for representing this configuration space, and for the rapid selection of desired alternatives. One approach that we have used in the past [16] seems particularly feasible: the hierarchical design is en-

coded as a tree, where each node is encoded using a binary vector containing bits of 1,0,X (unknown) values. This allows the use of Ordered Binary Decision Diagrams to represent and manage the design space symbolically. Architectural selections (to be used in the select() actions) can be performed symbolically, like the evaluation and search of a very large number of alternatives.

7   Summary, Conclusions, and Future Work

We have shown a systematic, technical recipe for building self-adaptive software systems. The approach is based on the well-established techniques of control engineering, and model-integrated computing. We have shown how the two-layer approach that separates main application functionality from supervisory, adaptation-related activities can be used to architect the system. We have illustrated how HFSMs can be used to model and implement reconfiguration logic, and how sophisticated decision logic can be incorporated into the design.

We are currently working on using the described approach to implement fault-adaptive controllers (FAC) [15]. A FAC is a controller architecture that is able to autonomously detect faults in physical plants, and reconfigure the regulatory controllers to maintain control in the face of failures. All the regulators, fault diagnostics, and reconfiguration logic is implemented in software. This problem domain is simpler than general-purpose self-adaptive applications, but it arguably offers an excellent opportunity to try out the ideas described above.

There are number of highly relevant research topics introduced by the proposed approach. Extending the formal modeling into the selection and construction procedures, verification and validation of reconfigurable systems for all possible configurations, and establishing some degree of assurance for the final systems' properties like schedulability and stability, just to name a few. However, the benefits offered by self-adaptive systems – their inherent ability to address flexibility and robustness in the same design – may one day far outweigh their shortcomings.

Acknowledgement

The DARPA/ITO SEC program (F33615-99-C-3611) has supported, in part, the activities described in this paper.

References

1. McLean, J and Heitmeyer, C. "High Assurance Computer Systems: A Research Agenda," America in the Age of Information, National Science and Technology Council Committee on Information and Communications Forum, Bethesda, 1995.
2. Kumpati S. Narendra, Anuradha M. Annaswamy: *Stable Adaptive Systems*, Prentice-Hall, 1988.
3. Karl Johan Åström and Björn Wittenmark: *Adaptive Control*, Addison-Wesley,1995.

4. Ken Dutton, William Barraclough, Steve Thompson, Bill Barraclough: *The Art of Control Engineering*, Addison-Wesley, 1997.
5. Karl J. Astrom (Editor): *Control of Complex Systems*, Springer, 2000.
6. http://trese.cs.utwente.nl/Workshops/OOPSLA2000/
7. Personal communication with engineers from a major aerospace manufacturer.
8. http://www.omg.org
9. Janos Sztipanovits and Gabor Karsai, "Model-Integrated Computing," *IEEE Computer*, pp. 110-112, April, 1997.
10. http://www.rational.com
11. David Harel, Michal Politi: *Modeling Reactive Systems with Statecharts: The Statemate Approach*, McGraw-Hill, 1998.
12. Ledeczi A., Bakay A., Maroti M.: Model-Integrated Embedded Systems, in Robertson, Shrobe, Laddaga (eds) Self Adaptive Software, Springer-Verlag Lecture Notes in CS, #1936, February, 2001.
13. IEEE Std 1232-1995. Trial Use Standard for Artificial Intelligence and Expert System Tie to Automatic Test Equipment (AI-ESTATE): Overview and Architecture, New York, IEEE Press. 1995.
14. Don Box, Charlie Kindel, Grady Booch: *Essential COM,* Addison-Wesley, 1998.
15. http://www.isis.vanderbilt.edu/Projects/Fact/Fact.htm
16. Neema S.: Design Space Representation and Management for Model-Based Embedded System Synthesis, ISIS-01-203, February, 2003.

Constraint-Guided Self-adaptation

Sandeep Neema and Akos Ledeczi

Institute for Software Integrated Systems, Vanderbilt University
Nashville, TN 37235, USA
{neemask,akos}@isis.vanderbilt.edu

Abstract. We present an approach to self-adaptive systems utilizing explicit models of the design-space of the application. The design-space is captured by a hierarchical signal flow representation that allows the specification of alternatives for any component at any level in the model hierarchy. Non-functional requirements and additional knowledge about the system are captured by formal constraints parameterized by operational parameters, such as latency, accuracy, error rate, etc, that are measured at run-time. The constraints and the models are embedded in the running system forming the operation-space of the application. When changes in the monitored parameters trigger a reconfiguration, the operation space is explored utilizing a symbolic constraint satisfaction method relying on Ordered Binary Decision Diagrams. Once a new configuration that satisfies all the constraints is found the reconfiguration takes place.

1 Introduction

This paper presents an approach to building self-adaptive embedded computing systems. Embedded computing systems are computer systems that are part of a larger physical system, where the embedded software is responsible for interacting with, coordinating and governing physical processes. This responsibility mandates that the embedded software obeys the rules imposed by the physical world, and reacts to changes in its operating environment in a timely fashion. This in turn implies that when the embedded system is functioning in a rapidly changing environment, the functional and performance demands (response times, rates) on the embedded software may change drastically over time.

Traditionally, and not without merits, the preferred approach of building embedded software has been to construct largely static, pre-programmed, pre-verified software, that can accommodate a diverse range of foreseeable operating scenarios. We argue that while this approach is very well suited for small-scale, relatively static systems working under predictable operating scenarios; it leads to brittle, inflexible and non-scalable software solutions. A better approach, as argued in [9], is to construct self-adaptive software that can restructure itself to better meet the changing performance and functional demands.

For the purpose of this paper we restrict the definition of self-adaptation to be a change in the system configuration, defined as a set of tasks, inter-task communication maps, and task execution schedules, with the goal of maintaining the *operational status* of the system. We precisely define the operational status of the system with the use of constraints. Constraints are logical expressions over the operating parameters

R. Laddaga, P. Robertson, and H. Shrobe (Eds.): IWSAS 2001, LNCS 2614, pp. 39–51, 2003.

of the system that evaluate to *true* or *false*. The system is said to be operational when all the constraints in the system are satisfied i.e. evaluate to true, otherwise, the system is not operational. Thus, the main steps in adaptation include: evaluating constraints, determining a new system configuration (that will meet all the constraints) when constraints are violated, and system reconfiguration. Inarguably many difficult issues arise when considering self-adaptation. Without diminishing the importance of other issues (that are being investigated by others, see the companion paper by Karsai et al.), the key question that we seek to address in this approach is how to construct and represent a *space of potential configurations*, and how to *decide the new system configuration*.

We present a model-based approach (see Model-Integrated Computing [2]) for construction and representation of the space of the potential system configurations, which we designate the *operational space* of the system. In a large-scale system with high-degree of variability this space could be extremely large. A large space is certainly preferable as it improves the opportunity to find a configuration that meets the constraints, however, an exhaustive search in a large operational space at runtime is simply infeasible. To overcome this challenge of searching for viable configurations, we present a symbolic constraint satisfaction technique based on Ordered Binary Decision Diagrams [7]. Symbolic methods represent the problem domain implicitly as mathematical formulae and the operations over the domain are performed by symbolic manipulation of mathematical formulae. The power of symbolic constraints satisfaction technique emanates from the ability to evaluate constraints over the entire space without enumerating point configurations.

The rest of the paper is organized as follows. The next section summarizes existing results in embedded model representation, as well as, design-space and constraint representation methods. Then, we describe our constraint-based self-adaptation technique in detail.

2   Background

2.1   Embedded Modeling

Our previous work on embedded model-integrated systems [1] forms the basis of this effort. The basic structure of these systems is illustrated in Figure 1. The Embedded Modeling Infrastructure (EMI) can be best viewed as a high-level layer at the top of the architecture, while a classical embedded systems kernel is located at the bottom. The component that connects these two layers is the translator that we call the embedded interpreter. The embedded models provide a simple, uniform, paradigm-independent and extensible API (EMI API) to this interpreter [1]. These models typically contain application models using some kind of dataflow representation. They may also describe available hardware resources and contain other domain-specific information.

Besides the kernel, the modeling system and the embedded interpreter, the fourth major component of the computing system is the set of software modules that perform the actual task of the embedded system. These are objects executable by the kernel and responsible for the core functionality of the system.

The EMI system provides capabilities for each of the three general tasks essential to self-adaptive systems: monitoring, decision-making, and reconfiguration. To facilitate the implementation of monitoring algorithms, convenient access to operational parameters, such as resource utilization, performance values, error rates etc., is required. The embedded models provide uniform representation of these parameters. Objects in the model may have designated attributes (monitor attributes) set by the underlying modules: either by the embedded kernel (in case of most operation system parameters), or by any of the application specific task modules that have information on the operation of the system.

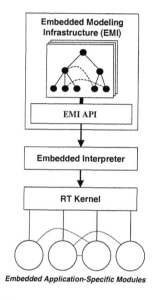

Fig. 1. Embedded Modeling

The second and most critical component of self-adaptive applications is the one making reconfiguration decisions. The constraint-based technique we are introducing in this paper provides an approach to his problem. The third task, reconfiguration, is done by the embedded interpreter utilizing the EMI API.

2.2   Design-Space Representation

Despite their numerous advantages, there is a lack of formalized methods for representing design spaces in embedded systems design research. In general, existing approaches can be grouped into two categories:

1. *Explicit Enumeration of Alternatives* – different design alternatives are explicitly enumerated. The design space is a combinatorial product of the design alternatives. Characteristically different designs may be obtained by selecting different combinations of alternatives.

2. *Parametric* – the design variations are abstracted into single or multiple parameters. The cross-product of the domains of the configuration parameters forms a parameterized design space. Physically different designs may be obtained from the parameterized design space by supplying appropriate values for the configuration parameters.

In the rest of this section, we present a review of some research and technologies where explicit representation of design space is considered.

2.3   Design Space Modeling with Alternatives

The Model-Integrated Design Environment (MIDE) for Adaptive Computing Systems (ACS) introduced in [4] targets multi-modal structurally adaptive computing systems. One of the key-features of this model-integrated framework is its support for explicit representation of design spaces for embedded adaptive systems. Representation of design spaces has special significance to multi-modal adaptive computing systems. The diverse functionality desired in the different modes of operation makes optimization decisions extremely difficult. Mode-level optimization does not imply system-level optimization as the reconfiguration cost involved in transitioning from a mode to another may offset any efficiency attained by a mode-optimized implementation. In order to address these challenges, a design flow has been developed that involves constructing large design spaces for the targeted system and then using constraints to guide the search through the large design space for system synthesis.

In this approach, an adaptive computing system is captured in multi-aspect models. The different modes of operation and the operational behavior of an adaptive system are captured as a hierarchical parallel finite state machine in a StateChart-like formalism [5]. The resources available for system execution are captured as an architecture flow diagram. The computations to be performed in the different modes of operations are captured as a hierarchical dataflow with alternatives. The basic dataflow model captures a single solution for implementing a particular set of functional requirements. In this framework the basic dataflow representation has been extended to enable representation of design alternatives. With this extension a dataflow block may be decomposed in two different ways. The first type is hierarchical decomposition in which a dataflow block can encapsulate a functionality described as a dataflow diagram. The second type is an orthogonal decomposition, in which a dataflow block contains more than one dataflow block as alternatives. In this case, the container block defines only the interface of the block and is devoid of any implementation details. The dataflow blocks contained within the container define different implementations of the interface specifications. With these extensions (i.e. hierarchy and alternatives), a dataflow model can modularly capture a large number of different computational structures together to form an exponentially large design space.

The alternatives in a dataflow may take many different forms. Alternatives may be technology alternatives that are different technology implementations of a defined functionality—e.g. TI-DSP C40 (software) implementation vs. a TI-DSP C67 (software) implementation vs. a VIRTEX® FPGA (hardware) implementation of a cross-correlation component. Technology alternatives minimize the dependency of the system design on the underlying technology, thereby enabling technology evolution. Alternatives may also be algorithmic alternatives that are different algorithms implementing a defined functionality (e.g. spatial vs. spectral correlation of a 2D image). It is generally accepted that the best performance can be obtained by matching the algorithm to the architecture or vice-versa. When different algorithm alternatives are captured, it may be possible to optimize the system design for a range of different architectures by choosing from different algorithm alternatives. Alternatives may also be functional alternatives that are different (but related) functions obeying the same interface specifications (e.g. a 3x3-kernel convolution vs. a 5x5-kernel convolution). Often in the design cycle of a system, functional requirements change when the system is scaled up, or better precision implementations of a function are desired due to improvements in sensor fidelity, availability of more compute power, etc. Functional alternatives are valuable in accommodating a large range of functional requirements in a design in such situations.

In summary, a design space composed by capturing alternatives can encapsulate a large number of characteristically different solutions for an end-to-end system specification. While large design spaces are valuable in improving design flexibility and optimization opportunities, determining the best solution for a given set of performance requirements and hardware architecture can be a major challenge. A constraint-based design space exploration method that meets this challenge is described in [6]. This paper advocates extending this approach to run-time for dynamic self-adaptation.

2.4   Generative Modeling

Modeling design alternatives explicitly provides much more flexibility than capturing a single point solution. However, it still requires the user to pre-design all the components and their possible interconnection topologies. The user (or an automatic tool) can pick and choose which alternative to select from a fixed set. A complementary approach, called generative modeling, is a combination of parametric and algorithmic modeling [1]. With this technique, the elementary components are modeled as before, but their number and interconnection topology are specified algorithmically in the form of a generator script. Generator scripts can refer to the values of architectural (numerical) parameters contained in the models. This approach is very similar to the VHDL generate statement; they both support the concise modeling of repetitive structures.

Generative modeling inherently supports dynamic reconfiguration. The generator scripts can be compiled as part of the runtime system. Runtime events can change the values of architectural parameters triggering the generator scripts. Note, however, that an extra level of indirection is needed here; the generators should not reconfigure the runtime system directly. Instead they should reconfigure a representation of the running system, the embedded models, in order to be able to analyze the system before the actual reconfiguration takes place [1].

2.5   Constraint Representation

Constraints are integral to any design activity. Typically, in an embedded system design constraints express SWEPT (size, weight, energy, performance, time) requirements. Additionally, they may also express relations, complex interactions and dependencies between different elements of an embedded system viz. hardware, middleware, and application components. Ideally, a correct design must satisfy all the system constraints. In practice, however, not all constraints are considered critical. Often trade-offs have to be made and some constraints have to be relaxed in favor of others. Constraint management is a cumbersome task that has been inadequately emphasized in embedded systems research. Most embedded system design practices place very little emphasis on constraints and treat them on an ad-hoc basis, which means either testing after the implementation is complete, or an over-design with respect to critical parameters. Both of these situations can be avoided by elevating constraints to a higher level in the design process. Two important steps in that direction are a) formal representation of constraints; and b) verification/pre-verification of the system design with respect to the specified constraints.

Principally, three basic types of design constraints are common to embedded systems: (a) performance constraints, (b) resource constraints, and (c) compositional constraints. More complex constraints are typically combinations of one or more of these basic types joined by first order logic connectives.

1. *Performance constraints* – Performance constraints express non-functional requirements that a synthesized system must obey. These may be in the form of size, weight, energy, latency, throughput, frequency, jitter, noise, response-time, real-time deadlines, etc. When an embedded computational system is expressed in a dataflow description, these constraints express bounds over the composite properties of the computational structure. Following are some common examples:
   - Timing – expresses end-to-end latency constraints, specified over the entire system, or may be specified over a subsystem e.g. (latency < 20).
   - Power – expresses bound over the maximum power consumption of a system or a subsystem e.g. (power < 100).
2. *Resource constraints* – Resource constraints are commonly present in embedded systems in the form of dependencies of computational components over specific hardware components. These constraints may be imperative in that they may express a direct assignment directive, or they may be conditionalized with other computational components. Following is an example of a resource constraint in plain English:
   - Imperative – component FFT must be assigned to resource DSP-1
   - Conditional – if component FFT is assigned to resource DSP-1 then component IFFT must be assigned to resource DSP-2
3. *Compositional constraints* – Compositional constraints are logic expressions that restrict the composition of alternative computational blocks. They express relationships between alternative implementations of different components. These are essentially compatibility directives and are similar to the type equivalence specifications of a type system. Therefore, compositional constraints are also referred to as typing constraints. For example, the constraint below expresses a compatibility directive between two computational blocks FFT and IFFT that have multiple alternate implementations: {if component FFT is implemented by component FFT-HW then implement component IFFT with component IFFT-HW}.

The Object Constraint Language (OCL), a part of the Unified Modeling Language (UML) suite, forms a good basis for expressing the type of constraints shown above. OCL is a declarative language, typically used in object modeling to specify invariance over objects and object properties, pre- and post- conditions on operations, and as a navigation language [8]. An extended version of OCL has been used in [6] to express the type of constraints specified above. The constraints are specified in the context of an object. A constraint expression can refer to the context object and to other objects associated with the context object and their properties. The OCL keyword *self* refers to the context object. Role names are used to navigate and access associated objects. For example, the expression self.parent evaluates to the parent object of the context object, similarly self.children evaluates to a set of children object of the context object.

A constraint expression can either express direct relation between the objects by using relational or logical operators, or express performance constraints by specifying bounds over object properties. Object properties can be referred to in a manner similar to associations. Property constructs supported in the derived constraint language include latency, power, resource assignment, etc.

3   Self-adaptive System Architecture

Figure 2 shows the overall architecture of a self-adaptive system under our approach. It should be noted that this architecture builds upon the EMI discussed earlier in the background section and in [1]. We improve upon the existing architecture by introducing a new reconfiguration controller that employs a constraint-based operation space exploration for determining the next configuration. Parameterized constraints and a symbolic constraint-based operation-space exploration form the essence of this new reconfiguration controller. Constraints in this approach provide a way of mapping operational requirements to reconfiguration decisions. The modeling paradigm, elaborated later in this section, allows capturing a large design space for the system implementation, along with constraints. The paradigm supports capturing both design-time and runtime constraints. The system design space is pruned using the design-time constraints, and a small subset of the design space is retained at runtime as the operation-space of the system. It is this reduced space that is explored at runtime using the parameterized runtime constraints. In the rest of this section, we elaborate upon the modeling paradigm for the embedded model representation, the constraint-based operation space exploration method, and the functioning of the reconfiguration controller.

3.1   Modeling Paradigm

The modeling paradigm, i.e. the modeling language, that supports designing embedded self-adaptive systems using constraint-based adaptation methods is a derivative of the one presented in [4] described previously. It has three primary components:

- application models that represent the desired functionality of the system using hierarchical signal flow diagrams with explicit alternatives, thereby capturing the design-space of the application,
- resource models that capture the available hardware resources and their interconnection topology,

- constraints that describe non-functional requirements, resource constraints and other information about the system and are parameterized by operational variables of the running system.

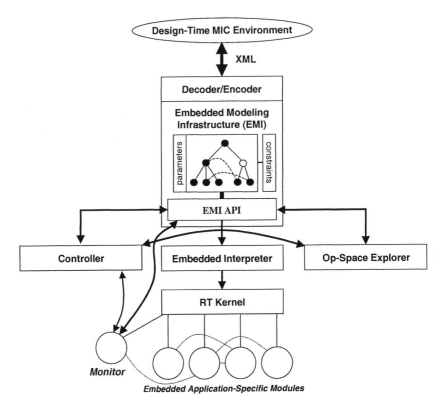

Fig. 2. System Architecture

The novel idea is the concept of parameterized constraints. Each constraint can be associated with one or more parameters that capture values that are continuously measured during the operation of the system. These parameters also have multiple thresholds specified. Whenever a value crosses a threshold, the controller is triggered which, in turn, starts the operation-space exploration.

Constraints are also prioritized. Constraints capturing critical requirements get the highest priority. These will always have to be satisfied. However, the system needs to have the flexibility to relax non-critical constraints in case there are no solutions in the operation space that satisfies all the constraints. Priorities specify the order of automatic constraint relaxation.

Note that currently generative modeling is not considered in our constrained-based approach to self-adaptivity. The main reason for this is the difficulty with symbolic constraint satisfaction. If the generator language is Turing complete, which is highly desirable for the expressive power, symbolic representation of the generator script is a very hard problem. A possible approach is to constrain the values of generative parameters and analyze the restricted (now finite) design space. This would diminish the advantages of generative modeling itself—the flexibility and the infinite design space. The only alternative is analyzing a single instance of the generative models that corresponds to a particular instantiation of the parameter set. However, the search for the new configuration in the parameter space needs to consider many such instances. Regenerating and analyzing every candidate would be computationally prohibitively expensive.

3.2   Operation Space Exploration

The objective of the operation space exploration is to find a single feasible solution from the space that satisfies all the critical constraints and maximally satisfies the non-critical constraints. The challenge of operation-space exploration emerges from the size of the space, complexity of the requirements and criteria expressed as constraints, and the strict resource and time bounds over the exploration process. This paper proposes the use of symbolic methods based on Ordered Binary Decision Diagrams (OBDD-s) for constraint satisfaction. The highlight of the symbolic constraint satisfaction method is the ability to *apply constraints to the entire space without enumerating point solutions*, whereas an exhaustive search by enumeration through the space is generally exponential time complexity. Symbolic analysis methods represent the problem domain implicitly as mathematical formulae and the operations over the domain are performed by symbolic manipulation of mathematical formulae.

The symbolic constraint satisfaction problem considered here is a finite set manipulation problem. The operation-space is a finite set. Constraints specify relations in this space. Constraint satisfaction is a restriction of the solution space with the constraints. Solving this finite set manipulation problem symbolically requires the solution of two key problems: (a) symbolic representation of the space, and (b) symbolic representation of the constraints.

Symbolic constraint satisfaction is simply the logical conjunction of the symbolic representation of the space with the symbolic representation of the constraints. Figure 3 illustrates the process of symbolic constraint satisfaction.

3.3   Symbolic Representation of the Operation Space

The key to exploit the power of symbolic Boolean manipulation is to express a problem in a form where all of the objects are represented as Boolean functions [7]. By introducing a binary encoding of the elements in a finite set, all operations involving the set and its subsets can be represented as Boolean functions. In order to represent the operation space symbolically, the elements of the operation space have to be encoded as binary vectors. The choice of encoding scheme has a strong impact on the scalability of the symbolic manipulation algorithms [7]. An encoding scheme has been developed in [6] after a careful analysis of the problem domain, taking into consideration the hierarchical structure of the solution space.

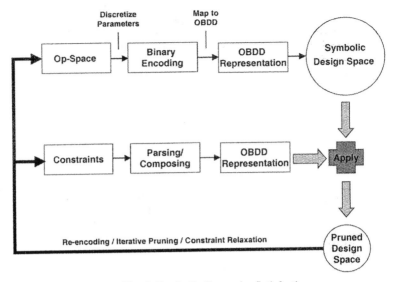

Fig. 3. Symbolic Constraint Satisfaction

The operation space captures feasible configurations for implementing the system functionality, and is represented as a hierarchical dataflow graph with alternatives, as described earlier. The dataflow is associated with a network of resources in defining the system configurations. This representation can modularly define a very large space. The complete operation space is a set of possible system configurations. The encoding scheme assigns encoding values to each node in the hierarchy such that each configuration receives a unique encoding value. Additionally, the encoding scheme must also encode the resource assignments of components along with performance attributes such as latency, throughput, power, etc. The performance attributes take numeric values from a continuous finite domain. However, for the purpose of encoding the domains of the attributes are discretized. The total number of binary variables required to encode the operational space is primarily dependent upon on the domain size and the quantization levels in the domain [6]. With this encoding the operation space is symbolically composed as a Boolean function from the symbolic Boolean representation of components. After deciding the variable ordering this Boolean representation is mapped to an OBDD representation in a straightforward manner.

3.4 Symbolic Representation of Constraints

Three basic categories of constraints are considered. Symbolic representation of each of these categories of constraints is summarized below.

1. *Compositional constraints* – Compositional constraints express logical relations between processing blocks in the hierarchical dataflow representation. Symbolically the constraint can be represented as a logical relation over the OBDD representation of the processing blocks trivially.
2. *Resource constraint* – Resource constraints relate processing blocks to resources. Symbolic representation of resource constraints is accomplished by expressing the relation over the OBDD representation of the processing block and resource.

3. *Performance constraints* – Performance constraints are more challenging to solve symbolically than the previously specified categories of constraints. There are two primary drivers of the complexity: 1) A system-level property has to be composed from component-level properties in a large design space, and 2) The property being composed is numeric, and may admit a potentially very large domain. Representing a large numeric domain symbolically as a Boolean function and performing arithmetic operations symbolically is a challenging problem with serious scalability concerns. In general, different performance attributes compose differently. An approach for expressing constraints over additive attribute symbolically has been detailed in [6]. The basic approach involves expressing linear arithmetic constraints over a group of binary vectors, each binary vector representing an integer variable, as a Boolean function. This function is then conjuncted with the representation of the operation space that encodes performance attributes of components as integer values for different binary vectors. The binary vectors are then quantified out from the resulting function. Thus, in effect a relation over the attributes of components is composed into a relation over the components of the operation space. Building on this basic approach more complex composition of system-level properties, and symbolic representation of different performance constraints has been shown in [6].

In addition to these basic categories of constraints, complex constraints may be expressed by combining one or more of these constraints with first order logic connectives. The symbolic representation of the complex constraints can be accomplished by composing the symbolic representation of the basic constraints.

3.5   Embedding Symbolic Constraint Satisfaction

The key issues in embedding the symbolic constraint satisfaction methodology outlined above are to manage the memory footprint of the OBDD data structures, and to control the potential non-deterministic exponential blow-up of OBDD-s. In the presented approach we have a rudimentary technique to manage both the memory footprint and the exponential blow-up by limiting the maximum node count in the OBDD data structure. Doing this forces the OBDD algorithms to throw an exception whenever the data-structure grows beyond the limit. Such an exception is handled by asserting the target constraint unsatisfiable within the given resource and time budget.

An additional optimization for embedding symbolic constraint satisfaction enables incremental constraint satisfaction. Thus, when a single or a small set of constraints is activated by a change in an operation parameter, and the change further constrains the operation space, then it does not necessitates re-exploration/re-application of all the constraints. Only the affected constraints are expressed symbolically as OBDD-s and re-applied. However, this approach does not work when the parameter change relaxes the constraint. In this case, it may be possible to avoid re-application of all the constraints by caching intermediate symbolic representation of the pruned operation. Caching, however, increases the memory requirements. Thus, a trade-off has to be made between the memory bounds and the time bounds of the exploration.

3.6   Reconfiguration Controller

The controller continuously monitors the operational parameters of the system. The embedded models capture the dependencies between the specified constraints and the operational parameters. The dependency specifications include multiple threshold levels for the operational parameters. Whenever any one of these parameters crosses any of the threshold levels, an operation space exploration is invoked with the affected constraints. Additional critical and non-critical constraints are also passed to the operation space exploration for satisfaction. The exploration process is time-bounded by specifying a maximum OBDD node count. The exploration process may result in an exception (for exceeding the maximum node count) or zero, one, or more possible configurations for the system implementation. The four scenarios are individually considered below:

1. *Exception* – In the event of an exception due to a non-critical constraint, the exploration continues with the specified non-critical constraint dropped from the constraint store. If the exception is due to a critical constraint then the system execution continues with the current system configuration, however, the system re-attempts exploration with an increased maximum OBDD node count. A number of re-tries limited by a pre-determined constant are made, until the exploration results in one or more configuration that satisfies all the critical constraints, and maximally satisfies non-critical constraints. The system continues to operate with the current configuration until a new configuration is found.

2. *Zero* – In this case the relaxation of non-critical constraints is attempted progressively. The progression continues until one or more configurations are found. If no configuration is found even after relaxing all non-critical constraints, no further attempts for exploration are made and the system continues to execute with the current configuration. It must be noted here that by progressively relaxing non-critical constraints and accepting the first configuration that emerges by relaxing constraints does not guarantee maximal satisfaction of non-critical constraints. The system sacrifices maximality in favor of finding at least one working configuration.

3. *One* – This is an ideal scenario, when the operation space exploration results in exactly one valid configuration. The system simply accepts the resulting configuration as the next configuration.

4. *Multiple* – The system can be compiled with several different strategies to handle this scenario. A simple strategy is to pick the first configuration from the result set, as they are all equally fit from a constraint satisfaction perspective. A more complex strategy attempts to evaluate the difference between the current configuration and the configurations in the result set. Configuration with the least difference is accepted as the next configuration.

Once the next configuration has been accepted, the reconfiguration controller passes the control to the system reconfiguration manager that performs the reinterpretation and reconfiguration process.

4   Conclusions

This paper presented an approach for constraint-guided self-adaptation of embedded systems. Embedded models of the system contain multiple potential system configurations captured as alternatives in an operation space. Parameterized constraints provide a way of capturing changing operational requirements. An embedded operation space exploration, triggered by changes in operational parameters, rapidly finds next system configuration that satisfies the current system configuration that satisfies the current operational constraints, which is then instantiated and deployed through our Embedded Modeling Infrastructure.

The main contribution of the work is the systematic approach to the reconfiguration controller, the key component of any self-adaptive system. The OBDD-based symbolic satisfaction of constraints parameterized by monitored operational variables makes the controller *reusable* across applications and even application domains. It can potentially replace the ad-hoc, highly application-specific, hand-crafted reconfiguration controllers of the past. Another principal benefit of this approach is that every system configuration that is deployed is *correct by design*, i.e. it already satisfies all the correctness criteria specified by the constraints.

An ideal application area for our approach is the domain of robust, fault-tolerant embedded systems. The operation space can contain various system configurations that are tailored for different system failure modes. Constraints capture the complex relationships between different failure modes and system configurations. The system can quickly find a new configuration and adapt after one or more component failures.

There are numerous open research issues associated with the approach and a lot of work remains to be done. The most difficult problem is the operation-space exploration within strict time bounds and utilizing possibly limited computational resources. A systematic approach to over- or under-constrained systems needs to be developed. Finally, the technique needs to be implemented and tested in real-world scenarios.

Acknowledgement

The research presented here was made possible by the generous sponsorship of the Defense Advanced Research Projects Agency (DARPA) under contracts F30602-96-2-0227 and DABT63-97-C-0020.

References

1. Ledeczi A., Bakay A., Maroti M.: "Model-Integrated Embedded Systems," in Robertson, Shrobe, Laddaga (eds): Self Adaptive Software, Springer-Verlag Lecture Notes in Computer Science, #1936, February 2001.
2. J. Sztipanovits, G. Karsai, "Model-Integrated Computing," IEEE Computer, pp. 110-112, April 1997.
3. Ledeczi A., et al.: "Composing Domain-Specific Design Environments," IEEE Computer, pp. 44-51, November 2001.
4. Bapty T., Neema S., Scott J., Sztipanovits J., Asaad S.: "Model-Integrated Tools for the Design of Dynamically Reconfigurable Systems," VLSI Design, 10, 3, pp. 281-306, 2000.
5. Harel, D., "Statecharts: A Visual Formalism for Complex Systems", Science of Computer Programming 8, pp.231-274, 1987.
6. Neema S., "System Level Synthesis of Adaptive Computing Systems", Ph.D. Dissertation, Vanderbilt University, Department of Electrical and Computer Engineering, May 2001.
7. Bryant R., "Symbolic Manipulation with Ordered Binary Decision Diagrams," School of Computer Science, Carnegie Mellon University, Technical Report CMU-CS-92-160, July 1992.
8. Warmer J., Kleppe A.: The Object Constraint Language: Precise Modeling With Uml, Addison Wesley Pub. Co. 1999.
9. Sztipanovits,J., Karsai G.: "Self-Adaptive Software for Signal Processing," CACM, 41, 5, pp. 55-65, 1998.

Model-Based Adaptivity
in Real-Time Scheduling

Árpád Bakay

Institute of Software Integrated Systems
Vanderbilt University
arpad.bakay@vanderbilt.edu
http://www.isis.vanderbilt.edu

Abstract. This paper presents an approach for building schedulers for real-time, especially soft real-time systems. It is based on two technologies, model-based computing, and self-adaptivity. The scheduler operation is based on on-line evolving models that reflect all significant information on the running system. We argue that despite the obvious overhead added by these computationally rather expensive technologies, these costs are returned as a result of more intelligent scheduling. A typical soft-real time device, an autonomous network probe device is used as a proof of concept application.

1 Introduction

Scheduling has long been a primary challenge of real-time systems engineering. Significant progress has been made in this area in the past 10-15 years. We find that most of the successful techniques take either of two approaches. Some solutions rely on certain particular timing properties of the application. Others – probably the majority – use techniques that are known to be sub-optimal, but sufficiently simple and robust for use in a wide range of applications. Although they are popular because of the implied guarantees, we find these latter, generic approaches to be painfully wasteful, especially when considering the production numbers of some of today's embedded real-time devices.

Obviously, to be more efficient, scheduling must be based on more and deeper information about the goals and means of the system. Organizing and processing this information drastically increases the complexity of the scheduling algorithm, and this is the reason why most solutions opt for some more simplistic approach. This paper investigates an alternative based on the application of two relatively remote technologies, model-based computing and self-adaptivity. These are used to develop a technique that enables the consideration of substantially more detailed information for scheduling decisions. Modeling is a viable way to structure information of a moderately large amount and complex structure, and we see it convenient to transform models into control information for schedulers. However, neither in theory, nor in practice is it possible to grasp every detail exactly in an a priori defined model. This is where adaptivity becomes very handy. We

R. Laddaga, P. Robertson, and H. Shrobe (Eds.): IWSAS 2001, LNCS 2614, pp. 52–65, 2003.

implement adaptivity as an autonomous and continuous update process on the evolving model of scheduling parameters. Such cooperation between the model and the adaptor is the key concept of this architecture.

It is conceivable, that our approach is less suitable for hard real-time systems than it is for soft real-time architectures. This is because non-determinism introduced by this technique is more tolerable if guaranteed performance is not as critical. Also, the fact that computing performance is not tailored to the absolute worst-case load, allows for more interesting scheduling policies. Accordingly, a realistic soft real-time system, a network traffic probe, is used as a platform for evaluating the concept.

2   Soft Real-Time Computing

We are witnessing a tangible shift of technological focus toward embedded and real-time systems. This research area has already been extensive in the past, and indeed, very remarkable real-time achievements date as far back as 30 years from ago [2]. Still the world of real-time applications is in a significant change. As one obvious trend, hardware performance and price are both changing drastically. Still, improvement of hardware is not the most prominent difference. The more dramatic change is occurring in the target market of these technologies: while early customers were typically high-profile, highly specialized fields with virtually endless budget (aerospace, military, power industry etc.), embedded systems of today are reproduced by the millions and marketed in shopping malls.

Even if we focus on the middle segment of the embedded market (like the automotive or telecommunication industry) the change of the target application areas results in a shift of technological focus for the developers and researchers involved in this field. *Reliability* used to be the typical single issue of no trade-off in earlier times. Today, however, profane concepts, such as *cost, efficiency, power consumption* and *ease of implementation* have become serious, sometimes dominant requirements.

Even in the case of truly critical applications, 100% reliability has proved to be a prohibitively expensive goal. We learned that simultaneous and total fault tolerance on all levels in an embedded computer system (hardware, operating system and run-time environment, application, I/O and communication channels) is not only impossible to achieve, but regularly exhibit end-to-end reliability inferior to that of fully distributed, redundant systems built of significantly cheaper components.

In the domain of real-time software, this tendency translates into some even more concrete phenomena. One is that although the price of computing performance is dropping by magnitudes, many real-time systems, now being mass-produced commodities, are increasingly concerned about the resource efficiency of the software. Obviously, power issues, where applicable, further call for the efficient use of a typically frugal hardware configuration.

These changes also affect *scheduling*, the basic, but critical functionality of any real-time operating environment. For a long time, hard-real time analysis used to be the exclusive focus of real-time scheduling research. Striving for maximum reliability is usually the prominent justifying argument behind the application of these strict techniques. With the advent of new priorities, hard real-time assumptions have proved to be prohibitively restrictive for many of the newer applications.

Rate Monotonic Analysis [1], the typical hard real-time design approach, presents a good example on the cost of guaranteed reliability.

- First, the basic formula requires a significant reserve in the system utilization factor (up to 31% for systems with many tasks).
- Second, this overhead is charged onto the combined worst-case timing utilization rate of the participating processes, a value that often exceeds the typical or mean timing parameters by magnitudes (consider the 'worst case performance' of most pattern matching algorithms).
- If aperiodic (sporadic) events are involved, they must be considered at their absolute maximum occurrence rate. Again, these may significantly differ from any sustained or typical frequencies.
- If tasks must synchronize to each other, synchronization delays must again be estimated for the worst case and additional utilization must be statically reserved for them.

In summary, scheduling based on worst-case data can lead to very low utilizations in actual running systems [3]. Meanwhile, several other areas of modern computing use technologies that bring improvement in the statistical sense while deteriorate worst-case figures. Virtual memory and caching are well known examples in the domain of computer hardware architectures. Theoretical arguments aside, their efficiency has been proven on millions of server and desktop systems. Their use would be certainly advantageous in real-time environments as well. Still, as far as rate monotonic and other worst-case analysis techniques are concerned, boosting technologies appear to have just the negative effect because of inferior worst-case characteristics.

It needs to be acknowledged, that the performance guarantee provided only by the pessimistic scheduling algorithms continues to be a very valuable feature. Those scheduling techniques have no alternatives in many high profile, safety-critical applications.

While Rate Monotonic Analysis seems to have expressed irrefutable rules of guaranteed, static real-time scheduling [1], extensive and valuable research has been done to provide alternatives which increase throughput while just minimally compromising (or hopefully preserving) worst case behavior. Because of obvious analogies, most solutions suggested are based on the existing and proven expertise of some related domains:

- *Queuing theories* have provided a useful foundation for telecommunication network modeling. Its applicability for real-time scheduling has been analyzed and demonstrated on several systems, especially ones in the telecommunication domain. This is no wonder, since the utility of these techniques largely depend on the validity of stochastic models originally developed for telecommunication services.

- *Traditional OS scheduling* has a remarkable experimental body of knowledge. Soft real-time systems certainly represent a transition between hard real-time and traditional interactive, multitasking architectures. Even closer problems are addressed by server applications. Of particular interest is the valuable experience in statistical performance-boosting technologies like caching and dynamic linking, areas hardly tangible by any purely theoretical approaches.
- Other directions have been based on the well-researched area of *production scheduling* [8]. Models developed for those environments (machine shops, storage areas, human resources) are certainly complex and are again based on real-world experience. These fields have well realized that scheduling is inseparable from resource management in general. It is questionable, however, how accurately those concepts transform into real-time scheduling and management of computer resources, where a single and fairly universal resource, processor time, dominates the scheduling challenge.
- *Rate monotonic analysis* and related technologies also serve as a base for further research approaches. These directions typically promise to preserve reliable scheduling while improving other qualities.

3 Extending Scheduler Intelligence

It is general rule, that the more information is available, the better decision can be made. It is also true for scheduling with the additional caveat that whenever a deadline is to be met, pondering on the decision consumes just the valuable resource we want to economize on. Decisions should be made *fast and correct*.

Most of the general R/T scheduling directions mentioned above resolve this dilemma with a rather determined approach to minimize design decision complexity, i.e. they opt for fast decisions. Telecommunication systems are dominated by the simple 'limited capacity FIFO' approach, which seems to be suitable for handling a large number of service requests with uniform probability parameters on a fixed number of service channels. Traditional operating systems implement more flexible service architectures (time-sharing enables them to process a variable number of requests simultaneously), but tasks are also considered uniform until the user explicitly sets nice values or a fair scheduler policy later modifies their relative priorities based on unusually high or low processor utilization. We have seen that pessimistic schedulers already do consider some a priori per-task information on worst-case execution time, periodicity, deadline, etc. But again, these are often just very rough estimates, while other parameters are ignored just because the analysis and the scheduler algorithm do not make use of them anyway. Shop scheduling algorithms, however, could theoretically utilize a much broader set of a priori task attributes. Still, research here is again mainly focused on proposing generic solutions for problems characterized by a very simple set of timing parameters.

Are speed and simplicity of decision making the only driving forces behind these designs? Hardly. There is also another, probably stronger argument: if a priori task information has to be used, someone must provide it. Supplying this kind of knowledge would typically be the responsibility of the person who assigns tasks to the system, but often this information is not readily available and would be too cumbersome to let these people specify it. Probably the real reason behind the popularity of simplistic schedulers is their convenient, 'fool-proof' nature.

A desktop operating system that keeps asking the user about anticipated timing characteristics before starting every program certainly seems to be impractical. Similarly, requiring a calling party to estimate the duration of a phone connection would also quickly deter subscribers. The full-automatic scheduling approach seems to be very appropriate in those areas.

Real-time systems are different, however. Tasks are not assigned by capricious users, but by the architects of the real-time system. Of course the real phisical environment will eventually make things happen, but in many cases the system architect is reasonably expected to be able to tell something about the timing and resource utilization characteristics of the triggering events and the tasks that get fired by them.

Pessimistic schedulability tests (like Rate Monotinic Analysis, Deadline Monotonic Analysys or Response Time Analysis [1, 2]) already require the specification of the tasks' temporal scope characteristics like the *maximum release rate, worst-case execution time* and task *deadline*. This already requires thorough analysis on real-time application components, and we believe that by just about the same effort it is possible to figure out numerous further interesting parameters like average *execution time* and *execution time vs. input data dependency*. If theoretical analysis is not possible, experimental or profiling results may still be available.

An advanced scheduling architecture could and should use these additional data to optimize real-time scheduling. Performance of scheduling decisions based on these estimated and incomplete task characteristics certainly cannot offer guaranteed schedulability, but they have a good chance to closely approach optimal throughput and efficiency in most cases. This is exactly what the expanding spectrum of soft real-time applications calls for.

These arguments form the philosophical background of the work presented here. To make this function, some implementation disciplines are also to be defined. *Model based computing*, a long-time research focus at the Institute of Software Integrated Systems of Vanderbilt University, is a very good candidate for effectively organizing and processing task-specific information. Modeling is thus a cornerstone of our approach.

Modeling alone, however, do not exempt the designer from determining task-specific characteristics. The possibility that a priori specified data will be inaccurate or completely unknown remains to be imminent. Another discipline, *run-time adaptivity* is expected to alleviate this problem. This mechanism again relies and operates on the model-based data, forming an obvious synergy of the two disciplines.

4   Model-Based Approach to Real-Time Scheduling

Models are sets of concepts representing real-world entities. As it is with real world entities, modeling elements often form a hierarchy of containment relations (e.g. a 'computing node' contains 'task'-s). Besides this hierarchy, modeling elements carry relevant information in attributes attached to them (e.g. 'deadline' for 'task'). The process of determining modeling element types, hierarchical composition rules, element attributes and some further relations described later, is called 'metamodeling'. In this way, metamodeling is the process of setting up a framework of concepts to work with in the subsequent model-building process.

As the examples above already suggested, modeling concepts of this work represent entities relevant to the scheduling problem: elements will be concepts like 'system', 'processor', 'task', 'component', 'assignment' etc.; attributes will be similar to 'estimated execution time', 'deadline', 'frequency', 'memory utilization', etc.

The set of generic modeling concepts used here are the ones defined by the Generic Modeling Environment (GME [5]), and used in dozens of successful applications in a variety of domains. This strong record and versatility has made us confident to use modeling, and we also benefit from a convenient set of tools provided by GME, as the editor and a range of converter and interpreter components. The environment also supports metamodeling, where metamodels are represented as UML class diagrams.

The two most basic modeling concepts are atomic modeling elements (*atoms*) that are not detailed any further, i.e. do not contain any other element, and unrestricted modeling elements (*models* for short) which usually contain other atoms or models. Further concepts defined by GME represent non-containment relations: *connections* connect elements; *references* provide aliasing or pointer support, while *sets* are used to identify a subset of elements contained within a model. See [5] for details, along with a description of some further modeling concepts.

The GME approach has been used for modeling different aspects of real-time environments, and we could certainly rely on this experience for a head start. Still, representing run-time knowledge for scheduling purposes remained a so far unresearched area, with important questions still remaining to be answered. As always, the most critical of these decisions were to be made right at the beginning, at the metamodeling phase. Modeling of a concrete system is usually a more organized and more straightforward activity. As it was mentioned, metamodeling is conceptually equivalent to drawing the UML diagram of the model database.

The first, and probably the most important question to be answered is the depth of the model to be used. It has been told in general that if more information is used, better decisions can be made. When scheduling properties are about to be calculated, this could also include the detailed control flow analysis on the application code of all the modules to be used, a precise inventory of all occurrences of thread synchronization (along with their timing characteristics), detailed analysis on virtual memory and cache usage, and so on. A similar

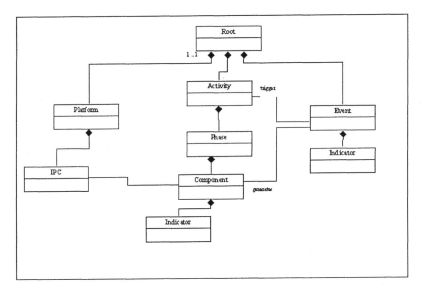

Fig. 1.

approach is used, but for worst-case execution time calculation as described in [4]. The computational cost of these extremely detailed analyses explodes with the inclusion of more and more detail. If the goal is real (i.e. not worst-case) execution time estimation, an increasing portion of it becomes highly dependent on input data, thus not computable until run-time. The scheduler would eventually end up carefully emulating each candidate task in run-time before actually scheduling some of them to run. The decision may be correct, but infinitely slow.

The remaining option -the one actually taken in this work- is to maintain a keen balance between decision speed and knowledge depth. Thus the previously mentioned idea of extracting model data from an automatic or manual line-by-line analysis of the application code has to be given up. Instead, the application programmer will be expected to provide a smaller amount of typically less accurate information belonging to a much higher level of abstraction. It is reasonable to refer to this information as *component characteristics*. He is expected to estimate characteristics based on engineering experience, design-time code analysis or profiling results of test runs. If none of them work, adaptive techniques described in the next section can be relied upon.

Our policy is to establish a set of structural and characteristic information that is sufficiently accurate but also minimal at the same time. We start with a relatively simple real-time system model and a small set of attributes, and provide functionality to effectively include user-defined extensions. It is not ruled out however, that based on experience with the first applications currently being implemented, additions to the model will be needed. Our proposed model structure is shown in Figure 1. Like most current design and analysis methodologies, this diagram also reflects a component-based approach. 'Component'-s are the most basic units of execution. They are not necessarily active (e.g.: dynamic libraries are also components). There is no requirement for a truly object oriented approach either: tasks of traditional real-time systems can also be components as long as they represent a single, indivisible unit of schedulability.

The diagram defines three kinds of root elements: *platform*, *events* and *activities*. There is a notable difference between the first and the latter two concepts. Platform describes an actual system, so it does not need to be instantiated. Events and activities, on the other hand, are still generic concepts, which get instantiated in large numbers along the operation of the system. So, in some respect these entities, as they are recorded in the sceduling model, should just be called event and activity *types*. (Even so, we continue using the short names, as they are less confusing.)

Platform describes the hardware and software resources available to the application programs. Simmetric multiprocessing (SMP) architectures are supported, so the number of processors and system memory are attributes of the platform entity. Other resources like I/O channels and IPC facilities are explicitly modeled within resources. Priority levels are also expressed as platform components. Another interesting and rather problematic attribute is the average *task switch time*. In short, platform contains a simple set of hardware related information considered to be relevant for scheduling. As a notable exception, processor speed is not represented anywhere, since other timing characteristics are usually expressed in terms of real time.

Events are concepts that trigger activities. Events can be external events (hardware interrupts), internal events (set by other activities), and timer events. The most important kind of event attributes, indicators, is described below.

Activities deliver something useful. Generally an activity is useless until it is fully executed. Reading and processing a new set of input data and updating output values is a typical single activity of a controller application. Logging the previous activity and refreshing the user interface are other examples of activities.

Activities are a sequence of **phases**, where each phase contains a set of **components**. Activities are strictly sequential, i.e. it is not possible to define alternative phases or fork and join schemes within a single activity. To do this, events and separate activities are used. Simple parallelism, however, can easily be represented as components within a phase.

Components of the same phase are to be executed in parallel. The most basic component is completely reserved for the parent phase, so it cannot be shared. Other components (typically resources) can be shared up to a certain extent, e.g. shareable by 'N' processes maximum. The *load factor* attribute of the component determines shareability if the factor is below 1. Some components (e.g. dynamic libraries) are shareable by an unlimited number of activities. They are associated by a load factor of 0, which of course still implies that the component is required in the parent phase.

The most important attributes of components are typical and maximal values for execution time and other resource utilizations. Timing is certainly the primary concept. As a general rule, only active components have a non-zero execution time, which also should include time spent in the associated reactive components, such as resources.

The pivotal concept of this approach is that attributes, like execution time and resource utilization estimates, are not constants, but dynamically computed functions of several other factors, such as *indicators, monitoring parameters* and *historical averages.*

Indicators are values carried either by an event that triggered the execution of the current activity or a component from a previous activity phase. They are defined by the application architect, and they must be manually computed from within the component that generated the event, or from the indicators container component. Indicators are either real-valued physical values or integral category codes (boolean variables are a special case of the latter). For example, if a timing attribute of component C2 is dependent on the 'packetsize' indicator of event 'E1', it will be expressed as

```
C2.exectimeestimate = 30.0 + 0.07 * E1.packetsize.
```

(The system uniformly represents all timing data as microseconds.) If memory usage of component C4 is dependent of the input data complexity categorized by the previous component C3 as one of (LOW, MED, HIGH), then

```
C4.memoryestimate = 48K + C3.complexity.lookup(MED: 85K,
                                                LOW: 17K
                                                HIGH: 198 K)
```

Monitoring parameters are standard attributes defined and calculated by the real-time scheduling environment. Actual execution time and resource usage data are automatically generated for all executing components. This is inevitable, since the adaptive intervention mechanisms all rely on these values. So they are also used internally, but it is straightforward to grant the attribute expression mechanism access to them. Of course, accessing the current monitoring values of a component is not possible until it has been started by the scheduler, but they are still useful to define averages (see below), to set intervention thresholds, and to be used for decisions on scheduling later activities.

Other monitoring parameters express the status of system resources (Platform.freeMemory, Platform.swappingRate, IOChannel.load, IOChannel.idle) or the activity-independent (global) state of individual components (Component.inMemory)

Averages are not shown in the input model, but they are virtual objects automatically generated whenever they are used by one of the expressions. Clearly they are essential as a feedback mechanism to implement adaptive scheduling. Averages can be simple moving averages on indicators or monitoring parameters like

```
average( exectimeactual, 50, 150)
```

which indicates the moving average of the current component's actual completion time, calculated by an attenuation factor of 50 (and with 150 as the initial value).

Other averages are bucketed averages, calculated and maintained separately on the options of the category indicator specified in the expression:

```
bucketaverage( exectimeactual, C1.complexity, 50, 150)
```

As it was mentioned before, average variables are set up automatically whenever such expressions are referenced. Two variables are only considered equivalent if all their four parameters are identical.

The above examples also introduce the *attribute expression language*, another key concept of our architecture. This is a language that supports arbitrarily complex expressions of constants, basic arithmetic operators, references to variables and some built-in functions. Still, it is a deliberately simple and limited-scope expression grammar, which is designed to express the most typical cases in a clear, although sometimes rather verbose, way. Another key design goal is the requirement for evaluation efficiency, since these expressions must be calculated in real-time by the scheduler. That is why subroutines and other convenience concepts are neither provided. Fortunately, as indicators are calculated by the components, more specialized calculations can often be 'squeezed' into the code of the generating component. This is in effect an arguably elegant, but fairly practical workaround for expression language limitations. Furthermore, it is also feasible and acceptable to introduce components and phases with the sole purpose of generating indicators.

Although the concept of dynamic (run-time evaluated) attributes has been introduced here, their use is not limited to components only. Other repositories of important attributes are the activity objects. While components express the cost of certain operations, activities define higher level, goal-oriented attributes:

- *Utility and deadline*: a measure of progress if the activity is completed by a given deadline. It is weel known, that utility is not necessarily a simple two-valued step function of meeting or missing a single deadline. To reflect this, our current approach tries to enhance utility expression in two ways. One is the linear approximation of utility values as shown in the following examples:

```
utility = 45           deadline = 50
utility = 45~20,10     deadline = 50,100
```

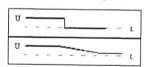

The other option is to use dynamic attributes for utility values. Suppose a data processing activity is triggered by an event generated by a pre-qualifier activity. Clearly the output of pre-qualification affects the utility of the subsequent activities. Utility is a very complex issue, and a significant body of research-based knowledge is available. The presented utility representation is a first and simple attempt, likely to be extended in the subsequent phases of the project.

Minimum latency: the time required to start up the execution of all components of the first phase, measured from the occurrence of the triggering event.

Hard or soft schedulability: the tolerance of this activity to being cancelled. Some processes can be scheduled tentatively, when it is not a problem if they are eventually terminated before completion. Others could leave some data inconsistencies when terminated, so they prefer not to be started at all if their deadline may be missed. Hard schedulable activities can also be represented by utility functions that turn negative after a deadline.

Periodicity: although activities are scheduled individually, it is important to know if an activity category represents a recurring operation. Moreover, some activities cannot be retriggered until their previous are finished.

While several additional, experimental, or secondary attributes have been defined, it is notable that priority itself is not represented directly. As it is seen at rate monotonic analysis, it appears that deadlines, execution times, and latencies sufficiently determine the effective priorities of the activities.

5 Scheduler Operation and Adaptivity

Having seen the model-based representation of the scheduling problem, it is now worth looking at it from the scheduler's point of view. Unlike the system architect who builds the static part of the model, the scheduler also has access to run-time data, and in effect works on an extended version of the model described above. In addition to the platform, events, and activities seen there, the scheduler also handles instantiations of the latter two: instances of currently pending events and currently executed activities.

A principal feature of the proposed scheduling approach is that it is not task, but activity based: each activity instance must compete individually for processor time and resources based on its actual, potentially data-dependent utility/cost ratio.

The evolution of the model is as follows: whenever an event happens (e.g. timer event), a new event is instantiated from the corresponding design-time event. The scheduler next evaluates activities connected to this event. Depending on the activity type, one or several of them are selected for execution, if they appear to be schedulable, considering:

the expected work load imposed by the new activities,
the current load factor of the system,
the currently executed activities
the utility of the current application.

If the system load is low or moderate, all candidate activities are scheduled. The new activity instances are added to the current set. This immediately affects system load, so later activities may not be immediately scheduled.

Activities may create new internal events. These may again trigger new activities exactly as described above. During execution, the design-time part of the model does not change, although some run-time variables like past performance averages, loaded/unloaded status, and event periodicy are bound to events and activities in general and not to any specific instance.

Having an activity scheduled does not guarantee that it will run to completion. The system is allowed to slightly overload itself with activities that probably cannot be all scheduled to finish by their deadline. All these excess activities must be soft schedulable, as the projected time requirements and resource utilization of hard schedulable ones must be well under the full range of resources.

Even if they are scheduled, activities may still be later discarded when it is obvious that they are no longer able to deliver utility above a certain threshold (e.g. they are going to miss their hard deadlines), or if their resources are needed by more important activities. Although it should never happen, even hard schedulable activities are potentially discardable, if their utility is exceeded by other, more urgent activities.

Note that tentative scheduling is only applied if only processor time is overloaded. Tasks are currently never scheduled if they are expected to cause the system to run out of any other resources.

Another interesting concept is the option for *prescheduled activities*. These activities are considered scheduled even before their triggering event actually happens. These are typically low-latency, high utility activities, since the main payoff in being prescheduled is a quick and practically guaranteed startup for the activity. Using prescheduled activities, the scheduling policy approximates the hard-real time discipline. Indeed, the strict schedulability criteria for rate monotonic scheduling is maintained for the whole set of prescheduled activities. Therefore, the set of prescheduled activities is in effect a little, guaranteed, deadline monotonic scheduler within this highly dynamic architecture.

The scheduling architecture can display *adaptive behavior* through the averaging mechanisms used in dynamic attribute expressions. Averages accumulate relevant historical information, and this is fed back to the decision-making process of new iterations. All this is based on the assumption that past characteristics of activities repeat themselves later. While this is not always true, it is most typically a good presumption, especially when no better estimates (e.g. data by human experts) are available.

As always, adaptivity introduces the concern of *stability*. It may happen that adaptive mechanisms result in runaway averages which completely overturn the balance of the scheduling mechanism. Unfortunately the adaptive control loop is non-linear and rather complex, so generic stability analysis techniques are inapplicable. Developing a suitable mechanism for monitoring adaptivity and system behavior in general is an agenda for further research.

As it has been mentioned before, another caveat, *scheduler performance* may also pose a problem. Although the model-based representation is in fact fairly lightweight, the presented dynamic scheduling architecture does not compare in efficiency with a static or less complex scheduler. On the other hand, it also has to be recognized, that if real-time efficiency and throughput are to be maximized for hardly predictable activities, scheduling definitely becomes a dominant issue. We assert that even a scheduler overhead of 10-15makes up for that loss.

6   Project Status and Challenge Problem

This research is an offspring from research done under the Darpa SAFER project [7]. At the current stage of the project, the conceptual design is accomplished, with detailed design and speculative analysis currently under way. Although the basic idea, model-based representation of fairly detailed schedulability-related information, has proven to be very perspective since its inception, several design iterations were tried and later overhauled by substantial changes. The current 'final' design, however, is no longer expected to change significantly until some practical experience has also been accumulated.

The proof-of concept implementation platform selected is the Java virtual machine, which runs a custom-developed simulated thread scheduler within the VM. Java is certainly not a mission critical real-time platform, but it has proved to be a very convenient experimental environment. The next step of the concept's evolution will probably include transferring to a truly real-time operating system platform with sufficiently versatile pluggable scheduler interface. Simultaneously, Real-Time Java, if it is available by that time, will certainly be another option to consider.

The challenge problem is from the area of network security monitoring. These devices are used to screen network data packets to identify suspicious traffic. Even some moderately complex processing on the currently typical 2x100 Mbps data flow is certainly a challenge for a real-time system. Moreover, several complementary or alternative approaches of traffic analysis exist, with vast differences in abstraction level, applicability area, screening capability, computational intensity, reliability, etc.

It is anticipated that network probes built on any hardware of limited budget will be unable to guarantee the execution of all these tests under all data rates and all traffic patterns. Hard real-time scheduling is thus not feasible. This is underlined by the fact that that network traffic is aperiodic in nature. There is a good chance, however, that under most traffic patterns the network probe is powerful enough to execute all or most of the important tests. Even under peak loads, a degraded but decent and valuable traffic probing can be provided.

The fact that many screening algorithms exhibit highly data-dependent performance makes our approach even more promising. By quickly looking at the data we expect to be able to estimate the performance of detailed tests with relatively high accuracy. Feeding back statistical averages of previous tests also appears to be feasible. All in all, chances are good for a successful demonstration of model-based adaptive real-time scheduling.

7   Conclusion

Soft real-time computation has received an increased amount of attention in the past few years. As a part of this, a core problem of real-time systems, scheduling has been researched. The key question seems to be how to extend scheduler intelligence and flexibility to accommodate workloads higher than what is permissible by hard real-time analysis techniques. Several valuable approaches have been proposed, but apparently additional research is needed to simultaneously satisfy requirements like sufficiently refined control on scheduling behavior, runtime efficiency, and ease of use by implementors of real-time applications.

Our approach intends to contribute to this work by proposing the application of model-based computing, a technology that has not been used so far directly to specify scheduler behavior. We expect that models will make it possible to describe hardware resources, processes, and process interactions in a clear and efficiently computable way. Moreover, placing models into the center of the scheduling mechanism allows the specification of self-adaptive behavior, which is expected to be useful whenever a priori information on component timing characteristics is not available or is not sufficiently accurate.

Considering all, we expect to develop a technology, which can emerge as one of the most viable architectures in certain segments of real time applications. Among many other researchers, we also believe that, – unlike in the case of hard real-time scheduling, – no single universally superior solution for the soft real-time scheduling will appear. That is why the nature and focus of the application area is also significant. Our first challenge problem, scheduling of a multilevel network security probe, is certainly a good representative of a rapidly expanding segment of real-world embedded systems characterized by aperiodic stimuli, high throughput, and somewhat relaxed fault tolerance requirements.

Acknowledgements

This paper and the work described in it was inspired by ideas and advice from my colleagues at ISIS/Vanderbilt, most notably Dr. Gabor Karsai, Dr. Akos Ledeczi and Miklos Maroti, whose valuable contribution I gratefully acknowledge.

References

1. Douglass, B. P.: *Doing Hard Time* (1999) Addison Wesley
2. Phillip A. Laplante, Eileen P. Rose, Maria Gracia-Watson: *An Historical Survey of Early Real-Time Computing Developments in the U.S.* (1995) Real-Time Systems, Volume 8, p 199-213
3. Burns, A., Wellings A. *Real-Time Systems and Programming Languages* (2nd ed, 1996), Addison Wesley Longman.
4. Park, A. *Predicting program execution times by analyzing static and dynamic program paths* (1993) Real-Time Systems, 5(1), 31-62
5. GME Ledeczi A., Maroti M., Bakay A., Karsai G., Garrett J., Thomason IV C., Nordstrom G., Sprinkle J., Volgyesi P.: *The Generic Modeling Environment, Workshop on Intelligent Signal Processing*, submitted, Budapest, Hungary, May 17, 2001
6. Gabor Karsai, Greg Nordstrom, Akos Ledeczi, and Janos Sztipanovits, *Specifying Graphical Modeling Systems Using Constraint-based Metamodels, IEEE Symposium on Computer Aided Control System Design,* Conference CD-Rom, Anchorage, Alaska, September 25, 2000.
7. Ledeczi A., Bakay A., Maroti M.: *Model-Integrated Embedded Systems, International Workshop on Self Adaptive Software*, Oxford, England, April, 2000. Springer Verlag 2001.
8. Chandru, V, Lee, C.Y., and Uzsoy (1993). *Minimizing Total Completion Time on Batch Processing Machines* International Journal of Production Research, Vol. 31, No. 9, 2097-2121.

Adaptive Agent Based System for State Estimation Using Dynamic Multidimensional Information Sources

Alvaro Soto and Pradeep Khosla

Robotics Institute, Carnegie Mellon University
5000 Forbes Avenue,
Pittsburgh, Pa, 15213, USA
{amsoto,pkk}@cs.cmu.edu

Abstract. This paper describes a new approach for the creation of an adaptive system able to selectively combine dynamic multidimensional information sources to perform state estimation. The system proposed is based on an intelligent agent paradigm. Each information source is implemented as an agent that is able to adapt its behavior according to the relevant task and environment constraints. The adaptation is provided by a local self-evaluation function on each agent. Cooperation among the agents is given by a probabilistic scheme that integrates the evidential information provided by them. The proposed system aims to achieve two highly desirable attributes of an engineering system: robustness and efficiency. By combining the outputs of multiple vision modules the assumptions and constrains of each module can be factored out to result in a more robust system overall. Efficiency is still kept through the on-line selection and specialization of the agents. An initial implementation for the case of visual information demonstrates the advantages of the approach for two frequent problems faced by a mobile robot: dynamic target tracking and obstacle detection.

1 Introduction

As the state of the art of computing technology is advancing, providing more powerful and affordable machines, computers are becoming widely used in the more diverse aspects of modern society. As computers start to perform new types of tasks in less structured and less predictable environments, there is an increasing need to provide them with a higher degree of awareness about the changing conditions of their virtual or natural surroundings.

From the seemingly endless information paths of the Internet to the case of a mobile robot collecting information from its environment, there is an increasing need for the development of automatic tools able to transform sensing information in useful knowledge.

As an example, in the Robotics domain the problem of understanding sensing information from the environment is highly relevant. While today it is possible to equip a robot with many sensors and sophisticated locomotion capabilities, the perception skills of most robots are still rather limited. In order to move robots out of labs to perform useful tasks in natural environments, it is needed to equip them with more

R. Laddaga, P. Robertson, and H. Shrobe (Eds.): IWSAS 2001, LNCS 2614, pp. 66–83, 2003.

powerful perception systems able to acquire useful knowledge from diverse sources of information. Today the main challenge for robots is not the controllability but the observability problem.

Although it is possible to argue in favor of a stateless or pure reactive machine, following the ideas presented in [1], in this paper we claim the need for maintaining an internal representation of the world that summarize the relevant knowledge needed by the agent[1] in order to act with diligence.

The basic scenario is an agent embedded in an unpredictable and dynamic environment. The agent is able to receive different types of information from its environment. As new information arrives the agent goal is to use the more adequate set of information sources in order to update the knowledge about its relevant part of the world.

In this sense our problem can be cast as dynamic state estimation based on multi-dimensional information sources. The key observation is that as the state of the world evolves the potential knowledge provided by different information sources can change dramatically. As a consequence there is a high variability about the more adequate set of information sources to complete a task. This stressed the need to incorporate suitable adaptation mechanisms that allow to combine and to select the more appropriate set of information sources in order to perform robust and efficient state estimation.

As an example consider ALVINN [2], a perceptual visual system designed to steer a car in natural environments using a neural net learning algorithm. After training, the main internal features learned by ALVINN were the edges of the road. With this knowledge ALVINN was able to demonstrate a reasonable performance, but it irremediable failed in situations where the edges of the road were obstructed by other passing vehicles, or were missing as on bridges or crossing points.

The main problem with ALVINN was its lack of adaptability to use alternative sources of information such as centerlines, other traffic, roadway signs, and so on. In contrast to ALVINN human drivers are remarkable robust to changes in the driving conditions. This great robustness of the human visual system can be explained by its extreme flexibility to adapt to the changing conditions of the environment by selecting appropriate sources of information.

In this paper we propose a new approach for the creation of an adaptive system able to selectively combine dynamic multidimensional information sources in order to perform state estimation. The system is based on an *intelligent agent*[2] paradigm. Each information source is implemented as an agent that is able to adapt its behavior according to the relevant task and environment constraints. The adaptation is provided by local self-evaluation functions on the agents. These functions are based on considerations about the level of uncertainty present at each time in the state estimation. Cooperation among the agents is given by a probabilistic scheme that integrates the evidential information provided by them.

---

[1] *We refer to these new types of machines as intelligent agents or just agents*
[2] *For a definition of an intelligent agent see section 2.1*

Using the power of probability theory for representing and reasoning under uncertainty, and elements from information theory to lead the inference engine to prominent hypothesis and information sources, the proposed system aims to achieve two highly desirable attributes of an engineering system: *robustness* and *efficiency.*

By combining the outputs of multiple information sources the assumptions and constrains of each module can be factored out to result in a more robust system overall. Efficiency is still kept through the on-line selection and specialization of the agents according to the quality of the information provided by each of them.

The research proposed in this work is particularly relevant for the case of dynamic visual tasks with a high variability about the subsets of visual attributes that can characterize relevant visual structures. This includes visual tasks such as dynamic target tracking, obstacle detection, and identification of landmarks in natural scenes. In particular, the advantages of the approach proposed here are demonstrated in two frequent problems faced by a mobile robot: dynamic target tracking and obstacle detection.

This paper is organized as follows. Section 2 describes our approach and its main components. Section 3 presents related work. Section 4 describes the implementation of the proposed system for the case of visual information. Section 5 describes the results of our implementation. Finally, section 6 presents conclusions and future lines of research.

2 Approach

2.1 Intelligent Agents

Even though there is a diversity of views about the correct definition of an intelligent agent, there is a general agreement that the main features that distinguish an intelligent agent are *autonomy, sociability, and adaptation* [3]. Autonomy provides the independency that allows the agent to exhibit an opportunistic behavior in agreement with its goals. Sociability provides the communication skills that allow the agent to interact with other artificial agents and humans. Adaptation provides the flexibility that allows the agent to change its behavior according to the conditions of the environment.

This work makes use of multiple agents that can simultaneously analyze different dimensions of the incoming information. These agents act as a group of experts where each agent has a specific knowledge area. This scheme provides a high degree of abstraction and modularity, which facilitate the design and scalability of the system.

2.2 Representation

Bayesian theory provides a solid mathematical framework for reasoning under uncertainty. Using the language of probability theory, a Bayesian approach provides mechanisms to combine information in order to reason about different hypothetical solutions to a problem.

In a Bayesian framework to dynamic state estimation the goal is to use the information available or evidence (e) to keep track of a probability density function (pdf) over a set of possible hypothesis (h) of the state of the world.

The core of the Bayesian technique is the so-called Bayes' Rule :

$$P(h/e) = \frac{P(e/h)*P(h)}{P(e)} = \alpha * P(e/h)*P(h) \qquad (1)$$

Bayes rules allows a convenient way to perform state estimation in terms of a likelihood function $P(e/h)$, and an a priori term $P(h)$. Equation (1) can be easily extended to the dynamic case:

$$P(h_t/\vec{e_t}) = \beta * P(e_t/h_t, \vec{e_{t-1}}) * P(h_t/\vec{e_{t-1}}) \qquad (2)$$

Assuming that the current evidence e_t can be totally explained by the current hypothesis h_t, and that the dynamic of the system follows a first order Markov process, it is possible to obtain (5) which is the standard way to perform Bayesian inference for the dynamic case.

$$P(h_t/\vec{e_t}) = \beta * P(e_t/h_t) * P(h_t/\vec{e_{t-1}}) \qquad (3)$$

$$P(h_t/\vec{e_t}) = \beta * P(e_t/h_t) * \sum_{h_{t-1}} P(h_t/h_{t-1}, \vec{e_{t-1}}) * P(h_{t-1}/\vec{e_{t-1}}) \qquad (4)$$

$$P(h_t/\vec{e_t}) = \beta * P(e_t/h_t) * \sum_{h_{t-1}} P(h_t/h_{t-1}) * P(h_{t-1}/\vec{e_{t-1}}) \qquad (5)$$

The recursive formulation of equation (5) requires knowledge about the observation model $P(e_t/h_t)$ and the system dynamics $P(h_t/h_{t-1})$. In practice, excepting the case of some finite state-space Hidden Markov models, the full Bayesian inference is only possible when the models have suitable analytical expressions. The more typical case is linear-gaussian models. For this case the state pdf remains Gaussian at all times, and the well-known Kalman Filter gives the optimal solution. For the case of nonlinear models it is possible to use the Extended Kalman Filter but still under a Gaussian assumption.

The Gaussian assumption severely limits the use of Bayesian inference for state estimation. High ambiguity is one of the inherent features that emerges in most unstructured environments. In this case the state pdf can have a complex multi-modal shape that cannot be accurately modeled by a Gaussian density. Fortunally stochastic sampling provides an alternative and efficient estimation approach for these cases.

In stochastic sampling a pdf is represented through a set of samples, each with an associated weight representing its probability. The great advantage is that it is possible to approximate any functional non-linearity and system or measurement noise. In this paper we approximate equation (5) using a particle filter approach, also known in the literature as bootstrap filter [4], condensation algorithm [5], or sequential Monte Carlo [6].

Figure 1 shows pseudo code for the operation of the algorithm. Starting from an initial set of samples that approximate the state pdf, the algorithm uses the system dynamic and its current belief to propagate the more prominent hypothesis. Then these candidate hypotheses are weighted according to the support received by the new incoming evidence represented as a likelihood function. The nice feature about the particle filter is the dynamic allocation of the sample hypothesis according to the current belief. This helps to avoid the problem of sample depletion, and allows a great efficiency in the representation in contrast to other stochastic sampling algorithms such as likelihood weighting.

$$At\ t = 0$$

$Sample\ h_i|_{i=1}^n\ from\ initial\ prior\ p(h)$

$set\ L_t = \{\ \pi_i, h_i\ \}|_{i=1}^n\ with\ \pi_i = p(\ h_i\ )$

$For\ t = 1,2,...$

   $For\ i = 1\ to\ n$

      $Sample\ h_{i-} \sim L_t$

      $Sample\ h_i \sim P(\ h_i\ /\ h_{i-}\ )$

      $Evaluate\ \pi_i = P(\ e_t\ /\ h_i\ )$

   end

   $Normalize\ weights\quad \pi_i = \dfrac{\pi_i}{\sum_i \pi_i}$

   $Set\ new\ L_t = \{\ \pi_i, h_i\ \}|_{i=1}^n$

end

Fig. 1. Pseudo code for Particle Filter algorithm.

Gordon et al. [4] originally presented this algorithm using some results by Smith and Gelfand. Isard and Blake [5] validated the filter using the factored sampling algorithm. Soto [7] presented a justification based on the composition algorithm. Recently independent results by Doucet [8] and Liu et al. [9] presented an interesting alternative view of the algorithm in terms of sequential importance sampling with resampling.

In summary, to be able to keep a sample version of the posterior density using a particle filter, one needs an initial approximation of the posterior density, and knowledge about how to evaluate the likelihood and propagation densities $P(e_t/h_t)$ and $P(h_t / h_{t-1})$. In general the dynamic of the process determine the level of exploration for new hypothesis, while the likelihood function can be obtained through an adequate metric that evaluates the fitness between each sample hypotheses and the observations. Section 4 describes an implementation of the algorithm and these functions for the case of multidimensional visual information.

2.3   Integration

The integration of information is performed using Bayes nets. Bayes nets take advantage of causal relations among random variables to allow an efficient graphical representation of joint probability distributions (jpds). The efficiency is gained by use of causal knowledge that provides conditional independence relations between the random variables. These independence relations allow partitioning the jpds in simpler local probabilistic models.

Figure 2 shows the typical tree structure of the Bayes nets relevant to this work. Agent nodes directly measure different dimensions of the incoming information. Abstraction nodes allow the integration of information and the updating of the state representation. Also, abstraction nodes allow introducing conditional independence relations among the agents. This decoupling of the information provided by the agents facilitates the construction of probabilistic models for applying Bayesian inference using equation (5).

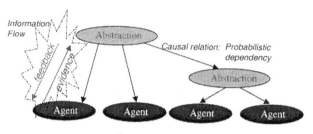

Fig. 2. Bayes Net.

Figure 2 can be considered as a hierarchical representation of the simpler case of just one abstraction node. In this case equation (5) can be expressed as:

$$Agents$$

$$P(h_t / \vec{e}_{1,t}, \vec{e}_{2,t}, ...) = \beta * \overbrace{P(e_{1,t} / h_t)} * \overbrace{P(e_{2,t} / h_t)} * ...$$

$$... * \underbrace{\sum_{h_{t-1}} P(h_t / h_{t-1}) * P(h_{t-1} / \vec{e}_{1,t-1}, \vec{e}_{2,t-1}, ...)} \quad (6)$$

$$Abstraction\ node$$

Equation (6) shows the nice decoupling between the evidence provided by each agent through a likelihood function, and the state updating performed by the abstraction node. The abstraction node acts as a central inference that keeps track of the state estimation represented by a set of sample hypothesis and their probabilities. Using the current estimations and the system dynamics, the abstraction node decides which hypothesis need further considerations and it sends this new set of hypothesis to each of the agents. According to its own local information sources, each agent evaluates the supporting evidence for each hypothesis, and it sends this evidence back to the abstraction node as a likelihood function. Finally the abstraction node uses this information to update its beliefs about the state of the world, and it starts a new iteration of the state estimation.

2.4   Adaptation

In contrast to most traditional applications of Bayes nets, where the structures of the nets are fix, the system intended in this research includes adaptation mechanisms that allows dynamic reconfiguration of the nets according to the characteristics of the incoming information.

The adaptation mechanisms are based on the evaluation of the level of uncertainty present in the state estimation and the evaluation of the quality of the information provided by each agent in terms of uncertainty reduction. The design goals are to perform a robust estimation keeping uncertainty low, and also to perform an efficient estimation avoiding the processing of irrelevant, misleading, or redundant information. In order to achieve these goals it is needed to introduce two performance metrics.

The first metric called uncertainty deviation (UD) is intended to evaluate the level of uncertainty in the state representation. The intuition behind this metric is to quantify the dispersion of the state representation with respect to the most probable hypothesis known as maximum a posteriori hypothesis (MAP). Equation (7) shows this metric; here d corresponds to a distance metric between hypotheses. In the implementation presented in this work for the case of visual information, d corresponds to the Mahalanobis distance[10].

$$UD = \sqrt{\sum_{h_i}^{|h|} d(h_i, MAP) * Pr(h_i)}   \quad (7)$$

The second metric is intended to evaluate the quality of the information provided by each agent in terms of uncertainty reduction. The intuition is that if an agent is providing good information its local likelihood should be close to the state pdf maintained by the abstraction node. So the problem reduces to quantify similarity between distributions. In this work we compare distributions using the Kullback-Leibler divergence [11], which is given by equation (8).

$$D(f,g) = \sum_i f(i) * log \frac{f(i)}{g(i)}   \quad (8)$$

$f(i)$= pdf for the state estimation
$g(i)$= local normalized agent likelihood

Using the previous performance metrics we introduce two adaptation schemes to the state estimation. The first scheme is performed by the abstraction node. Using the UD metric the abstraction node measures the level of ambiguity in its state representation. If this level exceeds a predefined threshold the central inference sends an activation signal to any inactive agent to start sending supporting evidence that can eventually reduce the current ambiguities. Also, in case that this level is lower than a predefined threshold, meaning that the uncertainty is low, the abstraction node stops the less informative agent in order to increase the efficiency of the state estimation. The selection of the less informative agent is performed in base to the relative values of the Kullback-Leibler divergence among the active agents.

The second adaptation scheme is carry out locally by each agent using the UD metric. In this case, given that each agent calculates a likelihood function, the MAP is replaced in equation (7) by the maximum likelihood hypothesis (ML). Using this metric each agent evaluates the local level of uncertainty in its information sources. If this level exceeds a predefined threshold the agent modify its own local actions in order to improve its performance. In case that after a number of cycles the agent still cannot improve its performance, it stops processing information becoming an inactive agent.

Section 4 describes an implementation of these adaptation mechanisms for the case of visual information.

3   Related Work

The idea of reducing uncertainty by combining knowledge from difference sources is by no account new. In several fields it is possible to find studies that recognize the relevance of integrating information in order to create more robust and flexible systems. Although all the abundant literature, there have been a gap between the conceptual idea and the production of working systems for real problems. Important issues such as the organization and control of the pieces of knowledge, and in special the development of mechanisms that allow the adaptation and feedback among the knowledge sources have not been tackled in depth, and they are still open questions. This section reviews some of the efforts that have appeared in the scientific literature of related fields.

3.1   Artificial Intelligence (AI)

In the AI domain the blackboard model for problem solving is one of the first attempts to adaptively integrate different types of knowledge sources. Using ideas independently proposed by Newell [12] and Simmon [13], Reddy and Erman implemented the first blackboard system as part of the HEARSAY and HEARSAY II speech understanding programs [14][15].

A blackboard model consists of 3 major components: the knowledge sources, the blackboard, and the control unit. A blackboard model divides a problem in *knowledge sources*, which are kept separate and independent. These knowledge sources interact through a *blackboard*, which is the global database that integrates the information. Finally, a *control unit* manages the opportunistic activation of the knowledge sources according to changes in the blackboard.

The blackboard conceptualization is closely related to the ideas presented in this work, but as a problem-solving scheme the blackboard model offers just a conceptual framework for formulating solutions to problems. In this sense, the work proposed in this research aims to extent the blackboard conceptualization to a computational specification or working system, providing specific mechanisms to perform probabilistic inference and adaptive integration for the case of dynamic multidimensional information sources.

3.2   Machine Learning

In the machine learning literature there is related work in the context of ensembles of classifiers. An ensemble of classifiers is a set of classifiers whose individual decisions are combined to classify new examples [16]. Each classifier can be considered as a different source of knowledge. Adaptation mechanisms are usually included in the policy used to combine the outputs of the individual classifiers. These kinds of techniques are currently receiving broad attention in the machine learning literature due to the capacity of the ensemble to improve performance over the individual classifiers that make them up. There have been several algorithms proposed to implement the ensemble of classifiers; among the more relevant are *Mixture of Experts* [17] and *AdaBoost* [18].

The work presented here differs in many ways with respect to the current algorithms used to build ensemble of classifiers. One of the main differences resides in the adaptation mechanisms. An ensemble of classifiers is an eager learner in the sense that the training is performed off-line and during operation each classifier acts as a blind data driven box. In contrast, one of the main features of the work proposed here is the on-line interaction or feedback between the knowledge sources.

3.3   Computer Vision

In the computer vision literature there have been a constant acknowledge about the importance of integrating information from different visual dimensions such as depth, color, shape, and so on. Several researchers have proposed a model of visual perception as a distributed collection of task-specific, task-driven visual routines with strong feedback among the visual modules [19][20]. However, all this constant acknowledge, there have been not many working systems that exploit these ideas and most of the work has been concentrated in the development of algorithms to extract knowledge from single visual cues.

Among the relevant works that have shown the gain in robustness of combining several visual modules, it is possible to mention [21][22][23][24]. Unfortunly, most of these works have not considered in their systems topics such as adaptation and uncertainty, being the works by Isard and Blake [5], and Rasmussen and Hager [23] some of the notable exceptions.

4   Implementation

An initial implementation of the ideas presented in this work has been developed for the case of visual information.

In contrast to other sensor modalities, vision can allow the perception of a large number of different features of the environment such as color, shape, depth, motion, and so on. Depending on the task and the environment, the quantity of information or entropy in each visual cue can fluctuate. For instance, while stereovision is usually a strong depth cue, in the case of images from a homogeneous grass field, the stereo decoding of depth is highly noisy. Even worse, it usually gives wrong information due to bad matches. Instead, in this case a visual cue such as texture or color conveys higher entropy.

An efficient integration of visual cues able to adapt to the changing conditions of the environment should increase the robustness of current visual system to successfully operate in natural environments. Following these ideas and using the state estimation presented in this work, we have developed an initial implementation of a visual system for online tracking of dynamic targets and obstacle avoidance.

4.1 State Representation

Bounding boxes were used to describe the state of a tracked target or a detected obstacle. These bounding boxes were modeled by their center position (x,y), width, and height. The rectangular box in figure 3 shows an example of a hypothesis used to perform state estimation. In all the examples shown in this work the state pdf was approximated using 1000 samples. Also for the dynamic of the system we use a stationary Gaussian model with sigma equal to 20 pixels.

4.2 Visual Agents

At this moment the implementation is based on two visual agents: Color Agent and Stereovision Agent.

4.2.1 Color Agent

The color agent uses as observation the hue histogram of the pixels inside each hypothesis in the sample set. A detailed description of the way in which we construct these histograms can be found in [25].

In order to express its observations in terms of a likelihood function, the color agent calculates the similarity between each hypothesis and a reference histogram. The metric used to evaluate similarity is a modified version of the cross similarity distance (csd) using a sigmoid type of function. The introduction of a sigmoid function allows accounting for slight variations in the image conditions and target appearance providing a more accurate probabilistic model. Equations (9) and (10) shows the likelihood function for the case of the color agent. Here all the histograms are previously normalized to the size of the reference histogram.

$$csd = (f_{cum}, g_{cum}) = \sum_{i=1}^{256} |f_{cum}(i) - g_{cum}(i)| \quad (9)$$

$$f_{cum}, g_{cum} := cummulative\ histograms$$

$$Likelihood = 1.0 - tanh(2.0 * \frac{(csd - cte)}{cte}) \quad (10)$$

A special agent called a detector selects the reference histogram automatically. The idea here is to divide the agents in two types: detectors and specialists. Detector agents are general tools able to explore the incoming information looking for possible structures without relying in specific illumination, views, posture, etc. Once possible candidate structures have been identified, it is possible to use specialist agents. These agents are more specific tools able to look for specific supporting evidence in order to provide more efficient and robust appearance models. In the case of color information the detector agent is based on a color segmentation algorithm based on the hue color component [25], while the color specialist agent is the one that estimates the likelihood function described above.

Figure 3 shows the reference and a hypothesis for the case of target tracking. The upper figure corresponds to the initial detection of a detector agent, while the lower one shows the csd and likelihood estimated by the specialist agent.

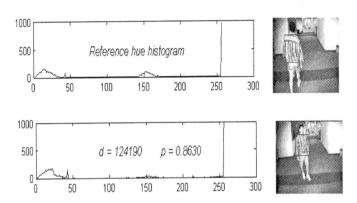

Fig. 3. Upper figure shows a reference target. Lower figure shows a state hypothesis.

4.2.2 Stereovision Agent

The stereovision agent uses as observation the depth values of the pixels inside each hypothesis in the sample set. The algorithm is based on depth segmentation and blob analysis, a detailed description of the algorithm can be found in [25].

In order to express its observations in terms of a likelihood function, the stereovision agent estimates four properties of the depth values: depth variance, heights of the depth blobs, blob shape, and number of points with valid depth values. Using these depth features the stereovision agent estimate a likelihood function using a multivariate Gaussian pdf given by equation (11):

$$Likelihood(\vartheta) = \frac{exp\{-0.5*(\vartheta-\mu)^T * B^{-1} * (\vartheta-\mu)\}}{(2\pi)^{1/2} |B|^{1/2}} \quad (11)$$

$\vartheta = feature\,vector\,(depth, height, blob\,shape, valid\,points)$

$\mu = mean\,of\,feature\,vectors$

$B = diagonal\,covariance\,matrix$

In the case of depth information there is also a detector agent. This agent initializes candidate targets or obstacles using the results of the depth based segmentation algorithm.

4.3   Software Architecture

The core of the software architecture is called CyberAries (Autonomous Reconnaissance and Intelligent Exploration System) which is a distributed multi-agent architecture developed by our research group [26][27]. CyberAries provides powerful inter-agent communication capabilities that greatly simplify the job of developing ensembles of cooperating agents.

On Cyberaries agents are independent processes that run concurrently and can be started on as-needed basis. The software mainly consists of an agent-framework environment and a distribution layer. The agent-framework provides all the operating system provisions such as concurrent processing or automatic scheduling, and also the application abstraction provisions such as memory management and resource categorization. The distribution layer is responsible for providing and balancing the communications, processing, and sensing resources among the active agents. If an agent needs to send a message or to access any resource, the distribution layer handles all the details of the connection, checking for availability and resource allocation.

5   Results

A preliminary version of the system proposed in this work has been developed for the case of single person tracking and obstacle detection.

Figure 4 shows four frames of the video sequence used for the case of single person tacking. The image at the upper left shows the intended target. After an initial detection given by the stereovision agent detector the system starts the tracking using the color and the stereovision specialist agents. The left image in figure 5 shows the set of sample used for the state estimation at frame 4, while the right image shows the MAP estimator for this case.

Due to the low ambiguity in the state representation, after five frames the system decided to operate just with the stereovision agent. In this case the system decided to discard the color agent due to the similarities between the color of the target and the rest of the scene. Figure 6 shows the normalized likelihood function provided by the stereovision and the color agents at frame 5. The clear unimodal shape of the likelihood function provided by the stereovision agent shows the low uncertainty present in the depth information. In the same way the highly spread shape of the color likelihood shows the high ambiguity present in the color information. In this case the difference in the level of ambiguity is properly captured by the UD index that it is used to stop the color agent.

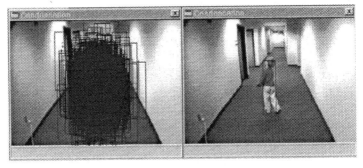

Fig. 4. Four frames of the video sequence used for target tracking

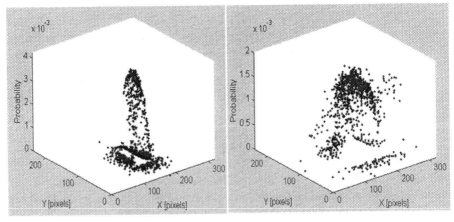

Fig. 5. (Left) set of hypothesis used for state estimation at frame 4. (Right) MAP hypothesis at frame 4.

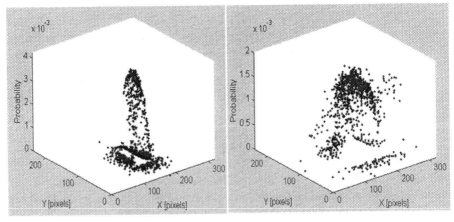

Fig. 6. (Left) likelihood function provided by stereovision agent for frame 5. (Right) likelihood function provided by color agent for frame 5. (for clarity only x and y are presented).

On frame 60 a second target enters the scene increasing the uncertainty in the state estimation based only on depth information. This is clearly shown in figure 7 by the bimodal shape of the state estimation. At this point the system automatically starts the color agent at frame 65. The 5-frame delay is set just to avoid unnecessary activations due to noise. Given that the color information of the distracting target differs from the intended target, the additional information provided by the color agent allows a drastic reduction in the uncertainty present in the state estimation (see figure 9).

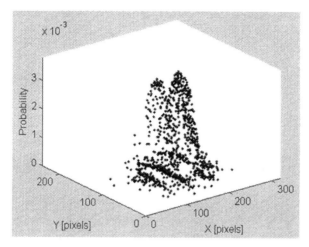

Fig. 7. State estimation at frame 60 (for clarity only x and y are presented)

As the second target moves away, the level of uncertainty decreases and the system again decided to operate just with the stereovision agent. Figure 8 shows the activation condition of the color agents for the whole sequence. Figure 9 shows the history of the UD index calculated at the abstraction node.

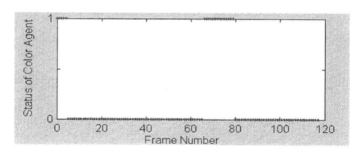

Fig. 8. Status of Color Agent (Active=1).

Table 1 shows the different performance in terms of average uncertainty and processing time for four tracking schemes: using just the color agent, using just the stereovision agent, combining the color and stereovision agents without adaptation, and using an adaptive integration of the color and stereovision agent. The important observation is that the adaptive integration of the information provided by the agents not only increases the performance of the system in terms of processing time, but also increase the robustness in terms of average uncertainty by considering the less reliable information provided by the color agent just when it was need it.

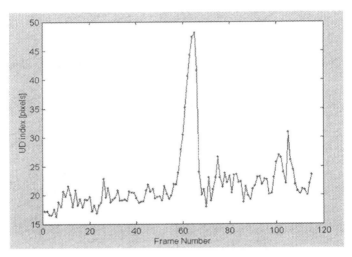

Fig. 9. Evolution of the UD index at the abstraction node.

Table 1. Comparative results for different operation cases

Modality	Average Uncertainty	Proceesing Time [hz] *
Color	67.4589 pix	5.23
Stereo	30.7798 pix	2.17
Color + Stereo	29.1677 pix	0.54
Color + Stereo (Ad)	24.7260 pix	2.11

*Pentium 600

Figure 10 shows an example of the performance of the system for the detection of obstacles using stereo and color information. The upper images show the detection based only on stereo for different time instants in the video sequence. From this figure it is clear that the effect of noise makes not possible a robust tracking of the features using just the stereo agent. The lower images show the combined tracking based on the color and the stereo agents. Combining both cues the system was able to keep track of all the structures during the complete video sequence consisting of 40 video frames.

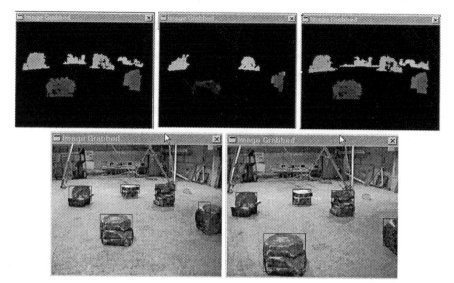

Fig. 10. Upper images show the structures detected by the stereo agent at some points during the robot motion. Lower images show the detection of the obstacles for the initial and final frame in the video sequence using information from the color and the stereo agents.

6 Conclusions and Future Work

This paper presented a new approach for state estimation based on the adaptive integration of dynamic multidimensional information sources. Using a synergistic combination of elements from probabilistic Bayesian reasoning and information theory the system allows the creation of a *robust* and *efficient* state estimation system.

The use of a probabilistic representation allows the introduction of uncertainty metrics able to quantify the quality of the information used in the state estimation. Furthermore the use of Bayesian reasoning in combination with an intelligent agent paradigm facilitates the design and scalability of the system. We believe that this is a natural and sound methodology to adaptively combine multidimensional information sources.

An initial implementation of the system for the case of visual information showed encouraging results. The comparative analysis with respect to the case of operation without adaptation and/or integration shows that the adaptive integration of information increases the robustness and efficiency of the system in terms of accuracy and output rate.

There are still further research avenues to improve the system. At this moment the determination of the adaptation thresholds is learned by examples. We are currently working in an automatic determination of these thresholds in based to an optimization function that considers performance requirements in terms of accuracy and output rate. Also at this moment the policy to active agent is fix. We are currently working in the implementation of learning algorithms to optimize the agent switching. The adaptive selection of the optimal number of samples used for the state representation is another important issue to consider because this variable plays an important role in the computational complexity of the system.

For the particular case of visual information, we are currently adding more information sources to the system. In particular we are adding agent based on motion, shape, and texture. Also for the case of multiple targets tracking it is important to add reasoning schemes for the case of target occlusion.

We believe that a synergistic combination of elements from computer vision, intelligent agents technology, probabilistic reasoning, and information theory is a viable way for the creation of a *flexible*, *robust* and *efficient* vision system for tasks such as target tracking.

References

1. Soto, A., and Nourbakhsh, I.: A Scenario for Planning Visual Navigation of a Mobile Robot. AAAI 1998 Fall Symposium Series, October 23-25, Florida, 1998.
2. Pomerleau D.: Neural Network Perception for Mobile Robot Guidance. Boston: Kluwer Academic Publishers, 1993.
3. Jennings, N., and Wooldridge, M.: Applying Agent Technology. Journal of Applied Artificial Intelligence special issue on Intelligent Agents and Multi-Agent Systems, 1995.
4. Gordon, N., Salmon, D., Smith, A.: A novel approach to nonlinear/non Gaussian Bayesian state estimation. IEE Proc. On Radar and Signal Processing, 140, 107-113.
5. Isard, M., and Blake, A.: Visual Tracking by Stochastic Propagation of Conditional Density. Proceedings of 4th European conf. on computer vision, 343-356, Cambridge, England, 1996
6. Kitagawa, G.: Monte Carlo filter and Smoother for Non-Gaussian Nonlinear State Space Models. Journal of Computational and Graphical Statistics, 5:1-25, 1996.
7. Soto, A.: Adaptive Agent Based System for Knowledge Discovery in Visual Information. Thesis Proposal, Robotics Institute, Carnegie Mellon University.
8. Doucet, A.: On Sequential Simulation-Based Methods for Bayesian Filtering. Technical report CUED/F-INFEG/TR 310, Department of Engineering, Cambridge University, 1998.
9. Liu, J., and Chen, R.: Monte Carlo Methods for Dynamics Systems. J. Amer. Statist. Assoc., Vol 93, 1032-1044, 1998.
10. Cox, I. J.: A Review of Statistical Data Association Techniques for Motion Correspondence. Int. Journal of Comp. Vision, 10:1, 53-66, 1993.
11. Cover T., Thomas J.: Elements of Information Theory. Wiley series in telecommunications, 1991.
12. Newell, A.: Some Problems of Basic Organization in Problem-Solving Programs. Conference of Self-Organizing Systems, Washington D.C.: Spartan books, 393-42, 1962.
13. Simmon, H.: Scientific Discovery and the Psychology of the Problem Solving. In models of Discovery, Boston, Mass: D. Reidel Publishing company, 1977.
14. R. Reddy, R., Erman, D., Richard, N.: A Model and a System for Machine Recognition of Speech", IEEE Transaction on Audio and Electroacustic AU-21:229-238, 1973.
15. Erman, D., Hayes-Roth, F., Lesser, V., Reddy, R.: The HEARSAY-II Speech Understanding System: Integrating Knowledge to Resolve Uncertainty". ACM Computing Survey 12:213-253, 1980.

16. Dietterich, T.: Machine Learning Research: Four Current Directions. AI magazine, 18 (4), 97-136, 1997.
17. Waterhouse, S.: Classification and Regression using Mixtures of Experts. PhD. Thesis, Cambridge University, October 1997.
18. Freund, S., Schapire, R.: A Decision Theoretic Generalization of On-Line Learning and an Application of Boosting. Proc. of the 2th European Conference on Computational Learning Theory, pp. 23-37, Springer-Verlag, 1995.
19. Ullman, S.: Visual Routines. Cognition, 18, 1984.
20. Zeki, S.: A Vision of the Brain. Oxford, Blackwell Scientific Publications, 1993.
21. Krotkov, E, Bajcsy, R.: Active Vision for Reliable Ranging: Cooperating Focus, Stereo, and Vergence. Intl. Journal of Computer Vision, vol. 11, no. 2, October 1993, pp. 187-203.
22. Darrell, T., Gordon, G., Harville, M., Woodfill, J.: Integrated Person Tracking Using Stereo, Color, and Pattern Detection. Proc. of the Conference on Computer Vision and Pattern Recognition, pp. 601-609, Santa Barbara, June, 1998.
23. Rasmussen, C., Hager, G.: Joint Probabilistic Techniques for Tracking Multi-Part Objects. Proc. of the Conference on Computer Vision and Pattern Recognition, Santa Barbara, June, 1998.
24. Isard, M., Blake, A.: ICONDENSATION: Unifying Low-Level and High-Level Tracking in a Stochastic Framework. Proceedings of 5th European Conf. on Computer Vision, 893-908, Cambridge, England, 1998.
25. Soto, A., Saptharishi, M., Dolan, J., Trebi-Ollennu, A., Khosla, P.: CyberATVs: Dynamic and Distributed Reconnaissance and Surveillance Using All Terrain UGVs. Proceedings of the International Conference on Field and Service Robotics, August 29-31, 1999.
26. Dolan, J., Trebi-Ollennu, A., Soto, A., Khosla, P.: Distributed Tactical Surveillance with ATVs. Proceedings of SPIE, Vol. 3693, AeroSense, Orlando, Fl., April, 1999.
27. Diehl, C., Saptharishi, M., Hampshire II, J., Khosla, P.: Collaborative Surveillance Using Both Fixed and Mobile Unattended Ground Sensor Platforms. Proceedings of SPIE, Vol. 3693, AeroSense, Orlando, Fl., April, 1999.

Confidence from Self-knowledge
and Domain Knowledge

Paul Robertson

University of Oxford, Dept. of Engineering Science,
19 Parks Road, Oxford, OX1 3PJ, England, UK
pr@robots.ox.ac.uk

Abstract. The GRAVA architecture supports building self-adaptive applications. An overview of the GRAVA architecture, its agent language and its reflective protocol are presented with illustrations from the aerial image interpretation domain.

Keywords: Aerial Image Analysis, Reflection, Code Synthesis, Agent Architecture.

1   Introduction

GRAVA is an architecture for building self-adaptive applications. In this paper we give a overview of the architecture and its protocols. The architecture is designed around an agent language embedded within a reflective architectural framework.

Autonomous agents are expected to operate in a decentralized manner without the intervention of a central control mechanism. This involves distributed algorithms for selecting which agents to run and when as well as dividing resources among the agents.

One approach to the agent selection problem that has been the focus of considerable attention, is the notion of a market based approach. The idea is that when an agent wishes to delegate a subtask to another agent capable of performing the subtask agents that are candidates to perform the subtask compete by bidding a price. This often works well, producing efficient solutions. However, two problems arise in such systems:

1. Selecting an appropriate basis for cost computations so that the bidding is fair.
2. Because the bidding is piecewise local, such systems are prone to find local minima and miss the global minima.
3. Agents not designed to work together can behave incoherently resulting in thrashing behavior. Ultimately multi-agent systems tend to work well only as a result of excruciatingly careful design. This makes implementing multi-agent systems a very complex and error prone programming exercise.

R. Laddaga, P. Robertson, and H. Shrobe (Eds.): IWSAS 2001, LNCS 2614, pp. 84–105, 2003.
© Springer-Verlag Berlin Heidelberg 2003

Our approach addresses these problems as follows:

1. The basis for cost computation is description length. Description length is the correct measurement in an interpretation problem because it captures the notion of likelihood directly: $DL = -log_2(P)$.
2. Monte Carlo sampling allows us to avoid the problem of finding unwanted local minima.
3. The problem of incoherent agents is addressed by dividing agents into contexts and then using reflection and self-adaptation to select an appropriate set of agents that are suited to the current state and which provably leads to a solution.

1.1   The Role of Reflection

Vision (and Robotics) systems lack robustness. They don't know what they are doing, especially when things change appreciably (i.e. in situations where technologies such as neural nets are ineffective).

Reflective architectures – an idea from AI – offer an approach to building programs that can reason about their own computational processes and make changes to them.

The reflective architecture allows the program to be aware of its own computational state and to make changes to it as necessary in order to achieve its goal.

However, much of the work on reflective architectures has been supportive of human programmer adaptation of languages and architectures rather than self-adaptation of the program by itself.

Our use of reflection allows the self-adaptive architecture to reason about its own structure and to change that structure.

1.2   Interpretation Problems

The problem of self-adaptive software is to respond to changing situations by re-synthesizing the program that is running. To do this we reify the software development process.

Layers of Interpretation: An Example. A key idea in the formulation of our reflective architecture is that problems can often be described in terms of interconnected layers of interpretation forming a hierarchy of interpretation problems. A simple and familiar example of such a layered view is the process of how large software projects are executed.

Large software projects, especially software projects of defense contrators, start out with a requirements document. This document says what the program should do but doesn't say how it should be done. Someone *interprets* the requirements document as a software system and produces a set of specifications for the components of the software system that satisfies the requirements. The

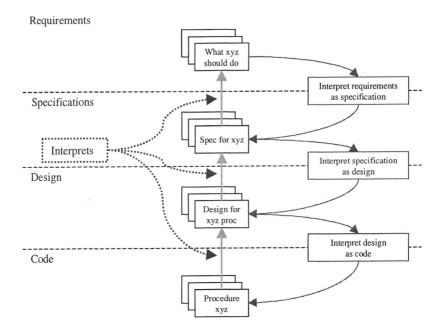

Fig. 1. Example of the relationship between levels of interpretation

specifications are then *interpreted* as a program design. The program design lays out the procedures that make up the program that implements the specification. Finally a programmer interprets the program design to produce a body of code. If care is taken to retain back pointers it is possible to trace back from a piece of code to the part of the design that it interpreted. Parts of design should be traceable to the parts of the specification they interpret and parts of the specification should be traceable to the parts of the requirements document that they interpret.

Figure 1 shows the relationship between different levels of interpretation in the software development example.

When requirements change, as they often do in the lifetime of a software system, it is possible to trace which pieces of the system are affected. In this example, at each level, an input is interpreted to produce an interpretation that is used as the input at a subsequent level.

Each component of the system "knows" what it is doing to the extent that it knows what part of the level above it implements (interprets).

2 Objects in the GRAVA Architecture

The architecture is built from a small number of objects: Models; Agents; Interpreters; Reflective Levels; and Descriptions.

All of these terms are commonly used in the literature to mean a wide range of things. In the GRAVA architecture they have very specific meanings. Below, we

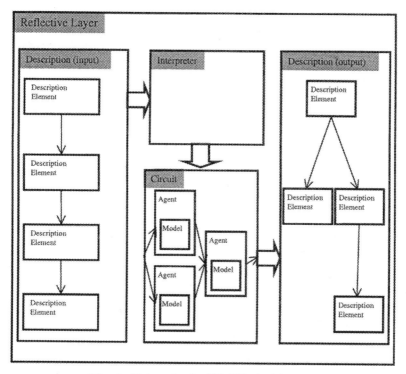

Fig. 2. Objects in the GRAVA Architecture

describe what these objects are and how they cooperate to solve an interpretation problem.

Figure 2 shows the objects that make up the architecture. A reflective layer takes an input description Δ_{in} and produces an output description Δ_{out} as its result. A description consists of a collection of description elements $< \epsilon_1, \epsilon_2, ...,$ $\epsilon_n >$. The output description is an interpretation ($I \in Q(\Delta_{in})$) of the input where $Q(x)$ is the set of all possible interpretations of x.

$$\Delta_{out} = I(\Delta_{in}) \tag{1}$$

The goal of a layer is to find the best interpretation I_{best} which is defined as the interpretation that minimizes the global description length.

$$arg \min_{I_{best}} DL(I_{best}(\Delta_{in})) \tag{2}$$

The interpretation function of the layer consists of an interpretation driver and a collection of connected agents. The interpretation driver deals with the formatting peculiarities of the input description (the input description may be an array of pixels or a symbolic description). The program is made from a collection of agents wired together. The program defines how the input will be interpreted. The job of the interpreter/program is to find the most probable interpretation of the input description and to produce an output description that represents that interpretation.

The GRAVA architecture allows for multiple layers to exist in a program and there are [reflective] links between the layers.

Below, we describe in greater detail the purpose, protocol, and implementation of the objects depicted in Figure 2. We maintain a dual thread in the following. On the one hand, we describe the GRAVA architecture abstractly, on the other, we also describe the actual implementation that we have developed.

Description. A description Δ consists of a set of description elements ϵ.

$$\Delta =< \epsilon_1, \epsilon_2, ..., \epsilon_n > \tag{3}$$

Agents produce descriptions that consist of a number of descriptive elements. The descriptive elements provide access to the model, parameters, and the description length of the descriptive element. For example, a description element for a face might include a deformable face model and a list of parameters that deform the model face so that it fits the face in the image. A description element is a model/parameters pair.

The description length must be computed before the element is attached to the description because the agent must compete on the basis of description length to have the descriptive element included. It makes sense therefore to cache the description length in the descriptive element.

The description class implements the iterator:

```
(for Description|des fcn)
```

This applies the function "fcn" to every element of the structural description, and this enables the architecture to compute the global description length:

$$DL(\Delta_{out}) = \sum_{i=1}^{n} DL(\epsilon_i) \tag{4}$$

To get a better fix on notation, this is implemented as:

```
(define (globalDescriptionLength Description|des)
   (let ((dl 0))
      (loop for de in des
         (set! dl (+ dl (descriptionLength de))))))
```

DescriptionElements. Description elements are produced by *agents* that *fit models* to the input.

Description elements may be implemented in any way that is convenient or natural for the problem domain. However the following protocol must be implemented for the elements of the description:

```
(agent <Element>)
```

Returns the agent that fitted the model to the input.

(model <Element>)

Returns the model object that the element represents.

(parameters <Element>)

Returns the parameter block that parameterizes the model.

(descriptionLength <Element>)

Returns the description length in bits of the description element.

Implementations of description elements must inherit the class DescriptionElement and implement the methods "agent", "model", "parameters", and "descriptionLength".

For readability we print description elements as a list:

(<model name> . <parameter list>)

Models. Fitting a model to the input can involve a direct match but usually involves a set of parameters.

Consider as input, the string:

''t h r e e   b l i n d   m i c e''

We can interpret the string as words. In order to do so, the interpreter must apply word models to the input in order to produce the description. If we have word models for "three", "blind", and "mice" the interpreter can use those models to produce the output description:

((three) (blind) (mice))

The models are parameterless in this example. Alternatively we could have had a model called "word" that is parameterized by the word in question:

((word three) (word blind) (word mice))

In the first case there is one model for each word. In the case of "three" there is an agent that contains code that looks for "t", "h", "r", "e", and "e" and returns the description element "(three)". In the second case there is one model for words that is parameterized by the actual word. The agent may have a database of words and try to match the input to words in its database.

Consider the two examples above. If the probability of finding a word is 0.9 and the probability of the word being "three" is 0.001 the code length of "(word three)" is given by:

$$DL(wordthree) = DL(word) + DL(three) = -log_2(p(word)) - log_2(p(three)) \tag{5}$$

$$= -log_2(0.9) - log_2(0.001) = 0.1520 + 9.9658 = 10.1178 bits \tag{6}$$

The second approach, in which a separate agent identifies individual words would produce a description like "(three)". The model is "three" and there are no parameters. The likelihood of "three" occurring is 0.001 so the description length is given by:

$$DL(three) = -log_2(p(three)) = -log_2(0.9 * 0.001) = 10.1178 bits \qquad (7)$$

That is, the choice of parameterized vs. unparameterized doesn't affect the description length. Description lengths are governed by the probabilities of the problem domain. This allows description lengths produced by different agents to be compared as long as they make good estimates of description length.

For a more realistic example, consider the case of a principle component analysis (PCA) model of a face [1]. A PCA face model is produced as follows. First a number n of key points on a face are identified as are their occurrences on all of the images. The shape of the face ψ_i is defined by a vector containing the n points. A mean shape is produced by finding the average position of each point from a set of example face shapes.

$$\bar{\psi} = \frac{1}{n} \sum_{i=1}^{n} \psi_i \qquad (8)$$

The difference of each face from the mean face $\bar{\psi}$ is given by:

$$\delta\psi_i = \psi_i - \bar{\psi} \qquad (9)$$

The covariance matrix S then is given by:

$$S = \sum_{i=1}^{n} \delta\psi_i \delta\psi_i^T \qquad (10)$$

The eigenvectors p_k and the corresponding eigenvalues λ_k of the covariance matrix S are calculated. The eigenvectors are sorted in descending order of their eigenvalues. If there are N images, the number of eigenvectors to explain the totality of nN points is N, typically large. However, much of the variation is due to noise, so that $p << N$ eigenvectors suffices to account for (say) 95% of the variance. The most significant of the eigenvector-eigenvalue pairs are selected as the principal components.

The resulting face model consists of a mean face shape $\bar{\psi}$ and a set of eigenvectors and weights such that any face shape ψ_p can be approximated by:

$$\psi_p = \bar{\psi} + \mathbf{Pb}, \qquad (11)$$

where $\mathbf{P}$ is the vector of eigenvectors and $\mathbf{b}$ is the vector of weights. The weights are a measure of how much the model must be distorted in order to match the face ψ_p.

The above formulation of a face shape model describes a parameterized model. The weights are the parameters and the mean shape and vector of eigenvectors is the model. Algorithms exist for fitting such shape models to data.

These algorithms first identify a key component and then, using the mean shape model, search for the other features (often edges) near the place where the mean suggests it should be. When the feature is found, its actual location is used to define a distance from the mean. This is repeated for feature points in the model. A set of weights is calculated which represents the parameterization of the model.

Agents. The primary purpose of an agent is to fit a model to its input and produce a description element that captures the model and any parameterization of the model.

We implemented the atomic computational elements in GRAVA as agents. The system manipulates agents and builds programs from them but does not go beneath the level of the agent itself. The agent allows conventional image processing primitives to be included in the GRAVA application simply by providing the GRAVA agent protocol. We might have used methods if we were building a language rather than an architecture. GRAVA agents are not autonomous agents. They depend upon other agents to reason about them and to connect them together to make programs.

An agent is a computational unit that has the following properties:

1. It contains code which is the implementation of an algorithm that fits its model to the input in order to produce its output description.
2. It contains one or more models [explicitly or implicitly] that it attempts to fit to the input.
3. It contains support for a variety of services required of agents such as the ability to estimate description lengths for the descriptions that it produces.

An agent is implemented in GRAVA as the class "Agent". New agents are defined by subclassing "Agent". Runtime agents are instances of the appropriate Agent class. Generally Agents are instantiated with one or more models.

The protocol for agents includes the method "fit" that invokes the agent's model fitting algorithm to attempt to fit one or more of its models to the current data.

```
(fit anAgent data)
```

The "fit" method returns a (possibly null) list of description elements that the agent has managed to fit to the data. The interpreter may apply many agents to the same data. The list of possible model fits from all applicable agents is concatenated to produce the candidate list from which a Monte Carlo selection is performed.

Interpreters. An *interpreter* is a *program* that applies *agents* in order to produce a structural description output from a structural description input.

A scene interpretation program may include agents for face recognition – such as the PCA face shape agent described above – and may include other agents that recognize other things that would be found in an image such as trees, buildings, and roads. The interpreter could be hand-assembled or it could be generated.

Monte Carlo Agent Selection. A recurring issue in multi-agent systems is the basis for cooperation among the agents. Some systems assume benevolent agents where an agent will always help if it can. Some systems implement selfish agents that only help if there is something in it for them. In some cases the selfish cooperation is quantified with a pseudo market system.

Our approach to agent cooperation involves having agents compete to assert their interpretation. If one agent produces a description that allows another agent to further reduce the description length so that the global description length is minimized, the agents *appear* to have cooperated. Locally, the agents compete to reduce the description length of the image description. The algorithm used to resolve agent conflicts guarantees convergence towards a global MDL thus ensuring that agent cooperation "emerges" from agent competition. The MDL approach guarantees convergence towards the most probable interpretation but it does not guarantee that the most probable interpretation will be found.

When all applicable agents have been applied to the input data the resulting lists of candidate description elements is concatenated to produce the candidate list.

The *monteCarloSelect* method chooses one description element at random from the candidate list. The random selection is weighted by the probability of the description element.

$$P_{elem} = 2^{-DL(elem)} \tag{12}$$

So, for example, if among the candidates, one has a description length of 1 bit and one has a description length of two bits, the probabilities of those description lengths is 0.5 and 0.25 respectively. The *monteCarloSelect* method would select the one bit description twice as often as the two bit description.

The monteCarloSelect algorithm is given below:

```
(define (probability DescriptionElement|de)
  (expt 2.0 (- (descriptionLength de))))

(define (monteCarloSelect choices)
  (callWithCurrentContinuation
    (lambda (return)
      (let* ((sum (apply + (map probability choices)))
             (rsel (frandom sum)))
        (dolist (choice choices)
          (set! rsel (- rsel (probability choice)))
          (if (<= rsel 0.0) (return choice)))))))
```

3   Reflective Interpreter for Self-adaptation

A reflective layer is an object that contains one or more "interpreter". Reflective layers are stacked up such that each layer is the meta-level computation of the layer beneath it. In particular each layer is generated by the layer above it.

A system can have an arbitrary number of levels. The example described in the introduction (Figure 1) has four levels. Most systems will have a small number of levels. Experience to date suggests that three levels is usually sufficient.

Each layer can reflect up to the layer above it in order to self-adapt.

```
(defineClass ReflectiveLayer
  ((description) ;; the (input) description for this layer
   (interpreter) ;; the interpreter for the description of this layer
   (knowledge)   ;; a representation of world knowledge at this level
   (higherlayer) ;; the meta-level above this
   (lowerlayer)));; the subordinate layer
```

A reflective layer is an object that contains the following objects.

1. *description:* the description that is to be interpreted. In the software development example the requirements level would contain a description of the requirement that is to be interpreted by the layer.
2. *interpreter:* a system consisting of one or more cascaded interpreters that can interpret the description.
3. *knowledge:* a problem dependent representation of what is known about the world as it pertains to the interpretation of the subordinate layer. The knowledge gets updated as the subordinate layer attempts to interpret its description. The knowledge is used in the synthesis of the interpreter for the subordinate layer.
4. *higherlayer:* the superior layer. The layer that produced the interpreter for this layer.
5. *lowerlayer:* the subordinate layer.

The semantics for a layer are determined by the *interpret, elaborate, adapt* and *execute* methods which we describe in turn below.

Figure 3 shows the relationship between reflective layers of the GRAVA architecture.

Reflective Layer "n" contains a description that is to be interpreted as the description for layer "n+1". A program has been synthesized (either by the layer "n-1" or by hand if it is the top layer. The program is the interpreter for the description. That interpreter is run. The result of running the interpreter is the most probable interpretation of the description – which forms the new description of the layer "n+1". Layer "n" also contains a compiler. Actually all layers contain a compiler. Unless the layer definition is overridden by specialization the compiler in each layer is identical and provides the implementation as a theorem prover that compiles an interpreter from a description. The compiler runs at the meta level in layer "n" and uses the knowledge of the world at layer "n+1" which resides in level "n". It compiles the description from level "n+1" taking in to account what is known at the time about level "n+1" in the *knowledge* part of layer "n". The compilation of the description is new interpreter at layer "n+1".

Below we describe the meta-interpreter for layers in GRAVA.

The interpret method is the primary driver of computation in the reflective architecture. The reflective levels are determined by the program designer.

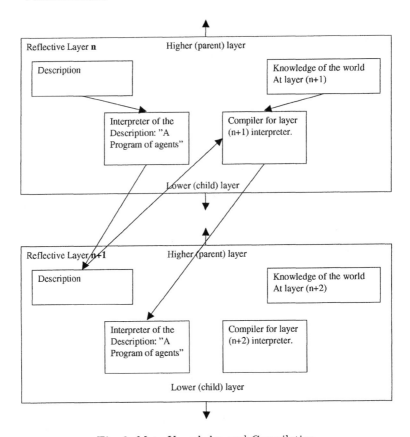

Fig. 3. Meta-Knowledge and Compilation

In order for the self-adaptive program to "understand" its own computational structure, each layer describes the layer beneath it. In self-adapting, the architecture essentially searches a tree of meta-levels. This is best understood by working through the details of the architecture.

The top level layer is manually constructed by the program designer. It must be because there is no higher level to defer to. That level defines its goal in the form of a description that must be interpreted. The collection of agents that interpret that description are provided by the human programmer. The program that those agents constitute is charged with the responsibility of producing the reflective layer immediately below. The lower level, once constructed, is then interpreted in order to bring about the desired behavior.

At some point the layers bottom out in a lowest level below which there is no further elaboration of layers. The lowest level layer has a description but no interpreter. The description at the lowest level is the result of the top level application of "interpret".

In the simplest of situations the top level application of "interpret" to the top layer results in the recursive descent of "interpret" through the reflective layers finally yielding a result in the form of an interpretation. Along the way however unexpected situations may arise that cause the program to need to adapt. Adaptation is handled by taking the following steps:

1. Reflect up to the next higher layer (parent level) with an object that describes the reason for reflecting up. It is necessary to reflect up because the higher level is the level that "understands" what the program was doing. Each level "understands" what the level directly beneath it is doing.
2. The world model (knowledge) that is maintained by the parent level is updated to account for what has been learned about the state of the world from running the lower level this far.
3. Armed with updated knowledge about the state of the world the lower level is re-synthesized. The lower level is then re-invoked.

We now explain the default interpret method.

```
1:(define (interpret ReflectiveLayer|layer)
2:  (withSlots (interpreter description lowerlayer) layer
3:    (if (null? interpreter)
4:        description          ;; Return the description
5:        (begin
6:          (elaborate layer);; Create/populate subordinate layer.
7:          (reflectProtect (interpret lowerlayer)
8:            (lambda (layer gripe) (adapt layer gripe)))))))

9:(define (reflectionHandler ReflectiveLayer|layer gripe)
10: (adapt layer gripe))
```

Line 3 checks to see if the layer contains an interpreter. If it does not the result of evaluation is simply the description which is returned in line 4. This occurs when the lowest level has been reached.

If there is an interpreter, the elaborate method is invoked (line 6). "elaborate" (described below) constructs the next lower reflective layer.

"reflectProtect" in line 7 is a macro that hides some of the mechanism involved with handling reflection operations.

(reflectProtect *form handler*) evaluates *form* and returns the result of that evaluation. If during the evaluation of *form* a reflection operation occurs the *handler* is applied to the layer and the gripe object provided by the call to reflectUp. If the handler is not specified in the reflectProtect macro the generic procedure reflectionHandler is used. The invocation of the reflection handler is not within the scope of the reflectProtect so if it calls (reflectUp ...) the reflection operation is be caught at the next higher level. If reflectUp is called and there is no extant reflectProtect the debugger is entered. So if the top layer invokes reflectUp the program lands in the debugger.

When the reflection handler has been evaluated the reflectProtect re-evaluates the *form* thereby making a loop. Line 8 is included here to aid in description. It is omitted in the real code allowing the reflectionHandler method to be invoked.

The handler takes care of updating the world model based on the information in *gripe* and then adapts the lower layer. The handler therefore attempts to self-adapt to accommodate the new knowledge about the state of the world until success is achieved. If the attempt to adapt is finally unable to produce a viable lower level interpreter it invokes reflectUp and causes the meta level interpretation level to attend to the situation.

```
1:(define (elaborate ReflectiveLayer|layer)
2:  (withSlots (lowerlayer) layer
3:    (let ((interpretation (execute layer)) ;; ll description
4:          (llint (compile layer interpretation)))
5:      (set! lowerlayer ((newLayerConstructor layer)
6:                        higherlayer: layer
7:                        description: interpretation
8:                        interpreter: llint)))))
```

The purpose of the elaborate method is to build the initial version of the subordinate layer. It does this in three steps:

1. Evaluate the interpreter of the layer in order to "interpret" the layer's description. The interpretation of $layer_n$ is the description of $layer_{n+1}$.
   Line 3 invokes the interpreter for layer with (execute layer). This simply runs the MDL agent interpreter function defined for this layer. The result of executing the interpreter is an interpretation in the form of a description.
2. Compile the layer. This involves the collection of appropriate agents to interpret the description of the lower layer.
   Line 4 compiles the new layer's interpreter. Layer n contains knowledge of the agents that can be used to interpret the description of layer $n + 1$. The description generated in line 3 is compiled into an interpreter program using knowledge of agents that can interpret that description.
3. A new layer object is instantiated with the interpretation resulting from (1) as the description and the interpreter resulting from compile in step (2) as the interpreter. The new layer is wired in to the structure with the bi-directional pointers (lowerlayer and higherlayer).
   In line 5, (newLayerConstructor layer) returns the constructor procedure for the subordinate layer.

The adapt method updates the world state knowledge and then recompiles the interpreter for the lower layer.

```
1:(define (adapt ReflectiveLayer|layer gripe)
2:  (withSlots (updateKnowledge) gripe
3:    (updateKnowledge layer))   ;; update the belief state.
4:  (withSlots (lowerlayer) layer
5:    (withSlots (interpreter) lowerlayer
6:      (set! interpreter (compile layer)))))
```

The representation of world state is problem dependent and is not governed by the reflective architecture. In each layer the world state at the corresponding meta level is maintained in the variable "knowledge". When an interpreter causes adaptation with a reflectUp operation an update procedure is loaded into the "gripe" object. Line 3 invokes the update procedure on the layer to cause the world state representation to be updated.

Line 6 recompiles the interpreter for the lower layer. Because the world state has changed the affected interpreter should be compiled differently than when the interpreter was first elaborated.

```
1:(define (execute ReflectiveLayer|layer)
2:   (withSlots (description interpreter knowledge) layer
3:     (run interpreter description knowledge)))
```

4 Program Synthesis

The purpose of the "compile" method described in Section 3 is to produce a collection of interpreters connected together that performs the function of interpreting the description that belongs to the layer. In this section, we explore the idea of compilation-as-proof, and then use the idea in our self-adaptive architecture.

An interpreter (as described above) is a coherent computational unit. It includes code for sequencing agent's over the input description and making Monte Carlo samples of the agents results. An interpreter therefore contains a collection of agents that the interpreter controls. In this section we develop the protocol for interpreters that permits them to be automatically selected, sequenced, and populated with agents by the compiler.

4.1 Compilation as Proof

The typical compiler can be thought of as the composition of several proof problems for example parsing, optimizing and producing machine code. The purpose of this discussion is to draw upon our intuitions of the compilation process and not to carefully model the behavior of a compiler so although such an exercise could be of interest in its own right, we restrict our discussion here to a single level of the compiler.

If we think of the task of the compiler as proving that the program can be computed by the target machine we can see that the resulting machine code is the axioms of the proof – the leaves of the proof tree.

The knowledge in the compiler can therefore be divided simply into two kinds

1. Knowledge of rules of inference and a procedure for applying them in order to arrive at a proof.
2. Knowledge of the relationship between the source code and the target code in the form of rules.

In this view, the compiler produces a tree-structured proof. The leaves of the proof are blocks of machine code. The machine codes are read off the fringe of the proof tree to produce the target machine language representation.

Consider the problem of interpreting a piece of source code as an assembly language program. Models of how to represent a source program fragment in assembly language can be applied in order to interpret the source code as assembly language.

Using the GRAVA agent/interpreter architecture the interpreter would sequence parts of the language over a collection of agents that can deal with the parts of the language. The interpreter part therefore is a code walker and the agents of the interpreter are the collection of agents that deal with each syntactic construct in the language.

Consider the problem of interpreting the expression **C=A+B**.

Compiling that expression involves proving that the expression is a part of the language. The proof looks like this:

1. C=A+B is an assignment (rule: assign-1) where the location is C and the expression is A+B.
2. C is a location (rule: location-1).
3. A+B is an addition (rule: addition-1) where A is a sub-expression and B is a sub-expression.
4. A is a de-reference (rule: dereference-1).
5. B is a de-reference (rule: dereference-1).

The simplest way of implementing this example is to treat it as a one step problem of interpreting the source expression as a sequence of machine instructions. However, in order to use this example to illustrate the components of the reflective architecture we develop this example here as a two step process. For readability and to avoid getting bogged down in unnecessary details we illustrate the essential components using pseudo code. Figure 4 shows the relevant portions of the assignment agent and its associated model.

The assignment agent is connected to two agents A1 and A2 from which is asks about the location of the left hand side (LHS) and the value of the expression. It tells its result to agent A3. It fits the model "store-1" which supports an "emit" method that assembles instructions to an instruction stream. Figures 5 and 6 show implementation templates for addition and de-reference respectively which are required for this example.

The proof tree is shown in Figure 7.

The resulting description that results from running the agents is shown below.

```
((location-of C) ; from assign-1
 ((location-of C)) ; from location-1
 ((register tmp1) ; from addition-1
  (deref-1 tmp1 (location-of A)) ; emits (LOAD tmp1 (location-of A))
  (deref-1 tmp2 (location-of B)) ; emits (LOAD tmp2 (location-of B))
  (add-1 tmp1 tmp2))            ; emits (ADD tmp1 tmp2)
 (store-1 tmp1 (location-of C)))); emits (STORE tmp1 (location-of C))
```

Running through the description in sequence applying the "emit" method on each entry results in the following instructions being assembled:

Agent: assign-1	
Consumes:	(A1=(location X) A2=(expression Y))
Produces:	(A3=(expression X=Y))
Fit:	(define (fit assign-1 agent) (withTemporaryRegister (R1) (let ((L1 (ask A1 `(location ,X)))           (E1 (ask A2 `(expression ,Y ,R1)))) (tell A3 (list L1 E1 (make store-1 val: R1 loc: L1))))))
Model: store-1	

	(define (emit store-1 mod output)
	  (withSlots (val loc) mod
	    (assemble output 'STORE val loc)))

Fig. 4. Agent and Model for Assignment

Agent: addition-1	
Consumes:	(A1=(expression X) A2=(expression Y))
Produces:	(A4=(expression X+Y) A3=(result))
Fit:	(define (fit addition-1 agent) (withTemporaryRegister (R1) (let ((R2 (ask A3 `(result)))           (E1 (ask A1 `(expression ,X ,R1))) (E2 (ask A2 `(expression ,Y ,R2)))) (tell A4 (list R2 E1 E2 (make add-1 val1: R1 val2: R2)))
Model: add-1	

	(define (emit add-1 mod output)
	  (withSlots (val1 val2) mod
	    (assemble output 'ADD val1 val2)))

Fig. 5. Agent and Model for Addition

```
(LOAD tmp1 (location-of A))
(LOAD tmp2 (location-of B))
(ADD tmp1 tmp2)
(STORE tmp1 (location-of C))
```

In the example given above we included only a single agent for each operation (assign-1 location-1 addition-1 dereference-1). We could provide arbitrarily many

Agent: dereference-1	
Consumes:	(A1=(location X))
Produces:	(A2=(expression X))
Fit:	(define (fit dereference-1!agent) (let ((R1 (ask A1 `(location ,X)))) (tell A2 (list R1 (make load-1 reg: R1 loc: L1)))))
Model: deref-1	
	(define (emit deref-1!mod output) (withSlots (reg loc) mod (assemble output 'LOAD reg loc)))

Fig. 6. Agent and Model for Dereference

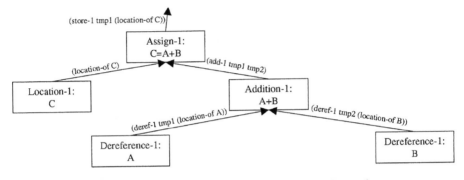

Fig. 7. Example Proof Tree for Compilation Example

agents for each operation in which case we would have to choose which one to select on the basis of the description length of the description elements.

A compiler is an interpretation program that interprets a high level language source program and produces a description that draws upon knowledge built in to the compiler about the target machine. Nowhere in the high level source code are the details of the target machine represented. Indeed the code may be compiled with different compilers for different target machines. The compiler embodies various kinds of knowledge essential to producing a good representation of the source:

1. Knowledge of the high level language.
2. Knowledge of certain time and space considerations of certain patterns used in the source program and transformations into more efficient forms.
3. Knowledge of the target machine its instructions, registers, and efficiency considerations.

The compiler may consist of several layers of interpretation problem in which the language is successively translated through intermediate languages until the target level is reached.

The purpose of the above example was to motivate the idea that compilation can usefully be viewed as a theorem proving activity. By adding "produces" and "consumes" to the protocol for agents and interpreters we can treat them as rules of inference and use a theorem prover to connect them up onto programs – just as we did above.

In compiling a program into machine code, we generally deal with certainty. The language that is being compiled is not ambiguous and the machine code can be relied upon to perform as expected. Computers are designed to operate reliably and high level languages are designed to be unambiguous.

The real world does not offer such certainty and programs that must interact with the real world inherit that uncertainty. The source specification may be ambiguous and the rules are not guaranteed to succeed. Instead we have a way of characterizing the likelihood of succeeding. Conventional compilers are a special case of a more general problem.

5   Uncertain Information and MDL

Because the real world doesn't offer us the kind of guarantees that we have managed to build for ourselves in the form of closed world computers programs are brittle when they attempt to operate in an unconstrained environment such as the *real world*.

The theorem prover developed below is "relaxed" in that the theorems it produces are guaranteed to be programs that produce the desired effect but only if the program terminates. The program may not terminate because (reflectUp ...) may be invoked prior to completion. Since there may be many agents and interpreters that can be connected up to be a valid program that satisfies the representation from which it was compiled there are many different proofs. We wish to find the compilation/proof that has the highest likelihood of completing without invoking reflectUp.

$$DL(interpreter) = -log_2(1 - P(invokesReflectUp)) \qquad (13)$$

For each interpreter the description length is determined by Equation 13. An individual agent can't invoke reflectUp because an individual agent may be unsuitable for a particular application and its failure is not cause to adapt the program. Instead another agent should do better. The interpreter then selects the agent that did best. It is the interpreter object that is in a position to invoke reflectUp.

We provide three ways for reflectUp to be invoked and cause self-adaptation of the program to occur:

1. An interpreter *pre-test* fails.
2. An interpreter *post-test* fails.
3. No agents are successful in interpreting part of the input that is being interpreted.

We add *pre-test* and *post-test* to the protocol for interpreters along with *produces* and *consumes*.

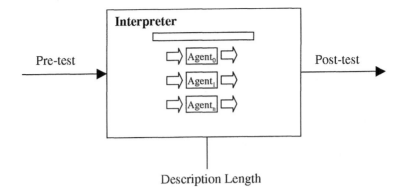

Fig. 8. Protocol for Interpreter Meta-Information

5.1   Protocol for Interpreters

An interpreter is a special kind of computational agent that contains agents which it sequences. To support those activities the interpreters support a protocol for meta-information shown in Figure 8.

1. *(pretest anInterpreter anInput)*
   Returns *true* if the input is suitable for the interpreter and *false* otherwise.
2. *(posttest anInterpreter anOutput)*
   Returns *true* if the output is acceptable and *false* otherwise.
3. *(descriptionLength anInterpreter anInput)*
   Returns the description length of the interpreter. The description length is $-log_2(P(success))$ where $P(success)$ is the probability that the interpreter will successfully interpret the scene.

5.2   Protocol for Agents

In order for agents to be selected and connected together by the theorem prover compiler they must advertise their semantics. The purpose of the compiler is to select appropriate agents and connect them together to form a program. To support those activities the agents support a protocol for meta-information shown in Figure 9.

1. *(consumes anAgent)*
   Returns a list of types that the interpreter expects as input.
2. *(produces anAgent)*
   Returns a list of types that the interpreter produces as output.
3. *(descriptionLength anAgent)*
   Returns the description length of the agent. The description length is $-log_2(P(correct))$ where $P(correct)$ is the probability that the agent will diagnose the feature in the same way as the specification.

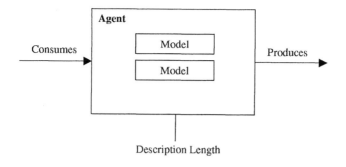

Fig. 9. Protocol for Agent Meta-Information

6 Conclusion

The GRAVA architecture is based on two ideas:

1. That for interpretation problems global MDL is the goal;
2. That global MDL can be approximated by Monte-Carlo sampling.

MDL provides a common currency or "gold standard" for use in market model agent systems. Because the architecture is specialized to solving interpretation problems there are problems for which it is not appropriate. Nevertheless a great many interesting problems can be cast in the form of interpretation problems.

Because the foundations upon which the architecture is built are well understood the behavior and performance of the architecture can yield to some level of analysis – such as convergence analysis. The architecture has some interesting characteristics:

1. Cooperation between agents at different semantic levels is an emergent property of the architecture.
2. Robustness within the limits of the programs domain is realized by virtue of measuring how local choices affect global description length.
3. There is an implicit information fusion model.

The third point is worthy of greater discussion. Most attempts at reasoning about uncertainty [4, 3, 2] attempt to bring together contributions so as to make a local decision. When local evidence is sufficient these methods work well but when the sources of evidence become less straightforward the approaches get bogged down. Numerous problems occur – most notably that required probabilities are often not available and that in order for the approaches to be tractable it is necessary to assume conditional independence. In any complex system the practical issues are immense.

The implicit information fusion model in the GRAVA architecture depends upon the effect that local decision has upon the global interpretation. A less probable interpretation of a feature will be selected if it gives rise to a shorter global description.

Conventioal architectures such as Schemas, Blackboards, Rule Systems, and Subsumption all attempt to find a single path towards a solution and manual hard wiring of control information is one of the major problems with those approaches. In GRAVA we have chosen a method that avoids those problems at the cost of having to pursue multiple paths. When multiple agents are available we choose one based on a Monte-Carlo sample.

It can be objected that our approach is computationally expensive compared to conventional approaches. There are a number of important observations on this issue:

1. Conventional architectures search for the first solution that can be found. They hoped that by making local decisions a reasonably good solution will result. They do not attempt to find the *best* solution. For interpretation problems it is often important to find the best solution (or one very close to it).
2. Processing is cheap. It is reasonable to have multiple parallel computations occurring at once. It is reasonable to have multiple processors, perhaps as many as one per agent or one per model. These are problems that scale well. You really can have one processor per model and derive benefit from the parallelism. There are of course within the single processor view numerous opportunities to build optimization methods. For example for certain problems we can do better than using Monte-Carlo sampling.

There are a few comments that should be made regarding the use of Monte-Carlo sampling to estimate the global MDL description. Most uses of Monte-Carlo sampling attempt to estimate a PDF by counting frequencies of occurrences. For complex situations a great many samples would be required before anything like an accurate estimate of the PDF would result. In our use we are able to measure the global description length by adding up the description lengths of the components. Since we only want the most probable solution and not the whole PDF we can get by with far less iterations than would be required to estimate the PDF with any accuracy. As successive samples are taken we always know which is the best solution so far and can terminate the search at any point. This allows us to trade off interpretation accuracy against computational cost.

In some agent architectures an agent is a wholly autonomous entity that determines its own applicability and negotiates to participate in the ongoing computation. The agents described in this architecture are woven together into a program. The choice of which agents may participate and where has already been made when the program was constructed (at run time). Agents in GRAVA are computational units that support the protocol for agents. The way that the agents are woven together into a program is similar to the way that methods are woven together in CLOS. The MDL approach to agent selection described here should be equally effective in other agent architectures as long as they are solving interpretation problems.

The architecture described in this paper has the novel attribute that it knows what it knows and it knows how to apply what it knows. As with Smith's [5] reflective architecture each reflective layer implements the layer beneath it. In Smith's architecture each level of interpreter implemented the level of interpreter beneath it. In the GRAVA architecture each layer implements not only the interpreter but also the program beneath it. The inclusion of a compiler in the reflection loop allows the meta-interpreter to respond to the changing state of the environment by recompiling lower layers as appropriate. Each layer contains the knowledge of:

1. What the layer beneath is trying to do.
2. What the current belief state is as to the state of the world as it pertains to the operation of the layer beneath it.

When the belief state changes at some level the code for lower levels is automatically updated. If new agents are added they are automatically used where appropriate.

Acknowledgements

Effort sponsored by the Defense Advanced Research Projects Agency (DARPA) and Air Force Research Laboratory, Air Force Material Command, USAF, under agreement number F30602-98-0056. The U.S. Government is authorized to reproduce and distribute reprints for Governmental purposes notwithstanding any copyright annotation thereon.

The views and conclusions contained herein are those of the authors and should not be interpreted as necessarily representing the official policies or endorsements, either expressed or implied, of the Defense Advanced Research Projects Agency (DARPA), the Air Force Research Laboratory, or the U.S. Government.

References

1. T.F. Cootes, G.J. Edwards, and C.J. Taylor. Active appearance models. In H. Burkhardt and B. Neumann, editors, *Proceedings, European Conference on Computer Vision 1998*, volume 2. Springer, 1998. pages 484-498.
2. A.P. Dempster. A generalization of bayesian inference. *Journal of the Royal Statistical Society, Series B*, 30:205–247, 1968.
3. W.B. Mann and T.O. Binford. Probabilities for bayesian networks. In *Proceedings Image Understanding Workshop*. Morgan Kaufman, San Francisco., 1994.
4. G. Shafer. *A Mathematiccal Theory of Evidence*. Prinston University Press, 1976.
5. B.C. Smith. Reflection and semantics in lisp. In *Proceedings 11th Annual ACM Symposium on Principles of Programming Languages, Salt Lake City, Utah*, pages 23–35, January 1984.

Self-adaptive Protocols

Katalin Tarnay

Nokia-Hungary, Köztelek u 6, H-1092 Budapest
katalin.tarnay@nokia.com

Abstract. A class of self-adaptive protocols is specified based on three main features of self-adaptive software: self-monitoring, dynamic dispatch and alternatives for protocol declaration and for behavior. A frame-based representation is introduced for communication protocols. As an example, a service discovery protocol is discussed from the point of view of self-adaptivity.

1 Introduction

Success generally follows activity. This rule is true in nearly every field of life, therefore it is interesting to attempt to make software more active. Self-adaptive software [1]is a promising solution for active software. This paper deals with a restricted type of software: the communication protocol. The problems related to protocols are two-sided, both theoretical and practical. Theoretical problems are strongly connected to formal description techniques.

The practical problems come from the changing network environment and from the frequent new user requirements. Self-adaptivity can solve many parts of these problems.

The goals are the followings:

- To introduce a new protocol representation, easy-to-use in protocol specification and testing,
- To apply principles of self-adaptivity in protocol development,
- To create self-adaptive test suites and thereby change the test scenario during the testing.

The basics of traditional protocol engineering [4] are summarized in Section 2, which is followed by a new frame-based protocol representation presented in Section 3. A new solution for changing protocol specification (based on self-monitoring) is introduced in Section 4. The next section deals with the self-adaptive test suite scenario. The final problem is to connect the service discovery protocols with self-adaptive protocols using self-adaptive components in the attributes of the service discovery protocol, Section 6 shows a solution for this relation. Finally, Section 7 summarizes the results, problems and it makes a suggestion for further research topics.

2 Protocol Engineering

A protocol specifies the information exchange between two communicating entities, and determines the syntactical, semantic and temporal rules of cooperation in such a

R. Laddaga, P. Robertson, and H. Shrobe (Eds.): IWSAS 2001, LNCS 2614, pp. 106–112, 2003.

way that one or more communication functions are fulfilled. The syntactic rules are given in the declaration part of the protocol specification and the semantic and temporal rules are given in its dynamic part. The communicating entities (Fig. 1) are composed of a controller, a transmitter, a receiver and a timer. The controller is the heart of the entity responsible for the semantic rules; these rules are specified with Communicating Extended Finite-State Machines (CEFSM). The transmitter and receiver are responsible for the syntactic rules, and the timer for the temporal ones. The entities communicate through a network considered as a service provider. The main goal of this cooperation is to offer some services to the users. The protocol specification is based on this model. To extend the usage of this model to the world of self-adaptivity in order to gain a self-adaptive protocol specification, it should be completed with some self-adaptive features. In our approach, these features are self-monitoring, dynamic dispatch and an offer of alternatives.

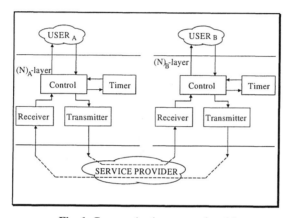

Fig. 1. Communicating protocol entities

The protocol engineering contains all steps of protocol development from textual description to final implementation. The main steps are demonstrated in Fig. 2.

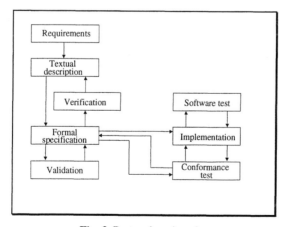

Fig. 2. Protocol engineering

The components of protocol engineering are the steps of the protocol lifecycle. The relation between the components plays an important role in deriving one component from the other. Nearly every component has its mathematical background, e.g. some kind of finite-state machines are used. The self-adaptivity should be built-in into the components of the lifecycle, for example to change from finite-state automata to learning automata. The relations among the components are also a significant part of protocol engineering. A new type of knowledge representation can make it easier to automate the derivation of the relations.

3   Frame-Based Protocol Representation

Communication protocols can be specified in many ways. The question is which specification can be used for every step of the protocol engineering effort. This paper uses frames for knowledge representation, first of all in the field of protocol specification and later in conformance testing.

The hierarchical structure of frames provides a good solution for representing a protocol. Every piece of information can be put into frames. The most important information is put into frames near the top of the hierarchy, and as we go lower in the structure we find frames containing specialized information about protocol messages, states and parameters. Protocol validation frames provide a good way for representing the reachability graph. They are especially useful in storing the information attached to the nodes, the protocol states and the contents of the channels. In this kind of representation each node is put in a frame, and a relation can be defined among them, which is represented by the arcs of the reachability graph. Since the frames provide a well-structured description of the protocol , they are a good basis for this implementation. The messages and state transitions are stored in frames, while the protocol activities are described with demons. In conformance testing the test suite structure, the test cases and the whole test scenario can be given according to the description of the protocols with In this paper the following syntax of frames is used:

    frame:name;
        slot:[list of values];
        (*comments*);
    end;

The name of the frames, slots and values are denoted with small letters, capital letters denote variables. The value in a slot can be a list, therefore a square bracket is needed. If a frame has only a name (and no slots or values are given) then we call it a primitive frame. If a frame has a name and some slots but no values, then it is called a generic frame. Finally, if nothing is omitted, we say it is a full-frame. The frames can be completed with additional information, called meta-information. Frames, slots and values can carry meta-information.

The frames can represent the declaration, transition, predicate (it is important for the service discovery protocol presented in Section 6) and a pattern. The next two frames are for event declaration.

First all inputs are listed in the input frame.

```
    frame:trans_inputs;
            asp_from_upper_layer:tconreq,tconresp,tdisreq,tdtreq;
                pdu:cr,cc,dr,dt:
    end:
```

All Abstract Service Primitives(asp) and Protocol Data Units(pdu) are described in a meta-frame. A generic frame for a Protocol Data Unit can have the following structure:

```
    frame:pdu;
            name[];
            code[];
            credit[];
            user_data[];
    end;
```

The next full-frame represents the state-transition:

```
frame:tdtreq/dt;
            is a transition;
            state1:open; (* dt can be sent*)
            input:tdtreq;
            output:dt:;
            state2:opw; (*dt can't be sent*)
            action:sn=sn+1;
            predicate:swue=swue+1;
            (*send_window_upper_edge=send_number+1*)
    end;
```

The connection establishment phase can be represented as a pattern frame:

```
frame:connection_establishment;
            is_a _pattern;
            inputs:tconreq,cc;
            outputs:cr,tconconf;
            transition:edge1,edge2;
    end;
```

4   Self-adaptive Protocol Model

The self-adaptive protocol model is an extended version of the basic model shown in Fig. 1. From our point of view three features (Fig. 3) are stressed:
- self monitoring,
- dynamic dispatch,
- set of alternatives.

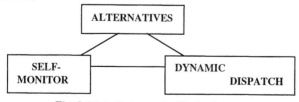

Fig. 3. Main features of self-adaptivity

The self-monitor lies between the receiver and the dynamic dispatch unit and receives and observes the incoming events during the normal operation as well as in erroneous cases. The traffic is analyzed in both cases. The self-monitor evaluates the received messages and controls the dynamic dispatch to select another protocol specification. The dynamic dispatch unit lies between the self-monitor and the controller. The controller contains a set of built-in alternatives that can be classified into two groups, one having many state-transition tables specifying the semantics of the protocol, and the other group having a set of data flow graphs describing the protocol data units. The dynamic dispatch unit controls the controller changing the state-transition tables and data flow graphs according to the decisions of the self-monitor.

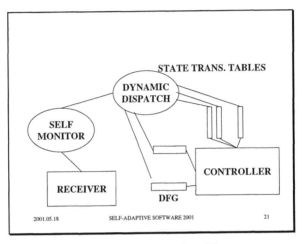

Fig. 4. Self-adaptive protocol model

This model is used for a self-adaptive transport protocol design [2]. The self-adaptive protocol can monitor and evaluate its own behavior and it has a repository for alternatives. If necessary, it changes itself without human interactions, affecting either the dynamic behavior or the declaration part, or both.

5   Self-adaptive Test Suite Scenario

Conformance testing is a type of approval, important for manufacturers and operators in every field of telecommunication. This test process is time-consuming, but good test coverage is needed to prevent undetected errors. Generally the errors come in bursts, therefore the probability of other errors around a detected error is higher then otherwise. Another point is that sometimes-extra testing can superfluous, e.g. testing the same protocol on another platform. Therefore a self-adaptive test scenario is suggested with dominant test cases always being executed. If an error is detected more test cases will be activated around the possible error sources, and the test scenario is changed during the test process. The whole test process is standardized in the telecommunication industry and every test case should have a verdict: passed, failed or inconclusive. The changes of the self-adaptive test scenario are guided by these verdicts.

This idea can be used in other fields of testing for increasing the reliability of the products and for accelerating the process to the market.

A system for frame-based test representation is initiated [3] specifying the test suite structure, test purpose and test cases similarly to the protocol frames shown above.

6   Service Discovery Protocols as Self-adaptive Protocols

A new and interesting field of protocol engineering is the development of service discovery protocols. The analysis of service discovery protocols as self-adaptive protocols seems to be a natural idea. With service discovery, devices may automatically discover network services including their properties, and services may advertise their existence in a dynamic way. Well-known examples are SLP, JINI, UPnP and Bluetooth SDP. The properties to be advertised are described as an n-tuple, generally in some kind of template. These templates can be easily specified in frame representations. A Web-trader can be seen in Fig. 5. The trader has a Service Offer Service process, a Matchmaker and a Shared Type Manager. The services send the service advertisements to the trader. If a client arrives and requires some services, the service requirement is sent to the trader, generally in the form of a template. The trader delivers the requirement to the Matchmaker, which matches the advertised and required features. After this step the client-server interaction can start.

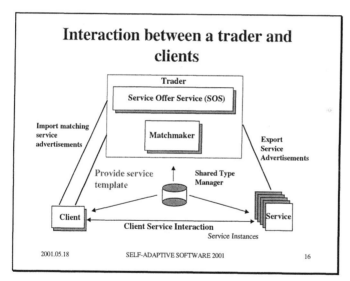

Fig. 5. A service discovery solution: the web trader.

This frame can contain meta-information. In the above example the client and server are the protocol entities. If both have complementary meta-frames with communicating finite-state machines, then these communicating finite-state-machines carry the rules of self-adaptivity.

7   Conclusion

This paper contains new approaches applying ideas of self-adaptivity of software to a promising field: communication protocols. A model is suggested for a self-adaptive protocol. The model shows how a protocol specification can be changed according to changes in the environment. A frame representation for protocols is introduced specifying the message declaration, the dynamic behavior and some more sophisticated steps. Conformance tests can also have a scenario guided by test verdicts. Finally an application to service discovery protocols using communicating finite-state machines has also been presented.

Self-adaptivity needs much new research to support adaptive protocol engineering. The driving force is derived from industry and the final goal is to establish easy-to-use computing in a ubiquitous networking environment

References

1. Robertson, P., Laddaga, R., Shrobe, H.: Results of the First International Workshop on Self-
2. Adaptive Software, IWSAS 2000, Springer Verlag, New York(2001)
3. Harangozo, Zs., Tarnay,K.: FDTs in Self-Adaptive Protocol Specification
4. (In this issue)
5. Adamis, G.,Tarnay, K.: Frame-based self-adaptive test case selection
6. (in this issue)
7. 4. Tarnay, K.: Protocol Specification and Testing,
8. Plenum Press, New York 1991

FDTs in Self-adaptive Protocol Specification

Zsuzsanna Harangozó and Katalin Tarnay

NOKIA HUNGARY, Köztelek u 6., H-1092 Budapest
{zsuzsa.harangozo,katalin.tarnay}@nokia.com

Abstract. In this paper a model of a simple communication protocol was introduced and described informally serving as an example to present usage of Formal Description Techniques (FDT) in protocol specification. The model was specified formally as well, using traditional FDT techniques: MSC and SDL languages. Our goal was to enhance the model with self-adaptive components, proving that it satisfies the approach for self-adaptivity published by DARPA in 1997, in order to show the world of communication protocols as a potential application field of self-adaptive software. We have presented that FDTs are applicable tools in specification method of self-adaptive protocols and mapping of self-adaptive components to FDT element has been shown.

1   Introduction

After some years spent in the field of testing communication protocols and reading proceedings of the first workshop on self-adaptive software (Oxford, 2000), we have felt inspired to deal with this exciting area. Having the feeling that we have to learn a lot to keep pace with the current research we think that there are any challenging white spots in the specific software area - in the field of protocols either. It seemed to be a good idea that's why to understand the philosophy of self-adaptive software, to create a simple example, a little prototype having specific characteristics related to self-adaptivity. Definition of DARPA on self-adaptive software was used to create the model [1]:

Self-adaptive software evaluates its own behavior and changes behaviour when the evaluation indicates that it is not accomplishing what the software intended to do, or when better functionality or performance is possible.

There are any FDTs supporting traditional protocol life cycle: requirement specification, specification, validation, implementation and conformance testing. These techniques will be presented in the Part 2.

The model of a simple protocol (M-TP) is introduced in Part 3 describing it by MSC (Message Sequence Chart) and SDL (Specification and Description Language), then it will be extended by self-adaptive components (M-SATP). We have an intuition that traditional formal techniques could be used in description of self-adaptive protocols. Our goal is to show the usability of traditional FDTs also in specification of SA protocols.

R. Laddaga, P. Robertson, and H. Shrobe (Eds.): IWSAS 2001, LNCS 2614, pp. 113–128, 2003.
© Springer-Verlag Berlin Heidelberg 2003

Part 4 of paper evaluates models and shows a possible mapping self-adaptive components to FDT symbols.

2   FDTs in Protocol Engineering

The protocol specifies the information exchange between two communicating entities determining the syntactic, semantic and temporal rules of the cooperation in such a way that one or more communication functions are fulfilled. The entities communicate through a network considered as a service provider. The main goal of this cooperation is to offer some services to the users. These services are the communication functions, e.g. file transfer or browsing. The syntactic rules define the messages, their structures and the data types composing the messages. The data models are based on abstract data types, the relations among data types can be modeled with data flow graphs. There were more attempts for data description languages in communication, but now the ASN.1 (Abstract Syntax Notation One) [7[8] seems to be the mostly widespread notation. The semantic rules specify the dialogue between the communicating entities. These entities can be considered as finite-state machines (FSM, EFSM and CFSM) or Petri nets in simple cases, either algebraic models (CCS, CSP) or formal grammar models in little more sophisticated cases. The labeled transition graph gives in any case a good orienteering for dynamic behavior modeling. Different standardized languages are used for system and system components, and other for the dialogue specification. SDL [5] is used for system, block and process specification and MSC [6] as a trace specification language. The temporal rules define the steps of cooperation in time. The theoretical background is based on timed automata. There are many attempts to design a suitable language, but still now MSC is the standardized language used wide-ranging in telecommunication.

The protocol engineering contains the whole life cycle of the protocol development. The subject of protocol engineering is the protocol design, implementation and testing. The main goal is to automate the whole process of protocol development. Formal methods support the protocol life cycle. The components of the protocol life cycle are the followings:

– requirements
– textual description
– formal specification
– validation
– implementation
– software tests
– conformance tests

The formal models and languages were shortly mentioned in the paragraph above. In the focus of our paper are the specification of the protocol and how this formal specification can be changed during the protocol's runtime. Two languages will be used for specification, SDL on system, block and process level and MSC for message exchange. Both languages are well defined in standard recommendations, but a very short overview will be given. Both languages are based on finite-state automata.

SDL is the language for specification of telecommunication systems and applications. SDL is a formal language in the sense of a formal syntax and formal semantics based on asynchronously communicating extended finite-state machines. The basic concept n SDL consists of communicating processes. A process instance is defined by a process definition. A process is either performing a state transition or waits for input. Every process has exactly one input queue, if two inputs are at a process simultaneously, they get ordered randomly.

The processes are built-in into blocks and the blocks into the system. This communication is through channels and signals are passing on the channels. The system is composed of one or more blocks and the blocks of processes. The processes specify the behaviour in a detailed way. The main graphical process symbols are input, output, state, decision, and task. It is important to mention the data type definition has ASN.1 format.

MSC is the other important language used in protocol engineering. This special trace language is for visualisation of selected system runs. It concentrates on message interchange by communicating entities and their environment. The clear graphical layout of MSC gives an intuitive understanding of the described system behaviour. The basic language elements include all constructs necessary to specify message flow: instance, message, environment, action, timer set and reset, and time-out, instance creation and stop. The fundamental language constructs are the instance and message flow. Vertical lines or columns with a heading represent the instance. The heading contains the entity name (process type, instance name). The message flow in time is represented by arrows, horizontal or downward slope. Structural language elements specify more general MSCs (coregion) and refine the time sequence chart with submsc.

3   Case Study: Specification of a Self-adaptive Protocol

First a simple transport protocol M-TP (Model of Transport Protocol) is introduced informally. The protocol has two classes; the difference between them is in the error handling capabilities. The two classes; Class0 and Class1 are specified first in MSC language describing the message exchange. Secondly a system level specification is presented in SDL/GR (graphical SDL). The goal of M-TP and its extension: M-SATP (Model of Self-Adaptive Transport Protocol) protocol is to assure reliable data transfer above the network (NW) layer independently from the error-rate of the environment. Foremost it will be dealt with the traditional M-TP protocol, which has USER and NW layer as operational environment (Fig. 1.).

M-TP ensures connection between two end-points, one of them acting as Initiator (INI) and the other as Responder (RES) (Fig. 2.). The Initiator part is able to send data to Responder entity by Data (DATA).req primitive, the Responder gives up the captured data - carried by DATA PDU between the two peer layers - to the USER layer using Data(DATA).ind primitive. If DATA is erroneous Data(ERR).ind primitive is given to USER of Responder. This protocol is asymmetrical, only Initiator is capable to send data for the Responder, and it has two operational modes:

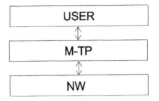

Fig. 1. Environment of M-TP

- Class0: Client broadcast mode, unreliable, and fast
- Class1: Mode reliable and slower

The protocol has a very simple error detection method: the data sent by Initiator includes a checksum field, checked by Responder. If Responder finds that data is erroneous, it sends Data(ERR).ind abstract service primitive to its USER layer, otherwise the data is sent up in primitive Data (DATA).ind.

Class0 mode:
In this mode the Initiator does not know whether the Responder received the data sent, because there is no acknowledgement - that is why the data transfer is faster.

This class is appropriate to have a good data transfer rate when the lower layer works in a reliable way. The TP-RES gives up either the data by Data(DATA).ind or its error message in Data(ERR).ind primitive to USER_RES. USER of Responder knows about the quality of receiving - if it is too bad then Class0 operation has to be replaced by a more reliable, but slower operational mode: Class1. The change in operation mode happens if USER layer decides and controls the event. Figure 2. contains the appropriate communicating entities as the nodes of graph; direction of labeled arcs shows that the messages are inputs or outputs of the entities.

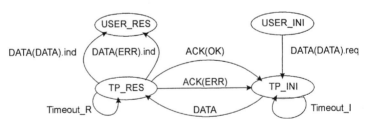

Fig. 2. M-TP operation in Class1 mode

Class1 mode:
The Responder should send an acknowledgement to its peer entity, when the data was received. There are two types of acknowledgements: ACK(OK) means the data received is errorless, in case of capturing ACK(ERR) the data was erroneous. The USER of Responder gets the received by TP_RES data in the same way as in Class0 mode.

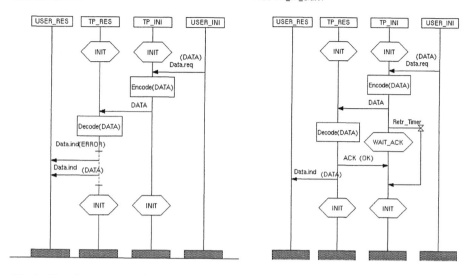

Fig. 3a. Requirement specification of Class0   **Fig. 3b.** Requirement specification of Class1

Here we show the expected behavior of Class0 mode, represented in graphical MSC/GR format. TP-RES and TP-INI instances (processes) are communicating with each other. The initial state of system is INIT state, in this case the DATA PDU is sent to TP-RES by the stimuli of USER of Initiator: the Data(DATA).req primitive.On the Initiator side data encoding is represented using the so-called 'task' symbol, on the peer side data is decoded in the same way. Depending on result of decoding in TP_RES instance, the USER can get Data(DATA).ind or Data(ERR).ind primitives, represented here as alternatives - the dashed line in TP-RES instance means 'coregion' in MSC (Fig.3a.).

Class1 means more reliable transfer, where TP_INI after sending the data to its peer sets timer called 'Retr_Timer' and goes to WAIT_ACK state. It makes a transition from there into the INIT state if Responder answers by ACK(OK) until the timer expired (Fig.3b.).

If timer expires and there is no acknowledgement, 'Retr_Timer' of Initiator is set again and a retransmission counter is incremented. The DATA PDU is repeated until ACK(OK) answer comes or the value of counter exceeds the maximum number of the defined retransmissions and an Alert is sent to the USER of Initiator. Figure 4. shows the case when data was received twice erroneously and the TP_INI entity has repeated the DATA.

3.1   M-TP Model

We have to describe in details how the operational methods will be changed from Class0 to Class1 and vice versa. Figure 5. depicts the way that USER_RES initiates this process by Change.req primitive.

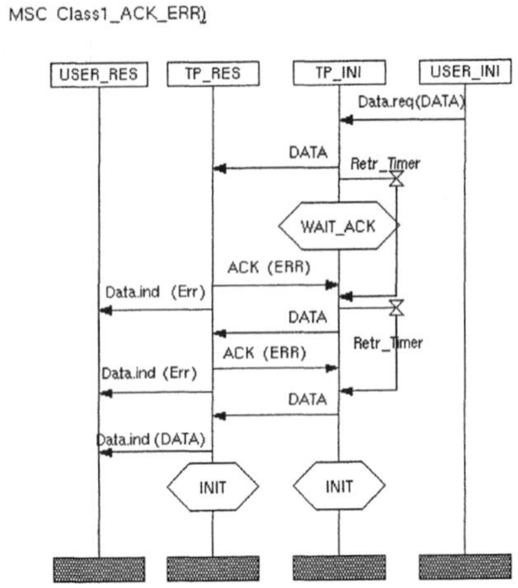

MSC Class1_ACK_ERR)

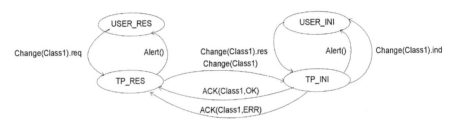

Fig. 4. TP-INI repeated 2 times the Data getting ACK(ERR) from Responder

Fig. 5. Switching from Class0 to Class1 using negotiation

It is refined neither in this graph representation nor in the following system level SDL/GR figure (Fig. 6.) whether TP_RES has already changed its mode to Class1 when it sends Change(Class1) PDU to its peer entity. The detailed specification of TP_RES block in SDL/GR will only provide us information. 'Alert' signals on both sides mean for USER that error was indicated in operation of lower layer. TP_INI receiving the Change(Class1) PDU tries to change its class to Class1, if it is success-ful then it informs its upper layer by Change.ind primitive. TP_RES entity has to be received acknowledgement if the other side was able to change its method or not. If the peer was not able to change its class the TP_RES should not continue by Class1. The negotiation is made by the M_TP protocol.

System representation in SDL/GR is based on 'block' and 'channel' symbols. Channels carrying signals represented in brackets provide interaction between the blocks. The signals via channels have to be defined in the system level. Blocks fig-ured as USER_RES and USER_INI are the two entities of the USER peer layer. The service provider for the USER layer is the M-TP protocol depicted here as TP_RES block and TP_INI block communicating via duplex (bi-directional) channel labeled as 'peer_to_peer'. Channel 'control_R' and 'control_I' are responsible for the com-munication of TP peer entities with the USER blocks. The signals sent are abstract service primitives (ASPs) defined in the MSC requirement specification (e.g.: Data.ind, Data.req).

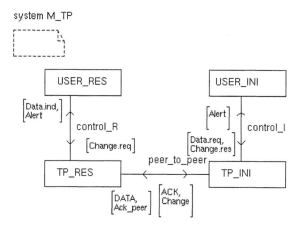

Fig. 6. System level of M-TP protocol in SDL/GR language

If the USER_RES decides on changing the operational class sends Change.req primitive and 'Change' protocol data unit will ask TP-INI peer entity to execute this modification, the result of execution is sent by TP_INI in 'Ack_peer' PDU.

3.2   Active Software Components

The presented model is a traditional, non self-adaptive protocol having active software components, namely error tolerance, changing behavior due negotiation between peer elements [2].

M-TP protocol shows error-tolerance, which can be changed to reach the goal of the reliable operation above a changing NW environment. Class1 replaces Class0 operation mode if USER would like to have a reliable data transfer provided by M-TP. This change does not happen autonomously in case of M-TP protocol; the USER layer stimulates it. Protocol was designed to be adapted to a changing environment, however this capability for adaptation does not mean self-adaptivity.

Other active software feature is the negotiation. The communication protocols have an initial negotiation to set some parameters, but there is no negotiation under operation. M-TP processes negotiate when Responder would like to change the operational mode.

We can claim that our traditional M-TP protocol has active software components as error-tolerance and negotiation of operations. It is designed to be adaptive that is to follow environmental changes. It is not self-adaptive, whereas its upper layer, even the USER is responsible to evaluate the operation: if there is too much error in Class0 mode it selects the mode Class1, if there is a good error rate but operation is slow it uses Class0.

3.3   Derivation of a Self-adaptive Model

In this part a simple self-adaptive protocol is derived on the basis of the introduced one. The idea of extending the M-TP into M-SATP is very simple: let's have an autonomous layer above the M-TP called as SA-CONTROL. This layer has the responsibility of USER to evaluate the state of NW, based on its continuos monitoring.

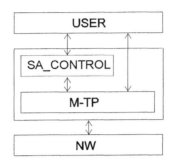

Fig. 7. Extended model of M_SATP was derived adding self-adaptive components to M_TP

Depending on NW state measured in real-time way, the SA_CONTROL selects the appropriate operation mode for the M_TP layer.

The possible operations have to be refined on an experimental basis. If network shows a certain change of error-rate the protocol class is changed: for $rate_K$ the optimal class is $Class_K$. The possible classes are members of a set having N elements and are mapped into a set which consists of error-rate intervals of connection:

$\{rate_0, rate_1, rate_2, rate_K, ..., rate_N\}$ => $\{Class_0, Class_1, Class_K, ..., Class_N\}$

This mapping can be not only one-to-one mapping and proposed classes are result of experiments. The 'rate-class' function is from real to integer mapping where for example:

$0 < rate_0 < 0.1$ means: 0 => $Class_0$, $0.1 < rate_1 < 0.28$ means: 1 => $Class_1$ and so on. Here we define a function based not on real measurements, it is only an abstraction enabling us to introduce other classes than the above-defined two to ensure the most optimistic operation if the error-rate of connection changes in real-time. So our initial model handling two operational classes was extended into N classes, reflecting that our operational environment is complex.

In this case instead of USER the transport layer itself will decide its operational changes based on a built-in knowledge. This knowledge is the previously measured 'rate-class' function experimented in an off-line way (Fig. 8.).

The negotiation on operational method between the peer entities is done by the elements of SA_CONTROL layer. These are the blocks SA_CONTROL_R and SA_CONTROL_I in SDL system level specification of M_SATP protocol.

Now M_TP layer supported by SA_CONTROL is functioning for its environment as a self-adaptive M-SATP protocol. USER is able to control the TP layer using 'Opt_Change.req' and 'Opt_Change.res' primitives, such way having a supervisory function [4] on the M_SATP protocol (Fig. 9.).

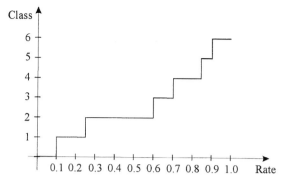

Fig. 8. Rate-Class function supporting decision

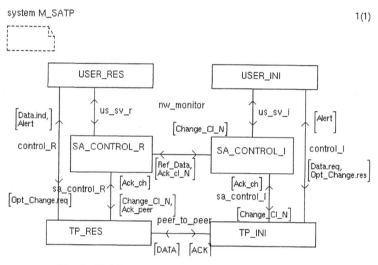

Fig. 9. SDL/GR system level specification of M_SATP

M_SATP follows the environmental changes in real-time way; noise (analogue or digital noise, distortion and other) increasing and decreasing on lower layer and provides an optimistic service for its user. In case of low noise M_TP protocol operates faster, otherwise it selects another class to provide more reliable data for its USER with decreased data transfer rate. The operation of SA_CONTROL layer will be refined.

3.4 Refinement of the Sa_Control Layer Operation

M_SATP protocol uses an independent 'nw_monitor' channel to measure and estimate the NW quality (Fig.9.), (Fig.10.). SA_CONTROL_I uses a data generator and sends periodically 'Ref_Data' to SA_CONTROL_R block having 3 processes. The 'Monitor_Evaluator' process continously counts the rate function. It means proportion of the number of received errors related to the number of received data.

$$rate(t) = NError(t) \ /NData \ (t) \tag{1}$$

The current rate value is compared to the actual 'rate-class' function in the 'Selector' process, which is able to make decision to change operational class. 'ClassN' signal is transferred to 'Control' process via 'sel_sr' signalroute and as a result 'Control' process sends 'Change_Cl_N' signal to TP_RES block via 'sa_control_R' channel. Here the new 'Class_N' process will be created and started. The previous process handles DATA sent by TP_INI until the peer answers.

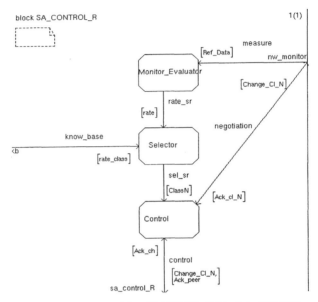

Fig. 10. Processes of SA_CONTROL_R block in SDL/GR

The peer SA_CONTROL_I block getting 'Change_Cl_N' via 'peer-to-peer' channel sends it to the lower TP_INI layer. It is done similarly on the responder side and block tries to create and start on the Initiator side the appropriate 'Class_N' process to interoperate with the Responder (Fig. 9.).

If the new operational class has been successfully created in both TP entities 'Ack_cl_N' is captured by the SA_CONTROL_R, and Control process sends 'Ack_peer' which stimulates in TP_RES block killing the old 'Class_K' process.

3.5   Hand-off Process

Here we examine the effect of transition from an old operational mode to a new one. Let's suppose that 'Ack_Cl_N' has not been received by the SA_CONTROL_R block which operates for example in Class0 (new) mode and the previous process Class1 has not been killed. On the peer side the Initiator mode has been changed to Class0 (new mode) and the old Class1 mode has been killed. In this case Initiator Class0 sends DATA using PID (process identifier) address of the new Class0 process on

Responder side. There is no asynchronous behaviour and data loss; the Class1 process will be killed when 'Ack_peer' is received.

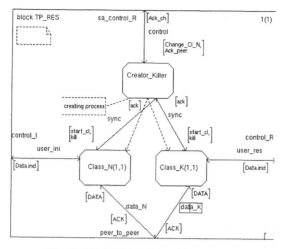

Fig. 11. TP_RES block level in SDL/GR

Let's see the case when the new process has been started on the Responder side but the demand 'Change_Cl_N' has not arrived yet to peer. In this case the old pair processes continues working - there is no data loss caused by hand-off (Fig. 11.).

3.6   Process Specification in SDL/GR

The behavior changes in TP_RES block creating a new process and killing the old one.TP_RES block having 'Change_Cl_N' signal via 'sa_control_R' channel creates Class_N process and starts it. If it is successful sends an 'Ack_ch' signal which inducts 'Change_Cl_N' sending to the peer via 'negotiation' signalroute of SA_CONTROL_R block (Fig. 10.).

The 'Creator_Killer' process waits 'Ack_peer' signal answers from 'Control' process of the control layer. Getting this signal Class_K the previous process is killed in TP_RES block (Fig.12.). The SA_CONTROL layer controls such way 'Creator_Killer' process assuring the appropriate operational mode ordered by SA_CONTROL_R.

3.7   Change Behavior Represented in MSC

In negotiation phase 'Change_Cl_N' signal has stimulated the Creator_Killer process to create the Class1 new mode on Responder side (Fig. 13). The new process creation is shown using dashed line in MSC. The Class1 process in NULL state is expecting the 'start_cl' signal.

Capturing this signal a transition is made to INIT state. If the negotiation phase terminated - an 'Ack_peer' signal received from Initiator side and in this case Class0 process is killed.

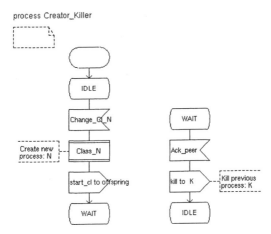

Fig. 12. Creator_Killer process in SDL/GR

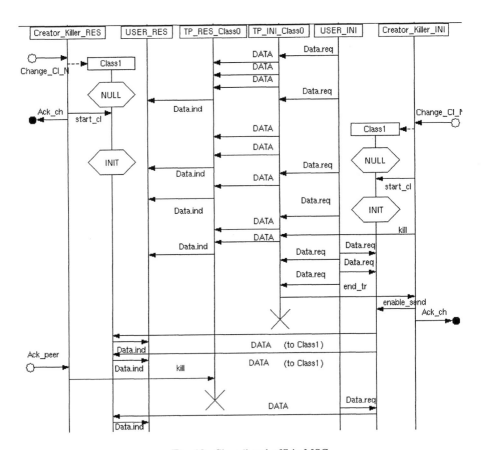

Fig. 13. Class 'hand-off' in MSC

4   Evaluation of Models and Usage of FDTs

The goal of this paper was to show that usage of traditional formal techniques is possible in self-adaptive protocol specification. The MSC and SDL languages have been in scope of our analysis.

M_TP protocol, a simple traditional transport protocol with two different operational classes was created to demonstrate the usage of the above mentioned techniques in the specification step of protocol life cycle. As a first step the goal and the behavior of protocol was described informally. Simple graphs were used to show the relationship among the peer layer entities.

The architecture of the protocol was planned in SDL, which is a good tool to depict the dependence of system elements. In the static part of SDL, the system level was presented where interaction of protocol with its service provider (network) and its service user was figured using blocks and signals carried by channels.

The required behavior of Class0 and Class1 operational methods was specified in MSC using ASP and PDU signals. MSC is capable to give a good view on the system operation in time.

Based on the SDL specification protocol behavior can be simulated, validating in such way the correctness of the previously imagined operation.

Error tracking is based on this method, before the implementation and the expensive testing phase protocol design errors (deadlocks, livelocks etc.) can be discovered. The goal in case of complex software systems is the same: to discover errors in the earliest phase of life cycle and not later - in the large software code.

M_SATP protocol having a self-adaptive characteristic was 'derived' from the simple transport protocol: M_TP, where the way to create model was the following:

– Complex environment: We have modeled a more complex environment having a characteristic property: the error-rate. It means proportion of the number of received errors related to the number of received data. The approach referred to the environment used in the traditional model was not enough - it was too 'binary': in case of an acceptable error rate the Class0 operation, else Class1 was used.

– Real-time decision related to change behavior: The behavior of traditional M_TP protocol was changed if the USER wanted so. The USER made the decision, however the adaptive behavior was implemented in M_TP layer, but it was stimulated in off-line way.

In M_SATP the decision is made by the SA_CONTROL_R Responder block, which is monitoring automatically the state of connection, selects the appropriate method for protocol operation (e.g. ClassN) and controls the lower sublayer: M_TP which executes switching to the selected class.

Behaviour of the self-adaptive model depends on the error-rate. A new sublayer makes this measurement: SA_CONTROL layer, which was added to protocol. The measurement is independent from the channel used by M_TP for real data transfer and it happens in parallel way operating in a 'pilot' channel (nw_monitor) and monitoring the connection.

Indicating a change of rate appropriate to the rate-class function a new class mode starts working on each side, after the negotiation, initiated by the SA_CONTROL_R layer and not by the M_TP.

The decision is made by a knowledge-based method; the previously measured rate-class function is the basis for Selector process to make decision to select the appropriate operational class.

– Negotiation: The negotiation with peer entity on changes happens between the entities of M_TP layer using the same channel where the data transfer was made.

In case of M_SATP self-adaptive variant the SA_CONTROL_R negotiates the possible change with its peer, enabling the data transfer part: M_TP to deal purely with its task: receiving the data sent by Initiator. Such way data transfer is not disturbed in time of negotiation phase.

– Learning: The rate-class function used in decision can be replaced by other functions if the system is capable to change the original one in order to access better behaviour. Let' s suppose that first time the system uses the proposed function and on Responder side after registration of switch times depending on the measured error rates in time of operation - the evaluation will show that the error rate is too high in appropriate situation. Analyzing the necessity of change SA_CONTROL will decide to use another function modified by the system.

Enhancing M_TP protocol with SA_CONTROL layer including self-adaptive components the derived M_SATP protocol has some important factors increasing quality and robustness of the original M_TP protocol:

– Less reaction time to the network changes: Separated 'nw_monitor' channel makes that the reaction time to the network changes is less than in case of one layer having only M_TP functionality.

– Larger data transfer rate: Because of the negotiation done by SA_CONTROL the M_TP could work parallel in a more robust way and has a larger data transfer rate.

– Effect of environmental changes: Protocol behaviour follows in real-time way the effect of environmental changes depicted in error-rate, making the system more tolerable. Time of transition from one mode to the other depends on the required negotiation time.

– Ability to be trained and self learning: Using knowledge base the operational modes can be changed in a flexible way: the user of M_SATP layer can add, remove, send and modify the database on-line way. The system is learning on its operational experiments (e.g.: results of measurements on class modifications in time) will select the best rate-class function depending on network behaviour, accessing the best error rate in the appropriate classes.

4.1   Use of FDTs in Case of CFSM Model

In this case study we have shown the specification steps of a self-adaptive protocol and presented that using of traditional FDTs (SDL and MSC) is possible. These languages are based on CFSM (Communicating Finite State Machines) automatons and the analyzed self-adaptive protocol is based on CFSMs.

The functionality of self-adaptive protocol is distributed in different protocol parts namely: Monitoring, Decision, Control process are in the upper layer and data transfer is in the lower one [3].

The goal for self-adaptive software is to answer environmental changes. The environment is very complex but should not include every possible effect shocking the protocol. We have to prepare our protocol to adapt in the best way to the changing network environment and to provide an optimal service related to error rate and data transfer rate to its USER. This environment has been modeled as a nonlinearly changing in time error-rate function. Our model follows in real time way the environmental changes.

4.2   Mapping Self-adaptive Components to SDL and MSC symbols

– Monitoring: The process and procedure symbols of SDL cover the task of monitoring which is important in our example: Monitor_Evaluator process (Fig. 10).

– Decision making: It is based on the comparison of knowledge base 'rate- class' proposal and the actually measured rate: the appropriate to this task SDL symbols are process or procedure, using two inputs: signal 'rate' and 'rate-class' and one output signalroute 'sel_sr': Selector process.

– Control: Usually process and procedure is responsible for control in SDL: Control process. In MSC a process is shown as an instance and a procedure can be depicted as an MSC procedure or a task.

– Changing behaviour in real-time way: Creator_Killer process (Fig. 11.) is responsible for process creation, start and stop actions which have appropriate symbol in SDL and MSC either.

Starting a process is made by a start signal. In SDL a signalroute is used to send signals for the created process (offspring) and it operates such a way in MSC either. Killing an old process is also possible: in SDL it is made using signalroute to the process and sending a kill message via; as a result the process is stopped and removed.

– The learning automata feature is a non-refined element of the system: An open question is: how a protocol can learn itself creating new operational modes in order to be adapted to network changes.

The first approach could be a process able to send a message to itself if the information read from the knowledge base is interpretable: the automaton uses rules to understand the information. If the new information is interpretable by the rules it will use it, for example it gets a list of functions and classes. Automaton is able to interpret the information and to modify the content adding new fields, removing the olds and rewriting some. These operations can be done using rules describing information.

This type of reflecting machine can be described as a process communicating with its environment. The knowledge base with its content is represented, as environment connected by signalroute to a process and signals are for example the different 'rate-class' functions. Describing 'rate-class' function is very simple using a simple grammar: we can use for example the well-known Backus-Naur form in our syntax. We think describing this self-learned automaton is possible by using SDL symbols (process, channel and procedure).

5   Conclusion

The usage of traditional FDTs as the Specification and Description Language and MSC was presented in case of self-adaptive protocol based on Communicating Finite State Machines.

These techniques are usable in CFSM based self-adaptive protocol specification because they are also based on this model.

Symbols supporting the behavioral changes in real-time way were shown: process creations, start, kill. The hand-off process was represented in MSC. The Monitor, Decision and Control components of self-adaptive protocol were mapped to SDL and MSC symbols. A possible model of knowledge based learning automata was described.

In this way we have proved the usability of FDTs in specification area of the protocol lifetime in case self-adaptive protocol.

Our future plans: based on this simple model to refine the protocol, to simulate its behaviour under a complex environment using SDL based simulation. We would like to insert error-tracing capability to the model and learn it to eliminate itself the bugs in real-time way. The whole life cycle of self-adaptive protocol could be covered if we focused on test case generation based on FDTs.

References

1. Robertson, P., Laddaga, R., Shrobe, H.,: Introduction: The First International Workshop on Self-Adaptive Software, IWSAS 2000, Springer-Verlag, New York (2001)
2. Laddaga, R.: Active Software, Self-Adaptive Software, IWSAS 2000, Springer-Verlag, New York (2001)
3. Robertson, P., Laddaga, R., Shrobe, H.: Results of the First International Workshop on Self-Adaprive Software, Self-Adaptive Software, IWSAS 2000, Springer-Verlag, New York (2001)
4. Karsai, G., Ledeczi, J., Sztipanovits, J., Peceli, G., Simon, Gy., Kovacshazy: An Approach to Self-Adaptive Software based on Supervisory Control, Self-Adaptive Software, IWSAS 2000, Springer-Verlag, New York (2001)
5. Specification and Description Language (SDL) ITU-T Recommendation Z.100 (11/1999)
6. Message Sequence Chart (MSC) ITU-T Z.120 (11/1999)
7. Specification of Abstract Syntax Notation One (ASN.1) ITU-T Recommendation X.208 (1988)
8. Abstract Syntax Notation One (ASN.1): Specification of Basic Notation ITU-T Recommendation X.680 (1994)

Frame-Based Self-adaptive Test Case Selection

Gusztáv Adamis[1] and Katalin Tarnay[2]

[1] Budapest University of Technology and Economics,
Magyar tudósok körútja 2.
H-1117 Budapest, Hungary
adamis@bme-tel.ttt.bme.hu
[2] NOKIA HUNGARY, Köztelek u 6.,
H-1092 Budapest, Hungary
katalin.tarnay@nokia.com

Abstract. This paper introduces frame representation for test notions such as test suite structure, test purpose and test cases. A self-adaptive approach to test case selection is suggested. These test cases are changed according to the detected error type. Some ideas are also presented on the creation of new rules for a test language standardized for protocol engineering. One well-known WAP protocol, called WTP is used to demonstrate our ideas and results.

Keywords: self-adaptive, frame representation, conformance testing, TTCN, WAP.

1 Introduction

1.1 General Overview

The conformance testing of communication protocols has a great importance in the coming age of ubiquitous computing. Ad hoc networks and changing configurations need flexible but reliable protocols. Exhaustive tests with full coverage are very time consuming and the full execution of such tests is nearly impossible. In one respect simple and quickly executable test cases are advantageous, but reliability and correct operation are important requirements that may not be met with only simple and quick tests. The erroneous parts of a protocol implementation should be tested more thoroughly then the errorless parts. Therefore a dynamic test case selection during the tests depending on the type or class of the detected errors seems to be a good solution.

Our goals are the following:

- to develop a frame-based test suite representation that is easy-to-use either for decomposition or for test case selection according to test purposes and protocol implementation,
- to introduce self-adaptivity to change test case selection during the conformance testing according to the detected errors,
- to define the basic terminology for frame-based knowledge representation of test suites and self-adaptive testing.

R. Laddaga, P. Robertson, and H. Shrobe (Eds.): IWSAS 2001, LNCS 2614, pp. 129–141, 2003.
© Springer-Verlag Berlin Heidelberg 2003

This paper is composed as follows. After this introduction the basics for conformance testing of communication protocols are summarized in Section 2. The test suite is specified as a net of frames. Section 3 describes first the frames used for test suite and test cases, then the net of frames. The next (fourth) section specifies the test purposes and the protocol implementation conformance statement (PICS), both represented as frames. The test case selection is derived from the resulting frame (meta-frame) of the above mentioned frames. Section 5 explains the methods for dynamic self-adaptive test case selection introducing a classification for test case execution. Section 6 contains some new ideas to augment the standardized test language of telecommunication protocols called TTCN (Tree and Tabular Combined Notation) with frame-based components. Finally the benefits and disadvantages of this methodology are summarized in Section 7 and some possible future research and development efforts are mentioned. New ideas are always illustrated by example in the second half of every section. The examples utilize a WAP protocol called WTP, because all aspects of WTP testing are known.

1.2   Example Protocol: WTP

In order to aid in comprehension, the main steps are represented with an example test suite used for an existing WAP protocol, called WTP [1]. This protocol and its test suite have a moderate complexity. The Wireless Transaction Protocol is defined to provide the services necessary for interactive "browsing" (request/response) applications. During a browsing session, the client requests information from a server, (either fixed or mobile) and the server responds with the information. The request/response duo is referred to as a "transaction" in this document. The objective of the protocol is to reliably deliver the transaction while balancing the reliability and the cost. WTP runs on top of a datagram service and optionally a security service.

The placement of WTP in the WAP architecture (Fig.1): WTP has been defined as a lightweight transaction oriented protocol that is suitable for implementation in "thin" clients (mobile stations) and operates efficiently over wireless datagram networks. The main features of WTP include:

Improved reliability over datagram services. WTP relieves the upper layer from retransmissions and acknowledgements, which are necessary, if datagram services are used.

- Improved efficiency over connection oriented services. WTP has no explicit connection set up or tear down phases.
- WTP is message oriented and designed for services oriented towards transactions, such as "browsing".
- Three classes of transaction service:
  o Class 0: Unreliable invoke message with no result message
  o Class 1: Reliable invoke message with no result message
  o Class 2: Reliable invoke message with exactly one reliable result message
- Reliability is achieved through the use of unique transaction identifiers, acknowledgements, duplicate removal and re-transmissions.

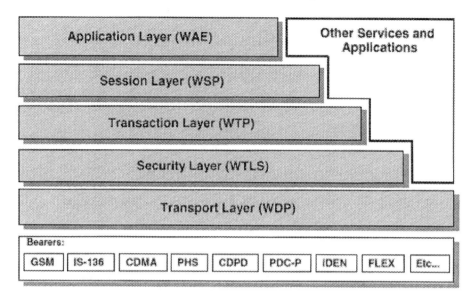

Fig. 1. WAP architecture

- No explicit connection set-up or tear down phases. Explicit connection open and/or close imposes excessive overhead on the communication link.
- Optionally user-to-user reliability: the WTP user confirms every received message.
- Optionally, the last acknowledgement of the transaction may contain out of band information related to the transaction. For example, performance measurements.
- Concatenation may be used, where applicable, to convey multiple Protocol Data Units in one Service Data Unit of the datagram transport.
- Message orientation. The basic unit of interchange is an entire message and not a stream of bytes.
- The protocol provides mechanisms in order to minimize the number of transactions being replayed as the result of duplicate packets.
- Aborting of outstanding transaction, including flushing of unsent data both in client and server. The user, canceling a requested service can trigger aborting.
- For reliable invoke messages, both success and failure are reported. If an invoke can not be handled by the Responder, an abort message will be returned to the Initiator instead of the result.

2   Conformance Testing

2.1   Basics of Conformance Testing

The primary objective of conformance testing is to increase the probability that different product implementations will actually interoperate. To achieve this goal every standardized protocol has a conformance clause containing all features necessary to compare different implementations and to repeat the development of the same implementation. Conformance testing verifies that an implementation meets the formal requirements of the conformance clause.

Conformance testing [3,9] is based on the formal specification of the protocol in addition to test principles. The protocol specification defines the message exchange and the components of the protocol. The test principle part contains the test requirements and test suites. In the later part of our paper we deal only with test aspects. The test requirements are composed of the Test Suite Structure (TSS) and of the Test Purposes (TP). The TSS has a hierarchical structure from top to bottom, with classified categories of tests. The first class contains capability tests for mandatory and optional features, the second class is for behavior test cases (valid/invalid syntax, connection establishment and release, data transfer, variations on timers, variations on parameters). Each test purpose focuses on a single conformance requirement. Each test case of the test suite is designed to achieve one of the specified test purposes.

The test suite has two representations, an abstract and an executable one. The Abstract Test Suite (ATS) is derived from the protocol specification guarded by test purposes. ATS contains the test cases for all possible protocol implementations, therefore test case selection for the implemented features is required to get the Executable Test Suite (ETS) for that particular implementation. Our goal is to introduce self-adaptive test case selection depending on the defined error class.

2.2   Test Suite Structure (TSS) and Test Purposes (TP) for WTP

The test suite is structured as a tree, and full coverage means to execute all test cases on each branch of the tree.

The test groups are organized in five levels [4] [5].

1. The first level creates two groups representing the availability of the optional SAR functions.
2. The second level separates the protocol plane in two functional modules INIT (Initiator) and RESP (Responder).
3. The third level is separated by transaction classes.
4. The fourth level represents the UACK function in case of Class1 and Class2.
5. The last level contains the standard ISO subgroups CA, BV, BO and BI.

The main test groups are the Capability group (CA), the Valid Behavior group (BV), the inopportune Behavior group (BO) and the Invalid Behavior group (BI).

- Capability (CA) tests: This test subgroup shall provide limited testing of the major IUT capabilities aiming to assure that the claimed capabilities are correctly supported, in accordance with the PICS.
- Valid Behavior (BV) tests: This test subgroup shall verify that the IUT reacts in conformity with the standard, on receipt or exchange of valid Protocol Data Units (PDUs). Valid PDU means, that the exchange of messages and the content of the exchanged messages are considered as valid.

- Inopportune Behavior (BO) tests: This test subgroup shall verify that the IUT is capable of a valid reaction, when an inopportune protocol event occurs. Such an event is syntactically correct but it occurs unexpectedly.
- Invalid Behavior (BI) tests: This test subgroup shall verify that the IUT reacts in conformity with the standard, on receipt of a syntactically invalid Protocol Data Unit (PDU).

3   Frame Representation of the Test Suite

A frame is the abstract and structured model of an object or a notion. The hierarchical structure of frames provides a good way to represent a protocol. Every piece of information about a protocol can be enclosed in frames. The most important pieces of information are enclosed in frames on the top of the hierarchy, and as we go lower in the hierarchical structure we get frames containing more detailed information about protocol messages, parameters and states. In protocol validation the frames provide a good way for generating the reachability graph.

In this paper the following syntax of frames is used:

```
frame: name;
Slot: [list of values]        /*comment*/
end;
```

The name of the frames, slots and values are denoted with small letters. Capitol letters denote variables. The values in a slot can be considered as a a list, therefore is the square bracket necessary.

If a frame has only a name, and no slots and values are given then we call it "primitive frame". If a frame has a name and some slots but no values, then it is called "generic frame". Finally if nothing is omitted, there is a "full-frame".

The frames can be completed with additional information, called meta-information. Frames, slots and values can carry meta-information. This method can also be used for describing the test suite structure of a protocol.

The TTCN test suites can be converted to generic frames. That is the suggested frame representation of a TTCN TSS (not all TTCN tables should be converted into frames). A TTCN-like test suite can be represented for example as a generic frame in the following way:

```
frame: test_suite structure;
    Standard: [];           /* reference to the specifica-
                               tion of the protocol*/
    PICS: [];               /* Protocol Implementation Con-
                               formance Statement */
    PIXIT: [];              /* Protocol Implementation Ex-
                               tra Information for Testing */
    test_groups:[];         /* List of the main functional
                               test groups */
    end;
```

All test groups can be considered as meta-frames, and a generic frame for test group has the following format:

```
frame: test_groups;
    selection_condition: [];          /* Condition describing
                                      when the test group is to be
                                      selected */
    test_subgroups: [];               /* List of the subgroups
                                      of the test group */
    test_cases: [];                   /* List of the test
                                      cases if the TSS is not struc-
                                      tured further on */
end;
```

In a similar way the subgroups are meta-frames and they can be displayed as frames:

```
frame: test_subgroups;
    selection_condition: [];          /* Condition describing
                                      when the test group is to be
                                      selected */
    parent_group: [];
    test_subgroups: [];               /* List of the subgroups of the
                                      test group if the subgroup is
                                      structured further on */
    test_cases: [];                   /* List of the test
                                      cases if the subgroup is not
                                      structured further on */
end;
```

The next test frame specifies the features of a test case:

```
frame: test_case;
    selection_condition: [];    /* Condition describing when
                                the test case is to be selected
                                */
    group: [];
    test_purpose: [];           /* the goal of the test case */
    default_behaviour: [];      /* refers to a TTCN Default Be-
                                haviour table, it may contain
                                e.g. error recovery procedures
                                */
    preambles: [];              /* the sequence of TTCN Test
                                Steps that carry the IUT into
                                the initial state of the test
                                case */
    body: [];                   /* refers to a TTCN Dynamic Be-
                                haviour Description table con-
                                taining the test case itself */
    postambles: [];             /* the (sequence of) TTCN Test
                                Step(s) that carry the IUT into
                                a well defined state after com-
                                pletion of the body of the test
                                case to be able to continue the
                                test with the next test case */
end;
```

The structure of the test steps and the default behaviours can be described in a very similar way:

```
frame: constraints;
    formal_parameters;
    type: [];                      /* type of information element:
                                   ASP, PDU, structured type */
end;

frame: ASP_constraints_inherits_constraints;
    type: ASP;
    ASP_type: [];                  /* the type of the ASP for
                                   which the constraint is defined
                                   */
end;

frame: ASP1_constraints_inherits_ASP_constraints;
    ASP_type: ASP1;
    first_field_of_ASP1: [];
    ....

end;
```

Definitions of other kind of constraints and other kind of elements of a test environment (like PCOs, Coordinating Points, Coordination Messages, Test Configuration etc.) can be given in similar ways.

By proper selection rules - based on the information given for the questions of the test input documents (PICS and PIXIT) - the selection of the test cases to be executed can be carried out automatically.

The model and method described above can be used in those cases, when we want to test a standardized protocol, or in general, a protocol whose abstract test suite has already selected those test cases from the ATS, which are necessary to be run to test the IUT in the given test arrangement. In other words, the method can help in creating the ETS from the ATS. But the expert systems may even help in the generation of the ATS itself.

We found it necessary first to create very simple, 'atomic' test cases. We call a test case atomic, if it contains exactly one state transition without decisions. That is, if the IUT is in state$_i$, and receives input(j), then generates output(k) and goes to state(m). More complicated state transitions (typically those that contain decisions) can be converted to this form, but of course we have to pay for it with the increasing number of test cases. [4] [5] [6]

Every frame can be described easily for WTP. As it was mentioned earlier, a full-frame has name, slots, and values. In the foregoing a generic frame for testing was presented, now the full-frame for WTP Test Suite Structure is the following:

```
frame: test_suite_structure;
    Standard: [WAP-WTP];
    Pics: [WTP];
    Pixit: [...];
    Test group: [no_SAR, SAR];
end;
```

A full-frame of test purpose for WTP capability test for Initiator:

```
frame: test_case[init/cl1/no-UCk];
     Initial condition:[ IUT...Invoke-PDU/Cl1];
     Stimulus:[noACK PDU arrives];
     ...
end;
```

4   Test Case Selection

4.1   Classification of Test Cases

For real protocols it is impossible to test all the possible situations. So when we generate an ATS to a protocol we can only say (after running the test) that the IUT conforms to the standard with the confidence of, say, e.g. 95%. But there are some situations, which must be checked that constitute the "normal" working of the protocol, and typically only those state transitions may be left out which represent some special, extra behavior. But sometimes we want to test how the protocol behaves under special circumstances ("worst case behavior test"). We must take into consideration these factors as well. We can assign a new slot to the frame description of the test case, which describes the "importance" of the state transition, that may take e.g. the following values: *dominant* (the test case checks a state transition which belongs to the "normal", desired behaviur of the protocol), *recessive* (the test case checks a state transition that happens very rarely during the "normal" working of the protocol, or leads either to erroneous or illegal state), *negligible* (the test case checks a state transition that never happens during the "normal" working of the protocol) [9].

When specifying protocols we consider a state transition takes place in 0 time. But this is not true in "real" testing. So not only the number of test cases can determine the transition time of a test, but also the time among the individual test cases The execution of a lot of simple test cases may take less time than the execution of a few complicated test cases. This fact can also be taken into consideration for example by adding an *estimated duration* slot to the frame description of a test case.

As a conclusion we can see that an expert system using frame and rule representations can be very useful in

– selection of ETS from an ATS,
– creation of ATS and its adjustment to specific test purposes.,
– classification of test cases as dominant, recessive and negligible tests
– activation of new test cases depending on the type or class of detected errors.

The first two points show the advantage of frame representation for different specifications in the field of conformance testing, these are the specifications of TSS, TP, ATS, ETS, test groups, test cases and test steps. The second two points give a guide to select test cases and to activate newer ones according to the test results. The traditional approach for test case execution is the following sequence, as the TSS of WTP presents:

- capability tests,
- valid behavior tests,
- invalid behavior tests,
- inopportune behavior tests.

The executable test cases are selected as PICS and TP specify the parameters. The selected set of test cases is too big, therefore our first suggestion is a second selection using the classification principle: dominant, recessive and negligible test cases. The next step is to introduce a third selection during the testing. If the tests are successfully executed, no more tests are needed besides the previously selected subset of dominant test cases. If one or more tests detected errors, then newer test cases should be selected depending on the error type. The detected events are either an input-output pair or a state-transition following input.

4.2   Test Case Selection Based on Test Purposes and on Protocol Implementation

For this kind of test cases it is very easy to define and formalize the test purposes. We can easily add preambles (that bring the IUT into the desired start state of the test case from the null state) and postambles (that bring the IUT to the null state) to these test cases.

Though it is possible to execute a test based on these test cases, but it may take quite a long time to perform it due to the large amount of these cases. From these atomic test cases we can generate more complicated test cases for different test purposes by the help of an expert system.

We have to add new pieces of information to the frame based test suite declaration like this:

```
frame: test_purpose;
    initial_state:;
    input_stimulus:;
    desired_output:;
    final_state;
end;
```

With the help of this information we can generate more complex test cases which check complete functions, services of the protocol, and take into consideration some specific situations like connection establishment where the initial message has been repeated due to expiration of a given timer, etc.

This way we can adjust the test suite structure to the specific requirements that we want to focus on.

4.3   Self-adaptive Test Case Selection

Self-adaptive test case selection during the testing is a quite new idea. Traditionally the test cases are selected before the testing in accord with the protocol implementation and the test purposes [3]. Therefore the test process is independent of the detected errors. This selection has a hierarchical structure for the test case selection. The test tree is structured for dominant, recessive and negligible layers as mentioned earlier. All three layers have additional sub-layers. The sub-layers are related to error types. The test scenario contains many decisions guided by the detected errors. The detected errors are classified according to the three possible verdicts: passed, failed and inconclusive. After error detection a new subset of test cases is selected.

The test scenario is changed during the test process. The frame representation can be built in into the test specification from test suite structure to test cases. The declaration part of the protocols can be made more flexible by converting the data flow graphs to frames.

5   TTCN and Self-adaptive Testing

In this chapter we examine how well suited both the current, and the new, development version of the TTCN are for writing self-adaptive test cases. At the end of this chapter we suggest to adding new features to the TTCN to support self-adaptive testing. The current version [10] of the TTCN language (TTCN2+) has several serious limitations preventing it from being an appropriate test specification language for self-adaptive testing. The most important insufficiencies are the followings:

• there is no built-in way to determine the order of the execution of the test cases (it can be specified only by informal comments);

• the selection of the ETS from the ATS is static. It means that those expressions (called Test Case Selection Expressions in TTCN) that determine - by the help of PICS or PIXIT entry values - which test cases are to be chosen are constants or constant expressions. That is the ETS will be determined BEFORE the test starts and there is no way to add new or omit previously selected test cases based on outcomes during the test;

• there are very few control transfer instructions, and most of them can only be used in a quite uncomfortable way, and in most cases we cannot avoid the usage of the GOTO construction; this may make it difficult to write more complicated test cases;

• the test suite parameters (like window size, timer values etc.) are constants. This may lead to problematic situations not only in the selection of the test cases, but in the description of the tests of self-adaptive protocols where these parameters can change their values due to adapting to the concrete situation. The solution to this problem may be the usage of test suite variables and assigning the values of the appropriate test suite parameters to them, but i.) since only global variables can be used in TTCN it can lead to naming conflicts; ii.) since the test suite parameter should be called in the same way as in the PICS/PIXIT, for its "substituting" test suite variable the standardized name cannot be used;

• to immediately assign a verdict to a test case causes the test case to be aborted. This problem can be avoided by using preliminary verdicts, but this may lead to complicated, hard-to-read test cases especially in sophisticated erroneous situations;

These problems, apart from the last one, are solved by the suggested use of a frame representation of the test suite.

The new release of the TTCN [2] (TTCN-3) is under development. This language is a(n almost) completely new language, not only a new version of it. The representation of the language is completely new. Instead of the need to fill in tables, as it was the case in the TTCN2+, the new language is very similar to the programming languages with a lot of new features.

We provide an overview of the features of TTCN-3 that makes it a suitable language for specifying self-adaptive test suites but we also point to some still existing problems.

In TTCN-3 it is possible to define a module control part for each test suite. In this part the selection of the test cases AND the order of the execution of the test cases can be determined. Here variable definitions & assignments, conditional (if) and control transfer instructions (loops) can be used. So it is possible to describe in a very straightforward way, for example if a test must be repeated several times. The conditional expressions used in if statements can be similar to the test case selection expressions of TTCN2+ but they may contain variables - so the selection is not static. But since the TTCN-3 follows the opposite extreme than the TTCN2+ in determining the scope of the variables (all variables are local), this means that the test cases cannot set the variables defined and used in the module control part for selecting the test cases directly.

The test cases in TTCN-3 are considered to be functions whose return values are restricted to be "verdicttype". They may have "in" (call by value) and "inout" (call by reference) parameters. The usage of "inout" parameters in the argument list of the test cases is the trick by which we can avoid the usage of global variables, but still be able to modify the values of the selection expressions in the module control part from a test case. Though it is a solution for the problem, it is not elegant, especially if the test case has too many parameters and/or a lot of selection controlling variables are to be modified. One could consider introducing the global variables in the TTCN-3 at least in the module control part - though we know, it can have a lot of other consequences.

The assignment of a verdict to a test case does not cause the termination of the test case. It may be continued e.g. by a further evaluation of the problem, by writing the cause of the error into a log file (new feature of TTCN-3) or setting the proper variables to select other test cases.

But in TTCN-3 the problem of the test suite parameters still exists. They are also constants and since there is no way to define global variables in TTCN-3 the solution will be more complicated than it was in TTCN2+.

We would suggest considering the addition of some features to TTCN-3 to support self-adaptive testing:

- test cases should have some attributes, like dominant, recessive or negligible;
- test cases should have an estimated duration that should be adjusted according to the real situation during testing
- it would be advisable to introduce the notion of 'linked test case'. This means that if we make a (typically not "pass") verdict at a given point of a test case, then we should be able to describe which other test cases are to be selected to examine the problem further.

6   Conclusion

The self-adaptive protocol [7,8] and the self-adaptive test scenario are interesting new research areas. Three ideas have been presented in this paper.

First a frame representation was demonstrated for tests which can lead to the use of new AI applications. The second idea was to change the test scenario in a self-adaptive manner during the conformance test process depending on the detected errors. The scenario can be guided by the test verdicts. Finally we presented how TTCN can create a better test language, and how they can be used to better support self-adaptive testing. In addition to this we give some suggestions to introduce new structures to TTCN3 to support our method.

The mobile communication has many problems starting from ad hoc networks to ubiquitous computing. The protocols have a key position to solve these problems, self-adaptivity can be a good tool to reach this goal.

References

1. Wireless Application Protocol Architecture Specification, www.wapforum.org
2. ETSI ES201 873-1 TTCN-3 Core language V2.1.0 (2001-10) ISO 9646/3 or IU-T X.292
3. Baumgarten, B., Giessler, A.: OSI Conformance testing methodology and TTCN, Elsevier, 1994
4. Adamis, G., Csopaki, Gy., Horváth, R.,-Pap, Z., Rétháti, Z.: Method for Development of Specification and Conformance Testing of WAP WTP, TUB study, Budapest 1999
5. Adamis, G., Csopaki, Gy., et al: Specification of WAP Protocols, BUTE study, Budapest 2000
6. Adamis, G., Csopaki, Gy., et al: Formal Specification of Test Processes, TUB study, Budapest, 2000
7. Harangozó, Zs., Tarnay, K.: FDTs in Self-adaptive Protocol Specification, (in this issue)
8. Tarnay, K.: Self-adaptive Protocols, (in this issue)
9. Tarnay, K.: Communication Protocol Models and Conformance Testing, 1991, DSc Thesis (in Hungarian)
10. ETSI, "Information technology – Open Systems Interconnection Conformance testing methodology and framework; The Tree and Tabular Combined Notation (TTCN-2++), TR 101 666 V1.0.0, May 1999.

Abbreviations

ASP	Abstract Service Primitive
ATS	Abstract Test Suite
ETS	Executable Test Suite
INIT	Initiator
PCO	Point of Control and Observation
PDU	Protocol Data Unit

PICS	Protocol Implementation Conformance Statement
PIXIT	Protocol Implementation Extra Information for Testing
RESP	Responder
TP	Test Purpose
TSS	Test Suite Structure
TTCN	Tree and Tabular Combined Notation
UACK	User Acknowledge
WAP	Wireless Application Protocol
WTP	Wireless Transaction Protocol

Model-Based Diagnosis
for Information Survivability*

Howard Shrobe

Artificial Intelligence Laboratory
NE43-839
Massacusetts Institute of Technology
Cambridge, MA 02139
hes@ai.mit.edu

Abstract. The Infrastructure of modern society is controlled by software systems that are vulnerable to attack. Successful attacks on these systems can lead to catastrophic results; the survivability of such information systems in the face of attacks is therefore an area of extreme importance to society. This paper presents model-based techniques for the diagnosis of potentially compromised software systems; these techniques can be used to aid the self-diagnosis and recovery from failure of critical software systems. It introduces *Information Survivability* as a new domain of application for model-baesed diagnosis and it presents new modeling and reasoning techniques relevant to the domain. In particular: 1) We develop techniques for the diagnosis of compromised *software* systems (previous work on model-base diagnosis has been primarily cconcerned with physical components); 2) We develop methods for dealing with model-based diagnosis as a mixture of symbolic and Bayesian inference; 3) We develop techniques for dealing with common-mode failures; 4) We develop unified representational techniques for reasoning about information attacks, the vulnerabilities and compromises of computational resources, and the observed behavior of computations; 5) We highlght additional information that should be part of the goal of model-based diagnosis.

1   Background and Motivation

The infrastructure of modern society is controlled by computational systems that are vulnerabile to information attacks. The system and application software of these systems possess vulnerabilities that enable attacks capable of compromising the resources used by the software systems. A skillful attack could lead to consequences as dire as those of modern warfare. In every exercise conducted by

---

* This article describe research conducted at the Artificial Intelligence Laboratory of the Massachusetts Institute of Technology. Support for this research was provided by the Information Systems Office of the Defense Advanced Research Projects Agency (DARPA) under Space and Naval Warfare Systems Center - San Diego Contract Number N66001-00-C-8078. The views presented are those of the author alone and do not represent the view of DARPA or SPAWAR.

R. Laddaga, P. Robertson, and H. Shrobe (Eds.): IWSAS 2001, LNCS 2614, pp. 142–157, 2003.

the government so far, the attacking team has managed to completely the target systems with little difficulty. There is a dire need for new approaches to protect the computational infrastructure from such attacks and to enable it to continue functioning even when attacks have been successfully launched.

Our presmise is that to protect the infrastructure we need to restructure these software systems as *Adaptive Survivable Systems*. In particular, we believe that a software system must be capable of detecting its own malfunction and it must be capable of repairing itself. But this means that it must first be able to *diagnose* the form of the failure; in particular, it must both localize and characterize the breakdown.

Our work is set in the difficult context in which there is a concerted and coordinated attack by a determined adversary. This context places an extra burden on the diagnostic component. It is no longer adequate merely to determine which component of a computation has failed to achieve its goal, in addition we wish to determine whether that failure is indicative of a *compromise* to the underlying infrastructure and whether that compromise is likely to lead to failures of other computations at other times. Furthermore, we wish to determine what kind of *attack* compromised the resource and whether this attack is likely to have compromised other resources that share a vulnerability. This paper focuses on the diagnostic component of self adaptive survivable systems.

2 Contributions of This Work

We build on previous work in Model-Based diagnosis [2–5, 8]. However, the context of our research is significantly different from that of the prior research, leading us to confront several important issues that have not previously been addressed. In particular, we present several new advances in representation and reasoning techniques for model-based diagnosis:

1. We develop representation and reasoning techniques for describing and reasoning about the behaviors and failures of *software systems* (most previous work has focussed on hardware, particularly digital hardware).
2. We develop mixed symbolic and Bayesian reasoning technique for model-based diagnosis. The statistical component of the technique utilizes Bayesian networks to calculate accurate posterior probabilities.
3. We develop a unified framework for reasoning about the failures of the computations, about how these failures are related to compromises of the underlying resources, about the vulnerabilities of these resources and how these vulnerabilities enable attacks.
4. We develop techniques for reasoning about *common-mode* failures. A common-mode failure occurs when the probabilites of the failure modes of two or more components are not independent. This issue has not been substantially addressed in the previous literature on model-based diagnosis.
5. We develop diagnostic techniques that lead to an estimate of the trustability of the computational resources that are used in a specific computation. These techniques also help us to assess which attacks have occurred and the likelihood that specific attacks have been successful.

These are crucial issues when failure is caused by a concerted and coordinated attack by a malicious opponent. There are many modes of attacking computational systems but the most pernicious attackers seek to avoid detection; therefore they attempt to scaffold the attack slowly, at a nearly undetectable rate. These scaffolding actions will typically appear as minor misbehaviors (i.e. they will cause the system to behave somewhat outside its normal range), but skillful attackers will space out the attacks so that the misbehaviors are infrequent and they will attempt to make the resulting misbehaviors seem as close to normal behavior as possible. This makes it crucial that our diagnostic techniques be capable of extracting information from low-frequency events that closely resemble normal modes of operation.

Attackers aim at high leverage points of the infrastructure, such as operating systems or middleware. This leads to common-mode faults, because once the operating system has been compromised all application components can be caused to fail simultaneously.

The paper first briefly reviews the current state of the art in model-based diagnosis; this work has mainly been concerned with breakdowns caused by the deterioration of hardware components. In particular, we adopt the framework in [4] where each component has models for each of several behavioral modes and each model is given a probability. We will then turn to the question of how to extend these techniques so as to apply them to the diagnosis of *software* systems. We extend our modeling framework to account for the fact that software systems are built in layers of infrastructure, with compromises to one layer affecting all higher levels. A software system has a great deal of hidden state; what we are actually capable of observing is the behavior of a specific *computation*; but this particular computation uses a variety of *resources* (e.g. the operating system and middleware, data-sets, etc.). These resources may have been subject to a variety of *compromises*, each of which might lead to a different misbehavior of the computation. Compromises to the resources occur because the resources possess *vulnerabilities* that allow specific *attacks* to take control of the resources for purposes other than those intended by the original designers.

We will finally present mixed symbolic and statistical diagnostic algorithms for assessing the posterior probabilities of the various behavior modes of each component in the model. We present an implementation and show an example of the reasoning process. Finally, we discuss the demands placed on the diagnostic component by our goal of self-adaptivity and conclude with suggestions for future research.

3   Related Research

Model-Based Diagnosis is a symptom directed technique; it is driven by the detection of discrepancies between the observations of actual behavior and the predictions of a model of the system. Almost all of the reported work in the area [2, 1, 3–5, 8] has been concerned with the diagnosis of physical systems subject to routine breakdown. Model-based diagnostic systems use simulation models that compute expected outputs given known inputs; they utilize dependency directed techniques to link each intermediate and final value to the selected behavioral model of any component of the system which was involved in producing that value.

The completeness of the diagnostic process is dependent on having bidirectional simulation models for each component of the system. Such models produce both a set of assertions recording what values are expected and a dependency network linking these assertions to one another and to assertions stating which components must be in a particular behavioral mode for those values to appear.

Our work builds on the framework in Sherlock [4] and on the probabilistic techniques in [8]. In Sherlock the description of a component includes multiple simulation models, one for each behavioral mode of the component. One distinguished mode is the normal mode, but behavioral models for known failure modes may also be provided. It is also typical to include a null model to account for unknown modes of behavior. Finally, each of the behavioral modes of a component is assigned an *a priori* probability. Sherlock uses these to guide a best first search for a set of behavioral modes, one for each component, such that the models for those modes predict the observed behavior. This is the most likely diagnosis. However, these techniques i depend on the assumption that the failure modes of the components are independent; as we will see this assumption doesn't hold in our environment. Later work [8] introduced techniques for applying Bayesian networks in the context of model-based diagnosis, allowing dependencies to be modeled; [10] presents techniques within this framework for generating several likely diagnoses in order of decreasing likelihood.

Because our focus is on detecting the intentional compromise of software components we are forced to face a number of new issues. These include: How to model software components in the spirit of model-based diagnosis; How to deal with the fact that a compromise to the computational infrastructure (e.g. the operating system) can manifest itself in the malfunction of many application components; How to deal with the fact that compromised components may behave in ways that are difficult to distinquish from normal behavior; How to reason about the system so as to extract as much information about possible compromises as we can. In particular, we deal with how to use both symbolic and Bayesian techniques.

4   Modeling Software Computations

Model-Based Diagnosis requires completely invertible models of the components in order to guarantee completeness of its analysis. But the components of a complex software system rarely have input-output relationship that are invertible. We therefore look for other, additional properties, that lead to more complete coverage. In particular, we concentrate here on descriptions of computational delay (or other *Quality Of Service* metrics). In our current implementation we use an interval of expected delay times (i.e. the computation should run no slower

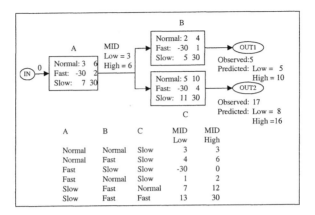

Fig. 1. Reasoning about software component delay

than x and no faster than y) as the behavioral models. Figure 1 shows the application of such models in a framework similar to Sherlock. When propagating in the forward direction we add the delay interval predicted by the behavioral model to the interval bounding the arrival time of the latest input. In the backward direction, we use interval subtraction (and only update the bounds on the last input to arrive). When more than one component predicts the bounds for a particular value (e.g. when a model for component A and a model for component C both predict bounds for the value labeled MID), we take the intersection of the two intervals to obtain the tightest bounds implied by the overall model. A discrepancy is detected when the lower bound of an interval exceeds the upper bound.

As in Sherlock we provide several behavioral models for each component, one characterizing normal behavior, others characterizing known failure modes and a null model to cover all other unexpected behaviors.

Notice that in Figure 1 there are six potential diagnoses, only one of which involves a single point of failure (in component C). The others involve multiple failures with one component running slower than expected and other components masking the fault at Out1 by running faster than expected. In the third diagnosis, component A runs in "negative time"! On the surface, such a diagnosis seems physically impossible and we might expect the diagnostic algorithm to reject it. But, the diagnosis algorithm is guided by our representational choices; the reason this diagnosis involves negative time is that the fast behavioral model of component A predicts a delay interval from -30 to +2.

Such behavior seems very unlikely, and indeed we assign a low likelihood to this model; however, it is not impossible. Suppose that both computations A and C are running on the same computer and further suppose that the computer has been compromised by an attacker. Under these circumstances, it's not impossible for component C to be delayed (because of a parasitic task inserted by the attacker) while component A has been accelerated, running in less than zero time because it has been hacked by the attacker to send out reasonable answers before it receives its inputs.

What we are able to observe is the progress of a computation; but the computation is itself just an abstraction. What an attacker can actually affect is something physical: the file representing the stored version of a program, the bits in main memory representing the running program, or other programs (such as the operating system) whose services are employed by the monitored application.

Thus, we require a more elaborated modeling framework detailing how the behavior of a computation is related to the state of the resources that it uses. In turn, we must represent the vulnerabilities of these resources and the attacks enabled by these vulnerabilities. Finally, we must represent how such attacks compromise the resources, causing them to behave in an undesired manner.

5   Common Mode Failures

A single compromise of an operating system component, such as the scheduler, can lead to anomalous behavior in several application components. This is an example of a *common mode failure*; intuitively, a common mode failure occurs when a single fault (e.g. an inaccurate power supply), leads to faults at several observable points in the systems (e.g. several transistors misbehave because their biasing power is incorrect). Another example comes from reliability studies of nuclear power plants where it was observed that the catostrophic failure of a turbine blade could sever several pipes as it flies off, leading to multiple cooling fluid leaks.

Formally, there is a common mode failure whenever the probabilities of the failure modes of two (or more) components are dependent. Early model-based diagnostic systems have assumed probabilistic independence of the behavior modes of different components [4] in order to simplify the assessment of posterior probabilities. Later work [8] allows for probabilistic dependence; however, it does not explore in detail how to model the causes of this dependence. We deal with common mode failures by extending our modeling framework to make explicit the mechanisms that couple the failure probabilites of different components.

We first extend our modeling framework, as shown in Figure 2, to include two kinds of objects: computational components (represented by a set of delay models one for each behavioral mode) and infrastructural components (represented by a set of modes, but no delay or other behavioral models). Connecting these two kinds of models are conditional probability links; each such link states how likely a particular behavioral mode of a computational component would be if the infrastructural component that supports that component were in a particular one of its modes (normal or abnormal). Each infrastructural component mode will usually project conditional probability links to more than one computational component behavioral mode, allowing us to say that normal behavior has some probability of being exhibited even if the infrastructural component has been compromised (however, for simplicity, figure 2 shows only a one-to-one mapping).

The model also includes *a priori* probabilities for the modes of the infrastructural components, representing our best estimates of the degree of compromise in each such piece of infrastructure. Following a session of diagnostic reasoning, these probabilities may be updated to the value of the *posterior* probabilities.

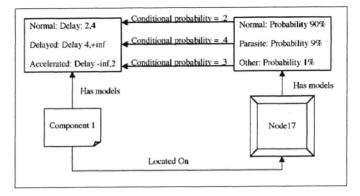

Fig. 2. Modeling computational and infrastructure components

We next observe that resources are compromised by attacks. Attacks are enabled by vulnerabilities in the resources. For example, many systems in the Unix family are vulnerable to buffer-overflow attacks; most networked systems are vulnerable to packet-flood attacks. An attack is capable of compromising a resource in a variety of ways; for example, buffer overflow attacks are used both to gain control of a specific resource and to gain root access to the entire system. But the variety of compromises enabled by an attack are not equally likely (some are much more difficult than others). We therefore add a third tier to our model to describe the ensemble of attacks assumed to be available in the environment. We connect the attack layer to the resource layer with Conditional probability links that state the likelikhood of each mode of the compromised resource once the attack has been successful.

Our model of the computational environment therefore includes:

– The components of the computation that is being observed
– A set of behavioral models for each component, representing both normal and failure modes.
– The set of resources available to be used by the computational components
– A set of behavioral modes for each resource, representing both normal and compromised modes.
– A map stating which resources are used by each computational component.
– Conditional probabilties linking the modes of the computations to the modes of the resources employed by that component.
– A list of vulnerabilities possessed by each computational resource.
– A description of which attacks are enable by each vulnerability.
– A list of attack types that are believed to be active in the environment.
– A description of which compromised modes of each type of resource can be caused by a successful execution of each type of attack. This is provided as a set of conditional probabilities of the compromised mode given the execution of the attack.

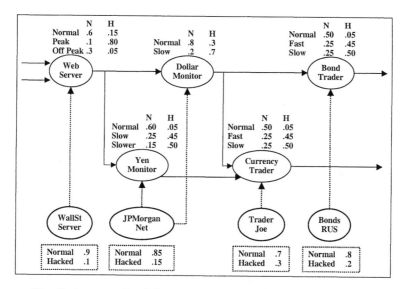

Fig. 3. An example of the extended system modeling framework

Given this information, simple rule-based inferencing (implemented in the Joshua inference system) deduces which specific resources might have been compromised and with what probability. This information is then used to construct a Bayesian network (in the IDEAL system).

6   Diagnostic Reasoning

Figure 3 shows a model of a fictitious distributed financial system which we use to illustrate the reasoning process. The system consists of five interconnected software modules (Web-server, Dollar-Monitor, Bond-Trader, Yen-Monitor, Currency-Trader) utilizing four underlying computational resources (WallSt-Server, JPMorgan, BondRUs, Trader-Joe).

For each computational component we show the conditional probability tables that describe how the behavioral modes of each computational resource probabilistically depend on the modes of the underlying resources (each resource has two modes, normal and hacked). Note that two computations (Dollar-Monitor and Yen-Monitor) are supported by a common resource (JPMorgan) and compromises to this underlying resource are likely to affect both computations. The failure modes of these two computations are no longer independent; this is indicated by the conditional probabilities connecting the behavior modes of the JPMorgan to those of both Dollar-Monitor and Yen-Monitor. The specific conditional probabilites supplied describe the degree of coupling.

Finally we show the *a priori* probabilities for the modes of the underlying resources. However, when attacks are present in the environment what matters is the conditional probabilities of the different modes of the resources given that an attack has taken place. We hypothesize that one or more attack types are present

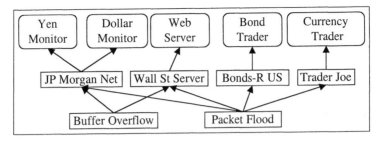

Fig. 4. An example of the three tiered system modeling framework

in the environment, leading to a three-tiered model as shown in figure 4. In this example, we show two attack types, buffer-overflow and packet-flood. Packet-floods can affect each of the resources because they are all networked systems; buffer-overflows affect only the 2 resources which are modeled as instances of a system type vulnerable to such attacks.

As in earlier techniques, diagnosis is initiated when a discrepancy is detected; in this case this means that the predicted production time of an output differs from those actually observed after an input has been presented. The goal of the diagnostic process is to infer as much as possible about where the computation failed (so that we may recover from the failure) and about what parts of the infrastructure may be compromised (so that we can avoid using them again until corrective action is taken). We are therefore looking for two things: the most likely explanation(s) of the observed discrepancies and updated probabilities for the modes of the infrastructural components.

To do this we use techniques similar to [4, 8]. We first identify all conflict sets, and then proceed to calculate the posterior probabilities of the modes of each of the computational components. We do these tasks by a mixture of symbolic and Bayesian techiques; symbolic model-based reasoning is used to predict the behavior of the system, given an assumed set of behavioral modes. Whenever the symbolic reasoning process discovers a conflict (an incompatible set of behavioral modes), it adds to the Bayesian network a new node corresponding to the conflict (see below). Bayesian techniques are then used to solve the extended network to get updated probabilities.

This approach involves an exhaustive enumeration of the combinations of the models of the computational components. This allows us to calculate the exact posterior probabilties. However, this is expensive and the precision may not be needed. It would be possible to instead use the techniques in [10] to generate only the most likely diagnoses and to use these to estimate the posterior probabilities; but we have not yet pursued this approach.

We instead follow the following approach: We alternate the finding of conflicts with the search for diagnoses. After each "conflict" node is added to the Bayesian network (see below) the network is solved; this gives us updated probabilities for each behavioral mode of each component. We can, therefore, examine the behavioral modes in the current conflict and pick that component whose current behavioral mode is least likely. We discard this mode, and pick the most

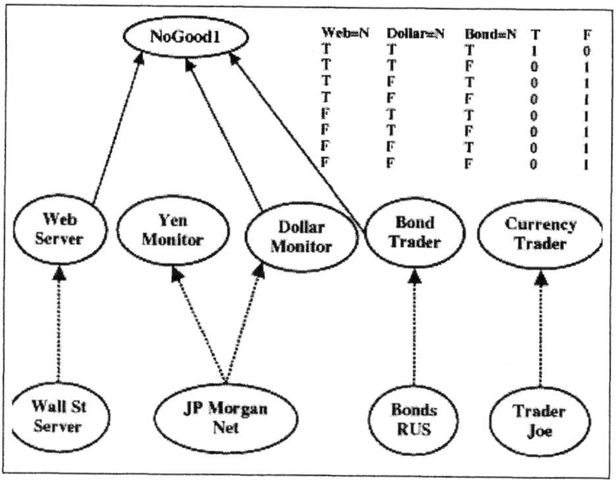

Web=N	Dollar=N	Bond=N	T	F
T	T	T	1	0
T	T	F	0	1
T	F	T	0	1
T	F	F	0	1
F	T	T	0	1
F	T	F	0	1
F	F	T	0	1
F	F	F	0	1

Fig. 5. Adding a conflict node to the bayesian network

likely alternative; we continue this process of detecting conflicts, discarding the least likely model in the conflict and picking its most likely alternative until a consistent set is found. This process is a good heuristic for finding the most likely diagnosis[1].

Our models of computational behavior (the delay models) are used to predict the behavior of the computational components and to compare the predictions with observations. When a discrepancy is detected, we use dependency tracing to find the conflict set underlying the discrepancy (i.e. a set of behavioral modes which are inconsistent). At this point a new (binary truth value) node is added to the Bayesian network representing the conflict as shown in Figure 5. This node has an incoming arc from every node that participates in the conflict. It has a conditional probability table corresponding to a pure "logical and" i.e. its true state has a probability of 1.0 if all the incoming nodes are in their true states and it otherwise has probability 1.0 of being in its false state.

Since this node represents a logical contradiction, it is pinned in its false state. Adding this node to the network imposes a logical constraint on the probabilistic Bayesian network; the constraint imposed is that the conflict discovered by the symbolic, model-based behavioral simulation is impossible. We continue to explore other combinations of behavioral modes, until all possible minimal conflicts are discovered. Each of these conflicts extends the Bayesian network as before, The set of such conflicts constitutes the full set of logical constants on the values taken on within the Bayesian network; thus, once we have augmented the Bayesian network with nodes corresponding to each conflict, the network has all the information available[2].

---

[1] However since the probabilities of the failure modes of different components are not independent, this is only a heuristic

[2] [8] builds logical reasoning directly into the Bayesian network system because the logical inferences needed are simple enough to be accomodated. However, our inference needs are more complex and not easily amenable to this approach

At this point, we have found all the minimal conflicts and added conflict nodes to the Bayesian network for each. We therefore also know all the possible diagnoses since these are sets of behavioral modes (one for each component) which are not supersets of any conflict set. For each of these we create a node in the Bayesian network which is the logical-and of the nodes corresponding to the behavioral modes of the components. This node represents the probability of this particular diagnosis. The Bayesian network is then solved. This gives us updated probabilities for all possible diagnoses, for the behavioral modes of the computational components and for the modes of the underlying infrastructural components. Furthermore, these updated probabilities are those which are consistent with all the constraints we can obtain from the behavioral models. Thus, they represent as complete an assessment as is possible of the state of compromise in the infrastructure. These posterior estimates can be taken as priors in further diagnostic tasks and they can also be used as a "trust model" informing users of the system (including self adaptive computations) of the trustworthiness of the various pieces of infrastructure which they will need to use.

7 Results

The sample system shown in Figure 3 was run through several analyses including both those in which the outputs are within the expected range and those in which the outputs are unexpected. Figure 6 shows the results of an analysis in which the outputs are within the expected range. Figure 7 and 8 show the results of an analysis of an abnormal case. Inputs are supplied at times 10 and 15 for the two inputs of Web-Server; each of the figures shows the times at which the the outputs of Currency-Trader and Bond-Trader are observed. There are four runs for each case, each with a different attack model. In the first, it is assumed that there are no attacks present and the *a priori* values are used for the probabilities of the different modes of each resource. The second run assumes only a buffer-overflow attack; the third run assumes only a packet-flood attack. The fourth run assumes both types of attacks. There are four columns in each of the results chart, one for each of these runs. The top chart in each figure shows the *a priori and posterior* probabilities for each resource being in its "hacked" mode. The middle chart shows the *posterior* probabilities for each mode of each computational component. The bottom bottom chart in each figure shows the *posterior* probabilites that each of the two types of attacks have occurred[3].

There are more than two dozen possible diagnoses in the abnormal case. It should be noted that even the most likely diagnosis is actually not all that likely; in addition the next several diagnoses are nearly equally as likely. The

---

[3] The implementation is in CommonLisp and uses the Joshua [7] rule-based reasoning system as well as the Ideal system [9] and in particular its implementation of the algorithm described in [6]. On a 300 MHz powerbook, the total solution time is under 1 minute. By far, the most expensive part of this is calculating the probabilities of the complete set of diagnoses. The most likely diagnosis and all conflict sets are located in less than 10 seconds)

Normal Case: 48 "Diagnoses"
　　　　　　30 Minimal Conflicts
Output of Bond-Trader Observed at 25
Output of Current-trader Observed at 28

Name	Prior	Posterior			
Wallst	.10	.04	.07	.09	17
JPMorgan	.15	.07	.08	.11	.19
Bonds-R-Us	.20	.18	.18	.15	.17
Trader-Joe	.30	.28	.28	.16	.18

Computations Using Each Resource					
Web-	Off-Peak	.40	.40	.40	.40
Server	Peak	.04	.05	.05	.08
	Normal	.55	.56	.55	.52
Dollar-	Slow	.23	.23	.25	.29
Monitor	Normal	.77	.77	.75	.71
Yen-	Really-Slow	.03	.04	.04	.05
Monitor	Slow	.21	.21	.21	.25
	Normal	.76	.75	.75	.70
Bond-	Slow	.29	.29	.27	.26
Trader	Fast	.23	.23	.24	.26
	Normal	.48	.48	.49	.48
Currency-	Slow	.09	.09	.07	.06
Trader	Fast	.52	.52	.48	.51
	Normal	.40	.39	.45	.43

Attack Types		Attacks Possible			
Name	Prior	None	Buffer-Overflow	Packet-Flood	Both
Buffer-Overflow	.4	0	.28	0	.30
Packet-Flood	.5	0	0	.23	.25

Fig. 6. Updated probabilities

most likely diagnosis is therefore not particularly informative for our two goals of recovering from the failure and steering away from compromised resources in the future. However, the posterior probabilities of the modes of the infrastructure components are, in fact, useful guides for the second of these goals. The posterior probabilities of the behavioral modes of the computational resources are useful guides for the first goal, because these probabilities aggregate the information contained in the individual diagnoses.

The most significant change is the increase in the probabilities that the resources named JPMorgan and Wallst-server are hacked. This changes the trustworthiness ordering of the resources: JPMorgan is *a posteriori* the least trustworthy resource, while the *a priori* listing ranks Trader-Joe followed by Bonds-R-US as the least trustworthy. This follows from the fact that the JPMorgan resources is utilized by the computations Yen-Monitor and Dollar-Monitor both of which are very likely to be in abnormal modes and the most likely explanation is that that JPMorgan causes a common-mode failure. Notice that in the last two columns when packet-flood attacks are possible, all the resources are much more likely to be hacked. Qualitatively, this is because all the resources are vulnerable

Slow Fault on both outputs   25 "Diagnoses"
                              34 Minimal Conflicts
Output of Bond-Trader Observed at 35
Output of Current-trader Observed at 45

Name	Prior	Posterior			
Wallst	.1	.27	.58	.75	.80
JPMorgan	.15	.45	.62	.74	.81
Bonds-R-Us	.20	21	.20	.61	.50
Trader-Joe	.30	.32	.31	.62	.50

Computations Using Each Resource					
Web-Server	Off-Peak	.03	.02	.02	.02
	Peak	.54	.70	.78	.80
	Normal	.43	.28	.20	.18
Dollar-	Slow	.74	.76	.73	.76
Monitor	Normal	.26	.24	.27	.24
Yen-	Really-Slow	.52	.54	.56	.58
Monitor	Slow	.34	.35	.34	.34
	Normal	.14	.11	.10	.08
Bond-	Slow	.59	.57	.76	.70
Trader	Fast	0	0	0	0
	Normal	.41	.43	.24	.30
Currency-	Slow	.61	.54	.62	.56
Trader	Fast	.07	.11	.16	.16
	Normal	.32	.35	.22	.28

Attack Types		Attacks Possible			
Name	Prior	None	.Buffer-Overflow	Packet-Flood	Both
Buffer-Overflow	.4	0	.82	0	.58
Packet-Flood	.5	0	0	.89	.73

Fig. 7. Updated probabilities

to the packet-flood attack. The misbehavior of the computational components provides evidence that JPMorgan is hacked which in turn provides evidence of a packet flood attack. But since packet-flood attacks affect all the resources, this increases the likelihood that other resources are hacked as well. The Bayesian network carries out the quantitative version of this argument.

It is worth noting that this propagation of trust can carry over to resources not used in the misbehaving computation. For example, assume that the environment contains another resource (call it "newbie") that is subject to the same attacks as the ones (e.g. JPMorgan) that participated in the faulty computation. The misbehavior in the computation is evidence that JPMorgan is "hacked" and this, in turn, is evidence that an attacked succeeded. But this would lend weight to the conclusion that other resources (e.g. Newbie) subject to this same attack had also been compromised. The Bayesian network would propagate probabilities in exactly this fashion leading to a posterior assessment that Newbie has been hacked (although this probability will be lower than the probability that JPMorgan is hacked).

Prob ability	Currency Trader	Bond Trader	Yen Monitor	Dollar Monitor	Web Server
.0898	Slow	Slow	Normal	Normal	Peak
.0876	Slow	Normal	Slow	Slow	Normal
.0855	Normal	Normal	slower	Slow	Normal
.0762	Slow	Normal	Really-Slow	Slow	Normal
.0641	Slow	Slow	Slow	Slow	Normal
.0626	Normal	Slow	Really-Slow	Slow	Normal
.0557	Slow	Slow	Really-Slow	Slow	Normal
.0468	Normal	Slow	Slow	Normal	Peak
.0416	Slow	Slow	Slow	Normal	Peak
.0321	Slow	Normal	Normal	Slow	Peak
.0306	Normal	Slow	slower	Normal	Peak
.0301	Normal	Normal	Slow	Slow	Peak
.0276	Slow	Slow	slower	Slow	Off-Peak
.0272	Slow	Slow	slower	Normal	Peak
.0268	Slow	Normal	Slow	Slow	Peak
.0262	Normal	Normal	slower	Slow	Peak
.0260	Fast	Slow	slower	Normal	Peak
.0235	Slow	Slow	Normal	Slow	Peak
.0233	Slow	Normal	slower	Slow	Peak
.0223	Fast	Normal	slower	Slow	Peak
.0221	Normal	Slow	Slow	Slow	Peak
.0196	Slow	Slow	Slow	Slow	Peak
.0192	Normal	Slow	slower	Slow	Peak
.0171	Slow	Slow	slower	Slow	Peak
.0163	Fast	Slow	slower	Slow	Peak

Fig. 8. Diagnoses

8   Conclusions and Future Work

The example above illustrates how model-based reasoning techniques can be used to extract information from a single run. Our example is intentionally fanciful since we are at the present concentrating on the development of the representational and reasoning frameworks. In future work we will explore realistic models of real systems.

The information extracted is probabilistic and it sheds light both on the question of where the computation might have failed, on what underlying resources might have been compromised and on what attacks might have succeeded.

It is notable that the identification of the most likely diagnosis is not particularly informative. For example, in the most likely diagnosis Yen-Monitor is in its Normal mode. However, the most likely behavioral mode for Yen-Monitor is its Slower mode which occurs in many of the remaining diagnoses. The posterior probabilites of the behavioral modes aggregate the probabilites from each of the possible diagnoses, producing an overall assessment that is more informative than any individual diagnosis. Of course, if there are very few diagnoses, or the most likely diagnosis is extremely probable, then the probabilities of its behavioral modes will approximate the overall posterior probabilities.

It is important to keep in mind why we are interested in the diagnoses at all. The goal of the system is to recover from the failure and to steer away from future trouble. To do this it needs to know how much of the computation has been completed successfully and how much remains to be done. Given such information the system would pick a rollback point for recovery that includes no failed part of the computation. Furthermore, the chosen rollback point would maximize the probability of continuing the restarted computation to completion. As we just saw, an individual diagnosis, even the most likely diagnosis, does not give us the information we need to do this. When the available evidence supports multiple diagnostic hypotheses, then our interest should shift from individual diagnoses to aggregate failure probabilities and this information is conveyed completely by the posterior probabilities of the failure modes. I.e. if the posterior probability that Yen-Monitor failed is high, then we don't actually care that there are multiple (multiple point of failure) diagnoses involving this failure nor do we care how likely each of these diagnoses is. Instead what we do care about is that it's very likely that Yen-monitor didn't do its job and that we should select a rollback point prior to its execution. Similarly, in choosing a recovery plan we should avoid using those resources whose posterior failure probabilities are highest[4].

This is to say that the goal of the diagnostic process should be to assess the overall posterior probabilities of the behavioral modes of the computational and infrastructure components. These give us evidence for which computational resources are to be to be trusted during the recovery process and during subsequent computations. This is a different definition of the goal of diagnostic activity than has been used in previous research on model-based diagnosis.

We have not yet addressed the details of how the system should use this information in forming a recovery plan. The general outline is that when assigning a computation to a resource it should choose that resource which is most likely to be in n mode that will successfully complete the computation. But the probabilities of the modes of different resources are not independent; they are linked by the Bayesian network. Having decided to use a particular resource because it's likely to be in an acceptable mode, the system should pin the Bayesian network into a state where the resource is believed to be in the desired state and

---

[4] Of course, gathering further evidence might reduce the number of possible diagnoses leading to greater resolution. However, in our context there are two difficulties with attempting to do this. First, it would take time and there might be tight timeliness contraints on the failed computation (e.g. suppose the computation was processing sensor data which must be acted on very quickly). Second, any attempt to gather more data would involve running the same, or similar, computations again when we know that something is compromised; this might lead to loss or destruction of data. Making this tradeoff correctly involves estimating the expected cost of new information and it expected benefit. It is possible that such and analysis would suggest that acting on the available diagnostic evidence is the best course of action

re-solve the network. Subsequent choices should be made in light of the updated probabilities.

We have also not yet addressed the question of what actions the system might take to obtain more information in future runs. The Minimum Entropy approach in [3] provides a useful framework. However, the current context provides more degrees of freedom; in addition to making new observations, we can also change the assignment of resources to computational components in a way that will maximize the expected gain in information. The details of this remain for future research.

References

1. Randall Davis. Diagnostic reasoning based on structure and behavior. *Artificial Intelligence*, 24:347–410, December 1984.
2. Randall Davis and Howard Shrobe. Diagnosis based on structure and function. In *Proceedings of the AAAI National Conference on Artificial Intelligence*, pages 137–142. AAAI, 1982.
3. Johan deKleer and Brian Williams. Diagnosing multiple faults. *Artificial Intelligence*, 32(1):97–130, 1987.
4. Johan deKleer and Brian Williams. Diagnosis with behavior modes. In *Proceedings of the International Joint Conference on Artificial Intelligence*, 1989.
5. Walter Hamscher and Randall Davis. Model-based reasoning: Troubleshooting. In Howard Shrobe, editor, *Exploring Artificial Intelligence*, pages 297–346. AAAI, 1988.
6. F.V. Jensen, S.L. Lauritzen, and K.G. Olesen. Bayesian updating in causal probablistic networks by local computations. *Computational Statistics Quarterly*, 4:269–282, 1990.
7. S. Rowley, H. Shrobe, R. Cassels, and W. Hamscher. Joshua: Uniform access to heterogeneous knowledge structures (or why joshing is better than conniving or planning). In *National Conference on Artificial Intelligence*, pages 48–52. AAAI, 1987.
8. Sampath Srinivas. Modeling techinques and algorithms for probablistic model-based diagnosis and repair. Technical Report STAN-CS-TR-95-1553, Stanford University, Stanford, CA, July 1995.
9. Sampath Srinivas and Jack Breese. Ideal: A software package for analysis of influence diagrams. In *Proceedings of CUAI-90*, pages 212–219, 1990.
10. Sampath Srinivas and Pandurang Nayak. Efficient enumeration of instantiations in bayesian networks. In *Proceedings of the Twelfth Annual Conference on Uncertainty in Artificial Intelligence (UAI-96)*, pages 500–508, Portland, Oregon, 1996.

Exercising Qualitative Control
in Autonomous Adaptive Survivable Systems

Jon Doyle[1] and Michael McGeachie[2]

[1] Department of Computer Science
North Carolina State University
P.O. Box 7535
Raleigh, NC 27605-7535, USA
Jon_Doyle@ncsu.edu
http://www.csc.ncsu.edu/faculty/doyle
[2] Laboratory for Computer Science
Massachusetts Institute of Technology
200 Technology Square
Cambridge, MA 02139, USA
mmcgeach@mit.edu

Abstract. We seek to construct autonomous adaptive survivable systems that use *active trust management* to adapt their own behavior in the face of compromises in the computational environment. Active trust management maintains probabilistic *trust models* that indicate the trustworthiness of different resources for different tasks, and uses these models in rationally adapting allocations of computational resources to tasks. Flexible adaptation of allocations to changing circumstances places great demands on the methods used to represent the utility information needed by rational decision-making mechanisms. This paper explains how to use qualitative preference specifications to exercise effective control over quantitative trust-based resource allocation by facilitating convenient specification and adaptation of the stable foundations of the trust manager's utility judgments.

1   Introduction

The engineering of autonomous systems generates very different demands on representations of decision-making information than those recognized and addressed in traditional decision theory and decision analysis. The traditional approaches mainly focus on manual methods for constructing quantitative utility models that guide rational decision-making systems. Decision theory provides the conceptual properties the utility models must satisfy, and decision analysis provides techniques for eliciting utility information from human informants. Once in place, however, decision making proceeds with the specific, fixed utility model so constructed, leaving all variability of decision to changing probabilistic measures of belief. Such fixed utility models serve poorly in designing autonomous agents, which must have the ability to adapt to face new situations and tasks by changing

R. Laddaga, P. Robertson, and H. Shrobe (Eds.): IWSAS 2001, LNCS 2614, pp. 158–170, 2003.

utility models as well as beliefs. Numeric utility models, of the sort constructed in traditional decision analysis, simply do not provide the conceptual structure needed to facilitate effective adaptation of utility models because mere numerical mappings need not expose the rationales or considerations underlying the assignment of different utility values to different alternatives.

This paper discusses the use of qualitative representations of the comparisons underlying numeric utility measures to provide guidance to autonomous systems. Rather than leave generic and qualitative utility considerations implicit in the decision-analytic process, we expose and represent these considerations directly in order to reason about them and to naturally separate those portions involved in some change from the portions persisting independent of the change. We use the task of guiding the response of autonomous systems to security violations to motivate and illustrate the methods, focusing in particular on the method of active trust management.

2   Active Trust Management

Computational system designers today find themselves in a hostile, even malicious, environment in which no one is safe and nothing is trustworthy. Automated processes scan networks seeking vulnerabilities, to which anyone can succumb anonymously without recognized enemies. Serious adversaries, in turn, can penetrate or defeat any known system; sufficient resources always mean success for the attacker willing to exploit all possible vulnerabilities, including those of the people operating the target systems.

This predicament poses problems for the traditional security idea of constructing a trusted computing base (TCB). Such trusted systems do not exist today, and little suggests they will exist in the future. Absent such a trusted base, however, the natural paranoia of security providers fosters paralysis. Attackers need only create a belief in the possibility that a system has been compromised to defeat it. Given the openness of modern societies and the ever expanding range of technologies, the TCB approach must suffer continuing fragility.

We believe that facing the security predicament without paralysis requires abandoning the all-or-nothing conception of trust underlying traditional TCB conceptions. We approach the problem of providing computational security using the notion of *Active Trust Management* (ATM) [1]. This approach involves three principal notions: construction of a probabilistic trust model, maintenance of the trust model through perpetual analytic monitoring, and rational trust-based resource allocation. We summarize each of these notions in turn.

2.1   Fine-Grained Probabilistic Trust Models

Abandoning all-or-nothing trust concepts requires recognizing that not all compromises affect all tasks, and that not every affected task matters.

Compromises differ in impact. Various computer systems at MIT have on occasion suffered intrusions in which an outsider uses a guessed user password to hijack a host's FTP server. The intruder stores pirated software or images on the server and advertises the location to friends, who then proceed to make copies from the server. Increasing levels of download activity eventually alerts users to the hijacking by making the compromised system slower and slower. This compromise clearly affects the trustworthiness of a host for performing demanding computational tasks. The same compromise, however, does not affect other properties of the host, such as privacy of user email, passwords, or file integrity. In contrast, systems suffering rootkit attacks aimed at gaining root privileges for the intruder need not compromise computational performance, but clearly compromise privacy and file integrity.

Affected tasks differ in importance. One might keenly miss an email service disused because intruders have replaced the normal process with one that copies all traffic to an enemy, but not care a whit about having a SETI@Home screen-saver starved of cycles.

Avoiding paralysis requires judging trustworthiness of resources in terms of the properties relevant to the performance of specific tasks. The trust model thus distinguishes many different properties of resources, some of common interest across tasks, but others of relevance only for certain task types or even task instances. In addition to this fine-grained differentiation between properties, the trust model also employs a fine-grained differentiation between degrees of trustworthiness. Toward this end, the model uses a probabilistic representation of the trustworthiness of each computational resource in the environment with respect to each property of interest.

Our trust models provide detailed decision-theoretic assessments of trustworthiness, suspicion, and related concepts as applied to information systems and their components, including attractiveness of a system as a target, likelihood of being attacked, likelihood of being compromised by an attack, riskiness of use of the system, importance or criticality of the system for different purposes, etc.

2.2   Perpetual Analytic Monitoring

Perpetual analytic monitoring seeks to keep the trust model current, reflecting the best estimates in light of observations. Such monitoring employs numerous different data sources, including sensors attached to different resources and diagnostic data streams generated by self-instrumenting task processes. We use the MAITA monitoring infrastructure [2] to provide the underlying monitoring framework and architecture. This architecture supports a network of distributed monitoring processes that analyze and correlate the sensor and diagnostic data streams, generating alerts or more refined data streams for further correlation or diagnostic stages.

Constructing and maintaining the trust model requires making estimates of the likelihood that a resource has been compromised in a particular way. Perpetual analytic monitoring thus must differentiate between different compromise events. To do this, MAITA employs abstract event descriptions called *trend templates* [3, 4], each of which characterizes a pattern of activities over several temporal intervals and in terms of several data streams, and a suite of mecha-

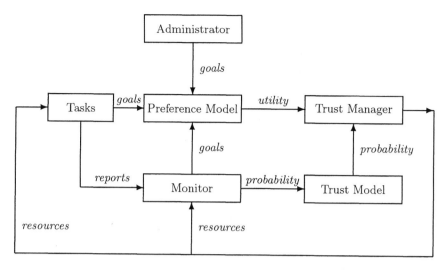

Fig. 1. The active trust management control loop.

nisms for matching trend templates to data in performing event recognition. The language for expressing trend template includes means for characterizing *landmark times* that represent possibly abstract divisions between different stages of events, algebraic relations between temporal intervals, and behavioral patterns of data values, such as constant, increasing or decreasing, and oscillating signals of different magnitudes, shapes, and frequencies. Matching processes employ various statistical criteria. The trust models themselves involve Bayesian network structures.

2.3   Rational Trust-Based Resource Allocation

The sensible response to possible or recognized compromises consists of making do with what one has, with doing the best one can with degraded resources. Active trust management interprets these common-sensical prescriptions as choosing resource allocations that maximize expected utility of task-suite performance. The estimates of expected utilities involved in these decisions depends on the probabilities captured in the trust model and maintained by the self-monitoring capabilities. The expected utility estimates also depend on a model of the utility of different task performance properties. This utility model reflects goals set by the processes charged with accomplishing primary system tasks, goals set by the system monitor, and goals set by external system administrators. The task and monitoring processes set and revise goals reflecting ongoing subactivities and changing priorities among these subactivities. One can expect that, in contrast to these internal autonomous changes, external guidance from administrators or users occurs only infrequently and episodically. Figure 1 depicts the flow of information and resources characteristic of active trust management.

3   Exercising Control in Active Trust Management

Control of active trust management takes several forms.

- An administrator or system process can establish and change the structure of the monitoring network in order to monitor different conditions. This structure reflects knowledge about relationships between different signals, such as independence or correlations, that exist independent of specific security concerns. It also reflects, however, the goals or concerns of a security manager, with specialized processes added to track temporary or specific concerns.
- An administrator or system process can adjust the models that guide alerting decisions. These models encode information about the likelihood different recipients will want to see different classes of alerts, at different times, via different communications paths, and in different forms. The models also encode the value of alerts to the sender and recipients in the different cases. In simple cases, alerting decision models consist of simple thresholds one can raise or lower, but more useful alerting models provide a more expressive representation of the preferences or utilities guiding the decisions.
- An administrator or system process can indicate the utility model guiding resource allocation decisions. This model, like the more sophisticated alerting models, involves expression of complex dependence of the utility of resource allocations on properties of task performance.

Putting these control mechanisms together, we find that exercising control over active trust management involves specification of goals and utility information. In the following, we consider means for specifying such goals and utility information in a coherent and coordinated way. We simplify and shorten the presentation by focusing on specification of resource allocation utilities. We take a similar approach to specification of alerting utilities.

3.1   Representational Concerns about Utilities

Though many computational decision-making methods rely on numeric utility functions, such functions provide poor representations for knowledge about task importance. Utility functions, of course, merely serve as numeric representations for orderings of relative preferability or desirability. They add irrelevant details to the underlying ordering, in the sense that many different numeric utility functions can represent the same underlying ordering.

In fact, utility functions and their underlying ordering really do not distinguish between essential and inessential aspects of preferability. Common judgments of preferability involve both fundamental preference relations and specific tradeoffs. One might, for example, judge the security of login services more important than the speed performance of those services. One might persist in that judgment even as one changes opinions on just how much more important login security is than login performance.

This confusion of preferential essence and accident impedes convenient specification of changes. One might start thinking performance more important than security for some purpose, and choose some specific tradeoff ratio. Later experience might provide evidence that this preference was wrong, that security is instead more important than performance. The natural inclination is to switch the underlying preference and figure out later the new tradeoff value. However, if all one has is a numerical utility function encoding the former tradeoffs, one lacks any simple means for adjusting it to reflect the switch in underlying preferences.

Worse still, an autonomous system seeking to maintain its own security can expect to encounter unforeseen circumstances and to occasionally modify its goals. Both of these events may call for modifying the utility function in even more fundamental ways than merely switching an existing preference, for they may call for adding new goals or conditions of interest, adopting new preferences, perhaps by means of inference from general principles set up to guide the system in facing novel circumstances.

3.2 Qualitative Preferential Information

To provide a framework for effective autonomous action in resource allocation, we step back from direct provision of numerical utility functions and augment utility functions with qualitative representations of preference information. Here we transcend the familiar non-numerical orders among individual outcomes underlying utility functions to express or capture abstract and generic preferences among qualities or properties of outcome classes. These qualitative expressions provide constraints on the orderings of individual outcomes, and provide a natural basis for reasoned construction of decision models appropriate to novel circumstances or types of decisions.

These qualitative representations of underlying preference structures augment rather than displace numeric utility functions, which remain important in calculations intended to optimize expected utility. We connect the two notions by providing mechanisms to automatically construct numeric utility functions from sets of qualitative specifications. This permits a human administrator or system process to exercise control through generic, qualitative expressions and the automated resource allocator to exercise control through concrete, numeric expressions.

4   Illustrating the Concepts

To help convey these abstract concepts, we illustrate the approach using a simplified form of the qualitative language under development and an imaginary but plausible application setting in which the trust manager operates to serve a company that performs computer animation for films. For simplicity of exposition, we start by examining how a human administrator can exercise control along the lines outlined in the preceding, and then consider means by which system processes might exercise similar control.

The company—let us call it Acme Animation Associates—does the usual things with its computers, such as logging in, handling email, maintaining marketing, operational, and financial databases, and running a web server. Acme's

Service	Performance goal	Security goal
login	P.login	S.login
mail	P.mail	S.mail
web	P.web	S.web
db	P.db	S.db
animation	P.animation	S.animation
seti	P.seti	S.seti

Fig. 2. Acme's ATM goals

Service	Service-specific preferences
login	S.login > P.login
mail	S.mail > P.mail
web	P.web > S.web
db	S.db > P.db
animation	P.animation > S.animation
seti	P.seti > S.seti

Fig. 3. Pure service preferences

core operation, however, consists of running animation processes that render films frame by frame.

Acme's system administrator, who we will call Al Greenspan, is charged with providing the underlying guidance to Acme's ATM system. To do this, he starts by identifying the fundamental goals in Acme's local setup. These include some standard goals, such as performance and security for individual services and the overall system, and may include addition goals appropriate to the special concerns of the local environment, in Acme's case, having to do with its animation activities. For simplicity, we suppose Greenspan starts by identifying only the performance and security goals for each of the standard services, to which, as an astronomy buff, he adds SETI@Home. This produces the goals displayed in Figure 2. Here one can think of "performance" as meaning something like "good performance". For the purpose of this illustration, we will only consider the coarse distinction between good and not-good (or bad) performance. More refined models can employ more refined categories of performance levels or characteristics.

With the system goals specified, and presumably with monitoring processes installed to observe and quantify these properties, Greenspan next specifies underlying preferences among these qualities. The first set of preferences relate only goals for the same service, as indicated in Figure 3. Greenspan also specifies some preferences that relate goals for different services, as given in Figure 4. Greenspan leaves a number of goals unrelated, as their relative ranking does not seem to matter to him as long as all get done.

With this initial specification of goals and preferences, Greenspan tells the ATM system to making his guidance effective by constructing a utility function over resource allocations compatible with the generic preferences he has speci-

Cross-service preferences
S.login >S.web
P.web > P.seti
P.db > P.seti
P.animation > P.seti
S.web >P.seti
S.db >P.seti
S.animation >P.seti

Fig. 4. Mixed service preferences

$$\begin{vmatrix} \text{P.web} = 10 \\ \text{S.web} = 3 \\ \text{P.db} = 15 \\ \vdots \end{vmatrix} >_a \begin{vmatrix} \text{P.web} = 12 \\ \text{S.web} = 80 \\ \text{P.db} = 1 \\ \vdots \end{vmatrix}$$

Fig. 5. A comparison between specific allocations

fied. This step is necessary because we distinguish preferences among qualities, as expressed in the preceding figures, and which we can more correctly notate as $>_q$, from preferences between individual resource allocations, which we can notate as $>_a$. The preferences among qualities do not refer to specific resource allocations, but only to properties of the allocations, such as whether the allocation in question provides good database performance or good web-server security. Preferences among allocations instead compare specific allocations of resources to tasks. If we suppose for simplicity that such allocations concern only allocation of units of CPU cycles to different tasks—hardly a desirable supposition in realistic situations—we might write one such comparison as in Figure 5. The ATM utility-construction task, then, consists of constructing a numeric utility function over individual allocations that conforms to the qualitative preferences, or roughly speaking, a function U such that $U(x) >_a U(y)$ if $x >_q y$. The ATM system constructs a suitable utility function and proceeds to allocate system resources.

The day comes, however, when trouble strikes and Greenspan is in the hot seat. Late one Friday (of course), the payroll manager confronts Greenspan because the production of payroll checks is not finishing as expected. On her heels the sales manager stomps in to inform Greenspan that someone has defaced Acme's web site with a crude insult to Acme's prime customer. Greenspan looks into the payroll problem first and determines that the ATM system is starving the database of cycles, giving preference, as usual, to the core animation processes. He promises to conduct a longer investigation to find out how the web intrusion occurred, but does notice he had specified that web performance was preferable to web security.

With these quick determinations, Greenspan modifies his guidance to the ATM system. For lack of a more specific solution to the defacement problem, Greenspan reverses his earlier guidance and tells the ATM system that good

Revised preferences
S.web > P.web
P.db.payday > P.animation.payday

Fig. 6. Changed and added service preferences

web server security is preferable to good web server performance. To address the payroll problem, Greenspan introduces some new goals and preferences. The new goals refine the existing goals for database and animation process performance by introducing goals specific to paydays. He then adds preferences that indicate database performance on paydays preferable to animation performance on paydays. We depict these revised preferences in Figure 6. Greenspan instructs the ATM system to reconstruct and install an updated allocation utility function.

To summarize, Greenspan expressed the principles underlying the desired ATM performance in fairly natural terms by stating and relating various qualitative goals for different services and at different levels of specificity. He was later able to state changes to these principles in natural ways. The ATM system, in turn, took care of translating these principles into quantitative guidance for the decision making mechanisms.

Autonomous responses to novel circumstances require some knowledge to guide the responses. The scenario sketched assumes a system unaware of the sorts of situations addressed by Greenspan's corrections. A more knowledgeable system might well prove capable of instituting some corrections on its own. Although it seems unreasonable to assume a general-purpose ATM system knows about customers and insults, having the system know about task deadlines seems perfectly reasonable. In the example above, the payroll task might have instead monitored its own progress, projected a failure to meet its deadline with the resources it was obtaining, and itself generated the temporary high priority for the payroll task relative to the core animation process without requiring any intervention by Greenspan to effect this correction.

Indeed, the flexibility of the architecture depicted in Figure 1 means that the an autonomous system need not make prior provision for all deadline dangers, but instead can choose to address some categories of deadline tasks by constructing responses only as impending deadlines draw uncomfortably near. In comparison with fixed schemes for deadline-dependent utility functions, such as those explored by Haddawy and Hanks [5], on-the-fly crisis management permits exploiting special characteristics of the specific circumstances faced at the time. In some cases, these special characteristics can provide value that outweighs the usual disadvantages of crisis-driven response. Indeed, in novel circumstances, prior provision proves impractical, and one must of necessity rely on crisis-driven responses.

5   Formal Tools

We have not yet mechanized all the capabilities alluded to in the illustration just presented. In the following, we describe two important formal techniques, namely a logic of generic preference capable of expressing both qualitative goals and preferences among them, and a utility construction method to make such guidance effective.

5.1   Specifying Preferences and Goals

The standard decision-theoretic framework for rational choice under uncertainty (see, for example, [6]) involves

- A set $\mathcal{A} = \{A_1, A_2, \ldots\}$ of *actions*,
- A set $\mathcal{S}$ of states or *outcomes* that can result from actions and in which the agent takes action,
- A probability distribution $Pr_A : \mathcal{S} \to \mathbb{R}$ for each action $A \in \mathcal{A}$ that assigns to states the agent's degree of belief that the states result from A,
- A *weak preference* order $\precsim_S$ over states that forms a complete preorder, that is, a complete reflexive and transitive order over alternatives, which compares desirability of outcomes, where $S \precsim_S S'$ means that the agent finds S' at least as desirable as S,
- A numerical *utility* function $u : \mathcal{S} \to \mathbb{R}$ that represent $\precsim_S$ in the sense that $A \precsim_S B$ iff $u(A) \le u(B)$,
- An *expected utility* function $\hat{U} : \mathcal{S} \to \mathbb{R}$ such that $\hat{U}(A) = \sum Pr_A(S)u(S)$,
- A weak preference order $\precsim_A$ of over $\mathcal{A}$, defined by requiring that $A \precsim_A B$ iff $\hat{U}(A) \le \hat{U}(B)$, so that the most preferred action in a set is one that maximizes expected utility.

One defines the two additional relations of *indifference* among alternatives, written $A \sim B$, so that $A \precsim B$ and $B \precsim A$, meaning that the agent finds whatever differences exist between the alternatives leave them equally desirable, and *strict preference*, written $A \prec B$, so that $A \precsim B$ but $B \not\precsim A$, meaning the agent finds B more desirable than A.

Our specifications of preferences and goals starts with a comparison relation between propositions, which represent generic outcome classes rather than the comparisons of individual outcomes of the standard formulation. We introduce notation for propositional preferences and goals by writing, when p and q denote sets of outcomes, $p \trianglerighteq q$ to mean the proposition p is weakly preferred to the proposition q, and $\trianglerighteq (p)$ to mean that p is a goal, which we interpret as shorthand for $p \trianglerighteq \bar{p}$, where $\bar{p} = \Omega \setminus p$ denotes the complement of p.

Wellman and Doyle [7] showed that we cannot usefully interpret propositional preferences of this kind in terms of simple lifting of preferences over outcomes. They instead proposed interpreting propositional preference as preference *ceteris paribus*, so that $\trianglerighteq (p)$ means that the agent prefers outcomes in p to outcomes in $\bar{p}$, other things equal. In particular, they interpreted the *ceteris paribus* clause in terms of a multiattribute representation of outcomes, so that propositional preference compares outcomes that vary on the attribute of interest but hold all other attributes constant.

Doyle, Shoham, and Wellman [8] then extended this to general comparisons $p \trianglerighteq q$ and proved the soundness of various principles for inferring propositional preferences from others. These sound inference principles included cases of dominance or sure-thing reasoning, such as inferring $p \trianglerighteq q$ from $pr \trianglerighteq qr$ and $p\bar{r} \trianglerighteq q\bar{r}$; goal inference, such as inferring $\trianglerighteq (p)$ from $\trianglerighteq (q)$ and $p \trianglerighteq q$; and goal combination, such as inferring $\trianglerighteq (p \wedge q)$ and $\trianglerighteq (p \vee q)$ from $\trianglerighteq (p)$ and $\trianglerighteq (q)$. Some of these proofs held only for propositions expressed in certain syntactic forms. Doyle and Wellman [9] later developed an alternative semantic basis for the logic that provides the results without the syntactic restrictions.

Other representations, logics, and semantics for propositional preferences have been investigated by a variety of authors, including Pearl and Tan [10, 11], Boutilier [12, 13], Bacchus and Grove [14, 15], and Shoham [16, 17]. Some of these focus on the notion of *utility independence* instead of individual propositional preference comparisons (see also [18]). Each of these systems has its own advantages and disadvantages. The logic of preference *ceteris paribus* supports significant inferential capabilities, but seems overly strong for some purposes. In particular, it does not provide a means for expressing preferences over more restrictive propositions that reverse preferences (form an exception to) preferences expressed over more general propositions. This poses problems for formalizing the revision of preferences, depicted in the illustration earlier, so that database performance dominates animation performance on paydays but animation performance dominates database performance otherwise. Addressing such needs may simply call for somewhat different formulation of goals, but might also require changing the underlying logic of propositional preferences. Such a change can have disadvantages, however. For example, logics based on conditional logics make expression of exceptional subcases easier, but in turn support almost no inferences. Solving these problems requires further research on qualitative preference, which continues as part of a larger investigation of qualitative decision theory [19].

5.2   Constructing Utility Functions

Our ongoing work [20] addresses the task of constructing a utility function over outcomes compatible with a set of qualitative preferences. We construct a utility function essentially by starting with presumptions of utility independence between all qualities and then using explicit statements of generic preference ceteris paribus to identify clusters of utility-dependent qualities. The construction exploits the presumptive utility independence to simplify the structure of the constructed utility function as much as possible, making the construction of low complexity in many cases. The method employs an intermediate representation that transforms individual preferential comparisons into small sets of relations between fundamental propositional classes, and applies various graph-theoretic algorithms to separate relations between fundamental classes into utility-dependent clusters. Further graph methods yield subutility functions over these clusters, and an additive scaling of the subutility functions yields a utility function compatible with the qualitative specification, as desired.

6 Conclusion

Autonomous adaptive survivable systems use active trust management, based on graded knowledge about the trustworthiness of resources for different purposes, to accomplish as much as possible with possibly degraded resources. While this performance may fall short of system needs in some circumstances, it represents the best one can do. Obtaining these results, of course, depends on one adequately characterizing the value of different computational outcomes in relation to each other. Systems operating with a changing population of circumstances and types of tasks make it imperative that human and automated controllers find it as simple as possible to specify and revise these values. The arguments and illustration presented in this paper indicate that qualitative propositional preferences provide a natural and effective means for exercising effective control over active trust management. Realizing the promise of this approach requires considerable further work, but the history of progress in effectively representing probabilistic information offers considerable hope that similar progress will obtain in bringing qualitative preference techniques into widespread use.

Acknowledgments

We thank the anonymous referee for helpful suggestions, and thank Howard Shrobe, Robert Laddaga, Peter Szolovits, and William Long for many useful discussions. This work was supported by the Defense Advanced Research Projects Agency of the United States of America under contract F30602-99-1-0509. Mike McGeachie is supported in part by a training grant from the National Library of Medicine, and a grant from the Pfizer corporation.

References

1. Shrobe, H., Doyle, J.: Active trust management for autonomous adaptive survivable systems. In Robertson, P., Shrobe, H., Laddaga, R., eds.: Self-Adaptive Software. Lecture Notes in Computer Science. Springer Verlag, Berlin (2001) 40–49 Revised papers from the First International Workshop on Self-Adaptive Software (IWSAS 2000).
2. Doyle, J., Kohane, I., Long, W., Shrobe, H., Szolovits, P.: Agile monitoring for cyber defense. In: Proceedings of the Second DARPA Information Security Conference and Exhibition (DISCEX-II), IEEE, IEEE Computer Society (2001)
3. Haimowitz, I.J., Kohane, I.S.: Automated trend detection with alternate temporal hypotheses. In: Proceedings of the Thirteenth International Joint Conference on Artificial Intelligence, Chambery, France (1993) 146–151
4. Doyle, J., Kohane, I., Long, W., Shrobe, H., Szolovits, P.: Event recognition beyond signature and anomaly. In: Proceedings of the 2001 IEEE SMC Workshop on Information Assurance and Security, United States Military Academy, West Point, New York. (2001) 17–23
5. Haddawy, P., Hanks, S.: Utility models for goal-directed decision-theoretic planners. Computational Intelligence **14** (1998) 392–429

6. Savage, L.J.: The Foundations of Statistics. second edn. Dover Publications, New York (1972)
7. Wellman, M.P., Doyle, J.: Preferential semantics for goals. In: National Conference on Artificial Intelligence. (1991) 698–703
8. Doyle, J., Shoham, Y., Wellman, M.P.: A logic of relative desire (preliminary report). In Ras, Z.W., Zemankova, M., eds.: Methodologies for Intelligent Systems, 6. Volume 542 of Lecture Notes in Artificial Intelligence., Berlin, Springer-Verlag (1991) 16–31
9. Doyle, J., Wellman, M.P.: Representing preferences as *ceteris paribus* comparatives. In Hanks, S., Russell, S., Wellman, M.P., eds.: Proceedings of the AAAI Spring Symposium on Decision-Theoretic Planning. (1994)
10. Tan, S.W., Pearl, J.: Specification and evaluation of preferences for planning under uncertainty. In Doyle, J., Sandewall, E., Torasso, P., eds.: KR94, San Francisco, CA, Morgan Kaufmann (1994)
11. Tan, S.W., Pearl, J.: Qualitative decision theory. In: AAAI94, Menlo Park, CA, AAAI Press (1994)
12. Boutilier, C.: Toward a logic for qualitative decision theory. In Doyle, J., Sandewall, E., Torasso, P., eds.: Principles of Knowledge Representation and Reasoning: Proceedings of the Fourth International Conference (KR'94), San Francisco, Morgan Kaufmann (1994)
13. Boutilier, C., Brafman, R.I., Hoos, H.H., Poole, D.: Reasoning with conditional ceteris paribus preference statements. In: Proceedings of Uncertainty in Artificial Intelligence 1999 (UAI-99). (1999)
14. Bacchus, F., Grove, A.: Graphical models for preference and utility. In: Proceedings of the Eleventh Conference on Uncertainty in Artificial Intelligence, Morgan Kaufmann (1995) 3–19
15. Bacchus, F., Grove, A.: Utility independence in a qualitative decision theory. In: Proceedings of the Fifth International Conference on Knowledge Representation and Reasoning, Morgan Kaufmann (1996) 542–552
16. Shoham, Y.: Conditional utility, utility independence, and utility networks. In Geiger, D., Shenoy, P.P., eds.: Proceedings of the Thirteenth Conference on Uncertainty in Artificial Intelligence, San Francisco, California, Morgan Kaufmann (1997) 429–436
17. Shoham, Y.: A symmetric view of probabilities and utilities. In Pollack, M.E., ed.: Proceedings of IJCAI-97, San Francisco, California, Morgan Kaufmann (1997) 1324–1329
18. Wellman, M.P., Doyle, J.: Modular utility representation for decision-theoretic planning. In: Proceedings of the First International Conference on AI Planning Systems. (1992)
19. Doyle, J., Thomason, R.H.: Background to qualitative decision theory. AI Magazine **20** (1999) 55–68
20. McGeachie, M.: Utility functions for ceteris paribus preferences. Master's thesis, Massachusetts Institute of Technology, Cambridge, Massachusetts (2002) In preparation.

Dynamic Change in Workflow-Based Coordination of Distributed Services

Prasanta Bose[1] and Mark G. Matthews[2]

[1] Information and Software Engineering Department, George Mason University,
Fairfax, VA 22030
prasanta.bose@lmco.com
[2] The MITRE Corporation, 7515 Colshire Drive,
McLean, VA 22012
mmatthew@mitre.org

Abstract. The rapid advances in distributed computing and network-based technologies have paved the path for a networked economy. In such a networked economy, software technologies for coordination of distributed services according to specific business policies or workflows will play an ever-increasing role. A critical success factor in such automation is the handling of dynamic changes in the workflow in a dependable manner. This paper introduces an integrated architecture, called SWAP, for dynamic adaptation of workflow policies. It develops systematic methods for the design of agents that perform workflow policy change coordination and uses model-checking methods to analyze safety properties. We use the domain of E-commerce for the ordering of products to demonstrate the concepts and methods of our approach.

1 Introduction

E-Commerce applications and supply chain management systems involve the coordination of distributed services according to specific business policies. Workflow management systems are gaining increasing importance in streamlining the business operations by automating the coordination of the services according to specific business policies, called workflows. The workflow defines a specific ordered execution of the services. The need to dynamically change workflow-based coordination policies is bound to arise in order to respond to changing user requirements, changing services and changing performance and availability of the shared network infrastructure and services. A major challenge is handling dynamic changes in such policies. In practice many organizations find it necessary to suspend or abort the work in progress in order to avoid the undesirable side effects of a change. This is an inefficient and ineffective change process because many organizations find it difficult and sometimes impossible to interrupt currently executing processes. Automated methods and tools are required to bring about the change in a dependable manner.

This paper considers dynamic structural changes to workflows [7]. An example of such a change can occur in the context of a business to business global coordination for customer order processing. Consider the following service coordination scenario: *The customer generates an order for a product leading to creation of an ordering job.*

R. Laddaga, P. Robertson, and H. Shrobe (Eds.): IWSAS 2001, LNCS 2614, pp. 171–186, 2003.
© Springer-Verlag Berlin Heidelberg 2003

The seller then checks the availability of inventory to meet the order needs specified in the job. Contingent on availability, the account manager checks the customer credit for the order. Contingent on valid credit and availability, the seller fulfills the order. The shipper takes the order and ships out the product to the customer and the account manager bills the customer for the order.

In the above coordination process, consider a scenario in which the shipping and billing activities are traditionally performed concurrently by the relevant services (Figure 1) and a dynamic change in the coordination is introduced specifying that the shipping activity is to be performed after the completion of the billing activity (Figure 2). Although the coordination may be "safe" before the change and safe for orders processed after the change, there may be problems with orders undergoing processing when the change is introduced. For example, jobs which have undergone the shipping activity but not the billing activity in the traditional workflow will never undergo the billing activity under the new workflow, resulting in a failure to bill some customers and thus violating the integrity constraint that jobs are billed if and only if they are shipped.

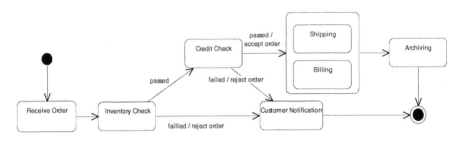

Fig. 1. Workflow Policy 1

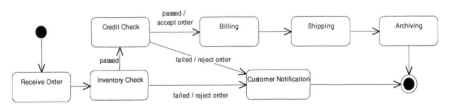

Fig. 2. Workflow Policy 2

Section 2 discusses the requirements and our approach for supporting dynamic change in workflow policies. Section 3 introduces SWAP and provides a brief description of the components and connections within the architecture. Section 4 provides a systematic approach to developing the change coordination mechanisms within the architecture. The approach is illustrated through the development of mechanisms supporting dynamic changes between the workflow policies in Figures 1-3. Section 5 provides details and examples concerning the analysis of the SWAP architectural specifications using the SPIN model-checker. Related work is included in Section 6 and Section 7 includes a conclusion and a discussion of future work.

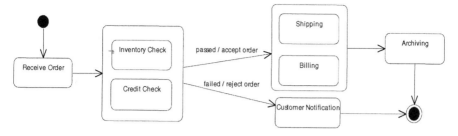

Fig. 3. Workflow Policy 3

2   Requirements and Approach for Dynamic Policy Change

In this paper we introduce SWAP, an adaptive workflow architecture for dependable policy switching. We also present systematic methods for developing the behavioral specifications of components in the architecture that bring about the dynamic policy changes while satisfying certain safety and correctness criteria. For simplicity, we consider a case in which the space of dynamic changes is defined by three workflow policy choices, shown in Figures 1-3 [7]. In Figure 1, the shipping and billing activities are performed concurrently. In Figure 2, all activities are performed sequentially. In Figure 3, shipping and billing is performed concurrently, as is inventory and credit checking. It should be noted that SWAP can be scaled to handle greater than three workflow policies and that SWAP is not limited to the case in which the policies are predefined at design time.

A major requirement in achieving a safe transition to a new policy is ensuring the validity of certain application specific coordination constraints for all jobs undergoing processing during the change. In the order processing domain, an example of such a constraint is that a job undergoes the billing activity if and only if the job undergoes the shipping activity. The key idea underlying the approach to change coordination is based on an understanding that ensuring the integrity of such constraints can be accomplished by: a) Using knowledge of the job processing state for the current workflow policy. b) Exploiting knowledge of the new policy to identify augmentations to the job status that determine the initial state of the new policy such that continued processing from that state would be a consistent progress of the processing state of the current policy without violating any application constraints (such as all accepted orders are to be billed and shipped). c) Executing a sequence of actions to bring about the change in activities of the policies and their respective states.

The key idea in our approach to meeting the above needs involves defining an agent[1]-based architecture that integrates dynamic policy change reasoning and coordination with workflow-based service coordination. The architecture uses tracking agents to track workflow policy execution states and a change coordination agent that utilizes the tracked policy states to plan change coordination actions. The major steps of the approach are: 1) Developing the behavioral specifications of the tracking agents, which use abstract specifications of policies in order to track the execution state of current policy based on monitored state. 2) Developing the behavioral specifi-

---

[1] We consider only behavioral specifications of agents.

cation of the state-dependent change coordination agent based on analyzing abstract behavioral specifications of policies to identify safe or valid transitions from a current policy execution state to a new policy execution state. 3) Verifying the correctness of the specifications and debugging of the change coordination components (tracking and change coordination agents) using the SPIN [9] model checker.

3   Architecture for Dynamic Policy Change

The approach to adapting workflow policies in response to a change in needs or constraints, or to handle an exception is based on an integrated layered architecture, called SWAP, that couples policy specification and change coordination with policy-based coordination of the services. Figure 4 shows the architectural components and connections in each layer modeled as a UML class diagram using stereotypes of the UML class. The architectural components in each layer, the connections between the components and the connections between the layers are briefly described in the following subsections.

3.1   Application Coordination Layer

The application coordination layer consists of agent representatives of the application specific service components required to perform workflow tasks (e.g., shipping, billing, and workflow scheduling agents). A workflow scheduling agent sequences the tasks to be performed by the service agents based on the workflow policy realized by that agent. A general application coordination agent (ACA) is introduced to accept jobs from client agents and to delegate the job to the active workflow scheduling agent. The agents interact via the application coordination event-channel (AChan) as depicted in Figure 4. Each workflow scheduling agent contains a control interface and associated methods to allow the change coordination agent to perform configuration and control actions. Workflow scheduling agents also include a monitoring interface and associated methods to allow tracking agents to track policy execution states.

3.2   Change Coordination Layer

In response to a communicated switching decision from the SWAP workflow administrator[2], the change coordination layer performs the set of actions required to realize the switching decision. The change coordination layer consists of tracking agents (TA1, TA2, and TA3), a change coordination agent (CCA), and a shared data space (CSpace). There is one tracking agent per workflow scheduling agent in the application coordination layer. A tracking agent interacts with the monitoring interface of its associated workflow scheduling agent via the change coordination event channel

---

[2] Although not depicted in Figure 4, change reasoning can be automated. The automated change reasoning approach in [3, 4] for distributed view maintenance can be applied to SWAP, as well. Here we assume that humans perform the change reasoning and an administrator inputs the workflow policy change decision into a SWAP administrative user interface.

(CChan). Each time a workflow scheduling agent experiences a qualitative change in one of its state variables, the change is propagated to the associated tracking agent which abstractly tracks the execution state of the workflow scheduling agent. The CCA accepts the communicated switching decision from the SWAP workflow administrator and, based on the current tracking information maintained by the tracking agents, executes the set of configuration and control actions required to bring about the dynamic switching between workflow scheduling agents within the application coordination layer. The CCA interacts with the control interface of the workflow scheduling agents via the CChan. The CSpace is used to communicate the tracking knowledge from the tracking agents to the CCA.

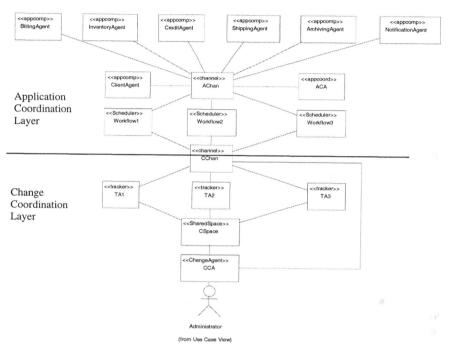

Fig. 4. SWAP -- An Architecture for Dynamic Change Management

3.3 Scheduler Agent Specification

In order to define a systematic method for design and analysis of the change coordination layer, we need to specify the design of the application coordination layer and in particular the scheduling agents which incorporate the workflow policies for service coordination. We consider a state-chart based behavioral specification of the scheduler agent and its concrete representation as a set of Event-Condition-Action rules for use by the scheduler agent to do task sequencing. The events model the receipt of an order and the completion of tasks. The conditions correspond to post-conditions resulting from task executions. The actions model the delegation of tasks to service agents.

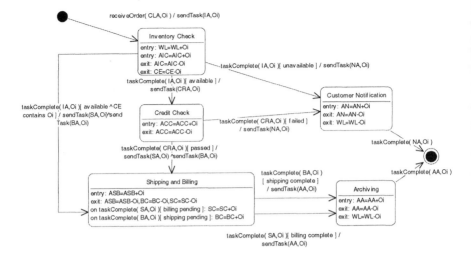

Fig. 5. Behavioral Specification for Policy 1 Workflow Instance

Figure 5 shows the state-chart based behavioral model for the sequencing of activities specified in Figure 1. Figure 5 also shows the concrete data elements maintained by the scheduler to track the status of the set of ordering jobs undergoing processing. For example, when the scheduler receives an order O_i from a client agent, the order is sent to the inventory agent for processing, the workflow instance enters the Inventory Check state, and upon entering the state O_i is added to the workload (WL) and awaiting inventory check (AIC) job queues. The behavioral specification of the scheduler then consists of the composite of the statecharts of the individual workflow instances currently in progress.

event[condition]→action
1.   receiveOrder(CLA,O_i)→sendTask(IA, O_i)
2.   taskComplete(IA, O_i)[inventory available]→sendTask(CRA, O_i)
3.   taskComplete (IA, O_i)[inventory unavailable]→sendTask(NA, O_i)
4.   taskComplete (CRA, O_i)[credit passed]→sendTask(BA, O_i)^sendTask(SA, O_i)
5.   taskComplete (CRA, O_i)[credit failed]→sendtask(NA, O_i)
6.   taskComplete(BA, O_i)[shipping complete]→sendTask(AA, O_i)
7.   taskComplete(BA, O_i)[shipping pending]→set(billing complete, O_i)
8.   taskComplete(SA, O_i)[billing complete]→sendTask(AA, O_i)
9.   taskComplete(SA, O_i)[billing pending]→set(shipping complete, O_i)
10.   taskComplete(AA, O_i)→end workflow instance
11.   taskComplete(NA, O_i)→end workflow instance
12.   taskComplete(IA, O_i)[inventory available^CE contains O_j]→ sendTask(BA,O_i) ^ sendTask(SA, O_i)

Fig. 6. Rule Set for Scheduler 1

Each scheduler in Figure 4 executes a set of rules to manage multiple jobs in accordance with a specific workflow policy. The rule set for scheduler 1 is depicted in Figure 6. For example, rule 1 in Figure 6 states that when scheduler 1 receives an order O_i from a client agent (CLA) the order is sent to the inventory agent (IA) for processing. As another example, rule 2 states that when the IA has completed its task and determined that sufficient inventory is available to support the order, the order is sent to the credit agent (CRA) for processing.

4   Change Coordination Layer: Design and Analysis

As discussed in the introduction, dynamic changes introduce safety concerns. Ensuring a safe transition to a new policy requires that certain integrity constraints in the application domain be maintained. The key idea underlying the approach to change coordination is based on exploiting knowledge of the new policy to identify augmentations to the job status that determine the initial state of the new policy such that continued processing from that state would be a consistent progress of the processing state of the current policy without violating any application constraints (such as all accepted orders are to be billed and shipped).

The above idea is translated into the following architectural design constraints of the change coordination layer: 1) Tracking agents are required to track the processing states of the workflow scheduler agents within the application coordination layer. 2) A unique change plan is required for each dynamic switch between specific policies supported by the system. The change plan specifies the sequence of actions required to maintain the integrity of the application specific constraints during the switch. 3) A change coordination agent is required to select the appropriate change plan, based on the change decision and the current tracked states, and to coordinate the sequence of actions contained within the change plan to bring about the dynamic switch in policies.

4.1   Design of Tracking Agent

The approach to developing the tracking agents in the architecture consists of the following steps: 1) Identify the key state variables of the workflow scheduling agents in the application coordination layer. The set of key state variables is referred to as the state vector. This step requires an analysis of behavioral specifications (e.g., Figure 5) developed as part of the application coordination layer. 2) Identify qualitative abstractions of the state variables. Qualitative abstractions are used to reduce the complexity of the tracker and change coordination agents. 3) Develop behavioral specifications for the tracker agents. A tracking agent specification consists of a state model with qualitative abstractions based on the state model of the corresponding scheduler agent. Choosing the right abstractions is critical to the approach for formal correctness analysis [10]. The above steps are elaborated below using examples.

Step 1: Identify key state variables. The key state variables are identified through domain analysis of the workflow policies and models developed in the application coordination layer. Since differences in the policies are limited to the scheduling agents, the key state variables representing the application specific processing state come from the set of explicit data elements manipulated by the scheduler in managing multiple jobs. For scheduler 1 (S_1), the state variables can be obtained from Figure 5. Likewise, the key state variables for schedulers 2 (S_2) and scheduler 3 (S_3) can be obtained from an analysis of their associated behavioral specifications. Table 1 contains a description of the key state variables resulting from this analysis.

Table 1. Key State Variables

	S_1	S_2	S_3
WL = array of orders in process (workload)	X	X	X
AIC = array of orders awaiting inventory check	X	X	
ACC = array of orders awaiting credit check	X	X	
ASB = array of orders awaiting shipping and/or billing	X		X
AN = array of orders awaiting notification	X	X	X
AA = array of orders awaiting archiving	X	X	X
CE = array of credit exceptions	X	X	
AS = array of orders awaiting shipping		X	
AB = array of orders awaiting billing		X	
SE = array of shipping exceptions		X	
AICC = array of orders awaiting inventory and/or credit check			X

Step 2: Identify qualitative state variable abstractions. The main goals in identifying qualitative abstractions are reducing the complexity of the tracker and change coordination agents and reducing the overhead associated with the tracking. In analyzing the state variables in Table 1, we have determined that it is not important for the tracker to know the individual job ids in each queue, or even the number of jobs in each queue. It is only important for the tracker to know if there are any (1 or more) jobs in a state variable job queue. Hence, the qualitative abstractions of empty (E) and non-empty (N) are used for all state variables in Table 1. This translates to a requirement for the scheduler to notify the tracker each time a state variable changes from an empty to a nonempty abstract value or vice versa.

Step 3: Developing tracking agent specifications. The tracking agent is developed through an analysis of the scheduler behavioral specifications and the key state variable abstractions. Figure 7 shows the specification for the tracking agents in SWAP. The tracking agents receive notification of abstract state variable changes (svchange event in Figure 7) from the schedulers, compute the current abstract state vector (sv), and write (send action in Figure 7) the current vector to the coordination space (CSpace) in the change coordination layer. In addition to the state variables, the states "idle" (I) and "processing" (P) are maintained by the tracker to indicate if the scheduler is currently processing orders. The state charts for all three tracking agents are identical, although the state variable changes received from the schedulers and the state vectors written to the CSpace differ.

4.2 Design of Change Coordination Agent

Scenario-based analysis is used in the approach to developing the change coordination agent in the architecture. The approach consists of the following steps: 1) Identify a set of workload scenarios that covers the state space of the tracker agent specifications. The workload scenarios correspond to jobs in different stages of processing. 2) Generate an event trace for each workflow policy against each workload scenario. An event trace captures the changes in the job-queue state variables as jobs undergo execution based on the workflow policy. 3) Systematically analyze the event traces for pairwise switching of policies such that certain integrity constraints (for example customers get billed if and only if the product gets shipped) are preserved. This involves identifying the workload constraints of the active policy in a given state (specified by the abstract state vector) in the trace and the matching workload constraints of the new policy to be activated in a specific state. 4) Generate the change plans. This involves combining the results obtained from the set of pairwise analyses performed in step 3 and resolving any discrepancies between analyses. The configuration actions (change plan) for activating the new policy then consist of setting up the workload state variables of the workflow scheduler agents according to the valid transitions obtained from the above analysis. 5) Model the change coordination agent (CCA). The CCA is modeled as a decision tree captured by a finite state machine model. The decision conditions are captured by the transitions and the actions (change plans) are captured by the activity states.

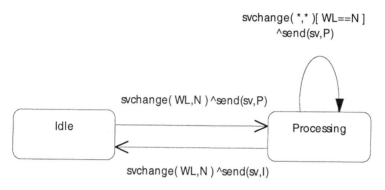

Fig. 7. Tracking Agent Specification

Step 1: Identifying workload scenarios. In this step we identify a set of workload scenarios that when executed cover the entire state space of the abstract state vectors of the tracking agents. Workflow 1 has seven state variables in Table 1. Since each variable has two possible abstract values, there are $2^7=128$ possible state vectors for tracker 1. An analysis of Figure 5 shows that only 49 of the 128 possible state vectors are reachable in the sense that those states will be encountered by the scheduler agent in the course of processing the jobs. For example, if WL=E all the other state variables must also be empty to be reachable. There are $2^9=512$ possible state vectors for tracker 2, of which 145 are reachable. There are $2^5=32$ possible state vectors for tracker 3, of which 17 are reachable. The following set of workload scenarios covers the entire state space of reachable vectors:

    a) Single order, inventory available, and credit passed
    b) Single order, inventory available, and credit failed
    c) Single order, inventory unavailable, and credit passed
    d) Single order, inventory unavailable, and credit failed
    e) Shipping exception from previous switch (valid for workflows 1 and 2 only)
    f) Credit exception from previous switch (valid for workflow 2 only)

Step 2: Generating event traces. Tables 2 and 3 show the event traces generated for workflows 1 and 3 in executing scenario a) above. The event traces show the state vectors encountered by the tracker as activities associated with jobs are completed. Table 2 does not include the state variable for credit exceptions (CE). The need for this state variable will be identified during the pairwise analysis in the next step. Due to the concurrency between tasks, there are four possible ordering of events in Table 3. We show the case in which the credit check completes before the inventory check, and the shipping activity completes before the billing activity. All four possible orderings must be considered during the analysis in the next step. Likewise there are two possible orderings of the events in Table 2 that must be considered.

Table 2. Workflow 1 Event Trace - Scenario a

id	event	WL	AIC	ACC	ASB	AN	AA
0	idle	E	E	E	E	E	E
1	order received	N	N	E	E	E	E
2	inventory check complete [available]	N	E	N	E	E	E
3	credit check complete [passed]	N	E	E	N	E	E
4	billing complete	N	E	E	N	E	E
5	shipping complete	N	E	E	E	E	N
6	archiving complete --> idle	E	E	E	E	E	E

Table 3. Workflow 3 Event Trace – Scenario a

id	Event	WL	AICC	ASB	AN	AA
0	Idle	E	E	E	E	E
1	order received	N	N	E	E	E
2	credit check complete [passed]	N	N	E	E	E
3	inventory check complete [available]	N	E	N	E	E
4	shipping complete	N	E	N	E	E
5	billing complete	N	E	E	E	N
6	archiving complete --> idle	E	E	E	E	E

Step 3: Analyzing event traces for pairwise switching. This step consists of analyzing pairs of event traces to identify the configuration actions and constraints on switching decisions to ensure safe and dependable switching.

For example, suppose a decision to switch from workflow 3 to workflow 1 is received while workflow 3 is in step 1 (i.e., id=1) of the event trace in Table 3. In this instance there is a single order with activities pending for both inventory and credit checking. In analyzing the traces in Tables 2 and 3, it is determined that step 1 of Table 2 is a consistent progress of the processing state. However, since the inventory and credit checking activities are serialized in workflow 1, the pending credit check in workflow 3 must be recalled. This job augmentation action is added to the change plans generated in the next step.

As another example, suppose a decision to switch from workflow 3 to workflow 1 is received while workflow 3 is in step 2 of the event trace in Table 3. In this instance there is a single order for which the credit check has already passed and an inventory check is pending. In this case there is no step in Table 2 that represents a consistent progress of the processing state. In this case we switch to step 1 of the trace in Table 2 and introduce the credit exception (CE) state variable which tells the workflow scheduler to bypass the credit check activity for this particular order. Rule 12 was added to the scheduler rule set in Figure 6 to handle this case. The behavioral specification in Figure 5 was also updated at this point to include the events and actions required to handle credit exceptions.

Step 4: Generating change plans. This step consists of merging the results from the set of pairwise analyses performed in the previous step into a set of change plans. A change plan consists of the set of condition-action rules, where conditions are predicates on the abstract state vector and actions perform augmentation to job queues and/or scheduler agent rules. Figure 8 shows the change plan for a decision to switch from policy 3 to policy 1. During the switch all the rules that evaluate to true will fire.

As an example, suppose a decision to switch from workflow 3 to workflow 1 is received while workflow 3 is in step 1 (i.e., id=1) of the event trace in Table 3. In this instance rules 2 and 3 of the change plan in Figure 8 will fire. The "CRA.recall(CPIP+CPIU)" action in rule 3 recalls the applicable credit checks as discussed in the first example of the previous step. The "WF1.CE=WF3.CC [results=passed]" action is step 3 populates the credit exception state variable as discussed in the second example in the previous step.

condition→action
1. WF3.state= =Idle→WF1.init(), WF3.init() // sets state variable values to null
2. WF3.WL= =N→WF1.WL=WL3.
3. WL WF3.AICC= =N→
CPIP=WF3.AICC-WF3.IC - WF3.CC //credit pending, inventory pending
IRL=WF3.CC[results==failed] // inventory pending, credit failed
CPIU=WF3.IC[results==unavailable] // inventory unavailable, credit pending
WF1.CE=WF3.CC[results==passed] // inventory pending credit passed
WF1.ACC=WF3.IC[results==available] // inventory available, credit pending
CRA.recall(CPIP+CPIU) // recall applicable credit checks
IA.recall(IRL) // recall inventory checks if credit failed
sendTask(NA,CPIU+IRL) // send unaccepted orders to NA
WF1.AIC=CPIP+WF1.CE
WF1.AN=CPIU+IRL
4. WF3.AN= =N→WF1.AN=WF3.AN
5. WF3.AA= =N→WF1.AA=WF3.AA
6. WF3.ASB= =N→WF1.ASB=WF3.ASB

Fig. 8. Change Plan for Switching from Policy 3 to Policy 1

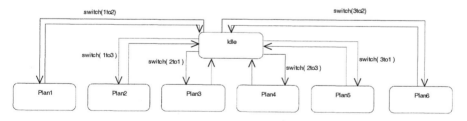

Fig. 9. Change Agent Behavioral Specification

Step 5: Developing change coordination agent specification. The change coordination agent specification is generated by analyzing the set of change plans and identifying the conditions under which each plan is applicable. Figure 9 shows the behavioral specification for the change coordination agent. Each leaf node in Figure 9 is populated with the rule set from the corresponding change plan generated in the previous step. For example, plan 5 in Figure 9 is populated with the rule set in the change plan in Figure 8. This plan would be executed upon the change coordination agent's receipt of the event "switch(3to1)."

5   Analyzing Correctness of Dynamic Change Coordination

We use the SPIN model checker to analyze the correctness of the architectural specifications of the change coordination layer. SPIN is a tool for analyzing the logical consistency of distributed systems, specifically data communication protocols. The system is described in a modeling language called Promela (Process or Protocol Meta Language). SPIN performs simulation of the system described in Promela to exhaustively check for system invariants, deadlocks, and trace properties. The Promela language defines constructs for describing processes and their asynchronous communication via channels. Processes are global objects. Message channels and variables can be declared globally or locally within a process. Process descriptions (called proctypes) in their basic form correspond to finite state models of components. A process declaration typically consists of i) a set of state variable declarations, ii) initial and final state declarations, iii) random or non-deterministic event declarations, and iv) transition declarations. A transition declaration specifies the current state, the message read event from a channel or some random event occurring, the next state and any output message event to a channel.

We first used SPIN to analyze the individual models for the three tracking agents, three workflow agents, and the change coordination agent. Once exhaustive checks were successfully executed by SPIN without errors, we integrated the individual models to allow SPIN to exhaustively check the SWAP change coordination layer as a whole. We have also encoded several workload scenarios and change decisions as SPIN processes to verify that the architectural specifications can support the workload scenarios and change decisions in a safe and dependable manner.

In our models we use Promela message types (mtype) to declare the abstract state variables and qualitative state variable abstractions. For tracking agent 1, the declaration is as follows:

```
mtype = {E, N, I, P, WL, AIC, ACC, CE, AN, AA, ASB,
KILL};
```

We then use the mtype declarations to define message structures (keyword typedef) that represent the monitored, tracked, and changed states as state vectors. For example, the typedef change declaration below is used to define the contents of the message passed from the workflow scheduler to the tracking agent when there is a change in the qualitative abstract value of a state variable. An instance of the structure is created through the declaration of the variable svchange as shown below.

```
typedef change {  mtype variable; mtype qvalue};
change svchange;
```

The state vector for workflow 1 is declared and instantiated as follows:

```
typedef  WF1SV {mtype WL1; mtype AIC1; mtype ACC1;
mtype CE1; mtype AN1; mtype AA1; mtype ASB1; mtype
state1};
WF1SV      TA1SV
```

We declared two channels in our model for testing tracker 1. The svupdate event channel is used for notifying the tracker of changes and the cspace channel represents the shared data space in the change coordination layer.

```
chan svupdate = [0] of {change};
chan cspace = [1] of {WF1SV};
```

A portion of the code for tracker 1 is included below.

```
active proctype   tracker1 (){
do
:: atomic {
if
:: svupdate? svchange; /* read change vector */
if
:: svchange.variable ==WL && svchange.qvalue==E-->
       TA1SV.WL1= svchange.qvalue;TA1SV.state1=I;
       cspace! TA1SV;
. . .
:: svchange.variable==ASB -->
       TA1SV.ASB1=svchange.qvalue; cspace! TA1SV;
:: svchange.variable==KILL --> break;
fi;
fi;}
od;};
```

The code within the do loop above waits for the workflow scheduler to write a state variable change svchange to the svupate channel. The tracker receives the update, modifies the state vector accordingly, and writes the new state vector to the cspace for use by the change coordination agent.

To analyze the correctness of the tracker agent, we create a process for the associated workflow scheduler. A partial listing of the Promela code for scheduler 1 is included below.

```
active proctype wf1   {
do
:: TA1SV.WL1==E--> svupdate! WL,N;
:: TA1SV.WL1==N-->
          if
          :: TA1SV.AIC1==E--> svupdate! AIC,N;
          . . .
          :: TA1SV.CE1==N--> svupdate! CE,E;
          fi;
:: TA1SV.WL1==N && TA1SV.AIC1==E && TA1SV.ACC1==E &&
TA1SV.ASB1==E &&        TA1SV.AN1==E && TA1SV.AA1==E &&
TA1SV.CE1==E --> svupdate! WL,E;
:: svupdate! KILL,E; break;
od;
};
```

The code within the do loop above identifies the set of valid qualitative state variable changes. The process continually writes valid changes into the svchange channel. The tracker1 process will then read the changes from the channel and update the state information accordingly.

```
(Spin Version 3.2.3 -- 1 August 1998)
proc 0 = tracker1
proc 1 = wf1
q\p  0  1
  2  cspace1!E,E,E,E,E,E,E,E,E,I
  1  .  monitor1!WL,N
  1     monitor1?WL,N
  2  cspace1!N,E,E,E,E,E,E,E,E,P
  1  .  monitor1!AIC,N
  1     monitor1?AIC,N
  2  cspace1!N,N,E,E,E,E,E,E,E,P
```

Fig. 10. Random Simulation Output for Tracker 1

Figure 10 shows the partial output of a random simulation of the specification for tracker1. The trace captures the message traffic between the workflow scheduling agent (wf1) and the tracking agent (tracker1). The figure shows the following sequence of events: 1) The scheduler is initially in the idle state. 2) An order is received by the scheduler resulting in an abstract change to the workload state variable. The change is written to the monitor channel by wf1 and read by tracker1. 3) The scheduler sends the order to the inventory agent adding the orderid to the AIC job queue resulting in an abstract change.

```
(Spin Version 3.2.3 -- 1 August 1998)
Full statespace search for:
        never-claim        - (none specified)
        assertion violations   +
        acceptance  cycles   - (not selected)
        invalid endstates    +
State-vector 44 byte, depth reached 1918,
errors: 0
   3061 states, stored
   1901 states, matched
   4962 transitions (= stored+matched)
   12516 atomic steps
unreached in proctype tracker1
        (0 of 56 states)
unreached in proctype wf1
        (0 of 40 states)
```

Fig. 11. Exhaustive Statespace Search Output for Tracker1

Figure 11 shows the output obtained from an exhaustive check of the tracking agent specification for workflow 1. The results are interpreted in the following manner. SPIN performed an exhaustive verification (full statespace search). The exhaustive search checked for assertion violations and invalid endstates. There were no assertion violations or errors. There were 3061 unique system states (states stored) generated during the search. In 1901 cases, the search returned to a previously visited state (states matched). Each state vector took 44 bytes of memory. The longest non-cyclic execution sequence was 1918 (depth reached). There were no unreachable states within the specifications.

6   Related Work

The SWAP approach described in this paper builds on existing research on workflow management systems, software architectures, and model checking to define a domain specific architecture for dynamic change coordination in workflow-based service coordination. We describe here only the work relevant to the research results presented in this paper.

There has been a significant amount of work conducted in the area of workflow models and workflow management systems. Workflow studies have been conducted by researchers in the area of organizational design, office information systems and software engineering [16,18,19]. Research in automation of workflow has resulted in several systems [6] that exploit existing distributed computing technologies. In most of the systems, adapting to dynamic changes in a dependable manner is not well addressed [11]. More recent work [7, 10, 11] has started to address such dynamic change concerns. Our work develops an integrated architecture for change management and develops a systematic method for the design and analysis of the change coordination mechanisms in the architecture to ensure safety properties during dynamic switching between policies.

The SWAP work on change coordination is related to recent work in the area of specifying and analyzing dynamic software architectures [1, 13] and on using architectural specifications to plan and analyze changes in the run-time system [14, 15]. The work of Oreizy et. al. [15] develops approaches to run-time software evolution based on exploiting an explicit architectural model of the system. The change coordination layer in SWAP exploits domain specific knowledge to identify the necessary components and their role in the change coordination process.

The work in this paper exploits current research on model checking of software systems and protocols, and architectural modeling and analysis. Model checking [5] of protocols and safety critical software systems have been investigated by a number of researchers in the area of formal methods. Model checking is a demonstrated success in hardware testing. Model checkers like SMV [12], and SPIN [9] have been used by researchers and industrialists to find bugs in circuit designs, floating point standards, and cache coherence protocols for multiprocessors. This work exploits SPIN technology to incrementally analyze and debug models that are created through a manual analysis process. The work also exploits existing UML [2] standards for object modeling to do architecture modeling.

7   Summary and Future Work

This paper addresses the problem of dynamic change in the context of a workflow-based coordination of services. The novel ideas of our approach are as follows: a) An integrated architecture that couples workflow policy change reasoning and coordination with workflow-based service coordination. b) A systematic method for determining the behavior of change coordination layer agents that bring about change without violating application domain specific workflow integrity constraints. c) Use of SPIN technology for model checking to analyze and debug the manually created specifications such that the safety properties are met. The above approach has also been applied to other domains [3, 4]. Future work is focused on i) generalizing the framework and methods based on results obtained in applying the framework to multiple task domains, and ii) development of tools that use SPIN model checker outputs to support the specification debugging process.

References

1. R. J. Allen, R. Douence, D. Garlan. Specifying and Analyzing Dynamic Software Architectures, Proceedings of the 1998 Conference on Fundamental Approaches to Software Engineering (FASE '98), March 1998.
2. G. Booch, J. Rumbaugh and I. Jacobsen, "The Unified Modeling Language User Guide", Addison Wesley, 1999.
3. P. Bose and M. G. Matthews, "Coordination of View Maintenance Policy Adaptation Decisions: A Negotiation-Based Reasoning Approach", Proceedings of the International Workshop on Self-Adaptive Software, Oxford, England, April 2000.
4. P. Bose and M. G. Matthews, "NAVCo: Negotiation-based Adaptive View Coordination", in Proceedings of the Automated Software Engineering Conference, 1999.
5. E. M. Clarke and J. M. Wing, "Formal Methods: State of the Art and Future Directions" ACM Computing Surveys, Vol. 28, No. 4, 1996., pp 626-643.
6. Dodac et. al., "Workflow Management Systems and Interoperability", NATO ASI Series, Springer Verlag, Berlin 1998.
7. Ellis, K. Keddara, G. Rozenberg, "Dynamic Change within Workflow Systems", Proceeding of the ACM Conference on Organizational Computing Systems, 1995, pp 10-21.
8. D. Garlan and M. Shaw. "Software Architectures: Perspectives on an Emerging Discipline", Addison Wesley Publishers, 1996.
9. G. J. Holzman, "Design and Verification of Computer Protocols", Prentice Hall, Englewood Cliffs, NJ 1991.
10. M. Kamath and K. Ramamritham, "Correctness Issues in Workflow Management", Distributed Systems Engineering Journal, Special Issue on Workflow Management, Volume 3, Number 4, December 1996.
11. M. Klein, C. Dellacros, and A. Bernstein, eds., "Workshop Towards Adaptive Workflow Systems" CSCW-98 Workshop Proceedings, ACM Press, 1998.
12. K. L. McMillan, "Symbolic Model Checking", Kluwer Academic Publishers, 1993.
13. J. Magee, J. Kramer. Dynamic Structure in Software Architectures. Fourth SIGSOFT Symposium on the Foundations of Software Engineering, San Francisco, October 1996.
14. P. Oreizy, N. Medvidovic, R. N. Taylor, "Architecture-based Runtime Evolution", ICSE 1998.
15. P. Oreizy et. al., "An Architecture Based Approach to Self-Adaptive Software", IEEE Intelligent Systems, 1999.
16. L. Osterweil, "Automated Support for the Enactment of Rigorously Described Software Processes," Proceedings of the Third International Process Programming Workshop, Computer Society Press, 1988, pp 122-125.
17. J. Robbins, N. Medvidovic, D. Redmiles, and D. Rosenbloom, "Integrating Architecture Description Languages with a Standard Design Method", Second EDCS Cross Cluster Meeting, Austin, Texas, 1998.
18. Seth, editor, Proceedings of the NSF Workshop on Workflow and Process Automation in Information Systems.
19. L. A. Suchman, "Office Procedure as Practical Action: Models of Work and System Design", ACM Transactions on Office Information Systems, vol. 1, no. 4, October 1983, pp 320-328.

SSCS:
A Smart Spell Checker System Implementation Using Adaptive Software Architecture

Deepak Seth[1] and Mieczyslaw M. Kokar[2]

[1] Northeastern University, Boston, MA 02115, USA
seth@coe.neu.edu
[2] Northeastern University, Boston, MA 02115, USA
kokar@coe.neu.edu
http://www.coe.neu.edu/~kokar

Abstract. The subject of this paper is a Smart Spell Checker System (SSCS) that can adapt to a particular user by using the user's feedback for adjusting its behavior. The result of the adjustment is manifested in a different ordering of the suggestions to the user on how a particular spelling mistake should be corrected. The SSCS uses the Adaptive Software Architecture (ASA). The ASA consists of a hierarchy of layers, each containing a number of components called *Knowledge Sources*. The layers are connected by a software bus called *Domain*. External elements include *User* and *Initiator(s)*. Initiators supply input data to the system. The system also includes an *Evaluator* that generates feedback. Each Knowledge Source is responsible for generating suggestions for correcting a specific type of error. Feedback is propagated to Knowledge Sources after the user makes a selection of the correction. In response to feedback, Knowledge Sources adjust their algorithms. In this paper we present the results of the evaluation of the adaptability of the SSCS.

1 Introduction

Spell checking applications are not only common in today's marketplace, but have reached a plateau; it is often difficult to distinguish between one application and the other because they offer almost the same features and functionalities. In general, spell checking applications present valid suggestions to the user based on each mistake they encounter in the user's document. The user then either makes a selection from a list of suggestions or chooses to ignore the suggestions and accepts the current word as valid. Regardless of how often this is done, the spell checking application will perform its task independent of the types of mistakes most commonly made by that particular user.

Most spell checkers available today tend to be inflexible because their interfaces present suggestions in alphabetical order. They are tailored to the needs of the general population rather than to the mistakes of a particular individual. There is a need for adaptive interfaces that can anticipate and adapt to the specific spelling mistakes of any user [10]. A self-adapting interface [9] monitors the user's activity and attempts to adjust its behavior automatically to be more

R. Laddaga, P. Robertson, and H. Shrobe (Eds.): IWSAS 2001, LNCS 2614, pp. 187–197, 2003.
© Springer-Verlag Berlin Heidelberg 2003

compatible with the particular user. By monitoring the user's activity, enough useful information about the user can be elucidated and an accurate model of the user can be generated [8]. An adaptive spell checker monitors the user's mistakes and is able to determine the types of spelling mistakes the user makes. Based on these mistakes, it presents suggestions to the user based on how frequently a particular type of mistake has occurred in the past, instead of simply displaying them in alphabetical order. We believe that an adaptive spell checker makes a good case study for self-adapting software.

In many cases, there are many different ways to correct an erroneous word. The spell checker needs to decide which correction to propose to the user. For the efficiency of the spell checking process, it is important that the right suggestion is presented as a default suggestion. In such a case, the user needs only to confirm the default suggestion and proceed with the next error. Otherwise, the user needs to scroll through a list of suggestions and pick one as the right one. Even worse, often the right suggestion is not on the list and thus the user needs to type the full word again. Our Smart Spell Checker System (SSCS) attempts to adapt to the user by learning most typical mistakes made by that particular user and incorporate this knowledge into the process of selecting the default suggestion that is put on the top of the list of suggestions.

The goal of the research presented in this paper was to implement and analyze an intelligent spell checker that adapts to the user's mistakes using a new paradigm in software architecture - self-adaptive software (cf.[2–4, 8]). This architecture is designed upon the structure of an adaptive controller [2, 5, 6] that uses the feedback mechanism to induce adaptability of the system. Towards this aim, we implemented a modular and flexible program, the SSCS, which incorporates some of the ideas of adaptive control systems [1]. The modularity of the architecture, called the Adaptive Software Architecture (ASA), allows easy additions of new components into the system, such as additional knowledge sources or domains to the overall system.

To demonstrate the adaptability feature of the SSCS, we evaluated the system against a non-adaptive system. The results of these comparisons were then mapped against a theoretical scenario. Finally, we analyzed the results and drew conclusions based on this study and proposed directions for future research.

2   Adaptive Software Architecture

The basic structure of the ASA is shown in Figure 1. The main components of this architecture are Knowledge Sources (KSs), Domains, Initiator and Evaluator. Knowledge Sources are the main working modules of an application. Domains act as software buses (also known as "blackboards" [7]) and connect the Knowledge Sources, Initiators and Evaluators. KSs take data from the Domain below, but the results are placed on either the Domain below or above, depending on a particular system configuration (design).

The input data are placed on the first Domain by the Initiator (the source of data) and consequently become visible to the KSs that are connected to the

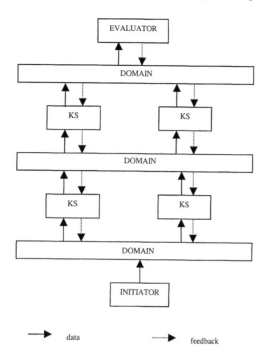

Fig. 1. Adaptive Software Architecture (ASA)

Domain. Each KS is equipped with a mechanism (knowledge) for making decisions on whether to process the data or not. The algorithms for data processing, decision-making, score generating and updating are also implemented in the KSs. After the first layer of KSs process the data placed on the first Domain, the results are placed either on the same Domain or on the next Domain (above), depending on the configuration of the system. If the new data are placed on the lower domain the same processing starts over. When the processing ceases, the second layer of KSs invoke their algorithms - first to make decisions on whether to process the data or not, and then their processing algorithms, if the decision is to process. When the processing reaches the highest Domain, the Evaluator assesses the quality of each of the results and gives feedback on whether the result was good or not. This feedback is then backpropagated through Domains and KSs so that it reaches only those KSs that participated in the processing, i.e., those KSs that made the decision to process. In response to the received feedback, the KSs adjust their processing algorithms so that the next time around the processing is different, tuned towards higher feedback scores.

3   Experimental Scenario

To investigate the adaptability of the system we use the application of spell checking. The input to the system is a text file containing a list of words. The goal of the system is to recognize erroneous words and then to attempt to correct the identified erroneous words and present suggestions to the user on what word should be used instead. The suggestions presented to the user are based on the mistakes made most often in the document.

The application, called here SSCS (Smart Spell Checking System) has been implemented as an instance of the Adaptive Software Architecture (cf. [2–4]) shown in Figure 1. The structure of the SSCS is shown in Figure 2. It consists of three domains (Input, Error and Evaluation) and nine KSs. Both the detection and correction of erroneous words are implemented within the KSs. The detection of erroneous words is implemented using a Dictionary and a User Defined Dictionary. The User Defined Dictionary contains words that the user wishes to be considered, in addition to standard dictionary entries. The following Knowledge Sources were used for correcting erroneous words:

- Left-Right Character Shifter
- Character Doubler
- End Character Appender
- Character Remover
- Subsequent Character Switcher

Each KS reflects one kind of typing mistake that has its source in the domain, i.e., in typing. The Left-Right Character Shifter corrects mistakes that arise due to misplacement of the hand on the keyboard. For example the UNIX command "cd" can be erroneously typed as "vf" or "xs". The Left-Right Character Shifter then replaces the characters with their neighbors on the keyboard and makes such a suggestion to the user. The Character Doubler assumes that a character was typed once instead of twice and corrects words by repeating characters that are potentially missing. For example, the erroneous word "siting" would be corrected as "sitting". The End Character Appender corrects erroneous words that have the end character missing. For example, the erroneous word "facto" would be corrected as "factor". The Character Remover corrects an erroneous word by removing a single character to produce a correct word. For example, "networjk" would be corrected as "network". The Subsequent Character Switcher swaps two consecutive characters in an erroneous word to generate a correct word. For example, "hta" would be corrected as "hat".

Each KS has associated with it a probability given by the equation:

$$P(t) = c/N$$

where c is the number of times that the correct suggestion was at the top of the list after t attempts, and N is the number of valid suggestions presented to the user. This value is a measure of the degree of success in generating the correct words selected by the user. Every time a user selects a word generated by a particular KS, the probability factor of that KS is incremented (the count c of correct words incremented by one). This value is used in determining the order of suggestions presented to the user. Suggestions generated by KSs that have a higher probability factor will be ahead of suggestions generated by other KSs.

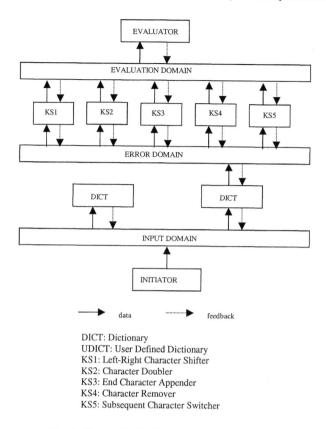

DICT: Dictionary
UDICT: User Defined Dictionary
KS1: Left-Right Character Shifter
KS2: Character Doubler
KS3: End Character Appender
KS4: Character Remover
KS5: Subsequent Character Switcher

Fig. 2. Smart Spell Checker System (SSCS)

The suggestions generated by the KSs are presented to the Evaluator. The Evaluator compares these words against a dictionary and displays the valid suggestions to the user. The user chooses a suggestion or selects Ignore. Based on the user's choice, feedback is generated and is passed back to the KSs.

4   SSCS Operation

The Initiator reads a text file and places the extracted words from the text file, one at a time, on the Input Domain. The extracted words are examined by both the Dictionary and the User-Defined Dictionary. If a word is present in the Dictionary or the User-Defined Dictionary, it is interpreted as a valid word and the Input Domain asks for the next word. If a word in not present in either dictionary, it is forwarded to the Error Domain.

All of the Knowledge Sources (Left-Right Character Shifter, Character Doubler, End Character Appender, Character Remover and Subsequent Character Switcher) attempt to correct the erroneous word based on their algorithms. For example, for the given erroneous word, the Knowledge Sources' algorithms will

Table 1. An example of generated suggestions

Knowledge Source	Erroneous Word	Generated Suggestions
Left-Right Character Shifter	jod	his, pkf
Character Appender	hai	haia, haib, haic, haid, haie, haif, haig, haih haij, haik, hail, haim, haio, haip, haiq, hair hais, hait, haiu, haiv, haiw, haix, haiy, haiz
Character Doubler	ben	bben, been, benn
Character Remover	caree	aree, cree, caee, care
Subsequent Character Switcher	hta	tha, hat

generate the words shown in Table 1. Note that these are not the suggestions that the user will see since only the words that pass the dictionary comparison test will be displayed.

Each Knowledge Source generates the above words as suggestions and forwards them to the Evaluation Domain. Along with these suggestions, it also forwards its probability value. The Evaluation Domain receives this information, concatenates the suggestions and probability of all KSs and passes them to the Evaluator. The Evaluator receives these suggestions and compares each suggestion against the words in the dictionary. The suggestions that exist in the dictionary are displayed to the user. The order in which they appear is based on the probability associated with the particular KSs that generated the suggestions. Therefore, words associated with errors that appear more frequently will be above those that are less frequent.

The KSs receive notification in the form of a feedback from the Evaluator whether any word from their suggestion was selected or not. All inputs to and outputs from a KS, including feedback propagation, are shown in Figure 3. After receiving feedback, KSs update their probability values according to the following formula:

$$P(t+1) = c \pm \frac{1}{N}$$

If the suggestion is accepted by the user, the probability increases, otherwise it decreases. Note that the selection of the default suggestion is based on the relative value of the probability with respect to the probabilities of other Knowledge Sources, and not just on the absolute value.

5   Measuring Adaptability

To assess the adaptability of the SSCS, we employed a "black box" approach by sending an identical input file to two systems and comparing the outputs; the first system is the SSCS, with the adaptability mechanism, and the second system is without any adaptability mechanism. We ran the same set of tests independently on the two systems using the same input words and selecting

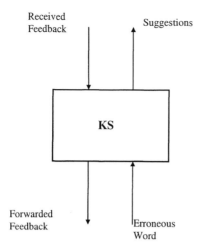

Received Feedback

Suggestions

KS

Forwarded Feedback

Erroneous Word

Fig. 3. Inputs and Outputs of a Knowledge Source

words in the same order for both the adaptive and non-adaptive systems. Based on their respective outputs, we then calculated the probability that the correct word was presented at the top of the list. For measurement purposes, we made the following assumptions:

- User errors can be processed by at least one of the Knowledge Sources
- Cases where user-defined words are processed were not included, since most spell checkers have a similar capability and, therefore, adaptation does not present any differentiation.

The main idea of our tests is presented in Table 2. One of our goals was to obtain results in terms of the number of suggestions that are spread over a range of numbers. This is difficult to achieve when using a randomly selected text file. We also wanted to be able to test all of the Knowledge Sources in action. Again, in a randomly selected file this is not necessarily the case. For these reasons, and keeping in mind that our real goal was to evaluate the adaptability mechanism of our architecture, we decided to generate a text file with artificially constructed words that satisfy the requirements of our test. Similarly, we pre-selected the user's choice of correct words. The test cases produced 9, 12, 15 and 18 suggestions, as shown in Table 2.

A sample of output displays of the SSCS with an input word "bc" that generates 9 suggestions is shown in Table 3. The "*" indicates which word was selected from the list of suggestions.

The first nine suggestions were generated by the following Knowledge Sources:

"vx" and "nv"	Left/Right Character Shifter
"bbc" and "bcc"	Character Doubler
"bca" and "bcz"	End Character Appender
"c" and "b"	Character Remover
"cb"	Subsequent Character Switcher

Table 2. Examples of test cases (artificial words)

Input Text	Number of Suggestions	Suggested words
bc	9	vx, nv, bbc, bcc, bca, bcz, c, b, cb
bcd	12	vxs, nvf, bbcd, bccd, bcdd, bcda, bcdz, cd, bd, bc, cbd, bdc
bcde	15	vxsw, nvfr, bbcde, bccde, bcdde, bcdee, bcdea, bcdez, cde bde, bce, bcd, cbde, bdce, bced
bcdef	18	vxswd, nvfrg, bbcdef, bccdef, bcddef, bcdeef, bcdeff, bcdefa bcdefz, cdef, bdef, bcef, bcdf, bcde, cbdef, bdcef, bcedf, bcdfe

Table 3. Examples of displays

	First Display	Second Display	Third Display	Fourth Display
1:	nv	bbc	nv	c
2:	vx	bcc	vx	b
3:	bbc*	bca	bbc	nv
4:	bcc	bcz	bcc	vx
5:	bca	c	bca	bbc
6:	bcz	b	bcz	bcc
7:	c	nv	c*	bca
8:	b	vx*	b	bcz
9:	cb	cb	cb	cb
10:	Ignore All	Ignore All	Ignore All	Ignore All

At the first display, the user picks "bbc", which is generated by the Character Doubler. When the next time suggestions are presented to the user in the second display, suggested words generated by the Character Doubler appear before the words generated by the other KSs. The same behavior can be observed in the third and the fourth displays.

The kind of test cases as presented in this paper was used to measure the adaptability of the SSCS, and not to test its functionality. For the adaptability test cases, we fed the same word into the initiator four times, and selected a word generated by a different KS every time. Normally, this would not occur in real interactions with a spell checker, but this test case was chosen to emphasize the demonstration of the adaptability mechanism.

The results of our tests are summarized in Figure 4. This figure shows a reference curve (marked with diamonds) obtained under the assumption that a word from a list of suggestions appears on the top of the list of suggestions (as default) randomly, i.e., the probability is

$$P(N) = 1/N$$

This kind of behavior was actually observed in a system without adaptability. In Figure 4, this behavior is represented by the triangle symbols. The SSCS, on the other hand, exhibits a different behavior. The probability of a correct suggestion being on the top of the list of suggestions presented by the system to the user only slightly decreases with the number of generated suggestions.

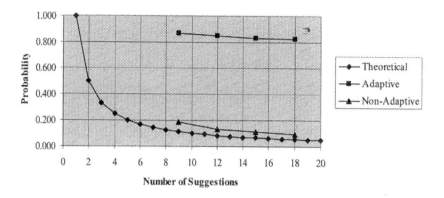

Fig. 4. Adaptability: Experimental Results

This is a desirable behavior, since it means that more knowledge sources can be added to the system without putting more burden on the user who otherwise would need to sift through a huge number of generated suggestions.

6   Conclusions and Future Research

The goal of the experiments presented in this paper was to demonstrate the usability of the idea of Adaptive Software Architecture [2–4] in constructing adaptive human-computer interfaces. As a case study, we selected the application of spell checking. The goal of the system was to pick the right word for a replacement of an erroneous word typed by the user and to adapt to the mistakes made by a particular user.

To achieve this goal, we mapped the ASA to the spell checking application, a Smart Spell Checking System (SSCS). Towards this goal, we had to select an instance of the architecture and populate particular components (Knowledge Sources) with domain specific knowledge. We implemented the system and tested it on various text files.

To evaluate the adaptability mechanism of the SSCS we developed a number of artificial test cases. The test cases consisted of artificial words, i.e., words that are normally not legal English words. We also generated annotations indicating which word was selected by the user as the right word. We ran this kind of tests and collected quantitative results that allowed us to develop characteristic curves of the SSCS, as shown in the paper. We ran the same experiments on the SSCS with the adaptive mechanism switched off. Additionally, we developed a theoretical performance curve of a non-adaptive system. We assumed that such a system would make its decisions randomly and thus the probability of right selection would depend only on the number of suggestions. This proved to be the behavior of our system without the adaptability mechanism.

Our adaptive system, on the other hand, performed much better and picked the right corrected word in more than 80% of the cases. Moreover, this kind of behavior was observed even with larger numbers of suggestions to pick from. The non-adaptive system's performance degraded significantly with the increased number of possible suggestions. This is a very encouraging result, since it indicates that the system can scale up to more Knowledge Sources. This feature is very important since the five Knowledge Sources developed in this experiment would not be sufficient for a real spell checker.

While the above implementation and results proved the possibility of building an adaptive spell checker, it is clear that more research surrounding the architecture and the adaptability measurement is needed. A more accurate measure of the SSCS's adaptability is to run the system using real words and using a full-fledged dictionary. The data points obtained from such a study would represent a more conclusive result as to how adaptable the system is.

It is clear that for a real spell checker more knowledge sources would need to be added. A larger number of KSs would produce more valid suggestions to the system and consequently would result in better coverage of spelling errors. At the same time the convergence to the real error distribution of a given user would become slower. The question of what is the convergence rate would have to be answered based on results collected using real human subjects rather than artificially generated text.

In order to make a decision on whether to use such an architecture in a real system one would need to first decide what should be the usability measure and then conduct more intensive studies to assess the impact of this kind of adaptability on the selected usability metric. One candidate for such a measure could be the time spent for correcting one error. This metric would tell what is the value added in terms of the productivity of people using this kind of spell checker. However, the goal of the study presented in this paper was merely to provide an indication of the adaptability of the proposed architecture. The spell checking application was just a case study to achieve this goal. Human factor studies were not within the scope of this research.

Acknowledgments

The authors would like to thank the members of the Software Engineering Project class for their work on the Adaptive Software Architecture: Bob Bamberg, Prasad Bandaru, Jianqing Huang, Amir Kompany, Tamnun Mursalin, Madhavi Narla, Firozur Rahman and Charles Tan.

References

1. K. J. Åström. *Adaptive Control*. Addison-Wesley, Reading, MA, 1989.
2. Y. A. Eracar. Raacr: A reconfigurable architecture for adapting to changes in the requirements. Master's thesis, Northeastern University, Boston, MA, 1996.

3. Y. A. Eracar and M. M. Kokar. An architecture for software that adapts to changes in requirements. *Journal of Systems and Software*, 50:209–219, 2000.

4. M. M. Kokar, K. Baclawski, and Y. Eracar. Control theory-based foundations of self-controlling software. *IEEE Intelligent Systems*, May/June 1999:37–45, 1999.

5. M. M. Kokar, K. M. Passino, K. Baclawski, and J. E. Smith. Mapping an application to a control architecture: Specification of the problem. *Lecture Notes in Computer Science*, 1936:75–89, 2001.

6. I. Mareels and J. W. Polderman. *Adaptive Systems: An Introduction*. Birkhauser, Boston, MA, 1996.

7. H. P. Nii. Blackboard systems. *AI Magazine*, (7(4)):82 – 107, 1986.

8. P. Robertson, H. Shrobe, and R. Laddaga. *Self-Adaptive Software. Lecture Notes in Computer Science, Volume 1936*. Springer-Verlag, 2001.

9. M. Schneider-Hufschmidt, T. Kuhme, and U. Malinowski. *Adaptive User Interfaces: Principles and Practices*. North-Holland, Amsterdam, The Netherlands, 1993.

10. K. P. Vaubel and C. F. Gettys. Inferring user expertise for adaptive interfaces. *Human Computer Interaction*, 5:95–117, 1990.

Design Principles for Resource Management Systems for Intelligent Spaces⋆

Krzysztof Gajos, Luke Weisman, and Howard Shrobe

MIT AI Lab, Cambridge, MA, USA
{kgajos,luke,hes}@ai.mit.edu
http://www.ai.mit.edu/projects/iroom/

Abstract. The idea of ubiquitous computing and smart environments is no longer a dream and has long become a serious area of research and soon this technology will start entering our every day lives. There are two major obstacles that prevent this technology from spreading. First, different smart spaces are equipped with very different kinds of devices (e.g. a projector vs. a computer monitor, vs. a TV set). Second, multiple applications running in a space at the same time inevitably contend for those devices and other scarce resources. The underlying software in a smart space needs to provide tools for self-adaptivity in that it shields the rest of the software from the physical constraints of the space, and that it dynamically adjusts the allocation of scarce resources as the number and priorities of active tasks change.

We argue that a resource manager can provide the necessary functionality. This paper presents a set of guiding principles for building high-level resource management tools for smart spaces. We present conclusions we arrived at after two years of exploring the topic in the Intelligent Room Project at the MIT AI Lab. The paper is based on a number of implemented and tested tools.

1 Introduction

For several years, our research group in the MIT AI Lab has been developing an "Intelligent Room" [8, 9, 5], a space that interacts with its users through sensory technologies such as machine vision, speech recognition and natural language understanding. Our room also is equipped with a rich array of multi-media technologies. These technologies are intended to provide a natural, human-centered interface to its users.

The Intelligent Room is designed to be a utility that must always be available and it must provide reasonable services to its users even though their needs are not easily predicted. It must continue to provide these services even if there are

---

⋆ The work presented here was supported in part by the Advanced Research Project Agency of the Department of Defense under contract number F30602–92–C0204, monitored through Rome Laboratory, and in part by the MIT Project Oxygen Alliance.

R. Laddaga, P. Robertson, and H. Shrobe (Eds.): IWSAS 2001, LNCS 2614, pp. 198–215, 2003.

equipment failures or if there is contention for the use of resources among the users or applications. It is also desirable that it be able to provide improved and additional services if higher quality equipment is added.

Finally, and most crucially to be truly human-centered it must be able to do all these things seemlessly while running, without intervention by programmers and systems wizards. In other words, the Intelligent Room must be a self-adaptive system in the spirit of [17, 16]. It must monitor the environment as well as its own state, have a variety of techniques for accomplishing its goals, and make intelligent choices about which technique to use in the current context.

This paper describes our experience with building such a system. The key insights are:

1. People should interact with the Intelligent Room not in terms of resources, but rather in terms of abstract services (e.g. "show me this information" rather than "print this on that printer")
2. The Intelligent Room should be capable of mapping a service request to a variety of solutions ("project the information," "display it on a PDA," "print it on a printer")
3. The Intelligent Room should choose a solution based both on how well the solution meets the users' needs and how well it minimizes the use of costly or rare resources and
4. It should make this decision at runtime so that it can respond to a changing set of requests and a changing environment.

1.1   What Is a Resource Manager for a Smart Space

What we mean by a resource manager is a system capable of performing two fundamental tasks: *resource mapping* and *arbitration* .

By resource mapping (a.k.a. match-making) we mean the process of finding out what actual resources can be taken into consideration given a specific request.

By arbitration we mean a process of making sure that, at a minimum, resources are not being used beyond their capacities. At best, arbitration ensures–via appropriate allocation of resources to requests–optimal, or nearly optimal, use of scarce resources.

This paper is concerned with management of higher-level resources. While OS level management (memory, CPU time, etc.) is of course important, and load-balancing of computationally intensive agents over multiple machines is also, we limit our focus to higher-level resources such as physical devices and large software components (see [28] and [22] for an example of a system that deals with resources in a smart spaces at the OS level). Our concerns lie with, for example, projectors, multiplexors, wires, displays, modems, user attention, software programs, screen real estate, sound input and output devices, CD players, drapes, and lamps.

1.2 Some Definitions

For clarity, we define here some potentially ambiguous terms.

Metaglue. Metaglue [10, 21, 26] is the multi-agent system forming the software base for all work at the Intelligent Room Project. Metaglue manages agent-to-agent communication via Java's RMI system. Agents can start and obtain references to other agents via a `reliesOn` method. All agents have unique IDs; part of an ID is the "occupation" which is the top-level interface the agent implements. Agents are also collected in societies so multiple users and spaces can have distinct name-spaces. Metaglue makes it easy to coordinate the startup and running of agents on any number of machines with differing operating systems.

Agent. Agents are distinct object instances capable of providing services and making requests of the resource manager. This means agents themselves are considered to be a type of resource (see below) because they provide services.

Device. A physical or logical device is something akin to a projector, screen, or user-attention; devices are often, but not necessarily represented by agents. Devices provide services and so are resources.

Service. Services are provided by agents and devices; a single agent or device can provide more than one service and any kind of service can be provided by a number of agents or devices. This is explained in more detail in Section 4.1.

Resource. A resource is a provider of a service. Both agents and physical devices are resources. For example, a physical LED sign is a resource (providing the LED sign hardware service) obtained and used by the `LEDSignText` Agent which is in turn a resource (providing `TextOuput` service and `LEDSign` service) that can be obtained and used by any other agent needing such a service.

2 Our Work to Date

This paper is based on our work on the Intelligent Room Project [8, 9, 5] at the MIT AI Lab, including otherwise unpublished research on resource management. Below we summarize our results relevant to this paper in order to give the reader a better idea of how we arrived at our observations.

Over the past two years we have developed several resource management tools for the Intelligent Room. The tools differed in approach and level of sophistication. At the two extremes we have Namer and Rascal [15]. Namer only does context-based name resolution (i.e. some service mapping but no arbitration). Rascal, on the other hand, is a very complex system that uses a rule-based language (JESS, [13]) for representing knowledge about agents' services and needs, as well as for service mapping, and uses a constraint satisfaction engine (JSolver, [7]) for arbitration. All of our resource managers implement a common interface which allows us to interchange them without changing any of the other code in the system. The reason for having several different resource management schemes was motivated by more than just the need to find the right solution: it is our assumption that different resource mangers will be used in people's various mobile personal spaces (with one or two devices and where computation is scarce) and large and well-equipped static spaces.

As mentioned before, Rascal is our most complex resource manager, conforming to most of the design principles laid out in this paper. Currently Rascal does not deal with issues of privacy and access control and we have only just began work on cooperation mechanisms.

Rascal relies on agents having external descriptions of themselves. Such descriptions include a list of startup needs, a list of provided services (each with a list of its own needs) and descriptions of all possible requests for resources the agent may make in its life-cycle.

Knowing startup needs and needs for providing particular services allows Rascal to ensure that before it assigns a particular agent to provide a service in response to a request, all of the needs of that new agent (and its underlings) can be satisfied. For example, if some agent requests a TextOutput device and the possible candidates are SpeechTextOutput and GuiTextOutput, Rascal will ensure that either speech generation is available for SpeechTextOutput or a computer screen is available for GuiTextOutput, before assigning either candidate to the requester. Additionally, knowing agent's startup needs also allows us to dynamically choose what particular machine an agent should be started on.

So far our software has been installed in six spaces of four different kinds: three small offices, one small living room, one large office (also used for small meetings), and a twelve-seat conference room. The instrumentation of these spaces varies widely; we have a single dilapidated projector and a couple of lights in one of the small offices on one hand, and six projectors and a large number of A/V devices in the conference room on the other. Our living room has two projectors, a TV, several cameras, and A/V equipment.

3 On-Demand Agent Startup – Reasoning about Absent Agents

An agent system in a smart space should have a way of autonomously starting agents on-demand and consequently the resource manager should be able to reason about agents that are not alive right now but could be brought to life if needed.

Because on-demand agent startup is one of the basic features of Metaglue, we have taken it for granted but many other agent systems do not support it. Hence we will now briefly argue why on-demand agent startup is a desirable feature of an agent system in charge of a smart space and then discuss the consequences for resource management.

3.1 Why Support On-Demand Agent Startup in Smart Spaces

Most agent systems deal with very dynamic, spontaneously created and often unstable collections of agents. Therefore, creators of such systems have to refrain from making assumptions about what is available in the system at any given time and usually have to resort to dynamic discovery, direct negotiation or other such techniques when an agent looks for a service or resource (e.g. [18, 23, 12]). This general attitude has been assumed by creators of agent systems controlling smart spaces. Standard Jini [2] implementation and Hive [20] are good examples of such systems.

Smart spaces, by the virtue of being based on stable physical environments, impose a special set of constraints on the underlying software infrastructure. It is true that a lot of adaptivity is still needed – new components can appear and disappear, people come and go, devices are brought in and removed–but at the same time we benefit from assuming certain level of persistence.

It is a feature of a physical space that most of its components are static in the sense that they are usually there. If one day a space contains lights, A/V equipment, projectors, and telephones, it is reasonable to expect that those devices would be present the next day as well. They will be there whether we are using them or not. This level of predictability can (and should) be reflected by the underlying software infrastructure. This is not to say, of course, that the software should not be capable of dynamically accepting new components.

On-demand agent startup is highly useful in any flexible space in a variety of ways. For example, it allows us to make multiple instances of an agent when we want to perform several versions of the same task. Furthermore, it allows us to have very complex interrelationships between agents and very large numbers of agents. Without on-demand startup one needs to craft elaborate startup scripts or hand-start all the agents in the system; both of these are infeasible when talking about collections of forty agents or more, especially when considering that the particular agents change depending on who is starting the system, the various tasks the system is to accomplish, and the room the system is being started in.

With on-demand startup, starting a single high level agent is sufficient to obtain a service provided by that agent. This agent will then request and, cause to be started, all other agents it needs in order to do its job well.

Even with the convenience argument set aside, the following example illustrates some additional benefits of being able to start agents dynamically.

Example 1. Let us assume that the phone service is provided by the phone agent. The agent needs a computer with a voice modem hooked up to a phone line in order to provide its services. Imagine a system consisting of several machines with voice modems hooked up to a single phone line (e.g. in a shared graduate student office). If we did not allow for on-demand agent startup, we would have to do one of the following:

1. Start the phone agent on a prespecified machine, running a risk that if that machine goes down the service is no longer available.
2. Start an instance of the phone agent on every machine with a voice modem and a connection – a rather misleading solution because each of the agents would be advertising phone service but only one of them would be able to provide it at a time because all of the machines share a single phone line.

Another immediate use for automatic agent startup has to do with robustness and recovery: if an agent providing a computational service goes down because of computer failure, it can be automatically restarted at a new location.

We understand that this point has much potential for debate, and so we will not dwell it as other aspects for and against it lie outside the realm of resource management.

3.2   Impact on Resource Management

If we assume that on-demand agent startup is supported by the underlying software architecture, then it stands to reason that the resource manager for such a system has to be able to reason about absent agents.

To the best of our knowledge, it is uncommon in agent architectures, even those in charge of smart spaces, to have non-alive agents be taken into account during any coordination efforts. It is our belief that taking potentially available agents into account allows a resource management system to make intelligent decisions about resource allocation as in Example 1 in the previous section. (See also Example 2 in Section 4.3.)

An important consequence of embracing on-demand agent startup is that we cannot rely on agents themselves to provide descriptions of their needs and services as they might not be running. The resource manager has to have access to such descriptions without having to instantiate any of the agents. Rascal requires agent programmers to create separate description files but other solutions could easily be created (e.g. descriptions could be cached by the resource manager).

Implicit in Example 1 in the previous section is the assumption that the system, and in particular the resource manager, has a way of starting agents on a specific computer or virtual machine. Metaglue provides such capability as one of its two main primitives. It is unclear to us at the moment to what extent other systems support it.

4   Representation

In this section we concentrate on what knowledge should be contained in the resource manager but not on how that knowledge should be encoded. In particular we argue that when building a resource manager for a smart space, the following key points should be observed:

- Represent resources in terms of the services they provide (e.g. text output) as well as their type (e.g. scrolling LED sign).
- Ensure that representations are rich enough to allow the requesters to get *the best* tools for the job. In particular we caution those using Java against using only interface names for describing resources.
- Ensure that the representation is capable of describing resources that are not represented within the agent systems by agents or other special proxy objects. Examples of such resources would be hardware that is not directly

controlled by the agent system but yet is crucial for system's performance (e.g. wires, low level computer components such as modems, third party software modules, etc.)

4.1 Services not Devices

To be truly useful, smart spaces have to be affordable, which implies that it should be possible to build them out of mass produced, interconnected components. This includes both the hardware and the software. Hence we can imagine that in the future we will be getting packaged software for our rooms and offices just as today we get it for our desktop computers. Creating such programs, however, may prove very difficult.

It is already difficult to keep desktop computers similar enough to make it possible for the same software to run on all of them. It will certainly be even more difficult when it comes to smart spaces. People take great pride in how they arrange their work and living environments and so creators of software for smart spaces cannot impose how those spaces should be arranged or equipped. While software creators for desktop computers can require that a computer should be equipped with a display, a CD-ROM and a sound card, they certainly cannot require the same level of uniformity among smart spaces. Thus we have to make it possible for applications to run in a variety of spaces with diverse devices and configurations.

The differences among desktop computers have been minimized by the use of software drivers for various devices installed in those computers. Hence, it does not matter what kind of a video card or a monitor one has - the drivers are going to make all cards and monitors "speak the same language" and provide the same services to all applications.

In intelligent spaces the situation will be even more difficult: not only will spaces have different kinds of displays, ranging from little TVs to large plasma displays, but some spaces may not have displays at all. Thus we have to express the abilities of various devices in smart environments in more abstract terms. As well as providing uniform interfaces to devices, as is done on desktop computers, we propose providing uniform interfaces to the services provided by those devices. This distinction is more profound than it may at first appear. It comes from the fact that each service can, in principle, be provided by a number of conceptually different devices and each device can provide a number of distinct services. For example, on one hand, the "short-text-output" service may be rendered by a computer display device, a speech output device or by a one line scrolling-LED display. On the other hand, the LED sign, as well as providing short text display, can provide simple graphics and animation.

We are not unique in suggesting that devices represented by device drivers are insufficient for a smart space; a somewhat different approach was suggested by Winograd [27]. Schubiger-Banz et al. [25] argue for "addressing by concept" in all ubiquitous computing environments (both spaces and/or collections of mobile devices). INS [1] uses "intentional names" for all networked resources. EasyLiving [6] also seems to represent resources in terms of services they provide.

4.2   Rich Representation – Rich Requests

We now examine how the services should be represented by the resource manager. The details are, of course, dependent on the particular implementation.

Open Agent Architecture OAA [19], which relies on a facilitator agent for all inter-agent communication and task brokerage, uses a PROLOG-based ICL (Interagent Communication Language) for describing agents' needs and capabilities. The language allows service providers to describe the agents in terms of tasks they can perform and not really in terms of resources they represent.

Decker [11] uses KQML for communicating needs and abilities of agents.

A common tendency among Java-based systems (e.g. Jini [2], Hive [20], Rascal [15, 14]), is to use the name of the interface (or interfaces) that the resource implements, and a list of attribute-value pairs for describing agents' capabilities.

In this last case, an agent's interface provides information on how the agent's capabilities should be invoked. It also often provides most of the information on what the agent does. One of the advantages of using interface names for describing agents is that interface "ontologies", i.e. APIs, are easily understood by programmers and some of them get adopted by large communities. But it has to be stressed again, that the interfaces should provide access to agent's services. Thus an agent can advertise a number of interfaces, one for each services it provides.

We agree with designers of Hive and Jini in that the types of interfaces implemented by an agent provide a lot of valuable information about agent's capabilities and expected behavior. We also agree with them in that the interface names are not sufficient for describing any agent fully.

Just having interfaces and nothing else be an agent's description is not enough. Often a number of parameters, some of them continuous, contribute to a service's full description. Display services need to be described in terms of resolution, size, color depth, brightness, etc. Having detailed descriptions of services allows for more precise requests: an agent that needs to show a map with a lot of detail, will request a high-resolution color display, not just a display. At the same time, a mail alert agent could deal with a very low resolution display as long as it is visible and so would ask for the display without additional parameters.

4.3   Abstract Resources

One important feature that distinguishes multi agent systems in charge of smart spaces from other multi agent systems is that they reside on the frontier between the physical and computational worlds. To function well, those systems have to not only accept but also embrace the physical world around them (we refer to this point again in Section 8).

As a consequence of this, it becomes necessary for the system to explicitly describe not only the services provided by its agents but also those provided by physical hardware and non-agent software present on available computers.

A common approach to this problem is to add agents to represent all needed physical and computational capabilities of the host environment. Hive, for example, uses "shadows" to represent physical devices accessible on or from particular computers. Metaglue has agents that represent individual devices. But how do we know where to start those shadows or agents? An unsatisfactory way is when startup has to be done by a human or by a script leaving the system with no way of reasoning about it or taking action on its own. In case of Metaglue, the device-controlling agents upon startup retrieve the name of a computer they should tie themselves to. In our view, the agents that directly interact with hardware or other software should be able to start dynamically (see Section 3) and dynamically find the computers with all necessary equipment and software.

Example 2. Currently in our system, the main way of providing the speech-input service is with personal wireless microphones connected to computers running third party speech recognition software. In our conference room we have several computers with the right software, several microphones, and an audio mixer that allows us to route microphone signal to any of the computers.

When any of our agents requests speech-input service, Rascal, our resource manager, checks the description of our speech input agent for all of the services that it will need to provide the service. Those will include a computer with a speech recognition engine, a microphone, and a connection between the two. Neither the speech recognition engine nor the microphones have software proxies in our agent systems yet the resource manager is able to reason about them. Rascal ensures that the speech-input agent starts on a computer with the right speech recognition engine and will award a microphone that is not being used for other tasks (e.g. teleconferencing) to the agent, and will ensure that there exists a connection between the two (see Section 8 for discussion of connections).

5   Arbitration

At the heart of resource management is arbitration. By our definition of a resource manager, when two or more agents vie for the same limited resource, the resource manager has to evaluate which gets what.

In this section we argue that arbitration is essential in any larger system embedded in a smart space because it allows individual agents and applications to be written without having to take other agents' and applications' needs into considerations. It also provides for the most basic (but not the simplest) apparently smart behavior of a space. Some arbitration schemes applicable in open agent systems, such as marked-based resource allocation, will prove less effective. Cost-benefit based on self-reported needs and preferences has proven a good solution especially when combined with access control (which limits requests by untrusted and potentially malicious or non-conforming agents).

In addition, in cases where a resource needs to be taken away from a requester to satisfy a new, more urgent, request, every effort should be made to find a replacement for the withdrawn resource.

5.1 Why Arbitrate

Arbitration allows for easier implementation of individual agents: the agent writer can view the world more selfishly than if there was no arbitration mechanism. With arbitration in place, the agent programmer can be sure that if any other agent needs resources more, the system will take care of necessary re-allocations (just like in properly multitasking operating systems programmers do not need to worry about yielding to other processes).

Another (obvious) benefit of arbitration is achieving apparent "intelligent" behavior of a space. Just like animals are expected to use their body parts intentionally and in a coordinated fashion, we also expect computer-steered spaces to be "aware" of the interface devices.

5.2 How to Arbitrate

The simplest way of resolving ties among requests is to award a resource to the most recent request. For many reasons this may prove to be insufficient. For example it would not be desirable for a new email notification to take over a screen during a video conference with one's boss. Hence there exists need for some analysis before allocating resources. Rascal, for example, uses a simple cost-benefit analysis (details in [15, 14]) to decide who should be awarded a particular service. This scheme relies on agents accurately and honestly reporting how urgently they need a resource. This approach is potentially problematic in that it allows for malicious or inaccuarate representation of one's needs.

A more natural and simple approach to arbitration in potentially open systems in smart spaces seems to be one in which some access control mechanism is used in conjunction with some priority-based scheme. In such a situation the access control mechanism would weed out requests from untrusted and unauthorized agents and then a priority mechanism would decide which of the trusted and authorized requesters should get what resources. In a model where agents can act on behalf of spaces or people, the role-based access control model [24] seems a viable option. We discuss the need for access control further in Section 10.1.

Other approaches had been developed with open systems in mind, notably some based on market mechanisms [3, 4]. Those approaches require existence of a central "bank" and some sort of currency. Such approaches, in their natural form, are not well suited for smart environments. It should not be possible, for example, for someone thousands of miles away to buy control of the room with their extra virtual currency.

Because resource managers can take resources away from requesters, it is reasonable for a requester to keep a resource even after finishing a task if it expects it may need the resource again in near future. For example, a email notification agent may want to keep its output channel as it is desirable for the sake of consistency in space's behavior for those notifications to come through the same channel unless there is a good reason to change.

5.3   Arbitration Should Allow for Clever Re-allocations

Consider the following scenario: a space is equipped with a TV set, LCD projector, VCR, video mux, and some computers. The VCR (that also acts as a TV receiver) can be connected to either the projector or to the TV set through the video mux. The computer, however, can only be connected to the projector.

The user is watching the news on the projector, this being the best resource to satisfy a request for a large display. Then the user hears some really important news and decides to share it with a friend while watching the rest of the newscast and so she requests her email agent. With our simpler resource management schemes in place, the projector would be taken away from the news and allocated to the email agent. The more desirable behavior, in this situation, would be for the newscast to be moved over to the TV set and the email to be then displayed on the projector.

The point here is that in many cases the only way to accommodate a new request is to take a resource away from one of the currently active requests. The disturbance can often be minimized, however, by reallocating the old request to a different service. The insight here is that the sets of services that can satisfy various requests overlap only partially and the relationships are often more complex than just proper inclusion (see Figure 1). The reason for it is two-fold: first, different kinds of devices can provide different sets of services; second, physical connections for different kinds of signals are routed differently (so, for example, in one of our spaces the video signal goes through a multiplexer and thus can be connected to either of the projectors or to a TV set, while VGA connections are hard wired).

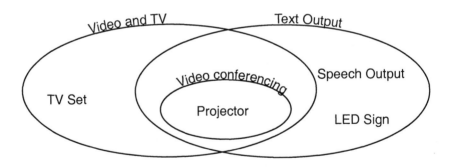

Fig. 1. Different kinds of tasks can be performed with different but overlapping possible sets of devices: both the TV set and the projector can be used for watching videos or tv while only the projector can be used for teleconferencing. At the same time, the projector, the LED sign or the speech output can be used for text output.

Allowing for re-allocations makes arbitration among requests much more complex: whenever a resource manager receives a request for a resource, it has to look for a solution that satisfies not only the new request but all of the old ones as well (as far as possible). In other words, a simple task of selecting the best resource for a request turns into a global constraint satisfaction problem.

One point to keep in mind, of course, is that re-allocations are costly. If we move the newscast from a projector to a TV,the user is bound to find it distracting. In some cases disturbance will be minimal, for example a mail notification agent will not mind a re-allocation if it happens between notifications—the next time it will simply use a different output device. It's more serious in case of agents that may have to rebuild a lot of their state after re-allocation. Some examples of this would be a camera which was carefully focused on a face or area of the room, or an Internet browser with all of its browser history.

Reasoning about the cost of a re-allocation has to be a part of the overall arbitration process. In Rascal, requesters can specify how costly a re-allocation would be to them and the cost can vary between zero and the cost of taking the service away altogether. The cost of a re-allocation in Rascal has two components: the fixed cost specified by the requester and the difference in utility between the new request and the old request (with the stipulation that it cannot be smaller than zero).

6 Ownership of Resources over Time (Resources vs. Tasks)

In this section we argue that many of the services provided by agents in a smart space (e.g. display service provided by a projector) are not tasks and therefore they should be managed differently from tasks. In particular requesters should be given ownership of resources over periods of time. Agents need to own their resources as they are often engaged in long-term jobs that can be changed or modified. We discuss all of this by comparing what we mean by resource management with task management performed by the faciliator agent in the Open Agent Architecture (OAA) [19].

Open Agent Architecture (OAA) is a good example of an agent system that could control a smart space and that also has a complex inter-agent facilitation scheme. What needs stressing, however, is that the OAA "facilitator agent" actually performs *task* management and not *resource* management. That is, the facilitator agent will break down a task into simpler sub tasks and allocate those to individual agents who can fulfill them best. It will not, however, ensure that all of the resources needed for the tasks are available and not in use by other agents. Hence OAA is well suited for a task like sending the current Boston weather report to all of requester's friends. The task will be broken into components, appropriate information obtained and message sent. OAA is not well suited for tasks that cannot be thought of as point-like in time. Implicit in the OAA model is the assumption that agents can never conflict over the use of scarce resources. Task management is, of course, very important but in a system that controls a physical space with a large number of scarce resources task management should work hand in hand with a resource manager.

It is more natural to think of many agents as having a life cycle, and going independently about their own long-term jobs. For example, an agent listening to and recording conversations in the room in order to be able to bring back audio snippets via keyword searching, needs resources over an extended period of time to complete its job. Showing a movie can be thought of as a task but it can be interrupted, modified, or abandoned in the middle. It can also prevent other agents from using a display for their jobs. In that sense, showing a movie is different from the OAA view of a task.

7   Third Party Resource Request Annotation

Once the core resource management system is in place, it should be easy to write modules that do specific types of reasoning and then use that reasoning to annotate requests to limit or reassess possible matches. Often knowledge of the world has direct impact on the appropriate nature of a specific resource to a specific request–this knowledge being outside either the resource manager's realm of expertise or the requesting agent's knowledge–and it is imparative that it be easy to have a third party entity contribute such knowledge.

For example, say a user is in a particular room and desires to play a song via his SongPlayer agent. The user would start his agent that would then ask for and locate the bits of the given file, and then attempt to gain access to another agent which would play the actual file. This, of course, would be a resource request for an agent with the ability to play sound.

However, there is also another criterion to the desired agent: location. If the user has been wandering from room to room, it is important that the sound playing agent used be in the room the user is in. This is knowledge that needs to be appended to the request, but neither the resource manager nor the song requesting agent would appropriately have this knowledge.

It would be a violation of normal notions of modularity if the SongPlayer agent had to check the user's location and annotate its resource request. It also seems unwieldy for the resource manager to be responsible for finding and maintaining this knowledge; certainly if this knowledge were in the resource manager's domain, then much other knowledge would be as well. Furthermore, the nature of a flexible agent system is knowledge itself is unlikely to be codified in a universal standard, and so the resource manager would be responsible for translating the output of various other agents into proper resource request annotations. Solving this problem is definitely an active area of research, but in this case it make for a massively large and unwieldy project in the writing of the resource manager.

The best solution we found is to have third party agents that extend the functionality of the resource manager. Authors write agents or functions which pattern match on resource requests and add then additional criterion to those requests as appropriate. In the example above, a distinct other agent which tracks the user eavesdrops on all resource requests and annotates any relevant ones to only consider physically local possibilities.

Request annotations should be able to happen in two ways. The first is modifying the request before a list of possible matches is generated. The second method is filtering the possible matches at the tail-end of the process, after the list of possible resources has been generated. Regardless of method, third party annotators allow for a real componotization of the agents; without them either one or the other agent on any given transaction needs to know too much about the significance of the job at hand. The idea is to have dumb objects wired together smartly to get thinking results, not to have heavyweight objects that are hard to write or maintain.

A further advantage of third party annotators is being able to provide the room with a way of dynamically adapting to equipment failures by writing modules that extended reasoning about certain particular resource allocation problems. For example, if we had an agent that could tell if a projector was broken by looking at the screen with a stearable camera, we could easily have an agent update the resource manager so all resource requests for projectors automatically remove that projector from consideration.

Furthermore, having the ability to have third party annotators should, we hope, serve nicely in the future when contemplating adding large features to the system such as access control (see Section 10.1). Once the model of requesting resources and receiving them is established, pretty much anything can be thought of as modifying or changing the appropriateness of a given resource to a given request–namely annotating a preexisting request.

8 Connections

One style of resource that deserves special attention are connections. Connections are a vital piece of the background of a smart space, and a system with a resource manager that fails to manage them is bound to end up in serious trouble.

The way our room is wired, we have several muxes and switches allowing for information to flow from source devices (cameras, VCRs, microphones) to output devices (projectors, TV sets, modems). Computers are also integrated into this web as either sources or sinks. We also have some trunk wires connecting muxes to muxes, for example, which can only carry one signal at a time. This, of course, is a limited resource. We are a long way from the time when the optimal carrier of all information signals (audio, video, etc.) is the same Ethernet, and until then we need to take into account the specialized wires in an intelligent space. This often means we do not have a fully connected graph of signal sources and sinks, and so the physical connections themselves are a limited resource that needs management.

Due to this, we enter all our connections into the manager as "connection resources". When an agent requests, say, a VCR and projector combination, they also request the collection of resources consisting of the path of connections leading from the VCR to the projector.

We keep the connection aspects of the system very much behind the scenes as an extension to the resource manager. Just because they are a crucial piece does not mean that they need to be in the forefront of a high-level agent programmer's attention. Agents can just ask for resources with the caveat that they are connected, and do not look at the resources involved in the connecting itself at all. The connection extension to the resource manager forges the actual path.

9 Special Requests

We have discovered a need for a few "special requests" for resources that seem to lie a bit outside the parameters discussed above. Happily, these are extensions of above, and can be added layers on top of the existing system. We will briefly discuss them in the following sub-sections.

9.1 "Screen Saver"

Many agents may want to use resources for a low-level background effect if the resources are not being used for something else. For example, the news ticker or weather forecast agent may want to use the LED sign if there is no better use for it.

The "Screen Saver" type of request gets automatically re-filled after the resource is taken away, used, and then released by some other agent. It is a way of the agent saying, in effect, "I want these resources whenever they are free. If you take them away, then give them back when they become free again."

The advantage of this approach is that it prevents a busy wait on the agent's side. Without "Screen Saver" requests, an agent would have to poll the resource manager from when it has lost its resource until it obtains it again.

An alternative solution would be to have blocking requests, which would also work. We have not closely examined this option, however.

9.2 Auto Upgrade

When a resource being used by an application is released, it is worth checking to see if other agents would be better served by getting that resource now that it is available. Agents can specially request that they do not mind being switched to a better resource at any time.

9.3 High-Urgency Short-Term Loans

Some requests are for more task-oriented reasons. In these cases, a resource may be needed only for a brief moment. For example, an alert agent might briefly need the speakers of the room to inform a room occupant that there is a call waiting. If the occupant was watching a movie, it would be much more smooth if the alert agent could just borrow the audio for a moment and then give it back. Without borrowing, the original agent would have to re-request the lost resources, and again we would have the polling situation described in the previous sub-section 9.1.

Loans, of course, make cost analysis in the resource manager even more difficult and we have found no easy answers as of yet.

10 Future

In this section we talk about two issues in resource management in smart spaces that we have identified as important but have not yet researched in depth.

10.1 Access Control

The real world is full of access control mechanisms. In particular, there are many ways in which access to spaces and enclosed equipment is restricted to certain people. The same is true of information. It stands to reason that agents acting on behalf of people should be subject to similar constraints their owners. If Alice does not have a key to Bob's office, then she is probably not supposed to be able to use his VCR either. We can take this parallel a step further and introduce some more interesting problems.

All members of our lab have a right to enter our conference room. They also have the right to control all of the a/v equipment, the lights, etc. To what extent should this right be extended to their electronic proxies? Should people be granted access to the devices when they are not physically present in a space, e.g. while on a trip to a faraway country? Should the access to the devices only be granted to authorized people on the condition that they are physically present in the space?

If we assume that physical presence is required of most people, let us take another scenario into consideration. Our research group has a meeting and one of the members is in a different city and needs to teleconference with us. During the meeting she needs to show us some of her results. Should she then be allowed to control our projectors and our slide show software? Should telepresence be treated equally with physical presence? Should perhaps one of the people physically present at the meeting grant her the permission? If so, who should have the rights to grant permissions to others?

As we said before, we are not clear yet how access control should be performed in a smart space but we are quite certain that the resource manager would have to be a part of the process. After all, it is the resource manager that grants agents access to particular resources. Thus the resource manager needs to be able to find out what resources the requester has rights to.

10.2 Cooperation

As research on smart spaces progresses, it becomes more and more likely that several spaces will be controlled by the same software. A number of people will be moving from one smart space to another and will expect to be able to make various requests in those spaces. They will also expect some of their agents to "follow" them. Building a single resource manager that would manage resources of all the spaces and all the people is clearly impractical. hence, there will have to be a number of resource managers, each representing a particular collection of resources and requesters. Given that spaces may border with each other or be enclosed by one another, and also given that agents acting on behalf of people will need to use resources provided by spaces, it is necessary for resource managers to communicate with one another to perform optimal resource allocation.

11   Contributions

We have outlined a number of issues that we found to be important in the design
of high-level resource management systems for smart spaces. Smart spaces are a
relatively new research area and few projects have reached a point where resource
management would become critical. We believe, however, that all projects will
eventually face these problems once their basic infrastructure is in place and
multiple, independently developed, applications are being ran in a space at the
same time.

Acknowledgments

Many people have contributed to the research presented here. In particular
Stephen Peters has provided us with a lot of help in implementing and testing some of the experimental resource management software. Stephen is also
working on representing multiple users and multiple spaces in our system. Rat-
tapoom Tuchinda is currently researching the issues of privacy and access control
in smart spaces.

References

1. W. Adjie-Winoto, E. Schwartz, H. Balakrishnan, and J. Lilley. The design and
   implementation of an intentional naming system. In *17th ACM Symposium on
   Operating Systems Principles (SOSP)*, Kiawah Island, SC, December 1999.
2. Ken Arnold, Bryan O'Sullivan, Robert W. Scheifler, Jim Waldo, and Ann Wollrath.
   The Jini Specification. Addison-Wesley, Reading, MA, 1999.
3. Jonathan Bredin, David Kotz, Daniela Rus Rajiv T. Maheswaran, Çagri Imer, and
   Tamer Basar. A market-based model for resource allocation in agent systems. In
   Franco Zambonelli, editor, *Coordination of Internet Agents*. Springer-Verlag, 2000.
4. Jonathan Bredin, Rajiv T. Maheswaran, Çagri Imer, Tamer Basar, David Kotz,
   and Daniela Rus. A game-theoretic formulation of multi-agent resource allocation. In *Proceedings of the Fourth International Conference on Autonomous Agents*,
   pages 349–356, June 2000.
5. Rodney Brooks. The intelligent room project. In *Proceedings of the Second International Cognitive Technology Conference (CT'97)*, Aizu, Japan, August 1997.
6. Meyers B. Krumm J. Kern A. Brumitt, B. and S. Shafer. Easyliving: Technologies
   for intelligent environments. In *Handheld and Ubiquitous Computing*, September
   2000.
7. Hon Wai Chun. Constraint programming in java with jsolver. In *First International
   Conference and Exhibition on The Practical Application of Constraint Technologies
   and Logic Programming*, London, April 1999.
8. Michael Coen. Building brains for rooms: Designing distributed software agents. In
   Ninth Conference on Innovative Applications of Artificial Intelligence (IAAA97),
   Providence, RI, 1997.
9. Michael Coen. Design principles for intelligent environments. In *Fifteenth National
   Conference on Artificial Intelligence (AAAI98)*, Madison, WI, 1998.
10. Michael Coen, Brenton Phillips, Nimrod Warshawsky, Luke Weisman, Stephen Pe-
    ters, and Peter Finin. Meeting the computational needs of intelligent environments:
    The metaglue system. In *Proceedings of MANSE'99*, Dublin, Ireland, 1999.

11. Keith Decker, Mike Williamson, and Katia Sycara. Matchmaking and brokering. In *The Second International Conference on Multi-Agent Systems (ICMAS-96)*, 1996.

12. Jacques Ferber. *Multi-Agent Systems - An Introduction to Distributed Artificial Intelligence*. Addison-Wesley, Reading, MA, 1999.

13. Ernest J. Friedman-Hill. Jess, the java expert system shell. Technical Report SAND98-8206, Sandia National Laboratories, 1997.

14. Krzysztof Gajos. A knowledge-based resource management system for the intelligent room. Master's thesis, Massachusetts Institute of Technology, Cambridge, MA, 2000.

15. Krzysztof Gajos. Rascal - a resource manager for multi agent systems in smart spaces. In *Proceedings of CEEMAS 2001*. Springer, 2001. To appear.

16. Robert Laddaga. Active software. In Paul Robertson, Robert Laddaga, and Howard Shrobe, editors, *Self-Adaptive Software*, number 1936 in Lecture Notes in Computer Science. Springer, 2001.

17. Robert Laddaga, Paul Robertson, and Howard Shrobe. Results of the first international workshop on self adaptive. In Paul Robertson, Robert Laddaga, and Howard Shrobe, editors, *Self-Adaptive Software*, number 1936 in Lecture Notes in Computer Science. Springer, 2001.

18. Victor Lesser. Reflections on the nature of multi-agent coordination and its implications for an agent architecture. *Autonomous Agents and Multi-Agent Systems*, 1:89–111, 1998.

19. David L. Martin, Adam J. Cheyer, and Douglas B. Moran. The open agent architecture: A framework for building distributed software systems. *Applied Artificial Intelligence*, 13(1-2):91–128, January-March 1999.

20. Nelson Minar, Matthew Gray, Oliver Roup, Raffi Krikorian, and Pattie Maes. Hive: Distributed agents for networking things. In *Proceedings of ASA/MA '99, the First International Symposium on Agent Systems and Applications and Third International Symposium on Mobile Agents*, August 1999.

21. Brenton Phillips. Metaglue: A programming language for multi agent systems. Master's thesis, Massachusetts Institute of Technology, Cambridge, MA, 1999.

22. Manuel Roman and Roy H. Campbell. Gaia: Enabling active spaces. In *Proceedings of 9th ACM SIGOPS European Workshop*, Kolding, Denmark, September 2000.

23. Tuomas W. Sandholm. Distributed rational decision making. In Gerhard Weiss, editor, *Multiagent Systems - A Modern Approach to Distributed Artificial Intelligence*. MIT Press, Cambridge, MA, 1999.

24. Ravi Sandhu, Edward Coyne, Hal Feinstein, and Charles Youman. Role-based access control models. *IEEE Computer*, 29(2), February 1996.

25. Simon Schubiger, Sergio Maffioletti, Amine Tafat-Bouzid, and Béat Hirsbrunner. Providing service in a changing ubiquitous computing environment. In *Proceedings of the Workshop on Infrastructure for Smart Devices - How to Make Ubiquity an Actuality, HUC 2000*, September 2000.

26. Nimrod Warshawsky. Extending the metaglue multi agent system. Master's thesis, Massachusetts Institute of Technology, Cambridge, MA, 1999.

27. Terry Winograd. Interaction spaces for 21st century computing. In John Carroll, editor, *Human-Computer Interaction in the New Millenium*. Addison-Wesley, 2001.

28. Tonomori Yamane. The design and implementation of the 2k resource management system. Master's thesis, University of Illinois, Urbana, Illinois, 2000.

Adaptivity in Agent-Based Systems via Interplay between Action Selection and Norm Selection

Henry Hexmoor

Computer Science & Computer Engineering Department, Engineering Hall,
Room 313, Fayetteville, AR 72701
hexmoor@uark.edu

1 Introduction

Beyond the ability for adaptation to an environment, Self-Adaptive Software (SAS) embodies the capacity and the initiative to adapt its own behavior. The adaptation is due to a need to maintain a desired or a reference relationship between a set of input and output signals. We may loosely divide SAS into adaptor and adapted components. The adapted component has an ongoing relationship with the environment. The adaptor detects and evaluates the need for change in the operation of the adapted component. In anthropomorphic terms, this detection and evaluation involves the cognitive processes of introspection and assimilation. However, an artifact may only need a supervisory control module. In a hierarchical system, the idea of adapted and adaptor can be extended to several levels with the higher level adapting the function of lower level. Hierarchical architectural systems are well studied. However, self-adaptive software is more than hierarchical control or application of adaptive techniques such as neural nets or genetic approaches. SAS adaptation is at the mission level. To the extent it is adaptive, a SAS system perceives the environment, computes trends, and compares the system performance to the operationally defined reference metrics and not to concrete quantities. For instance, in a game of football, the coach monitors the game and each player very closely and decides on strategies and swapping players. The coach's decision is at the operational level. The coach as the adaptor component of the team understands nuances of the game and the overall state of the game at a global, functional level. But in its most general form, to understand the environment and to adjust to it is the wholly grail of AI.

We focus on agent-based systems, which represent an important class of potentially self-adaptive systems. An important paradigm in agent-based systems is to consider intentional notions of Belief, Desire, and Intention (BDI agents). BDI agents possess update/revision functions for each intentional component. Beliefs are adapted to the agent's current state of mind and changes in the environment. Desires or specific goals are adapted to the agent's beliefs and attuned with the changing environment. Intentions over specific actions are adapted agent' beliefs and desires. These adaptations create adaptivity for the agent at a behavior level called action selection. Action selection is a cognitive process of finding the most appropriate and the most relevant action to perform [12, 18, 19]. Adaptivity at the action selection is limited to individual rationality. Agents that operate among other agents must reason about other agents and possess social rationality. Coordination with other agents provides yet another form of adaptivity. Coordination strategies are varied among domains. In

R. Laddaga, P. Robertson, and H. Shrobe (Eds.): IWSAS 2001, LNCS 2614, pp. 216–226, 2003.
© Springer-Verlag Berlin Heidelberg 2003

this paper we will investigate selection of social norms as coordination strategy among agents.

Actions selected based on norms may be in conflict with action selected entirely on individual concerns, i.e, based on action selection. To avoid such a conflict, we suggest treating *action selection* as the adapted component and the *norm selection* as the adaptor, Figure 1. Here norm selection will suggest modes of action selection as normative patterns.

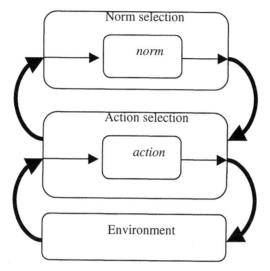

Fig. 1. Norm selection guides action selection

Interaction between layers is continuous. The following is a simplified outline of introducing norms to the agent's top-level decision-making loop. As the descriptions in the steps will illustrate, the interaction between layers is nontrivial. In general norm selection will be over a larger temporal horizon than action selection and in that respect, the process of action selection will cohere to adopted norms. Of course actions will need to be coherent but that is beyond this discussion. For a discussion of coherence see [21].

1. Perceive the environment and update beliefs in the world model. Both action selection and norm selection share the results of this process.
2. Consider options for individual goals, and norms. Adopt the most compatible goals and norms. I.e., processes of norm selection and action selection are concurrent and interacting but norm selection will be the dominant process.
3. Consider plans to implement adopted goals, and norms that lead to options for action selection. Both action selection and goal selection will inform planning. Subsequently, planning will determine actions to be performed.
4. Formulate intentions to act and perform planned actions.

The remainder of this paper begins with a discussion of norms and norm selection. This is followed by sections that take on utilitarian and intentional views of dealing with norms. We then feature teaming as a special class of norms. The paper ends with concluding remarks about self adativity in agent based systems.

2   Norm Selection Guides Action Selection

Selection of a normative pattern of interaction is often articulated by a person's discourse that cites predominant situated mental attitudes for choosing the normative pattern. For example, if you ask a person proctoring an exam "why are you monitoring your students so closely" the answer might be "I don't trust them they have cheated before". In this example, the person is engaged in a normative pattern of keeping a watchful eye on students and expresses that *trust* was the main reason for adopting this specific normative pattern. By exploring the connection between mental attitudes, normative patterns of interaction, and action selection we wish to develop agents that can self-adapt. We aim for a calculus over mental attitudes that will modify the agent's in-the-field decision making and lower the need for human supervision. Our model borrows from social human behavior. Human's ever-changing mental attitudes regulate selection of normative patterns needed for survival and success. The contribution to adaptive software is the understanding and algorithmic duplication of these mental attitudes. This paper is a preliminary report on developing computational framework that supports adaptation in software in similar ways that humans perform this task.

For a rational agent, action selection is guided by its situated attitude governing its relationship to its environment and other agents. But possessing social attitudes might be unnecessary for agents. In fact it might be argued that attitudes are absent in biological systems. For instance, it can be argued that a combination of behavioral pattern recognition, imitation, and instinctual attunement is sufficient to produce complex relationships such as teaming in Vervet monkeys[1]. We suggest that if an agent is allowed to have nontrivial autonomy about whether and how it will choose the complex relationship (such as teaming), it must be able to reason about mental ingredients that lead it in its choice and use of those relationships. The monkeys do not have our level of requisite autonomy. Perhaps, they engage in teaming by default and not by choice.

Norms are "often viewed as emergent properties of utilitarian agents' behavior" and "no theory of the acquisition of normative attitudes as grounded upon agents' representations has yet been provided" [11]. Norms can be useful when two or more interacting agents are aware of each other's norms, and use it in their individual deliberation. The general purpose of norms is in anticipation of expected mental and physical actions of other agents. There are many types of norms. Some norms govern intra-personal interactions such as "reactivity"[2]. Some norms govern interpersonal interactions such as "communal laws". Social norms can in general influence an agent's behaviors and plans as well as the agent's mental states with respect to goals, beliefs, and intentions. Some norms can either be a collection of disjoint rules of thumb as in "look before crossing" and are domain specific. Other norms might be a cluster of related norms and are adopted in entirety. For example, "friendship", and "teaming" are well-developed clusters of social norms useful in an agent society [7]. A recent domain independent technique for collecting communication norms is a *conversation policy*, which is a model of the structure and content of a type of agent conversation for a certain communicative function [13]. Norms can be specified formally

---

[1] Chris Hill at U of Arkansas suggested this example.
[2] "reactivity" is a pattern of personal habits/skills/routine [12, 19].

and systematically or informally and heuristically. Norms are not mutually exclusive and an agent may enact one or more of them concurrently. An external observer can often detect many of the active norms. In social situations most people are aware of effectiveness of their action selection under the influence of a norm. For instance, people know when a negotiation scheme (as a cluster of norms) has become fruitless, their role choice is ineffective, and their team membership is a hindrance. This can be used to assess related goal status and perhaps utilities.

Here are a few clusters of norms. In this paper we will focus only on teamwork.

- Teamwork is a class of interpersonal social conventions that bond a number of individuals to a goal. The bond might be loose or rigid, [17].
- Situated action and reaction is a class of intra-personal methods for coping in the world that connects sensing to acting with minimum of mental processing. In their repertoire, many agent architectures provide a tier for this kind of interaction [10].
- Control and monitoring is a class of systematic methods in which the agent monitors its environment for predetermined outcomes. The mechanisms can be interpersonal or intra-personal. For instance, an agent may select a master-slave role for agents in its surrounding. [8].
- Negotiation is an interpersonal template for interaction that an agent may use in order to bring about desired changes [22].
- Social role adoption and adaptivity is an interpersonal skill for choosing a role that best fits the agent's capabilities and objectives [23].

It is very interesting but at present omitted from our consideration is: (a) emergence of norms in agents or in the society of agents, (b) changes in norms, (c) how an agent acquires a norm as a pattern of activity, or (d) how an agent violates or modifies a norm. Instead we are interested in the following: (a) how an agent instantiates (i.e., enacts) a norm, and (b) what mental ingredients of an agent are responsible for characterizing and sustaining a norm.

2.1   Identifying a Norm

We suggest the following minimal list of norm characteristics.

- Involve two or more agents, each of whom shares the norm.
- Agents have power to not choose them.
- There need not be any direct rational account of the norms available to the agents.
- There are explicit or implicit sanctions and rewards for norm adoption.

While strategies might fit the above requirements, norms dwell in pragmatics of interaction whereas strategies are means-end techniques. Norms and values (i.e., principles) are both influences on behavior. The agent must be able to respond to changing conditions and this requires that the agent be able to drop current norms, obligations and intentions in favor of norms, obligations and intentions that better fit the changed environment. Norms therefore cannot be unconditionally adopted. Norms are not defaults or exceptions. Defaults and exceptions can be used for similar purposes as norms. e.g., in coordination. However, unlike defaults and exception, agents deliberate about norms. Obligations are strong norms and are derived from it. We consider interdictions, bans, and other similar terms as kinds of norms. Norms might produce goals for an agent but the norm is not the goal itself but the surrounding social context. Some researchers have treated norms as constraints. Constraints are a knowledge encoding method regulating an agent's actions. Norms that might resemble constraints preserve the teleological foundations of such encoding so the agent can perform reasoning. Norms are a subset of social laws and the agent's pragmatics of using them.

To recapitulate, we divide norms into two classes. The first class is a set of conventions or behaviors for a given situation. The second class of norms is valuations of behavior for deliberation and prediction. The second class of norms varies from societal or institutional to personal or individual. These norms also vary from absolute or global to relative and local.

2.2   Norm Selection

The problem of off-line norm selection has been studied in [14, 20]. Simplicity and minimality as criteria used for norm selection where alternative norms are available. In contrast to this approach, we focus on the process of norm formation and its relation to mental attitudes. This will allow us to account for both the choice and dynamics of social norms.

Here, like [1], and in contrast to a collective decision, we take an individualistic view of the choice of norm that will affect the agent itself and others. A possible approach to norm selection by an agent can be in terms of rule-utilitarianism where an agent chooses a norm that maximizes social welfare of agents it cares about. This would mean a kind of machine learning that would use feedback to reinforce choices of norm. However attractive, such feedback is hard to compute as well as unintuitive.

Another basis for norm selection can be based on a system of mental attitudes with varying intensity. These models will prescribe the proper combination of mental attitudes as reasons to adopt a norm. An agent equipped with such a system and endowed with abilities to form mental attitudes over such things as power, autonomy, sociability, etc., will then instantiate the norms that comply with its accompanying system of decision.

In the next section we will discuss the relation between norms and utilities.

3   Utilitarian View of Norms

We limit our consideration of norms relative to goal achievement. Furthermore, we assume agents are all self-interested. We assume the agent has a goal that it can accomplish. However, when it chooses to consider interaction with another agent, it will consider applicable norms, which in turn affects its action selection.

Let's assume an agent's norms with respect to a goal can be grouped into disjoint sets. Assume norms in a set are consistent and the agent must pick one set from among its norm sets. Examples of norm sets are collaboration or competition.

It is conceivable to reason about norms explicitly. However, we believe that reasoning about norms is often indirect and through mental attitudes. The indirect nature of reasoning about norms is explored in section 3. By using utilities, we can model arbitration among norms explicitly. I.e., the agent can weigh one norm against another. This is the focus of this section.. A common objection to this approach is unavailability of utilities. Other objections are along the lines of inadequacies of decision theory and its unrealism in human decision-making. However, this kind of explicit reasoning with utilities can be used in problem solving and planning. Let's define a norm.

Definition: Norm = (O, R, G, U).

- O is the content of the norm set which is being considered for norms selection. This is independent of G, which is being considered for action selection.
- R is a social marginal utility function that considers the social gains and losses with respect to G.
- G is the agent's goal that invokes the norm set. Norms are indexed by goals. This is the connection between the agent's individual and social rationality.
- U is an individual marginal utility function that considers the agent's gains and losses with respect to G. The gains and losses might be rewards, penalties, and other valuable s such as reputation.

Rules 1 (below) is suggested for selecting a norm at the norm selection layer when a goal is considered at the action selection layer.

Rule 1: Norm selection for one goal
An agent considering a goal G and norm sets $N_1...N_m$ will pick the norm set N_i, which maximizes its goal achievement utility. If all norms for G will produce a negative utility, no norm is selected and the goal is reassessed.

Rules 2 (below) is suggested for selecting a goal at the action selection layer when a norm is considered at the norms selection layer.

Rule 2: Goal selection for one norm
An agent considering a norm N with content as goal G and other goals $G_1...G_m$ will pick the goal G iff the utility of the norm (and its corresponding content G) is higher than utilities of all $G_1...G_m$.

Rule 3 (below) is suggested for selecting a norm at the norm selection layer when multiple goals are considered at the action selection layer.

Rule 3: Norm selection for multiple goals
An agent considering goals G_1, G_2, ..., G_m and corresponding norm sets $N_{11}...N_{1m1}$, $N_{11}...N_{1m2}$, ..., and $_{N11}...N_{1mm}$ will pick one norm set for each goal (Norms N_1, ..., N_m) with the constraint that $U_1 + ... + U_m$ is maximized.

At times, utilities due to norm selection can have such an effect as to influence the goal selection. The agent may not be able to select a norm since the utility losses outweigh any gains it might have. This agent must be prepared to pay the sanction penalties for non-adoption of norm corresponding to the goal. If the sanction penalty is larger than the utility of the goal, the goal should be dropped. An example is robbery. The thief may think about the penalty of the sanction and when it is considers it to be higher than any gains, it should drop it. What happens if the agent has several goals and is faced with some sanctions that each outweighs utility of the corresponding goal? Naturally, the utility maximizing agent will not drop the goals and will be prepared to pay the sanctions.

4   BDI and Deliberative View of Norms

We now turn to defining norms indirectly in terms of mental attitudes. Since agents deliberate about their mental attitudes, norms based on mental attitudes are deliberative norms.

Mental attitudes arise out of the agent's deliberation on motivations, which we will take for granted in this paper. To use a production system metaphor, these are the agent's situated attitudes that the agent will use for conflict resolution among competing courses of action. We suggest that if a sufficiently sophisticated agent is questioned about its choice of a specific norm or a norm class, it should mirror typical human response and present the mental attitudes that led to its choice of template. These mental attitudes are sometimes colloquially referred to with phrases such as "in the spirit of ...", which imply a "mood" or a predominant feeling. This might suggest the notion of personality. However, unlike personality, which dictates an anthropomorphic emotional state of the agent such as fear and tenacity, for agents we will focus on self-evaluative qualities, which are derived from an agent's experience. We are focusing on the space of relationships among mental attitudes and how that leads to its choice of action selection template, Figure 2. Much of this diagram is a simplified relationship between the Beliefs, Desires, and Intentions of an agent from the popular BDI paradigm [24]. The most important parts for us are the *adopted norms* and *adopted intentions* along with accompanying motivational attitudes. Motivations are instantiations of an agent's high-level objectives and reasoning which produce such an instantiation. Motivations can be thought of as the agent's *desires* and might be amorphous and abstract. Goals are concrete and more readily achievable. "brf" is belief revision function and *percept and communications* are used as inputs to revise old beliefs. "Option generation" is a function that maps beliefs and old desires and old intentions to updated desires. In addition to functionality described in [24] we have this function take into account agent's deontological commitments as well. This is the main function for the action selection layer in Figure 1. "Selection function" maps beliefs, desires, prior deontological commitments, as well as agent's adopted roles to adopted norms. This is the main function performed in the norm selection layer in Figure 1. *Adopted roles* are a result of negotiating plans with other agents. *Negotiation* might be negligible or substantial and there are normative considerations as well. Fuller treatment of plans and roles is beyond our scope in this paper.

In social situations most people are adept at being conscious of their own mental attitudes and detect mental attitudes of others. People might even command or suggest adoption of these mental attitudes from other people as in "follow the rules" or "don't be impulsive". This is shown in Figure 2 as the environment's direct effect on beliefs. Unlike bi-valued logics, mental attitudes can be more accurately understood as having quantity as in a mass noun. For instance, 'sociability' is like 'water' in its measurability. There are metrics for some nouns like 'water' whereas others like 'cloud'; 'ink blot', and our attitudes lack such well-developed metrics. Common parlance such as "fairly sociable" or "highly impulsive" motivate us to consider attitudes as having possibility values, as in fuzzy logic.

The following is a partial list of mental attitudes of general interest to us: cooperation, autonomy, exploration, impulsiveness, commitment, responsibility, trust, conformance, sociability, dependence, and power. Defining these terms is difficult and can take much space that we don't have here. In this paper we will rely on the reader's intuitive understanding of these terms. Next we redefine norms in term of mental attitudes.

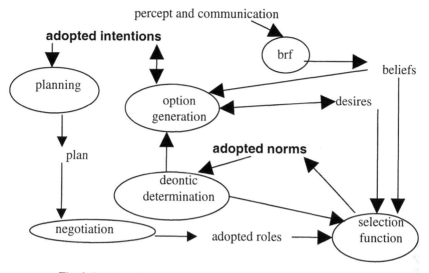

Fig. 2. Relationship between norm selection and intention selection

Definition: Norm = (O, R, G, A)
- O is the content of the norm set which is being considered for norms selection. This is independent of G, which is being considered for action selection.
- R is the marginal deontological effects of adoption/rejection of the norm.
- G is the agent's goal that invokes the norm set. Norms are indexed by goals. This is the connection between the agent's individual and social rationality.
- A is a set of mental attitudes along with degrees for each. The mental attitudes are characterized by using the notions of belief, desire, and intention. The degrees of mental attitudes form a required pattern against which we will match the agent's actual mental attitudes.

A is a set of mental attitudes the agent somehow chooses. The mechanisms of selecting a mental attitude are very much an area of research in Ecommerce and multi-agency for which we will not provide an answer in this paper. Utilitarian approaches have been applied in such mechanisms for mental attitude determination [4, 5, 6]. There are many discussions of mental attitudes found in the literature, e.g., [7, 8, 9].

An agent at any given time will have a pattern of mental pattern of mental attitudes with respect to an adopted goal. For instance, the agent will experience a degree of autonomy, a level of trust, and so on. Norm selection turns into matching the existing pattern of mental attitudes to required patterns of mental attitudes for each norm.

Rule 4 (below) revisits Rule 1 and is suggested for selecting a norm at the norm selection layer when a single goal is considered at the action selection layer.

Rule 4: Norm selection for one goal

An agent considering goal G, norm sets $N_1...N_m$ each with required mental attitudes and their corresponding degrees and actual mental attitudes $A_1...A_N$ will pick the norm set N_i with the closest match between actual mental attitudes and the required mental attitudes.

Rule 5 (below) revisits rule 2 and is suggested for selecting a goal at the action selection layer when a norm is considered at the norm selection layer.

Rule 5: Goal selection for one norm

An agent considering a norm N with content as goal G and other goals $G_1...G_m$ and actual mental attitudes $A_1...A_N$ will pick the goal G iff the actual mental attitudes match the required attitude of N more than required attitudes of any of the Norms corresponding to goals $G_1...G_m$.

Rule 6 (below) revisits rule 3 and is suggested for selecting a norm at the norm selection layer when multiple goals are considered at the action selection layer.

Rule 6: Norm selection for multiple goals

An agent considering goals G_1, G_2, ..., G_m, corresponding norm sets $N_{11}...N_{1m1}$, $N_{11}...N_{1m2}$, ..., and $N_{11}...N_{1mm}$ and actual mental attitudes $A_1...A_N$, will pick one norm set for each goal (Norms N_1, ..., N_m) but with the constraint that maximizes the match between degrees of actual mental attitudes and degrees of required attitudes in norms.

With utility analysis of norms, norm selection was shown to influence the goal selection and at times lead the agent to abandon its goals. This is also possible in the attitude formulation of norms. The content of the norm can be the negation of the norm's goal. This is the case where the norm for a goal prohibits that goal. If the actual mental attitudes activate the norm strongly, then the goal and its norm counteract. The agent might abandon such a goal. If the goal is part of a series of related goals, as long as the number of counteractions is fewer than the number of goal, the agent might be inclined to execute the goals. We have been very sketchy here and there is a lot of room for formalization, which we leave for future work.

5   Teaming

Teaming is a cluster of norms for collaboration. We have developed a utilitarian approach for deciding to team [15, 16] and an attitude-based approach [2, 17]. Our model of selecting a team as a cluster of norms includes consideration of four conditions: (1) joint intentions, (2) group autonomy, (3) joint awareness, and (4) joint cooperation. We claim these conditions that an agent needs to consider to form a team. Once a team is formed there will be conditions beyond the ones we will review that the agent will use to remain in a team or exit it.

The central attitudes in considering to form a team are the notions of group autonomy and cooperation. Agents jointly intend a goal if and only if as a group they are jointly autonomous toward that goal plus they choose to attempt actions toward it. Group autonomy in a group of agents is when each member of the team believes in adequacy of joint abilities of the group and perceives adequate mutual (among group members) and external (from agents outside the group) permission to exercise their ability. Joint awareness in a group is when each agent in the group believes that together with the group it has joint ability toward the desired state and believes that it has joint intention to achieve that state. Joint cooperative condition is met when all member of the team believe that they will share in the benefits with the group and they have joint responsibility to achieve the group objective. Responsibility is in turn the condition that if an agent can do an action to facilitate the desired group goal will intend to do it.

Perhaps other attitudes such as trust toward potential and actual team members are relevant. It is shown that agents that learn to trust one another are more likely to cooperate [3]. It is intuitive that with more trust among agents, there will be more motivation for teamwork.

6   Conclusion

Norms affect action selection in social agents. We showed that reasoning about norms guide norm selection as well as affect choice of goals. Norms might be arbitrated by utilities. Alternatively, an agent may deliberate about mental attitudes to determine norms. We have sketched some relationships between norms and goals.

In many artificial systems, designers hard-code norms on agent systems. We believe by allowing an agent to select its own norm that fits its attitudes, we increase its adaptivity. Agent system engineering needs to be extended to account for norm classes so that agents can adapt to social contexts. Much remains to be done in extending the agent communication language and agent inference mechanisms to encode notions of mental attitudes such as autonomy, trust, power, etc.

Acknowledgements

This work is supported by AFOSR grant F49620-00-1-0302.

References

1. E. Alonso, 1998. How Individuals Negotiate Societies, Proc. of the Third International Conference on Multi-Agent Systems (ICMAS-98), pp. 18-25. July 3-8, Paris. IEEE Computer Society Press.
2. G. Beavers and H. Hexmoor, Teams of Agents, In the Proceedings of IEEE SMC, Arizona.
3. A. Birk, 2000. Boosting Cooperation by Evolving Trust, **Applied Artificial Intelligence Journal**, Taylor and Francis.
4. S. Brainov, 1996. Altruistic Cooperation between Self-Interested Agents. In Proceedings of **European Conference on Artificial Intelligence**, 519-523, John Wiley & Sons.
5. S. Brainov, 2000. The role and the Impact of Preferences on Multiagent Interaction. In **Intelligent Agents VI**, Lesperance and Jennings (eds.), 349-363, Springer-Verlag.
6. S. Brainov and T. Sandholm, 1999. Power, Dependence and Stability in Multiagent Plans. In Proceedings of **AAAI'99**, pages 11-16, Orlando, Florida.

7. C. Castelfranchi, 1990. Social Power. In Demazeau Y. and Muller J.-P. eds. Decentralized AI - Proceedings of the *First European Workshop on Modeling Autonomous Agents in a Multi-Agent World*. 49-62. Elsevier Science Publishers.

8. C. Castelfranchi., and R. Falcone, 2000. Trust and Control: A Dialectic Link

9. C. Castelfranchi, F. Dignum, C. Konker, and J. Treur, 1999. Deliberative Normative Agents: Principles and Architectures, pp. 364-378, **ATAL-99**.

10. W. Clancey, 1997. **Situated Cognition: On Human Knowledge and Computer Representations**, Cambridge University Press.

11. R. Conte, R. Falcone, and G. Sartor, 1999. Introduction: Agents and Norms: How to fill the gap? **AI&Law Special Issue on Agents and Norms**. R. Conte, R. Falcone, and G. Sartor (Eds), vol 7, no 1, p 1-15.

12. R. Cooper, T. Shallice, and J. Farringdon, 1995. Symbolic and continuous processes in the automatic selection of actions. In Hallam, J., (ed.) **Hybrid Problems, Hybrid Solutions**. IOS Press. Amsterdam. pp. 27-37.

13. M. Greaves, H. Holmback, and J. Bradshaw, (1999). What is Conversation Policy? In *Proceedings of the Autonomous Agents '99*, **Workshop on Specifying and Implementing Conversation Policies**, Seattle, WA, May 1999.

14. D. Fitoussi and M. Tennenholtz, 2000. Choosing social laws for multiagent systems: minimality and simplicity. Artificial Intelligence, 119(2000) 61-101.

15. H. Hexmoor and H. Duchscherer, 2000. Shared Autonomy and Teaming: A preliminary report. In Proceedings of **Workshop on Performance Metrics for Intelligent Systems**, NIST, Washington, DC.

16. H. Hexmoor and H. Duchscherer, 2001. Efficiency as a Motivation to Team. In Proceedings of **FLAIRS 2001**, FL.

17. H. Hexmoor and G. Beavers, 2001. Towards Teams of Agents, In Proceedings of the International Conference in Artificial Intelligence, H. R. Arabnia, (ed), (**IC-AI'2001**), Las Vegas, CSREA Press.

18. P. Maes. 1989. How to Do the Right Thing. **Connection Science Journal**, Vol. 1, No. 3, pp. 291-323.

19. T. Norman, and T. Shallice, 1986. Attention to action: Willed and automatic control of behavior. In Davidson, R., Schwartz, G., and Shapiro, D., (eds.) Consciousness and Self Regulation: **Advances in Research and Theory**, Volume 4. Plenum, New York, NY. pp. 1-18.

20. Y. Shoham and M. Tennenholtz, 1995. Social laws for artificial agent societies: Off-line design. Artificial Intelligence 73(1995) 231-252.

21. P. Thagard, 2000. **Coherence in Thought and Action** (Life and Mind: Philosophical Issues in Biology and Psychology), MIT Press.

22. D. Walton, 1989. **Informal Logic: A Handbook for Critical Argumentation**, Cambridge, Cambridge University Press.

23. R. Werner, 1989. Cooperative Agents: A unified Theory of Communication and Social Structures. In L. Gasser, M. Huhns, editors, **Distributed Artificial Intelligence**, Volume II.

24. M. Wooldridge, 2000. **Reasoning about Rational Agents**. The MIT Press.

Probabilistic Dispatch, Dynamic Domain Architecture, and Self-adaptive Software

Robert Laddaga, Paul Robertson, and Howie Shrobe

Massachusetts Institute of Technology
Artificial Intelligence Laboratory
{rladdaga,paulr,hes}@ai.mit.edu

Abstract. In this paper we report on a beginning effort in the self adaptive software research area of improving function or method dispatch. We extend type-signature based method dispatch in a dynamic object oriented programming language with probabilistic dispatch, where the choice of method to use is determined by statistical means. This research direction is part of a larger self adaptive software effort at the MIT Artificial Intelligence Laboratory, called Dynamic Domain Architectures.

Keywords: Self-adaptive Software, probabilistic dispatch, aspect oriented programming, method dispatch, dynamic object languages

1 Introduction

The first International Workshop on Self Adaptive Software [16] identified several key research areas. One of these areas was to improve function or method dispatch, by applying decision theoretic concepts [12]. In this paper we report on a beginning effort in that research area. We extend type-signature based method dispatch in a dynamic object oriented programming language with probabilistic dispatch, where the choice of method to use is determined by statistical methods. This research direction is part of a larger self adaptive software effort at the MIT Artificial Intelligence Laboratory called Dynamic Domain Architectures (DDA). We begin by describing the background and context of DDA. Afterwards we compare DDA to other research directions. Finally we describe our probabilistic dispatch, and how it might be applied in practice.

2 Dynamic Domain Architectures

A Dynamic Domain Architecture structures a domain into service layers; each service is annotated with specifications and descriptions of how it is implemented in terms of services from lower levels. Like other domain architectures, a Dynamic Domain Architecture provides multiple instantiations of each service, with each instantiation optimized for different purposes. Thus, it serves as a well-structured software repository. Typically, the application is a relatively small body of code utilizing the much larger volume of code provided by the framework. Typical

R. Laddaga, P. Robertson, and H. Shrobe (Eds.): IWSAS 2001, LNCS 2614, pp. 227–237, 2003.

domains of concern for military embedded software systems include sensor management, navigation guidance and control, electronic warfare, etc.

A Dynamic Domain Architecture is, however, different from the domain architectures developed in earlier DARPA programs (e.g. STARS and DSSA). In earlier systems, the Domain Architecture was a static repository from which specific instantiations of the services were selected and built into the run-time image of the application. Neither the models nor the deductions used to select specific instantiations of the services are carried into the runtime environment. In a Dynamic Domain Architecture, however, all the alternative instantiations, plus the models and annotations describing them are present in the run-time environment, and multiple applications may simultaneously and dynamically invoke the services.

Dynamic Domain Architectures allow late binding of the decision of which alternative instantiation of a service to employ. Like Dynamic Object Oriented Programming (DOOP) systems, the decision may be made as late as method-invocation time. However, Dynamic Domain Architectures go further than DOOP, allowing the decision to be made using much more information than simple type signatures. The models which describe software components are used to support runtime deductions leading to the selection of an appropriate method for achieving a service. Dynamic Domain Architectures recognize that in many open environments (e.g., image processing for ATR) it isn't possible to select the correct operator with precision, a priori. Therefore, Dynamic Domain Architectures support an even later binding of operator selection, allowing this initial selection to be revised in light of the actual effect of the invocation. If the method chosen doesn't do the job well enough, alternatives selections are explored until a satisfactory solution is found or until there is no longer any value to be gained in finding a solution.

Dynamic Domain Architectures remove exception handling from the purview of the programmer, instead treating the management of exceptional conditions as a special service provided by the run-time environment. The annotations carried forward to run time include formal statements of conditions which should be true at various points of the program if it is to achieve its goals. The DDA framework generates runtime monitoring software that invokes error-handling services if these conditions fail to be true. The exception-management service is informed by the Dynamic Domain Architecture's models of the executing software system and by a catalog of breakdown conditions and their repairs; using these it diagnoses the breakdown, determines an appropriate scope of repair and possibly selects an alternative to that invoked already; it then restarts the computation. Finally, a DDA framework provides an embedded language in which the developers of other frame- works can access its state-variables and infuence its goal and plan structure.

2.1   Domain Modeling

The idea of domain architecture dates back to the Arpa Megaprogramming initiative where it was observed that software reuse could best take place within the context of a Domain Specific Software Architecture. Such an architecture would identify important pieces of functionality employed by all applications within the domain, and would then recursively identify the important functionality supporting these computations. In a visual-interpretation domain, for example, typical common functionality might include region identification, which in turn might depend on edge detection, which in turn might depend on filtering operations (eg, convolutions).

This process of identifying and structuring the common functionality is the first component of a process termed Domain Analysis. Domain Analysis structures common functionality into a series of "service layers," each relying on the ones below for parts of its functionality. The second component of Domain Analysis is the identification of variability within the commonality. Returning to our visual-interpretation example, there are several different approaches to region identification, dozens of distinct edge-detection algorithms, and many different ways to perform filtering operations. When looked at in even finer detail, there may be an even greater number of variant instantiations of any of these operations. Variations arise due to different needs for precision, time and space bounds, error management, and the like.

The power of Domain Analysis is that its identification of common functionality lets one view the code in a new terms: the bulk of the code is in the service-layer substrate and implements functionality common to many applications. Each application consists of a thin veneer of application-specific code, riding on top of this substrate of service layers. However, the substrate contains many variant instantiations of each service. Although each instantiation is relevant to only some of the applications, Domain Analysis lets us see these as variants of a common conceptual service. Before the Domain Analysis was performed, each application stood alone using its particular instantiations of the common services and was ignorant of the fact that other applications used the same conceptual services but with different instantiations.

2.2   Dynamic Object Oriented Programming

The Lisp community, with its close connection to artificial intelligence research, has independently discovered some of the same ideas, but has packaged them in a more dynamic but less formal framework. This approach was first identified and termed "super-routines" in a paper by Eric Sandewall [17] [18]. Sandewall noted that it is often the case that a whole class of computations are instances of some very general pattern of computation, where the members of the class differ only in the details. He termed this higher-level structure a "super-routine" and noted that data-driven programming techniques could dynamically determine which subroutine was relevant at run time. As object-oriented programming ideas developed in the Lisp and Smalltalk communities, several researchers began to understand that the Dynamic OOP facilities common in these languages were exactly what was needed to build a super-routine.

The high-level common services of a Domain Architecture are precisely the same idea as Sandewall's notion of a super-routine (rediscovered in another context by another community a decade later). Unlike the Static Domain Architectures, the runtime environment of the systems Sandewall characterized all included many variant instantiations of the common services, and dynamically invoked a particular instantiation based on run-time conditions.

The mapping between the super-routine (or Domain Architecture) idea and the features of DOOP is straightforward: each high-level abstract operation (or Domain Architecture service) is identified with a generic function; the different instantiations are provided by different methods, each with a unique type signature. Method invocation performs the dynamic run-time selection of the appropriate instantiation of the service. This style of building extensible, domain specific architectures has become known as "open implementation" [8]. Dynamic OOP also provides significant facilities for managing exceptional conditions. In the case of Lisp, these facilities were motivated by the needs of adaptive planning systems. In particular, the facilities provided to signal exceptional conditions allow the error-handling code access to the environment of the exception and this, in turn, allows the handler to characterize the nature of the breakdown. Facilities similar to the signalling of the exception are used to transfer control from the error handler to an appropriate "restart" handler. Once the error handler has characterized the nature of the breakdown, it invokes a repair mechanism, not by name, but by description. Finally, the language provides facilities to specify what cleanup work must be done to perform the appropriate recovery work as rollback to the restart position takes place.

What is needed is to enrich this infrastructure with extensive models of the software's structure, function and purpose and to build in facilities for noticing if an operator has failed to achieve its purpose. We must carry into the run-time environment all the descriptive information as well as all the variant instantiations of operators present in the development environment, and we must use this information reactively to control the physical system in which the software is embedded. We call such a framework a Dynamic Domain Architecture because it incorporates and extends ideas from the two traditions of Domain Architectures and Dynamic Object Oriented Programming.

2.3 Services Provided

A Dynamic Domain Architecture is far more introspective and refective than conventional software systems. This allows many tasks which currently burden the programmer to instead be synthesized from the models within a framework or to be provided as system services.

1. The synthesis of code that selects which variant of an abstract operator is appropriate in light of run-time conditions. (This includes decision theoretic or probabilistic dispatch).
2. The synthesis of monitors which check that conditions expected to be true at various points in the execution of a computation are in fact true.
3. Diagnosis and isolation services which locate the cause of an exceptional condition, and characterize the form of the breakdown which has transpired.

4. Alternative selection services which determine how to achieve the goal of the failed computation using variant means (either by trying repairs or by trying alternative implementations, or both).
5. Rollback and recovery services which establish a consistent state of the computation from which to attempt the alternative strategy.
6. Allocation and reoptimization services which reallocate resources in light of the resources remaining after the breakdown and the priorities obtaining at that point. These services may optimize the system in a new way in light of the new allocations and priorities.
7. The synthesis of connections to reactive executives that manage physical components of concern to the DDA framework.
8. The synthesis of connections to other DDA frameworks with whose state-variables, goals and plans the current framework interacts

2.4   Influences from Artificial Intelligence

Our ideas on Dynamic Domain Architectures stem from several trends in AI and software engineering. The idea that programs can be viewed as instances of plans and that they exhibit a goal-directed structure dates back at least to the work on the Programmer's Apprentice [15, 19, 14]. DDA frameworks build in diagnostic services which draw on the work on model-based diagnosis [4–6, 3]. The idea of formalizing a domain architecture and even the idea of dynamic invocation go back to a little referenced but nevertheless seminal paper by Sandewall [17]. There is a host of more modern work similar in spirit to ours. These include ideas of decomposing systems in cooperating frameworks, using advanced object oriented techniques to build integration techniques, generating the integration code that links frameworks in to larger ensembles. We briefy survey some of that work below:

2.5   Subject-Oriented Programming

Subject-oriented programming [7] allows the natural specification of an application in terms of the composition of domain and task specific decompositions. The decompositions can cut across normal object-oriented organization involving partial definitions of classes and methods. These decompositions address subject-oriented design paradigms such as product lines, evolutionary development, and multi-team collaborations. Subject-oriented programming permits a user to specify the composition of these separate components as a set of rules for managing their combination and resolving conficts.

The limitations of pure object-oriented programming have been recognized for a longtime in the LISP community. The Common Lisp Object System (CLOS) provides the ability to decompose applications along object and procedural lines. For example, multimethods allow a developer to define a set of methods on a particular class or set of classes outside the usual class definition. This permits additions or modifications to object-oriented programs to be specified as separate files or libraries in language without resorting to outside compositional support. Mixin classes, method combination, and runtime namespaces increase the compositional power even further. Finally, procedural macros provide one more tool for specifying behavior that cross-cuts the usual object or procedural boundaries without tangling the source.

2.6   Product Lines, Scalable Libraries, and Software Generators

A product-line architecture (PLA) [2] is a design for a family of similar applications. A generator is a tool that takes a specification for a composition of scalable libraries and produces a high-performance application. In [20], the authors propose an object-oriented building block called a mixin-layer. The idea here is that often additions to software are not localized to a single class but instead span several classes. They show how to compose these layers using an implementation of the Gen Voca theory [1].

Our work demonstrates another set of techniques for implementing scalable libraries. In contrast to their work, our CLOS-style substrate is not as constrained as their object-centric foundation (e.g., C++). For example, multimethods can already be added outside of class definitions. On the other hand, one strength of their approach is the view that libraries are composed to build applications. We would like to research more mechanisms for specifying the composition of our frameworks.

2.7   Aspect-Oriented Programming (AOP) and AspectJ

Aspect-oriented programming [10] is a style of programming that complements object-oriented and procedural programming by providing an alternative decomposition of a program into features of a particular domain, called aspects, that cross-cut multiple classes and/or procedures. These aspects can then be merged with the object-oriented and/or procedural parts of a program using a weaver to form an application.

AOP is a generalization of subject-oriented programming in that it goes beyond merely combinations of aspects, but addresses semantic and performance issues as aspects in their own right.

AspectJ [13] is an implementation of AOP for Java. It provides a mechanism for combining methods and fields defined in separate aspects. In particular, advise methods can be combined with existing methods and fields can be added. The focus on method combination and method dispatch functionality is very useful, and similar in spirit to the work we report here.

Aspects can be easily plugged in or out of applications by invoking a weaver at compile time. Unfortunately, this is a static operation. Pattern matching is used to specify the domain of the aspects, that is, the methods to which method combination is to be applied.

We maintain that AspectJ is limited in a number of key areas. First, aspects can be woven in only at compile time. Second, the forms of method combination are limited. Third, the system is not user extensible. Fourth, the semantics are opaque. In contrast, our meta-object approach, overcomes all of these limitations.

Refection and metaobject protocols [9] are a powerful way to implement AOP. A refective language is embodied in a base language and several meta languages which control the semantics and implementation of the given base language. The meta languages provide hooks that allow a user to implement cross cutting functionality, functionality to which no single base language has access.

3 Probabilistic Dispatch

Probabilistic dispatch is a class of method dispatch mechanisms, each of which select the most likely method to execute on any given call. This requires a fundamental dispatch capability, plus the ability to evaluate candidate methods as to their probability. The intention is that the probability numbers assigned to methods reflect the likelihood that a method will be the right method for the particular invocation at hand. Of course, there are many ways that the probability numbers could be computed, many timescales at which the numbers could be updated, and many sources and forms of input that might be utiltized by the probability computing algorithm.

We have prototyped our probabilistic dispatch facility in the dynamic object language Yolambda [11]. Yolambda is based on Scheme, but has a class based type system, and significant meta-object programming capabilities. Among other things, Yolambda allows us to program new method combination routines, as well as rewrite method dispatch. Accordingly, we use Yolambda's method combination mechanism to provide selection between implementations.

For any particular computation, we start by implementing several different ways of making the needed computation. These alternate methods are available to be executed on any function call that meets the syntactic requirments of the call. Next we implement a function that can compute probabilities of success for each of these methods, ideally in ways that depend on the arguments and context of the current call. The method combination mechanism invokes the probability assignment function, and then dispatches the call to the most likely method.

3.1 Solution Details

We have a collection of methods $(M_0 M_1 \ldots M_n)$, each of which implements a solution. Method combination is responsible for determining what method or methods should be applied on a given call.

Method combination has a way of computing the probability of success of each method, and finds the method most likely to succeed, puts it at the head of the ordering, and applies it. If the chosen method cannot complete, it performs a "(callNextMethod)" in order to pass the responsibility on to another (the next most likely) method. To do this, callNextMethod recomputes the probabilities of the remaining methods (since they may have changed) and again picks the best one and applies it. As the methods learn things about the problem, probability estimates produced for the other methods may change.

If multiple methods have the same probability, we need another procedure for choosing the method to be applied. We can have a number of different (but similar) method combination operators that behave differently in this case:

1. Deterministic: Pick the one that occurs earliest in the program code. (call this combination operator PROB+DETERMINISTIC)
2. Random: Pick at random one of the set of (equally most probable) methods. (call this combination operator PROB+RANDOM)

An alternative method combination operator would not pick the most probable but would pick one of the methods at random, but weighted by their probabilities. (call this combination operator MONTECARLO).

Next we describe how these method combination operators work with a very simple example, that does little to obscure the mechanism (but also does very little to motivate the approach).

3.2 Dice Rolling Example

In this example we have six methods: roll-1 roll-2 .. roll-6 that have equal probability and which return their respective number. The method combination operator PROB+DETERMINISTIC will initially roll a "1" because the methods are equally likely, and "roll-1" comes first. It will follow this behavior each time it is invoked.

The method combination operator PROB+RANDOM will randomly pick a method among the six methods, for the first roll. It will do the same on subsequent rolls as well, but outcomes will be equally distributed among the six methods, if we invoke the method enough times.

The method combination operator MONTECARLO will randomly pick a method among the six methods, for the first and subsequent rolls.

We now modify the example to make "roll-1" twice as probable as the other methods. In other words, we model a loaded die.

In this case, PROB+DETERMINISTIC will always roll a 1 because it is most probable. PROB+RANDOM will always roll a 1 because it is the most probable choice.

MONTECARLO will randomly produce a number between 1 and 6 but "1" will occur twice as often as the other digits if sampled enough times.

For this next modified example, the outer call to "roll" takes an argument which is the digit that it should roll. Initially, all the methods have equal probability, as in the first, unmodified example. We try it on "(roll 3)".

PROB+DETERMINISTIC tries 1. Since it doesn't match 3 it does (call-NextMethod) that causes 2 to be tried, because it is the first of the remaining equally likely methods (note that the probability of "roll-2" is now 1/5 instead of 1/6). "roll-2" also fails, so "roll-3" is tried next and succeeds.

PROB+RANDOM tries numbers at random, without replacement, until "roll-3" is tried. MONTECARLO tries numbers at random, without replacement, until 3 is reached.

If the example is now modified in the same way as the second modified example, then the probability of "roll-1" is made double that of the other methods. PROB+DETERMINISTIC tries "roll-1", since it is the most probable. Since it doesn't match 3, "roll-1" does (callNextMethod) that causes "roll-2" to be tried, because it is the first of the remaining, equally likely methods. "roll-3" is tried next and succeeds.

PROB+RANDOM tries "roll-1", since it is the most probable. Since it doesn't match 3, "roll-1" does (callNextMethod) that randomly causes one of the other methods to be tried, because the remaining methods are equally likely. Eventually, "roll-3" will be tried and will succeed, or all the other methods will have been tried and discarded, and "roll-3" will be tried and will succeed.

MONTECARLO tries methods at random, without replacement, until "roll-3" is reached. "roll-1" is twice as likely to be selected as any other method, until it has been tried and discarded from consideration.

In the next modification, we assume that we have some learning from experience, and that we are now making the second call of "roll" with an argument. All the method combinations now assign equal proabability to "roll 1" and "roll 3", say 1/4 for each, and 1/8 for each of the other four methods.

PROB+DETERMINISTIC tries "roll-1", since it is first among the two most probable methods. If the result doesn't match the argument, "roll-1" does (callNextMethod) that causes "roll-3" to be tried, because it is most likely remaining method. If the result still doesn't match the argument, "roll-3" does (callNextMethod) that causes "roll-2" to be tried, because it is the first of the remaining, equally likely methods.

PROB+RANDOM tries "roll-1" or "roll-3", randomly, since they are the most probable methods. If the result doesn't match the argument, the chosen method does (callNextMethod) that causes the other of the most likely methods to be tried, because it is the most likely of the remaining methods.

MONTECARLO tries methods at random, without replacement, until the result of a method equals the argument. "roll-1" and "roll-3" are each twice as likely to be selected as any other method, until they have been tried and discarded from consideration.

3.3 Suggested Applications

We are working on more realistic and interesting examples, including:

1. Airline planning example: We have various methods for finding a well priced airline trip using one or more online reservation systems. We will write code to parse the results of the pricing queries, and also write code to assign intial probabilities to methods, and dynamic probability updating methods.
2. Diagnose a computer hack attempt using methods and probabilities from an attack taxonomy database.

These examples are suggestive of the sorts of applications we envision using probabilistic dispatch. Other examples include autonomous vehicle navigation and control, image understanding applications, cryptography applications, medical imaging and diagnostic applications, web search, data mining and transaction processing.

3.4   Expected Utility Dispatch

We consider probabilistic dispatch to be the first of several decision theoretic approaches to raising the abstraction level of method dispatch. A clear extension of probabilistic dispatch is a method combination operator that computes the expected utility of a collection of methods, and chooses the method that maximizes expected utility. This type of approach is very useful in situations where the method most likely to give the "best result" may not be the method to choose, because of other reasons, such as expected time to deliver the result.

4   Conclusion

We have described an approach to expanding method dispatch to include a very general sort of probabilistic (or utility or expected utility) computation of the appropriate set of methods for a given generic function call. That expanded form of dispatch gives us access to dynamically controlling the application of method dispatch via virtually any computation that will return a probability or utility value.

This facility has very broad application, including dynamically changing method calling in response to a wide variety of enviromental or historical considerations. It also lets us easily segregate, design and program cross cutting concerns such as memory utilization, power utilization, or user or environmental preferences. All the modularity and efficiency of AOP can be achieved with this sort of mechanism.

Generic function dispatch is already a well understood facility in DOOP languages, so the extended facility will not be hard for programmers to learn. Since it involves no language changes, but only sufficient meta-object protocol capabilities to program method dispatch, it is easy for "power users" to program this capability for other programmers to use.

Potential applications include web search, transaction systems, embedded software and autonomous systems. It is a crucial foundation for self-adaptive software (self monitoring and self repairing software).

References

1. D. Batory and S. O'Malley. The design and implementation of hierarchical software systems with reusable components. *ACM TOSEM*, 1992.
2. D. Batory and Y. Smaragdakis. Object-oriented frameworks and product-lines. *Submitted for publication*, 1999.
3. R. Davis. Diagnostic reasoning based on structure and behavior. *Artificial Intelligence*, 24:347–410, 1984.

4. R. Davis and H. Shrobe. Diagnosis based on structure and function. In *Proceedings of the AAAI National Conference on Articial Intelligence*, pages 137–142. AAAI, 1982.

5. J. deKleer and B. Williams. Diagnosing multiple faults. *Artificial Intelligence*, 32(1):97–130, 1987.

6. J. deKleer and B. Williams. Diagnosis with behavior modes. In *Proceedings of the International Joint Conference on Artificial Intelligence*, 1989.

7. W. Harrison and H. Ossher. Subject-oriented programming (a critique of pure objects). In *Conference on Object-Oriented Programming: Systems, Languages, and Applications*, pages 411–428, 1993.

8. G. Kiczales. Beyond the black box: Open implementation. *IEEE Software*, (January), 1996.

9. G. Kiczales and J. des Rivieres. *The art of the metaobject protocol*. MIT Press, Cambridge, MA, USA, 1991.

10. G. Kiczales, J. Lamping, A. Menhdhekar, C. Maeda, C. Lopes, J. Loingtier, and J. Irwin. Aspect-oriented programming. In Mehmet Axkçsit and Satoshi Matsuoka, editors, *ECOOP '97 — Object-Oriented Programming 11th European Conference, Jyväskylä, Finland, Volume 1241 of Lecture Notes in Computer Science*, pages 220–242. Springer-Verlag, 1997.

11. R. Laddaga and P. Robertson. *Yolambda Reference Manual*. Dynamic Object Language Labs, Inc., 1996.

12. R. Laddaga, P. Robertson, and H. Shrobe. Results of the first international workshop on self-adaptive software. In R. Laddaga P. Robertson and H. Shrobe, editors, *Self-Adaptive Software*, pages 242–247. Springer-Verlag, 2000.

13. C. Lopes and G. Kiczales. Recent developments in aspectj(tm). In S. Demeyer and J. Bosch, editors, *Object-Oriented Technology: ECOOP'98 Workshop Reader, Volume 1543 of Lecture Notes in Computer Science*, pages 398–401. Springer-Verlag, 1998.

14. C. Rich. Inspection methods in programming. Technical Report 604, MIT A.I. Lab, 1981.

15. C. Rich and H. Shrobe. Initial report on a lisp programmer's apprentice. Technical Report 354, MIT A.I. Lab, 1976.

16. P. Robertson, R. Laddaga, and H. Shrobe. *Self-Adaptive Software, Volume 1936 Lecture Notes in Computer Science*. Springer-Verlag, 2000.

17. E. Sandewall. Why superroutines are better than subroutines. Technical Report LiTH-MAT-R-79-28, Linkoping University, 1979.

18. E. Sandewall, C. Stromberg, and H. Sorensen. Software architecture based on communicating residential environments. In *Fifth International Conference on Sofware Engineering, San Diego*, 1981.

19. H. Shrobe. Dependency directed reasoning for complex program understanding. Technical Report 503, MIT A.I. Lab, 1979.

20. Y. Smaragdakis and D. Batory. Implementing layered designs with mixin layers. In *European Conference on Object-Oriented Programming*, 1998.

Self-modeling Systems

Christopher Landauer and Kirstie L. Bellman

Aerospace Integration Science Center
The Aerospace Corporation, Mail Stop M6/214
P. O. Box 92957, Los Angeles, California 90009-2957, USA
{cal,bellman}@aero.org

Abstract. This paper is about systems with complete models of themselves (down to some very low level of detail). We explain how to build such a system (using careful system engineering, and our Wrapping approach to flexible integration infrastructures for Constructed Complex Systems), and why we want to do so (it is at least interesting, and we believe it is essential for effective autonomy). The long-term goal is the use of these models to understand modeling processes, so that computing systems can be built that can do their own modeling and construct their own abstractions, which we believe is important for computational intelligence.

Key Phrases: Computational Reflection, Constructed Complex Systems, Integration Science, Knowledge-Based Polymorphism, Model-Based Design and Analysis, Problem-Posing Programming Paradigm, Wrapping Infrastructure

1   Introduction

In this paper, we show that it is possible to build systems with complete models of themselves (down to a surprisingly low level of detail), through some careful software system engineering, and theoretical considerations of biological principles. We address the two major difficulties with such a program: how to manage self-reference without contradiction, and how to avoid infinite regress in the circular definitions.

We explain why we want to do this, based on our earlier studies of autonomy and intelligence in Constructed Complex Systems [45, 46, 52, 56, 58], and on our belief that abstraction and modelling are essential capabilities for intelligent systems [38, 47, 49, 55, 57]. This desire is not a new idea. The *meta-circular interpreters* of [1, 69] were intended to have some of these properties. In particular, reasoning about the interpreter program can lead to conclusions about all of the programs written in the language. Because such a system has access to its own source code, it can examine and specialize that code to particular application contexts [20, 27].

We explain what a self-modeling system is, its architecture, the active processes that make it work, and its life cycle of process development and definition construction. This explanation depends on some careful distinctions between

R. Laddaga, P. Robertson, and H. Shrobe (Eds.): IWSAS 2001, LNCS 2614, pp. 238–256, 2003.

processes, definitions, descriptions, and interfaces, and on a particular notion of actors and actions. Our definitions of these terms in this paper are provisional, but they do seem to suffice for our purposes.

Finally, we show how to build these systems, using our previous research results on the Wrapping approach to integration infrastructure [10, 36, 37, 58, 59] (and other papers to be found in their references), the Wrapping expression notation *wrex* [43], and the Problem Posing Programming Paradigm [44], which lead to new methods of software system development [48, 59], and have led us to begin developing a new area of study that we call "Integration Science" [14, 15].

For lack of space in this paper, we do not discuss the representational mechanisms used, the symbol systems that a system uses to express its own models, and the "Get Stuck" theorems that limit the way symbol systems can be used [12, 42, 50, 53], or the method of conceptual categories [51, 54], which is a very flexible knowledge representation mechanism that is used to keep track of all of these models and processes, and the assumptions and limitations each model entails. Descriptions of those methods can be found in the references. We have made no attempt at a complete or even representative survey of this area, since it is only beginning to attract widespread interest. We present our own results and intentions, and relate them to some of the existing work that we know about.

2 Autonomy and Intelligence

We start with a description of our attitude about autonomy and intelligence in Constructed Complex Systems, which are large, heterogeneous, usually distributed, systems mediated or managed by computing systems [45, 47, 50].

There are many versions of autonomy in the literature, and even many different ways to define and measure some kind of gradations of autonomy, but there is little consensus as yet. We think that the reason is that the appropriate set of differences among the levels has not been proposed. There do seem to be two properties that are common to many of the definitions of autonomy: independent action (which we call autonomous behavior) and independent tasking (which we call autonomy), the former being much more prevalent.

For us, however, it is the latter property of autonomy, that is, the ability to construct one's own goals, that is more important. A thermostat, a batch program keypunched onto computer cards, and even a rock, are all autonomous according to the first property alone, but we do not find these examples at all interesting. We want our autonomous systems to help construct their own goals, rather than merely attempting to carry out goals that are provided exclusively from the outside. To that end, they need to be much more capable of self-analysis and have much more flexibility of decision processes than computer systems usually do. We have argued that intelligence and autonomy in computing systems requires that they are Constructed Complex Systems, and proposed a knowledge-based architecture for them [47, 49], as well as a set of aspects or characteristics of intelligence in systems that are subject to measurement and evaluation [38].

We believe that many properties and mechanisms usually ascribed to intelligence [5] are in fact necessary for any biological system to exist and persist "out in the real world" [16]:

- autonomy,
- use of controlled sources of variation for adaptability,
- multiple layers of symbol systems (complex representational mechanisms),
- infrastructure commonalities,
- methods of exploiting side effects,

and many other mechanisms not yet identified (of course, all individual biological systems eventually fail, which leads to other considerations at other levels of aggregation and time scale, such as treating whole populations as individual biological systems). In general, biological systems have many interesting and useful properties, few of which are known, and none of which are well-understood, and we believe that careful theoretical thinking about them is therefore important [45].

Our theoretical work on biological systems produces hypotheses about properties and possible mechanisms [16, 41], and we expect to use them to build more interesting computing systems. Constructed Complex Systems need many of those properties and mechanisms to deal with the kinds of complex environments in which we place them, and to deal with the others that use them, both humans and other computing systems.

We believe that any computing system that is intended to support human activities will also need many of those properties and mechanisms, because human users need better clerks [54]. We want clerks that support humans to be

- industrious,
- controllable,
- knowledgeable,
- adaptive,
- inventive,

and many other properties not normally associated with computing systems. We think that tools for designing, building, and managing constructed complex systems are an important special case [57, 58].

We study properties of and mechanisms for intelligence and autonomy [52, 65]: we observe, identify, or postulate important or interesting properties [13, 41, 45], we invent mechanisms that we expect to provide those properties, we define requirements for and specifications of algorithms for the mechanisms, and we implement those algorithms in complex computing systems for study [38].

3   Approach

There are many approaches to building autonomous systems, ranging from those based on a distributed or reflective infrastructure [28, 33, 52], those that are expected to display realistic or comfortable behaviors [11, 21, 66], to those that are more simply reactive [9, 19] (see also [18] for a survey of many different styles of implementation),

There are also many interesting descriptions of agent cooperation, that is, how autonomous systems coordinate their activities or negotiate task or resource partitions. When the agents are not very similar, the coordination processes matter much more than otherwise. Recent results obtained with heterogeneous but cooperative agents [70, 71] show the value of teamwork and common goals (see also [24] for a particularly interesting description of multi-agent systems).

Our approach to all of these difficult design problems is to build model-based analysis systems [56], with the models carrying the essential information for the system to use. Thus we generally work along the lines of [5, 65], but with significant differences in detail. We want as little as possible to be built-in, and as much as possible to be modeled explicitly and therefore analyzable. Ideally, everything is described using explicit models that are analyzable, which implies that self-analysis is possible. The reason we want these characteristics is simple: purely reactive agents are way too slow to operate effectively in complex environments; we need *anticipatory agents* [23], with models of their own processes, so they can identify anomalies in their behavior or in their environment's behavior [32].

The main hard problem is to define the connection between the models (descriptions) and the processes. This connection must be effective in both directions, from descriptions to processes (by interpretation), and from processes to descriptions (by model construction, analysis, and validation), though the system does not need to analyze those processes for which it is already given a description (besides, this is hard). We would, however, like to have some method of validation that the description does in fact describe the process (this is also hard in general).

Such a system may therefore need bootstrap processes that exist separately from the models and are not derived from them (at least at first), but we claim that this will not be necessary after the first implementations. The reason is that we start with some method of converting process descriptions to processes, and one of the descriptions describes that method. The original conversion program is written in some language for which previously existing conversion tools exist, or converted by hand into an executable program. After that first run, subsequent conversions are computed using the description of the conversion process and the process produced in the previous cycle. The process is illustrated in Figure 1.

An example of this kind of processing is the "moby hack" of Ken Thompson that was in some early internal versions of the UNIX operating system [72], in which an executable version of the C compiler would compile special code into the login program and into the C compiler itself, code that was not present in the source code for either one of them. Since the C compiler could recognize the source code for both of those programs fairly reliably, it could add in compiled code that was not present in the source code (this covert code had the recognition algorithms and code insertion functions in it, among other things).

The attempt to remove the bootstrap process entirely has generated much heat and little light, but there are several new mathematical developments that lead to interesting approaches and possibilities. The most common response to

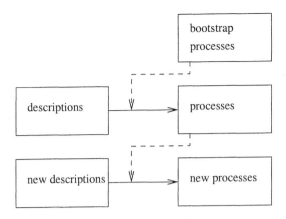

Fig. 1. Bootstrap Conversion Process

the problem is capitulation, such as in [33], where multiple agents each examine the rest to avoid the circular self-analysis, and in all other approaches that separate the "watchers" from the "watched".

There are also many different kinds of arguments that it cannot be done, such as those in [23], referring to Löfgren's linguistic complementarity: "no language can be completely defined within itself" [60], and those in [29] that show that infinite regress or circularity in definitions is unavoidable. It turns out that the necessity of grounding all the definitions externally or otherwise, which is essential for the usual kind of inductive definitions [2], is not the only possible approach. Co-inductive definitions can also be useful and much more powerful [30], do not need complete grounding, and it is shown in [25] that circularity in a set of definitions can be a powerful and well-defined computational tool. Similarly, well-foundedness is not necessary for meaningful definitions [40]. Non-well-founded Sets have a theory as good as (i.e., as consistent as, if not as well known as) ordinary Set Theory [3, 8].

Similarly, [60] describes the well-known tension between interpretability and describability: the more expressive a language is, the harder it is to interpret. We can avoid much of the difficulty if the symbol system (i.e., the language itself) can change, a possibility we have considered and advocated for some time [42, 50]. It does not change the fact that there is a trade-off; it merely moves it farther away.

Even though our diagram shows the connection from descriptions to processes going in only one direction, we can easily imagine inductive inference processes [6] helping to produce descriptions of observed process behavior in some cases (though this process is difficult in general [73, 74]).

4   Terminology

In order to make our intentions easier to describe and understand, we provide some term definitions and distinctions that we use in the rest of the paper. These definitions are to be regarded as provisional, and only applicable in the context of this discussion.

For this paper, *actors* are active entities (particular hardware configurations or executable files in a particular operating system environment), *processes* are the behaviors (actors acting), *actions* are events (instantaneous) or transitions (not necessarily instantaneous) or trajectories (to allow for continuous changes), *definitions* are programs (they always require interpreters), *descriptions* are meta-knowledge (semantics of the processes and their uses), and *interfaces* are also meta-knowledge (only the interaction syntax and protocols).

Any system has a range of symbolic constructs and activities, which can roughly be categorized as expressions of different kinds, according to the processes that can be applied to them:

(kind of expression) : (supported activities)
process : activation
process definition : interpretation
process description : analysis
process interface : comparison

The last three are models of some phenomenon (the first one is the phenomenon itself). The step from definition to description is not always one of losing information, since many analyses that we might want to perform are undecidable in general from the definition alone (e.g., termination).

Similarly, we distinguish the definitions from the descriptions by taking the definitions as just the running code, either executable programs or executable interpreters with process descriptions. On the other hand, specifications of behavior are always descriptions. They are most detailed when they uniquely define that behavior, but they are still just descriptions (models).

5   Architecture

We describe very briefly the main concepts and entities of the Wrapping approach to Constructed Complex System infrastructure, since it underlies our confidence that we can do as we claim. It is necessarily fairly cryptic, but all of the details can be found in the references, especially [41, 43, 45, 58].

We have raised to an architectural principle the notion of multiplicity. No one model or method suffices to define a complex system completely [16, 17], so that multiple models must coexist and be used in concert. We must recognize that there is almost never just "one way" that suffices for all tasks or descriptions; we will need to have several methods. The system infrastructure must therefore support multiplicity in system components and models. This even applies to model resolution, temporal and otherwise [63–65].

The structure of a Wrapping system is based on two kinds of entities: descriptions and processes. The descriptions are called *Wrapping*s. They describe all computational resources in a system, not only *how* to use them for particular problems, but also *when, whether,* and *why.* They are organized into *Wrapping*

Knowledge Bases, or *WKBs*, that can be viewed as context-dependent mappings from *posed problems* (i.e., information service requests) in a particular context, to computational *resources* (i.e., information service providers) that can be applied to the given problem in the given context. These mappings are described by the WKBs, which is why we call the process Knowledge-Based Polymorphism.

The processes that provide the information services are called *resources*, and though our implementations have generally assumed that the collection of resources is fixed, there is nothing in the approach that requires it, since it is quite simple to imagine a resource whose service is to find other resources for particular problems in particular contexts. This distinction between information service requests (called *problems*) and information service providers (called *resources*) is the essence of the Problem Posing Programming Paradigm [43, 44]: any programming or modeling notation can be interpreted using this distinction, which allows tremendous flexibility in making the connections from problems to appropriate resources, and makes interconnecting multiple languages much simpler.

The programs that read Wrappings and connect the resources to each other are called *Problem Managers*. which can be thought of as varyingly sophisticated planners. The last important aspect of Wrappings is that these PMs are also resources, and they also have Wrappings that can be used to select them in appropriate contexts. That means that the system is Computationally Reflective in a strong sense: it has models of the situations of use of all of its parts. All resources are selected as defined in the Wrappings, according to appropriate context, including both the system's basic planning and integration functions and the basic Knowledge Base reader functions, which means that they can all be replaced; these systems have no privileged resources at all.

The Wrapping theory therefore has four basic features:

1. ALL parts of a system architecture are *resources*, including programs, data, user interfaces, and everything else;
2. ALL activities in the system are *problem study*, (i.e., all activities *apply* a resource to a *posed problem*), including user interactions, information requests and announcements within the system, service or processing requests, etc.;
3. *Wrapping Knowledge Bases* contain *Wrappings*, which are explicit machine-processable descriptions of all of the resources and how they can be applied to problems to support what we have called the Intelligent User Support (IUS) functions [10]:
   - *Selection* (which resources to apply to a problem),
   - *Assembly* (how to let them work together),
   - *Integration* (when and why they should work together),
   - *Adaptation* (how to adjust them to work on the problem), and
   - *Explanation* (why certain resources were or will be used);
4. *Problem Managers (PMs)*, including the *Study Managers(SMs)* and the *Coordination Manager (CM)*, are algorithms that use the Wrapping descriptions to collect and select resources to apply to problems. The PMs are also resources, and they are also Wrapped. These PMs are usually defined as structured sequences of steps.

The Wrapping information and processes form expert interfaces to all of the different ways to use resources in a heterogeneous system that are known to the system. The most important conceptual simplifications that the Wrapping approach brings to integration are the uniformities of the first two features: the uniformity of treating everything in the system as resources, the uniformity of treating everything that happens in the system as problem study. The most important algorithmic simplification is the reflection provided by treating the PMs as resources themselves. These uniformities are the coordinative processes for our desired flexibilities of resource selection and problem posing (it is a fundamental philosophical principle of ours that every flexibility must have a corresponding coordinative mechanism to manage it). These ideas have proven to be useful, even when implemented and applied in informal and *ad hoc* ways.

A Wrapping is not simply an interface "to" a resource; it is an interface to the "use" of a resource. We Wrap "uses" of resources instead of resources in and of themselves, since many analysis tools have grown by accretion over the years, and common ways to use them have developed their own style. We gain conceptual simplicity by separating the styles of use into different descriptions. Similarly, combinations of resources that often work together may have a single Wrapping for the combination, in addition to separate Wrappings for separate ways to use the resources by themselves.

Because the Problem Managers are also Wrapped, the entire system is Computationally Reflective [34, 39, 52, 61, 62], so that all of our integration support processes apply to themselves, too. It is these descriptions of all the resource uses that underlies this ability of the system to analyze its own behavior, and thereby provide the great power and flexibility of resource use.

Another source of flexibility in these systems is to have many different resources that address the same problem. For example, in pattern recognition systems, an analysis algorithm may exist with different sets of assumptions. Simple versions of an analysis algorithm depend on assumptions about the data. As different classes of assumptions are identified, different versions of the algorithms become more interesting or more appropriate. There is therefore a lattice (or at least a partially ordered set) of input spaces defined by those sets of constraints.

The algorithm can be essentially the same in all cases, but the programs are very dependent on the data structures used to account for the properties of the input spaces. Even when a "most general" method exists, which is not always, it is often much more effective to find an applicable special case, since the appropriate specializations can save much time and produce much more accurate results, when they apply.

This approach leads, ideally, to a kind of generic programming [43], in which a series of different programs are all derivable from a single algorithmic description, according to different context and usage conditions. We generally write these generic programs in *wrex*, our Wrapping expression notation, which is nearly semantically neutral, making very few design decisions in advance [68]. The semantics of expressions in *wrex* is defined by the resources that the system can

```
define
CM [ <usr> ]:
    [
    <cxt> = Find context [ <usr> ],
    for ever :
        [
        <prob> = Pose problem [ <usr> ],
        <res> = Study problem [ <usr>, <prob>, <cxt> ],
        Present results [ <usr>, <res> ]
        ]
    ],
```

Fig. 2. Default Coordination Manager (CM) Step Sequence, in *wrex*

attach to their constituents and arrangements (by interpreting them as organized sets of problems).

For example, one of the PMs is the *Coordination Manager* (or *CM*), which is a kind of heartbeat that drives some Wrapping systems, by performing a sequence of steps that manage all of the system activity. It is shown in Figure 2 as written in *wrex*. In particular, the steps are intended to cycle through a loop of getting a problem posed and using one of the other PMs, called the *Study Manager* (or *SM*) to study it. However, that behavior depends on the resource applied to the problem "for ever :" in the program (much more about *wrex* can be found in [43, 44]).

The design choices in Wrappings are useful and interesting for high-autonomy systems, but they lead to several questions about how to implement such systems.

Why do high autonomy systems require anticipatory modeling?

They don't. However, reactive systems are much too slow in a complex environment, so anticipation of environmental effects, and modeling of the potential effects of actions, are necessary to keep up with alternative contingencies.

Why do high autonomy systems require reflective complex architectures?

They don't. However, they do require

- self- and situation-monitoring,
- selection from alternatives that are already in progress,
- heterogeneous-initiative behavior (not just mixed-),
- continual contemplation for learning

We think that these are enough reasons to want reflection (if the system has access to descriptions of what it needs to do, what it is doing, and what it can do, then it can make better choices).

Why do high autonomy systems require knowledge-based architectures?

They don't. However, biological systems have an enormous and mysterious capability for generative processes to create the variation spaces within which activities are constrained [16], and then from which they are selected ("controlled sources of variation"), and until we have such generative processes in computing systems, we have to replace them with something else. We have chosen to use explicit knowledge bases and interpreters thereof.

6   Sustainment

The next step is to determine what processes need to be available to make this kind of a system sustainable. Such a system has at least the two kinds of components mentioned: the descriptions and the processes. Descriptions are not active; declarative statements do nothing. Processes provide the "spark of agency", accounting for all activity in a system.

We want the descriptions to be complete, that is, to describe all of what the processes do, in some modeling notation or notations that can be interpreted by other processes (which must of course also be part of the system, in order to close the loop).

We want a rich enough set of notations (or fragments of notational systems) that everything we want to describe can be conveniently described. Each notation fragment has to have an interpreter, which defines how that notation fragment is to be understood or activated, and an integrator, which defines how that notation fragment interacts with others, and all of those interpreters and integrators are written in at least one of those notations or fragments.

At least one of the interpreters needs to have an alternative definition in some existing compilable notation (most likely some ordinary programming language), so that the first processes in the system can be built.

But we also want the system to be Wrapping based [45], since it provides such a flexible infrastructure, so we need to have some knowledge-base definition notations and their interpreters. We could presumably write all of this in C, for example, as we did in the earlier Wrapping implementations [48], or in some other common programming language, but the resulting code would be too far removed from the compiled processes to be easily understood (and of course, there are even undecidability issues in trying to devise descriptions of behavior from code), and we would like better and more natural notations for the Wrappings.

Such a notation must express the appropriate conditions on resource use: under what contexts is the resource applicable, for what problems is it appropriate to use, what are its context and input requirements, what products or services does it provide, and how is it to be used in that context for that problem. The same resource can be used for many problems in different contexts, and even for the same problem in different ways in different contexts, and many resources may apply to the same problem in any context.

These notations are generally divided into three kinds: those that describe context spaces, those that describe problem spaces, and those that describe resource spaces. The context spaces define subject areas, application domains, and the corresponding concepts and local terminology that can be used to define problems and processes. The problem spaces define collections of terms and concepts associated with particular classes of problems, so that they can be stated clearly and distinctly, according to particular contexts. The resource spaces define collections of activities and processes that can be used to address various problems in their appropriate context. The notations that describe these spaces range from simple lists of alternative labels to complex interrelated syntactic structures. The interpreters for the notations can be selected according to context conditions (as are any resources in a Wrapping-based system).

7 Dependencies

As we have mentioned earlier, and shown elsewhere (see the Wrapping references), a Wrapping system depends on the Problem Managers (PMs) and their step functions, the Knowledge Bases (KBs) and their readers, the symbol dictionaries, and the other infrastructure and application domain resources. The other resources can be written in any languages, and compiled or interpreted by the corresponding programs.

All of our earlier Wrapping implementations define their knowledge bases and many other informational data files using "keyword-value" pairs, with each file being defined as a sequence of records, and each record containing a sequence of elements that are keyword-value pairs, using a fixed set of keywords, and values that are expressions with a type that depends on the keyword. Any of the file formats can use a kind of "tuple template" notation, which formalizes the process of associating the types of expressions to the corresponding keywords, and which sequences of keywords are valid for any given file format. Such a tuple template notation at least needs to have some of the usual basic datatypes, namely, boolean, string, and integer, and some expression-forming combinations for them (logical connectives, arithmetic, etc.). More expressive versions can have more types and more combinations., and more flexible sequence constraints. The interpretation of such a notation requires a program written in C or some other basic programming language.

The dictionaries need to map resource names (strings) to program addresses (address symbols in object files), so they depend in our earlier implementations on the UNIX "dlopen()" library, and on the C compiler to make the function calls. This is essentially the only operating system dependency (Scheme, Smalltalk, Snobol, and many other languages have the ability to use string data as program symbols directly).

We have written PMs and PM steps in C and in *wrex*, so they depend on having a C compiler or a *wrex* interpreter written in C, which depends in turn on the C compiler and a Wrapping system. So if we want to use the *wrex* definitions instead of the C programs, then the dependency graph has a cycle that needs to be broken in some way.

It turns out that a translator from *wrex* to C in a Wrapping context is enough. It requires C code for the syntax recognition and parsing, which already exists in earlier *wrex* interpreters, and some new C code for the output generation, which is not hard. We can write such a "w2c" program in *wrex* or in C (we have parts of this program written in C already). As soon as we can write a *wrex*-to-C converter in C, we can start this bootstrapping process and avoid the circularity,

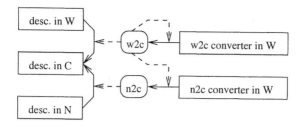

Fig. 3. Adding New Notations

including other languages via their C or *wrex* definitions. These relationships are shown in Figure 3.

We have written Knowledge Base interpreters with tuple template conventions (they could as easily be written in XML or any other syntax description notation, as long as we also have a reader and an information extractor), and the Knowledge Base readers and interpreters in C (we have neither an explicit definition for the notational conventions used in our earlier implementations or any XML work on the syntax).

We have written the dictionaries using C, and we could write them in an address mapping notation (we do not have an explicit definition for the notation, but the association rules are very simple in this case, mapping string data to address symbols).

8   Languages and Notations

We have described in this paper a system organization that extends the self-modeling down much further than in the usual Wrapping implementations. In this section, we describe some of the language relationships that are necessary for this kind of model-based system to work.

The history of our Wrapping development has repeatedly moved from processes to descriptions of those processes, which must be written in some notation. As we have studied the minimal essentials in a Wrapping system, we have made transformations from processes (e.g., a *wrex* parser) to notations that define the relevant notation (e.g., various styles of Backus-Naur Form for *wrex* syntax definition [4]) and the processes that transform an expression in the notation into a process (e.g., a C program for a table-driven parser generator or interpreter like the Cocke-Kasami-Younger parser [4], as modified by Vaughn Pratt [67] and extended by the first author [35] to produce an extremely simple and flexible chart parser [31] with some convenient complexity properties [26]). These transformations mean that more and more of the operation of a Wrapping system is made explicit and therefore interpretable. Our goal is to make the entire system consist of a set of descriptions and processes derived from those descriptions using interpreters, which are also among those descriptions.

We can use here again the strategy of multiple layers of constraints, using well-known grammatical description mechanisms that define different classes of languages with different levels of expressive power [4]): from regular sets at the simpler end through context-free grammars, and then extended attribute grammars.

This movement towards making everything more explicit requires that the resources are written in *wrex* or other notations for describing processes, models, and data structures. For these to be used effectively, the system needs translators from at least one of those notations (say N, which might or might not be *wrex*) into some programming language. These translators can be written in N or *wrex* or anything else, but at least one of them needs to be written in a programming language that can be compiled, to start the bootstrapping process. These relationships are also shown in Figure 3.

We can also use almost any other programming language to write models, and it provides an extra degree of flexibility to have compilers written in several of those languages for the others. While there are some efficiency arguments against using multiple languages, we prefer the counter argument that different languages are more appropriate for different kinds of resources or resource uses, so that having multiple languages makes the resources easier to write.

We also think that we can eliminate the ordinary programming languages altogether, except at the beginning, in favor of *wrex* and a collection of domain-specific notations. This would work by having the original *wrex*-to-C translator written in both *wrex* and C, translated thereby to an executable program, and used thereafter to convert *wrex* programs and other descriptions into C, including itself. This process would allow the context-based changes of interpretation to be incorporated into the translators at each stage, thus greatly facilitating the gradual transitions from semantic differences discovered or invented by the interpreters into syntactic ones expressed in the notations themselves.

9   Conclusions

We have already shown earlier that we can build Computationally Reflective systems based on Wrappings, which are self-modeling down to a resource level, but resources are generally fairly large units of program code that cannot be further decomposed within the system. We think that this kind of self-modeling can be extended down to a very small descriptive unit level, such as single statement expressions or small fragments of modeling notations and programming languages.

In this paper, we described a system architecture, based on Wrappings, in which all executable parts of the system have explicit descriptions (in various notations) that are used to produce those parts (by compilation, translation, or interpretation). In this sense, the system has a complete description of its own behavior-generating steps, which it can use to analyze its own behavior. We think that this is a good first step towards a system that has a much more complete description of its own behavior than most programs do.

Furthermore, we have studied the basic representational mechanisms that such a system might use, and shown that they have inherent limitations unless the system can change its own symbol system (these are the "Get Stuck" theorems [42]). We have begun to study how a system might be able to avoid some of these limitations, by having processes that analyze and evaluate its own representational mechanisms (and the corresponding interpreters), and use the detected deficiencies to help change them [12, 38].

References

1. Harold Abelson, Gerald Sussman, with Julie Sussman, *The Structure and Interpretation of Computer Programs*, Bradford Books, now MIT Press (1985)
2. Peter Aczel, "Inductive Definitions", Chapter C.7, pp. 739-782 in [7]
3. Peter Aczel, *Non-well-founded Sets*, CSLI Lecture Notes Number 14, Center for the Study of Language and Information, Stanford U., U. Chicago Press (1988)
4. Alfred V. Aho, Jeffrey D. Ullman, *The Theory of Parsing, Translation, and Compiling, Volume I: Parsing*, Prentice-Hall (1973)
5. James S. Albus, Alexander M. Meystel, *Engineering of Mind: An Introduction to the Science of Intelligent Systems*, Wiley (2001)
6. Dana Angluin, Carl H. Smith, "Inductive Inference: Theory and Methods", *Computing Surveys*, Volume 15, Number 3, pp. 237-269 (September 1983)
7. Jon Barwise (ed.), *Handbook of Mathematical Logic*, Studies in Logic and the Foundations of Mathematics, Volume 90, North-Holland (1977)
8. Jon Barwise, Lawrence Moss, *Vicious Circles: On the Mathematics of Non-Wellfounded Phenomena*, CSLI Lecture Notes Number 60, Center for the Study of Language and Information, Stanford U. (1996)
9. Randall D. Beer, Roger D. Quinn, Hillel J. Chiel, Roy E. Ritzmann, "Biologically Inspired Approaches to Robotics", *Communications of the ACM*, Volume 40, Number 3, pp. 30-38 (March 1997)
10. Kirstie L. Bellman, "An Approach to Integrating and Creating Flexible Software Environments Supporting the Design of Complex Systems", pp. 1101-1105 in *Proceedings of WSC'91: The 1991 Winter Simulation Conference*, 8-11 December 1991, Phoenix, Arizona (1991)
11. Kirstie L. Bellman, "Emotions: Meaningful Mappings between an Individual and its World" (invited paper), *Proceedings of a Workshop on Emotions in Humans and Artifacts*, 13-14 August 1999, Vienna, Austria (1999)
12. Kirstie L. Bellman, "The Challenge for a New Type of Computational Semiotics: The Roles and Limitations of Diverse Representations in Virtual Worlds", *Proceedings of VWsim'01: The 2001 Virtual Worlds and Simulation Conference, WMC'2001: The 2001 SCS Western MultiConference*, 7-11 January 2001, Phoenix, SCS (2001)
13. Kirstie L. Bellman and Lou Goldberg, "Common Origin of Linguistic and Movement Abilities", *American Journal of Physiology*, Volume 246, pp. R915-R921 (1984)
14. Kirstie L. Bellman, Christopher Landauer, "Integration Science is More Than Putting Pieces Together", in *Proceedings of the 2000 IEEE Aerospace Conference (CD)*, 18-25 March 2000, Big Sky, Montana (2000)
15. Kirstie L. Bellman, Christopher Landauer, "Towards an Integration Science: The Influence of Richard Bellman on our Research", *Journal of Mathematical Analysis and Applications*, Volume 249, Number 1, pp. 3-31 (2000)
16. Kirstie L. Bellman and Donald O. Walter, "Biological Processing", *American Journal of Physiology*, Volume 246, pp. R860-R867 (1984)

17. Richard Bellman, P. Brock, "On the concepts of a problem and problem-solving", *American Mathematical Monthly*, Volume 67, pp. 119-134 (1960)
18. Jeffrey M. Bradshaw (ed.), *Software Agents*, AAAI Press (1997)
19. Rodney Brooks, *Cambrian Intelligence: The Early History of the New AI*, MIT (1999)
20. Olivier Danvy, Robert Glück, Peter Thiemann (eds.), *Partial Evaluation, Proceedings of the International Seminar*, 12-16 February 1996, Dagstuhl Castle, Germany, Springer Lecture Notes in Computer Science, Volume 1110 (1996)
21. Kerstin Dautenhahn, "Socially Situated Life-Like Agents", pp. 191-196 in *Proceedings VWsim'99: The 1999 Virtual Worlds and Simulation Conference*, part of *WMC'99: The 1999 SCS Western Multi-Conference*, 18-20 January, San Francisco (1999)
22. Kerstin Dautenhahn (ed.), *Human Cognition and Social Agent Technology*, Benjamins (2000)
23. Bertil Ekdahl, Eric Astor, Paul Davidsson, "Towards Anticipatory Agents", pp. 191-202 in M. Wooldridge, N. R. Jennings (eds.), *Intelligent Agents - Theories, Architectures, and Languages*, Springer LNAI 898 (1995); also on the Web at URL "http: //citeseer. nj. nec. com/ ekdahl95towards. html" (availability last checked 17 February 2002)
24. Jacques Ferber, *Multi-Agent Systems*, Addison Wesley Longman (1999); translation of Jacques Ferber, *Les Systèmes Multi-Agents: Vers une intelligence collective*, InterEditions, Paris (1995)
25. Joseph Goguen, Kai Lin, and Grigore Roşu, "Circular Coinductive Rewriting", pp. 123-131 in *Proceedings of ASE'00: The 15th International Conference on Automated Software Engineering*, 11-15 September 2000, Grenoble, France, IEEE Press (2000)
26. Susan L. Graham, Michael A. Harrison, Walter L. Ruzzo, "An Improved Context-Free Recognizer", *ACM Transactions on Programming Languages and Systems*, Volume 2, No. 3, pp. 415-462 (July 1980)
27. John Hatcliff, Torben Æ. Mogensen, Peter Thiemann (eds.), *Partial Evaluation: Practice and Theory, Proceedings of the DIKU 1998 International Summer School*, 29 June - 10 July 1998, Copenhagen, Denmark, Springer Lecture Notes in Computer Science, Volume 1706 (1998)
28. Barbara Hayes-Roth, Karl Pfleger, Philippe Lalanda, Philippe Morignot, Marka Balabanovic, "A Domain-Specific Software Architecture for Adaptive Intelligent Systems", *IEEE Transactions on Software Engineering*, Volume SE-21, No. 4, pp. 288-301 (April 1995)
29. Francis Heylighen, "Advantages and Limitations of Formal Expression"; on the Web at URL "http: //citeseer. nj. nec. com/ heylighen99advantages. html" (availability last checked 17 February 2002)
30. Bart Jacobs, Jan Rutten, "A Tutorial on (Co)Algebras and (Co)Induction", *EATCS Bulletin*, Volume 62, pp. 222-259 (1997)
31. Martin Kay, "Algorithm schemata and data structures in syntactic processing", Report CSL-80-12, Xerox PARC (1980); reprinted in Barbara Grosz, Karen Sparck-Jones, Bonnie Lynn Webber (eds.), *Readings in Natural Language Processing*, Morgan Kauffman (1986)
32. Catriona M. Kennedy, "A Conceptual Foundation for Autonomous Learning in Unforeseen Situations", Tech. Rpt. WV-98-01, Dresden Univ. Technology (1998); also on the Web at URL "http: //citeseer. nj. nec. com/ kennedy98conceptual. html" (availability last checked 17 February 2002)

33. Catriona M. Kennedy, "Distributed Reflective Architectures for Adjustable Autonomy", in David Kortenkamp, Gregory Dorais, Karen L. Myers (eds.), *Proceedings of IJCAI-99 Workshop on Adjustable Autonomy Systems*, 1 August 1999, Stockholm, Sweden (1999); a similar note is on the web at URL "http://citeseer.nj.nec.com/kennedy99distributed.html" (availability last checked 17 February 2002)

34. Gregor Kiczales, Jim des Rivières, Daniel G. Bobrow, *The Art of the Meta-Object Protocol*, MIT Press (1991)

35. Christopher A. Landauer, "Table Parser Description", informal report (available from the author), Pattern Analysis and Recognition Corp. (1977)

36. Christopher Landauer, "Wrapping Mathematical Tools", pp. 261-266 in *Proceedings of EMC'90: The 1990 SCS Eastern MultiConference*, 23-26 April 1990, Nashville, Tennessee, Simulation Series, Volume 22(3), SCS (1990); also pp. 415-419 in *Proceedings of Interface'90: The 22nd Symposium on the Interface (between Computer Science and Statistics)*, 17-19 May 1990, East Lansing, Michigan (1990)

37. Christopher Landauer, "Wrapping Mathematical Tools for Design Analysis", *Proceedings of SOAR'90: The 1990 Conference on Space Operations, Automation, and Robotics*, 26-28 June 1990, Albuquerque, New Mexico (1990)

38. Christopher Landauer, "Some Measurable Characteristics of Intelligence", Paper WP 1.7.5, *Proceedings of SMC'2000: The 2000 IEEE International Conference on Systems, Man, and Cybernetics (CD)*, 8-11 October 2000, Nashville Tennessee (2000)

39. Christopher Landauer, Kirstie L. Bellman, "The Role of Self-Referential Logics in a Software Architecture Using Wrappings", *Proceedings of ISS '93: the 3rd Irvine Software Symposium*, 30 April 1993, U. C. Irvine, California (1993)

40. Christopher Landauer, Kirstie L. Bellman, "Mathematics and Linguistics", pp. 153-158 in Alex Meystel, Jim Albus, R. Quintero (eds.), *Intelligent Systems: A Semiotic Perspective, Proceedings of the 1996 International Multidisciplinary Conference, Volume I: Theoretical Semiotics, Workshop on New Mathematical Foundations for Computer Science*, 20-23 October 1996, NIST, Gaithersburg, Maryland (1996)

41. Christopher Landauer, Kirstie L. Bellman, "Computational Embodiment: Constructing Autonomous Software Systems", pp. 42-54 in Judith A. Lombardi (ed.), *Continuing the Conversation: Dialogues in Cybernetics, Volume I, Proceedings of the 1997 ASC Conference*, American Society for Cybernetics, 8-12 March 1997, U. Illinois (1997); pp. 131-168 in *Cybernetics and Systems: An International Journal*, Volume 30, Number 2 (1999)

42. Christopher Landauer, Kirstie L. Bellman, "Situation Assessment via Computational Semiotics", pp. 712-717 in *Proceedings ISAS'98: the 1998 International MultiDisciplinary Conference on Intelligent Systems and Semiotics*, 14-17 September 1998, NIST, Gaithersburg, Maryland (1998)

43. Christopher Landauer, Kirstie L. Bellman, "Generic Programming, Partial Evaluation, and a New Programming Paradigm", Paper ETSPI02 in *Proceedings of HICSS'99: The 32nd Hawaii Conference on System Sciences (CD), Track III: Emerging Technologies, Software Process Improvement Mini-Track*, 5-8 January 1999, Maui, Hawaii (1999); revised and expanded version in Christopher Landauer, Kirstie L. Bellman, "Generic Programming, Partial Evaluation, and a New Programming Paradigm", Chapter 8, pp. 108-154 in Gene McGuire (ed.), *Software Process Improvement*, Idea Group Publishing (1999)

44. Christopher Landauer, Kirstie L. Bellman, "Problem Posing Interpretation of Programming Languages", Paper ETECC07 in *Proceedings of HICSS'99: The 32nd Hawaii Conference on System Sciences (CD), Track III: Emerging Technologies, Engineering Complex Computing Systems Mini-Track*, 5-8 January 1999, Maui, Hawaii (1999)

45. Christopher Landauer, Kirstie L. Bellman, "Computational Embodiment: Agents as Constructed Complex Systems", Chapter 11, pp. 301-322 in [22]

46. Christopher Landauer, Kirstie L. Bellman, "Agent-Based Information Infrastructure", in *Proceedings of Agents'99/AOIS'99: Workshop on Agent-Oriented Information Systems*, 1 May 1999, Seattle, Washington (1999)

47. Christopher Landauer, Kirstie L. Bellman, "New Architectures for Constructed Complex Systems", in *The 7th Bellman Continuum, International Workshop on Computation, Optimization and Control*, 24-25 May 1999, Santa Fe, NM (1999); in *Applied Mathematics and Computation*, Volume 120, pp. 149-163 (May 2001)

48. Christopher Landauer, Kirstie L. Bellman, "Lessons Learned with Wrapping Systems", pp. 132-142 in *Proceedings of ICECCS'99: the 5th International Conference on Engineering Complex Computing Systems*, 18-22 October 1999, Las Vegas, Nevada (1999)

49. Christopher Landauer, Kirstie L. Bellman, "Architectures for Embodied Intelligence", pp. 215-220 in *Proceedings of ANNIE'99: The 1999 Artificial Neural Nets and Industrial Engineering Conference, Special Track on Bizarre Systems*, 7-10 November 1999, St. Louis, Mo. (1999)

50. Christopher Landauer, Kirstie L. Bellman, "Symbol Systems in Constructed Complex Systems", pp. 191-197 in *Proceedings of ISIC/ISAS'99: The 1999 IEEE International Symposium on Intelligent Control*, 15-17 September 1999, Cambridge, Massachusetts (1999)

51. Christopher Landauer, Kirstie L. Bellman, "Relationships and Actions in Conceptual Categories", pp. 59-72 in G. Stumme (Ed.), *Working with Conceptual Structures - Contributions to ICCS 2000, Auxiliary Proceedings of ICCS'2000: The 8th International Conference on Conceptual Structures*, 14-18 August 2000, Darmstadt, Shaker Verlag, Aachen (August 2000)

52. Christopher Landauer, Kirstie L. Bellman, "Reflective Infrastructure for Autonomous Systems", pp. 671-676, Volume 2 in *Proceedings of EMCSR'2000: The 15th European Meeting on Cybernetics and Systems Research, Symposium on Autonomy Control: Lessons from the Emotional*, 25-28 April 2000, Vienna (April 2000)

53. Christopher Landauer, Kirstie L. Bellman, "Symbol Systems and Meanings in Virtual Worlds", *Proceedings of VWsim'01: The 2001 Virtual Worlds and Simulation Conference, WMC'2001: The 2001 SCS Western MultiConference*, 7-11 January 2001, Phoenix, SCS (2001)

54. Christopher Landauer, Kirstie L. Bellman, "Conceptual Modeling Systems: Active Knowledge Processes in Conceptual Categories", pp. 131-144 in Guy W. Mineau (Ed.), *Conceptual Structures: Extracting and Representing Semantics, Contributions to ICCS'2001: The 9th International Conference on Conceptual Structures*, 30 July-03 August 2001, Stanford University (August 2001)

55. Christopher Landauer, Kirstie L. Bellman, "Intelligent System Architectures with Wrappings", in *Proceedings of CASYS'2001: The Fifth International Conference on Computing Anticipatory Systems*, 13-18 August 2001, Lièege, Belgium (2001)

56. Christopher Landauer, Kirstie L. Bellman, "Architectures for Autonomous Computing Systems", *Proceedings of ANNIE'2001: The 2001 Artificial Neural Nets and Industrial Engineering Conference, Special Track on Bizarre Systems*, 4-7 November 2001, St. Louis, Missouri (2001)

57. Christopher Landauer, Kirstie L. Bellman, "Abstraction Based Software System Design", *Proceedings of ANNIE'2001: The 2001 Artificial Neural Nets and Industrial Engineering Conference*, 4-7 November 2001, St. Louis, Missouri (2001)

58. Christopher Landauer, Kirstie L. Bellman, "Computational Infrastructure for Experiments in Cognitive Leverage", in *Proceedings of CT'2001: The Fourth International Conference on Cognitive Technology: Instruments of Mind*, 6-9 August 2001, Warwick, U.K. (2001)

59. Christopher Landauer, Kirstie L. Bellman, "Wrappings for One-of-a-Kind System Development", Paper STSSV04 in *Proceedings of HICSS'02: The 35th Hawaii International Conference on System Sciences (CD), Track IX: Software Technology, Advances in Software Specification and Verification Mini-Track*, 7-10 January 2002, Waikoloa, Hawaii (Big Island) (2002)

60. Lars Löfgren, "Phenomena of Autonomy with Explanations in Introspective Language"; on the Web at URL "http: //citeseer. nj. nec. com/ 176143. html" (availability last checked 17 February 2002)

61. Pattie Maes (ed.), Special Issues of *Robotics and Autonomous Systems*, Volume 6, Nos. 1 and 2 (June 1990); reprinted as Pattie Maes (ed.), *Designing Autonomous Agents: Theory and Practice from Biology to Engineering and Back*, MIT / Elsevier (1993)

62. Pattie Maes, D. Nardi (eds.), *Meta-Level Architectures and Reflection, Proceedings of the Workshop on Meta-Level Architectures and Reflection*, 27-30 October 1986, Alghero, Italy, North-Holland (1988)

63. Alex Meystel, "Multiresolutional Architectures for Autonomous Systems with Incomplete and Inadequate Knowledge Representations", Chapter 7, pp. 159-223 in S. G. Tzafestas, H. B. Verbruggen (eds.), *Artificial Intelligence in Industrial Decision Making, Control and Automation*, Kluwer (1995)

64. Alex Meystel, *Semiotic Modeling and Situation Analysis: An Introduction*, AdRem, Inc. (1995)

65. Alexander M. Meystel, James S. Albus, *Intelligent Systems: Architecture, Design, and Control*, Wiley (2002)

66. Paolo Petta, "The Role of Emotions in a Tractable Architecture for Situated Cognizers", (invited paper), *Proceedings of a Workshop on Emotions in Humans and Artifacts*, 13-14 August 1999, Vienna, Austria (1999)

67. Vaughan Pratt, "LINGOL - A Progress Report", working paper 89, MIT (January 1975); also available via World-Wide Web at URL "http: //boole. stanford. edu /pub /lingol75 .ps .gz", 26kb (availability last checked 20 October 1998)

68. Mary Shaw, William A. Wulf, "Tyrannical Languages *still* Preempt System Design", pp. 200-211 in *Proceedings of ICCL'92: The 1992 International Conference on Computer Languages*, 20-23 April 1992, Oakland, California (1992); includes and comments on Mary Shaw, William A. Wulf, "Toward Relaxing Assumptions in Languages and their Implementations", *ACM SIGPLAN Notices*, Volume 15, No. 3, pp. 45-51 (March 1980)

69. Guy L. Steele, Jr., Gerry J. Sussman, "The Art of the Interpreter, or, the Modularity Complex", (Parts Zero, One, and Two), AI Memo 453, MIT (1978)

70. Peter Stone, *Layered Learning in Multiagent Systems: A Winning Approach to Robotic Soccer*, MIT Press (2000)

71. V. S. Subrahmanian, Piero Bonatti, Jürgen Dix, Thomas Eiter¡, Sarit Kraus, Fatma Ozcan, Robert Ross, *Heterogeneous Agent Systems*, MIT Press (2000)

72. Ken Thompson, "Reflections on Trusting Trust", *Communications of the ACM*, Volume 27, Number 8, pp. 761-763 (August 1984), also at URL "http: //www. acm. org/ classics/ sep95/" (availability last checked 17 February 2002); see also the commentary in the "back door" entry of "The Jargon Lexicon", which is widely available on the Web, and in particular, version 4.3.1 can be found at URL "http: //www. tuxedo. org/ ~ esr/ jargon/ html/ entry/ back- door. html" (availability last checked 17 February 2002)

73. Pierre Wolper, "Temporal Logic can be More Expressive", pp. 340-348 in *Proceedings of FoCS 1981: The 22nd Annual IEEE Symposium on the Foundations of Computer Science*, 28-30 October 1981, Nashville, Tennessee, IEEE (1981)

74. Pierre Wolper, "Specification and Synthesis of Communicating Processes using an Extended Temporal Logic", pp. 20-33 in *Proceedings of PoPL 82: The Ninth Annual ACM Symposium on Principles of Programming Languages*, January 1982, Albuquerque, New Mexico, ACM (1982)

From Wetware to Software:
A Cybernetic Perspective of Self-adaptive Software

A.G. Laws, A. Taleb-Bendiab, S.J. Wade, and D. Reilly

School of Computing and Mathematical Sciences,
Liverpool John Moores University
Liverpool L3 3AF
A.Laws@livjm.ac.uk

Abstract. The development and application of software engineering practices over the last thirty years have undoubtedly resulted in the production of significantly improved software. However, the majority of modern software systems remain intrinsically fragile and highly vulnerable to environmental change and require continuing and problematic manual adaptation. In this paper and given the problems inherent in manual software adaptation, the authors argue that imbuing the software system with the ability to self-adapt offers a potentially profitable route forward. For support of this claim, the authors draw on the emerging discipline of self-adaptive software, which seeks to devolve some of the responsibility for maintenance activity to the software itself. Realizing such auto-adaptive capability proves to be a challenging problem. The authors contend that many of the themes, problems and goals currently identified in the field of self-adaptive software bear a striking resemblance to problems that have long formed the basis of enquiry in the well-established field of cybernetics. Classical cybernetics, drawing on mathematical models of the adaptive processes of biological organisms, seeks to identify the general principles of control and communication required for organisms to survive in a changing environment. Consequently, cybernetics appears to offer the potential to apply naturally developed adaptation strategies to software artifacts. Therefore, after discussing these theoretical foundations, this paper reports their practical application by presenting the initial findings from the development of an experimental, agent based, adaptive In-Vehicle Telematics System (IVTS) for use by the Emergency Services.

Introduction

Software engineering has been defined as the application of a systematic, disciplined, quantifiable approach to the development, operation and maintenance of software; that is, the application of engineering to software [15]. Since the establishment of software engineering as a discipline over thirty years ago [32], many techniques have been introduced in pursuit of this goal: structured programming, high-level languages, object-oriented analysis & design and formal process modelling to name but a few [30]. However, while the progress represented by these initiatives and the significantly improved software systems that have resulted is undeniable, the majority of modern software systems nevertheless remain intrinsically fragile. Nowhere is this

R. Laddaga, P. Robertson, and H. Shrobe (Eds.): IWSAS 2001, LNCS 2614, pp. 257–280, 2003.

more apparent than in those systems that attempt to model real world situations. Here, the abstractions and assumptions made in attempting to capture the unbounded, unspecifiable richness of the real world in the finite and static medium of software, inevitably result in systems that are incomplete models of that real world and thus deeply riven with uncertainty. Such systems remain highly vulnerable to change, requiring continuing and increasingly problematic manual intervention, adaptation and evolution, activities upon which software engineering approaches do not appear to have had significant impact. This in turn, suggests that some fundamental problems of software development and usage remain unaddressed and consequently unresolved by current conventional engineering solutions.

It would of course, be unfair to say that these issues have been completely ignored by the software community and a number of relevant research thrusts have made some progress in addressing these concerns. Contributors to the field of software evolution, for example, have long argued that while the technical innovations of software engineering may have delivered local improvements in developmental productivity and a reduction in the need for post-implementation fault-fixing, there is little evidence to suggest that their adoption has improved the overall ability to effectively maintain a software system embedded in an evolving environment.

Some evidence of a growing awareness of the limitations of a purely technical and engineering approach to software development and evolution can be seen in the recent emergence of new approaches to these activities such as; evolutionary programming, intentional programming, model-based programming and self-adaptive software [20]. Although such approaches have yet to gain widespread acceptance in the software community, further evidence of a significant change of viewpoint can be seen in a recent research agenda for software engineering presented by Brereton *et al.*, in which they state:

> *"Software evolution will also remain a major difficulty...it may be possible to evolve software by learning from biological models, through which the evolution of incredibly complex structures has been achieved.".* [8].

One approach to addressing the problems inherent in the manual adaptation of software would be to attempt to minimize the human involvement in such exercises by devolving the responsibility for some adaptive changes to the software itself. Such an approach has been termed "self-adaptive software" and was described by the DARPA Broad Agency Announcement that introduced the field as:

> *"...software that evaluates its own performance and changes behaviour when the evaluation indicates that it is not accomplishing what the software is intended to do, or when better functionality or performance is possible."* [19].

However, realizing such an approach raises significant problems of its own and while the field of software evolution appears to have much valuable experience to offer to the area of self-adaptive software, the authors argue that the most valuable contribution is perhaps in the identification of the value of assuming a more biologically oriented view of software. For the authors contend that many of the themes, problems and goals currently identified in the field of self-adaptive software bear a striking resemblance to problems that in a different context, have long formed the basis of enquiry in the well-established field of cybernetics.

Classical cybernetics, drawing on mathematical models of the adaptive processes of biological organisms, seeks to identify the general principles of control and communication required for organisms to survive in a changing environment. Such is the generality of cybernetic thinking that the principles involved are entirely applicable to both biological and man-made entities and hence provide a bridge between biological and man-made worlds. Consequently, cybernetics appears to offer the potential to apply naturally developed adaptation strategies to software artifacts.

Moreover, a further cybernetic development in the form of the managerial cybernetics of Beer's Viable System Model (VSM) [4, 5], identifies the necessary and sufficient systems that must exist for any purposeful entity to survive in a changing environment and as such offers a conceptual blueprint for the design of self-managing software systems. While the apparent applicability of cybernetic theory to the notion of self-adaptive software is certainly of some academic interest, the worth of such a claim can only be determined in practical application. As yet no means currently exist to fully realize a cybernetic "pattern" of software development, although recent developments in software agents, particularly multi-agent systems, exhibit significant conceptual similarity to a cybernetic approach and hence provide a practical and immediate means to explore and apply these ideas.

Consequently, the remainder of the paper is organized as follows. The first section presents a brief review of the field of software evolution. In the next section, a review of the literature of the field of self-adaptive software is presented, thus facilitating a discussion of the main goals, themes and problems identified in the area. The following section begins with a cybernetic tutorial that serves to highlight the appropriateness of the approach to self-adaptive software and also allows the nature and meaning of the term *adaptation* to emerge. This serves as a foundation for the introduction of the main vehicle of enquiry used in this paper, namely the Viable System Model (VSM). The next section presents both an integration of the previous discussions and demonstrates their application through the development of a robust and theoretically defensible adaptive software architecture realizable by means of multi-agent software. The penultimate section continues with a brief case study that integrates the previous concepts and is drawn from an on-going research project in dependable services provision. Finally, the paper concludes with a discussion of the implications and future possibilities of this work.

Considerations from Software Evolution

In the thirty years since the establishment of software engineering as a discipline and given the remarkable progress in the use of computing technology during this time, it is perhaps not surprising that the processes involved in the initial development of software systems have received significantly more attention from the software community than those involved in maintaining installed systems. However, over this period of time and with a growing understanding of the causes and effects of continued software maintenance on software systems, has come the growing recognition that software systems under these circumstances display very different characteristics to other, physically engineered products. As Lehman comments:

> "...software must evolve, undergoing continuous adaptation and change. It must be treated as an ever to be adapted **organism**, not as a to be produced once **artifact.**" [24].

Yet the current state of the art in software engineering is to attempt to foresee every circumstance that the software may encounter and to provide functionality to cope with those situations. Limited adaptability is provided in the system through the use of alternative control paths activated by run-time decisions [17]. Changes in the situation, other than those catered for by such adaptability, require time-consuming, error-prone manual intervention to adapt the software accordingly. Such continued change quickly degrades the overall quality of the software and leads to an increasingly complex and fragile structure that is difficult to understand and dangerous to change. A spiral of decline builds with increasing speed as increased complexity makes further maintenance more error-prone requiring more maintenance that again increases complexity.

Nevertheless, if the standard definition of software maintenance given below is compared with the description of self-adaptive software provided in the preceding section of the paper, the close relationship between the aims of self-adaptive software and those of the field of software maintenance and evolution are demonstrated.

> "Modification of a software product after delivery to correct faults, to improve performance or other attributes, or to adapt the product to a modified environment." [15].

Of course, while self-adaptive software intends to devolve the responsibility for such activities to the software itself, the field of software maintenance and evolution has, nevertheless, accrued much valuable theoretical understanding and experience of the causes and effects of these activities, knowledge that is highly applicable to the development of self-managing, adaptive software.

To begin this discussion the modelling aspects of software systems are considered. Lehman has described any software program as:

> "...a model of a model within the theory of a model of an abstraction of some portion of the world or of some universe of discourse." [23].

Further consideration of this notion led to the development of a software classification scheme derived from the relationship between the software and the environment in which it is executed. Based on the degree of homomorphism required to obtain a suitable mapping between the problem domain to be addressed and the subsequent software model, the resulting scheme allows software to be categorized into three main classes, namely *S, P* and *E-type software.* [23]

S-type software addresses those types of problems where a completely isomorphic mapping between problem domain and the resulting software is obtainable and hence fully specifiable. The correctness of the software solution obtained is determined solely by comparison with the specification and although the software produced may not be strictly change free, any changes performed would generally be restricted to program-internal issues of elegance, efficiency or correctness.

Problem domains for which an isomorphic mapping to software cannot be obtained because of physical resource limitations results in *P-type* software. Reducing the problem to manageable proportions requires the introduction of approximation and assumption, necessitating a homomorphic weakening of the mapping between the problem domain and the software solution. Selection of the particular assumptions and approximations used to achieve such a restricted mapping relies on human judgment and the resulting solution must reflect that human viewpoint to some extent. Uncertainty is necessarily introduced in the resulting software by the process of abstraction and assumption selection. The appropriateness of the derived mapping is evaluated by comparison with the real environment; differences are then identified and corrected. However, the changes noted generally reflect a changed perception of the problem domain, not that the problem has changed.

The last software category, *E-type* software is defined as software that addresses an application, activity or problem in a real-world domain [29]. Given the finite nature of software and the unbounded nature of the real-world, the software system is, of necessity, an incomplete model of the operational domain. Although closely related to the previous category, the vital difference is that the installed software system becomes part of the world that it models and hence changes the nature of the problem situation it was introduced to address. This can lead to new possibilities and applications and, in combination with the incompleteness of the system, leads to the establishment of an intrinsic feedback loop and an inevitable, continuing need for change in the system. Interestingly, in the light of the following discussion, Lehman, while admitting to the logical impossibility of this in a finite domain model, asserts that the software system must contain a model of itself and its own operation in the operational domain. The lack of such a model is highlighted as another source of incompleteness and imprecision in the software [28].

The success of initially deploying such a software system in the real world relies upon the validity of the assumptions selected to model that world. As long as those assumptions hold then the system should operate effectively, however, changes in the world may unexpectedly violate any of those assumptions at any time. Lehman has characterized this situation in an Uncertainty Principle, namely:

> "In the real world, the outcome of software system operation is inherently uncertain with the precise area of uncertainty also not knowable." [25].

Consequently, changes to the software are undertaken to maintain, refine or enhance the currency of the software as a model of the environment in which it executes. As Lehman comments more succinctly:

> "System evolution is its adaptation to reflect a changing valid assumption set." [24].

Furthermore, Lehman has captured the trends inherent in evolving software in the eight "Laws of Software Evolution" [23, 27]. While these encapsulate much of the thinking outlined above, the eighth and final "law" has particular relevance to this discussion by making explicit the role of feedback in software evolutionary processes. The eighth "law" is stated as:

> "*Software evolution processes constitute multi-level, multi-loop, feedback systems and must be treated as such to achieve any significant improvement over any reasonable base.*" [26].

Therefore, given the intention of self-adaptive software to assume at least some of the responsibility for the adaptation of a software system, it seems reasonable to expect that such systems will undertake, in some form, activities that are not entirely dissimilar to their counterparts in the processes of manual software adaptation. Consequently, it seems reasonable to expect a form of the eighth law of software evolution to apply to such software systems and therefore suggests that they can be expected to be constituted as a form of multi-level, multi-loop feedback systems.

Self-adaptive Software

Although the relatively recent emergence of the field of self-adaptive software naturally renders the available literature limited, the noticeably rapid progress in the area has nevertheless allowed a clearer definition of the key themes, goals and problems of the area to emerge. Therefore, in this section, those key concerns and the metaphors adopted to guide development in the area are briefly rehearsed in order to contextualize the remainder of the paper.

As noted previously, the fundamental ambition of the self-adaptive software initiative is to devolve some of the responsibility for evolutionary activity to the software itself. Essentially, this requires embedding equivalent elements of the human software evolution process in the software itself, thus allowing autonomous adaptation to local conditions during runtime. Effectively, such software must be capable of detecting the need for change, either to address changing external conditions or for internal performance-related reasons, determine which elements to change and how they should be changed, planning and enacting the change and finally verifying the effectiveness and robustness of the resulting solution.

To date, progress towards realizing such software has mainly been informed by three guiding metaphors, namely control systems theory, dynamic planning systems and self-aware systems.

Classical control theory considers three distinct elements of a system. An external environment, the productive element of the system generally consisting of physical objects and viewed as a factory or plant interacting with and providing products or services for that environment and an automated control unit charged with ensuring the plant meets its obligations to the environment. The basic structure of the plant, given its physical makeup, generally remains fixed over the lifetime of the control system. Consequently, much interest has focussed on providing increased flexibility in the control element of the system and over the course of time, the control community has developed a hierarchy of progressively more complex control models, each designed to provide increasing adaptive capability in the control unit.

The simplest form of plant management is achieved by providing the control unit with the goal of the system and a model of the plant. The unit then uses explicit feedback control to monitor and evaluate performance in terms of the goal and thence select appropriate control actions from a fixed response set to ensure the control goal is met. Whilst establishing the basic features of such a control system, the approach relies upon the constancy and consistency of the plant model and the stability of both the goal and the environment.

Adaptive control approaches attempt to address both changing goals caused by unexpected environmental disturbances and uncertainty in the plant model by parameterising both the controller and the plant model and providing estimating mechanisms to adjust the plant model and subsequent control actions. Further flexibility to address structural changes in the system may be provided by the inclusion of databases of plant models and associated controllers and selection mechanisms to match the appropriate model and controller to the situation, thus facilitating a degree of reconfigurability in the control mechanism.

The reconfigurability described above is largely directed towards the control elements of the system because of the inherent difficulties in changing the physical aspects of the plant. Such limitations are, of course, not so apparent when the plant element itself is a software system. Kokar *et al.* have shown that by adopting the above approach and extending the model to incorporate both a high-level specification database and component database, reconfiguration of both the control elements and software plant of the system may be achieved [18].

In order to achieve this and as identified by other authors, this implies that the software must be supplied with the capability of *"awareness"* of its goals and/or intentions and a means of evaluating the performance of the current system configuration both in terms of the current intention and the external environment [21, 34]. Such performance evaluation remains a challenging problem and in complex multi-part systems suggests the need to quantify or metricate system components in order to determine those that contribute to or detract from performance and hence identify candidate components for replacement.

This, in turn suggests that to perform such an evaluation the software system must be provided with accounts or models of both its internal configuration and capability and of the external environment, models that must themselves be capable of adaptation to reflect changing internal or external circumstances [17]. Essentially, the system must be provided with a degree of *"self-awareness"* and the ability to reflect upon that knowledge to perform the deliberative processes of performance evaluation, reconfiguration and subsequent adaptation. Implicitly, these latter activities depend both upon the ability of the system to plan and enact changes during run-time and the provision of appropriate alternative components or methods for use in response to a negative evaluation [34]. Such a view is complementary to the notion of dynamic planning, another of the key guiding metaphors of the self-adaptive software area. Here, the system plans its actions rather than simply executing algorithms, those plans and possibly the system itself being subject to change when an evaluation determines that the plan is not being met [21].

Clearly, embedding such mechanisms in the operational software itself would, of necessity introduce significant complexity and performance overhead into the executing software. Indeed, as Robertson *et al.* [34] comment:

> *"Managing complexity is a key goal of self-adaptive software. If a program must match the complexity of the environment in its own structure, it will be very complex indeed! Somehow we need to be able to write software that is less complex than the environment in which it is operating yet operate robustly.".*

As indicated by a number of commentators in the field, this issue may partially be addressed by transferring such system complexity to a supporting architecture responsible for model maintenance, performance monitoring and evaluation and subsequent adaptive activities [33, 12]. Such a separation of concerns then leaves relatively simple operational units free to pursue their respective objectives [34].

This brief review of the field of self-adaptive software has served to introduce the major guiding metaphors of the area. Noticeably, although a control systems approach forms the basis of the majority of contributions to the field, this approach is commonly enhanced to a greater or lesser extent, by overlaying elements drawn from the remaining metaphors. While this suggests a significant consensus of opinion regarding the value of these approaches, how they may be architecturally integrated remains less clear. In the following sections we begin to address this problem, initially by examining some classical cybernetic concepts. Building on this theoretical foundation, a cybernetic architecture that effectively encompasses and integrates elements of control theory, self-awareness and dynamic planning is introduced.

Managing Complexity

In this section, some fundamental concepts of cybernetic thinking are introduced and their relevance to the field of self-adaptive software is indicated. We lay the foundations of this discussion by considering the more general lessons learned from the cybernetic study of adaptive organisms surviving in a changing environment. Central to this approach is the notion of the state-determined system, in which both the organism under consideration and the environment in which it exists are represented by a set of variables that form the state-determined system. Consequently, the environment of the organism can be defined as:

> *"...those variables whose changes affect the organism and those variables that are changed by the organism's behaviour."* [1].

There are a number of immediate outcomes from this viewpoint. The first leads directly to a means to define the notion of complexity, put simply complexity can be defined as:

> *"...the property of a system of being able to adopt a large number of states or behaviours."* [13].

This in turn points to a means by which complexity may be at least notionally measured. In cybernetic terms, this measure is termed *variety,* where variety is defined as:

"*the number of possible states of a system.*" [13].

However, perhaps the most fruitful outcome is the identification of feedback within the organism/environment system and what this implies in terms of adaptation. The idea that the environment affects the organism and the organism affects the environment introduces some important concepts into the discussion and is perhaps best addressed by a biological digression.

If body temperature is considered as one of the variables describing the state of a human organism, then changes in environmental temperature may provoke a bodily response in the organism. So, if the environmental temperature falls, causing a fall in body temperature, shivering is induced to generate heat in an attempt to return the body temperature variable to an acceptable level, i.e. 37°C. Similarly, if the environmental temperature rises, causing a rise in body temperature, the human organism responds by perspiring in an effort to dissipate heat and again return the body temperature variable to a constant, acceptable level. These bodily responses are performed automatically without conscious effort and represent short-term adaptation to local environmental conditions. These processes are termed *homeostatic* in nature [9], where homeostasis is defined as:

"*the physiological process by which internal systems of the body (e.g. blood pressure, body temperature, acid base balance) are maintained at equilibrium, despite variations in external conditions.*" [31].

It should also be noted that the variables under homeostatic control mentioned above are critical to the survival of the human organism and although each may deviate around a norm, prolonged differences indicate the survival of the organism may be threatened. Of course, the human organism may attempt to influence the environment should the autonomic bodily responses outlined above fail to alleviate the condition caused by the environmental disturbance, so shade or external heat sources may be sought in high or low temperatures respectively. In some respects, these latter actions could be considered as a dynamic re-planning exercise undertaken to compensate for the inability of the autonomic systems to adequately correct the situation.

However, this leads to the view that one form of adaptation is aimed at the maintenance of the internal stability of the organism as represented by its critical variables or as Ashby puts it:

"*...a form of behaviour is adaptive if it maintains the essential variables within physiological limits.*" [1].

Such physiological control is required for the continued existence of the organism with death as a consequence of control failure. It should, however be noted that the autonomic responses detailed above represent a form of error-correcting, i.e. reactive feedback control, in that the bodily temperature has already changed before corrective measures are undertaken. Such error-controlled reflexes are relatively primitive and are, in fact only used as a reserve measure. Higher organisms develop more sophisticated control measures where temperature changes are sensed at the level of the dermis and corrective action taken before bodily temperature change occurs. Such "cause-controlled" regulation acts in a feed-forward fashion, predicting and preventing change before it occurs [3].

Nevertheless, as yet no allowance has been made for a "purpose" or reason for existence for the organism. If the discussion is turned to consider man-made systems, then the purpose of such systems is, in general terms, to create some beneficial or desired change in the environment of the system. To accomplish this, the system must have the ability to influence and cause change in other elements that make up the environment. In effect, the system must attempt to exert a form of "control" over some part of it's environment. This can be considered as "operational control", or control of one system by another. Internal physiological control is still required, but an additional set of variables (essential or otherwise), determined by the purpose of the system is selected and maintained within tolerances set by the controlling system. So, if operational control fails, although the system may continue to survive, it has to a greater or larger extent failed in its purpose.

The notion of control has some important implications that may be explored by recourse to the state-determined system considered earlier. For, if each of the possible states a system is capable of assuming is represented as a point, i.e. one point represents the set of values held by the variables that describe the system at that time, then it is possible to view the system as following a trajectory through a multi-dimensional phase space of all possible states of the system. As the state of the system changes, different points are assumed in that space. If the acceptable states for the system i.e. those representing homeostatic and operational stability, are notionally grouped inside a boundary, then as long as the trajectory assumed by the system stays within that boundary the system can be considered to be in homeostatic control.

Now if two such systems are coupled such that the output of each forms the input of the other and each is pursuing local homeostasis as depicted in Figure 1 below:

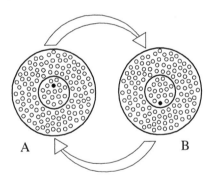

Fig. 1. Self-Vetoing homeostasis in coupled systems.

Then as long as the representative point for each system remains within the boundary of acceptable states, both systems can be considered to be operating normally. Furthermore, each system can recognize that the other is in normal operation through the variables in each system that represent environmental variables to the other. However, should for example, the representative point in system A move outside the acceptable boundary, that event should register in system B and cause an appropriate change of state in that system, the type of change required being indicated by the original change in A. Meanwhile, system A must undertake a trajectory of state changes designed to return it's representative point to an acceptable position. The danger is that changes in A and registered in B may drive the representative point in system B over the boundary to unacceptability which, of course is registered in A and may cause the planned trajectory to be adjusted. B must now plan it's own trajectory back to stability. The operation of the loop continues until both systems arrive back at acceptable states. In effect, each system acts as a controller of the other and "vetoes" any state that the other system adopts that is unacceptable to itself regardless of whether it is in the acceptable range of the other system.

Such a process is termed *self-vetoing homeostasis* and represents a form of *negotiated* adaptation. It is clear that such a process should result in adaptive stability in both systems and aids both in adjusting to the operation of the other even when extraneous disturbances not shown on the diagram affect either system. The concept is based on Ashby's homeostat [1], a mechanism designed to achieve stability after disturbance. Although many systems can achieve this, Ashby attempted to isolate a property he called *ultrastability* [1]. An ultra-stable system is capable of returning to stability after it has been disturbed in a way not envisaged by the designer.

A difficulty in this process lies in the time taken to reach dual stability, if environmental disturbances arrive faster than the time taken for the homeostatic loop to complete operations, then the system may oscillate interminably. This can be addressed with recourse to what may be described as a reward and punishment scheme. Although initial adaptive attempts may be based on trial and error, those that result in beneficial effects are reinforced by positive feedback while those that have detrimental effects are discouraged. The result is a type of hill-climbing approach to adaptation, although ineffective approaches are retained to prevent the system being stranded on local optima. A further outcome of this process is the growth of organization within each system, trajectories leading to effective and timely adaptation can be "ear-marked" for future re-use, resulting in a growing "map" of effective routes back to stability. In effect, the system "learns" both to adapt to new or changed circumstances and decreases its reaction time to previously occurring disturbances [5].

We now turn the discussion to consider the management of complexity that began this section. If a system is considered to be interacting with its local environment and that system is, in turn, being "managed" by a management unit and each pair of this triad is striving for homeostatic equilibrium. Then, while the management unit is attempting to control the system, the system is in turn, attempting to control the environment. However, it is clear that the complexity and hence variety exhibited by the system will typically far exceed the complexity of the management unit. Similarly, the complexity and consequent variety apparent in the environment will again generally far exceed the variety of any system that is trying to control it can display. Indeed, an environment such as the natural world is so complex and possible states so numerous that they are effectively uncountable. In such situations, the extent of variety exhibited precludes the control or management of the situation by any means that rely on enumerating or dealing sequentially with the states [35].

Yet, each controlling element must in some sense, absorb the variety of the element it is trying to control. To do otherwise would allow the controlled situation to assume states for which the controller had no response. That is, control can only be attained if the variety of the controller is at least as great as the situation to be controlled. This is Ashby's Law of Requisite Variety, which may be more succinctly stated as "only variety destroys variety" [2]. However, as noted above, there is a natural varietal imbalance between the environment, the system and the management unit under consideration. Classical cybernetics offers two means to address this imbalance, the variety of the controlled situation is reduced or *attenuated* to the number of states that the controller can address, e.g. in programming terms, the user's input is regulated to ensure that the program receives an input it can deal with.

The variety of the controller may be *amplified* to match or exceed that of the controlled situation and the standard example of this is the notion of delegation, i.e. the devolution of responsibility to enhance managerial control. In practice, amplification and attenuation are used in conjunction to attempt to achieve the requisite varietal balance as illustrated in Figure 2 below.

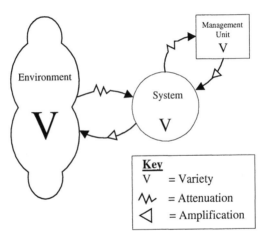

Fig. 2. Varietal control through attenuation and amplification.

Furthermore, in order to ensure effective control or regulation of a controlled situation requires that the controller models the situation to be controlled, otherwise the situation may adopt states that are meaningless in terms of the controller. This requirement, known as the Conant-Ashby theorem, states:

"Every good regulator of a system must be a model of that system." [3].

So ideally, an optimal regulator will be an isomorphic model of the situation to be controlled. However, when such isomorphism is not possible as in highly complex systems, then the regulator must be, i.e. contain, a strongly homomorphic model of the situation.

The Viable System Model –
A System Architecture for Complexity Management

The Viable System Model [3, 4] provides a theoretically supported cybernetic model of organization. Viable systems may be defined as being robust against internal malfunction and external disturbances and have the ability to continually respond and adapt to unexpected stimuli allowing them to survive in a changing and unpredictable environment. The model specifically attempts to imbue the system with the ability to adapt to circumstances not foreseen by the original designer and identifies the *necessary* and *sufficient* communication and control systems that must exist for any organization to remain *viable* in a changing environment. In doing so, the model does not attempt to specify nor prescribe the activities that must occur in each system, instead activities are described or typified by a cybernetic rationale to allow either the design of activities to match the cybernetic criteria or for actual activities to be identified by their system type and hence assigned to the appropriate element of the model. Such a generalized approach allows the model to be applied to any organization regardless of size. The six major systems advocated by the model are detailed in Table 1. below.

The major systems (i.e. S1s, S3, S4 and S5) are structured hierarchically and connected by a central 'spine' of communication channels passing from the higher level systems through each of the S1 management elements. These provide high priority communication facilities to determine resource requirements, accounting for allocated resources, alerts indicating that a particular plan is failing and re-planning is necessary and the provision of the "legal and corporate requirements" or policies of the organization.

The systems described above concern the management structure at one level of the organization, and consequently specify the communication and control structures that must exist to manage a set of S1 units. However, the power of the model derives from its recursive nature. Each S1, consisting of an operational element and it's management unit, is expected to develop a similar VSM structure, consequently, the structure of systems is open ended in both directions and may be pursued either upwards to ever wider encompassing systems or downwards to ever smaller units. However, at each level the same structure of systems would occur although their detail would necessarily differ depending on context. This recursivity allows each level in the organization relative autonomy bounded by the overall purpose of the system as a whole. Such cooperation and coordination within and between S1 units on the same hierarchical level and between sets of S1's on different levels is provided by communication channels operating over an organizational range and tailored locally to each viable entityWhile the overview of the VSM given above has been necessarily brief, hopefully that description has conveyed the apparent conceptual completeness of the model in its identification of the mechanisms of adaptation required by systems attempting to survive in a changing environment.

Table 1. The major systems of the Viable System Model

System Identifier	System Type
System One (S1) Operations	System One performs the productive operations of the organization. An organization may be composed of a number of S1s, each providing a distinct product or service. Each S1 consists of an operational element controlled by a management process and in contact with the operational environment and is in some respects is similar to the plant/management arrangement adopted by control system theory.
System Two (S2) Coordination	System Two is concerned with coordinating the activities of S1 units. It is essentially anti-oscillatory in that it attempts to contain or minimize inter-S1 fluctuations. This is achieved by the provision of stabilizing, coordinating facilities such as scheduling and standardization information that is disseminated over all S1s, but tailored locally to suit individual S1 needs.
System Three (S3) Control	System Three is concerned with the provision of cohesion and synergy to a set of S1 units. The management processes contained within this system will be concerned with short-term, immediate management issues, such as resource provision and strategic plan production, although strategic in this situation refers to planning with existing resources rather than in the normally accepted sense.
System Three* (S3*) Audit	System Three* (read as System Three Star) provides facilities for the intermittent audit of S1 progress and provides direct access to the physical operations of a particular S1 allowing immediate corroboration of that progress. This essentially provides additional data over and above that provided by normal reporting procedures.
System Four (S4) Intelligence	System Four is concerned with planning the way ahead in the light of external environmental changes and internal organizational capabilities. To this end, S4 'scans' the environment for trends that may be either beneficial or detrimental to the organization and constructs developmental organizational plans accordingly. To ensure that such plans are grounded in an accurate appreciation of the current organization, the intelligence function contains an up-to-date model of organizational capability.
System Five (S5) Policy	System Five determines the overall purpose of the organization i.e. defines the activities that are performed by S1s. As such S5 represents the policy-formulation or normative planning function. Policy formulation is informed by a "world-view" provided by S4 and representing the current beliefs and assumptions held by the system about the environment and models of current organizational capability populated by data flowing from the lower level systems in the organization.

In the authors view, the explanatory power of the model is, at least in part, demonstrated by some of the interesting parallels it highlights between the cybernetic theory embodied in the model and a number of separate research threads current in the computing arena. As such, the model appears to offer a means to structure and integrate these threads and hence provides a substantial theoretical foundation for the realization of self-managing software systems. Consequently, the next section begins by considering some recent research efforts in the light of cybernetic viewpoint provided and then continues with a modest case study that demonstrates the practical implementation of these ideas.

A Viable Architecture for Self-adaptive Software

In order to move towards a practical application of the ideas mooted here, the authors now consider currently available technologies in terms of their contribution towards system viability as required by the precepts of the VSM. Given that the effectiveness of the model derives from the synergistic interaction of its composite systems and the consequent emphasis on communications between systems, the discussion begins with a consideration of communicating software units and in particular, the most versatile of these, namely software agents. A software agent may be defined as:

> "...software components that communicate with their peers by exchanging messages in an expressive agent communication language."
> [14].

Consequently, a relatively simple software entity may be considered as an agent simply through its ability to communicate. More typically however agents are larger entities that exchange information and provide services either to other agents or human users. Such interoperation allows communities of agents to address problems too extensive for a single software entity.

However, the most appropriate means by which a community of agents may be effectively organized to ensure coordinated interoperation remains an open question. Two approaches have been explored, namely *direct* communication where agents are responsible for their own coordination and what may be termed indirect communication where communication and co-ordinative responsibilities are devolved to "system agents" or facilitators.

There are some notable disadvantages to direct communication, in that embedding the necessary communication and negotiation elements within individual agents leads to significant implementation complexity. Similarly, although the approach works well with a relatively small number of agents as the number of agents involved rises, the cost of broadcasting needs and capabilities becomes prohibitive.

Indirect communication seeks to address these disadvantages by organizing agents into a *"federated system"*, whereby a degree of agent autonomy is surrendered in return for the efficiency-enhancing services of a facilitating agent to handle communication and coordination tasks. Consequently, in this approach, agents do not communicate directly with each other, but via facilitators. To provide the facilitator with the necessary means to provide its services, meta-level information regarding the needs and capabilities of agents are registered with local facilitators. Application-level information and requests both to and from the agent are also passed by the facilitator using the meta-level information to route messages appropriately. However, consideration of how such a federated system may be structured raises the question of a suitable system architecture.

The notion of "architecture", derived from fields such as building construction and more recently applied in areas such as network and computer hardware engineering, concerns the identification of high-level, structural *design patterns* that can be used to determine how major elements of an overall construct or system may be organized and hence physically realized. Recently, much research effort has been devoted to the application of the underlying principles of architectural design patterns in the software arena to produce software architectures. Considerable impetus for this approach has been provided by the growing availability of software components provided by object-oriented technologies. This has led, both to component-based architectures where systems are constructed using commercial, off-the-shelf (COTS) elements and, when used in conjunction with concurrent and distributed processing technologies, to the development of *loosely-coupled*, distributed, object-based architectures.

The construction of component-based software architectures is very similar to more traditional architectural applications in that the architecture is created by "plugging" COTS elements into the overall architecture. This is achieved by means of a three stage process, namely:

1. Connection – of the component to other neighbouring components via connectors attached to ports on the component.
2. Registration – of the component so that the overall architecture is made aware of the presence of the new component, the services it produces and the services it needs to function.
3. Configuration – of the component to tailor it to suit the architecture so that the desired services are provided.

Such an approach facilitates component maintenance, upgrades, personalization and more generally, a "plug and play" view of software architecture.

We now extend and apply this cybernetic approach and consider each S1 of the VSM in terms of an intelligent, intentional software agent [22]. To demonstrate, a conceptual, architectural outline of such an agent is determined, using both the principles of the VSM and Bratman *et al.*'s Intelligent Resource-Bounded Machine Architecture (IRMA) [7] terminology and design as a constructional guide.

IRMA incorporates a number of key symbolic data structures to underpin the architecture, namely: a plan library representing a subset of the agent's beliefs, and explicit representations of beliefs, desires and intentions. In addition, the architecture includes a reasoning process for reasoning about the world; a means-ends analysis process to determine which plans may be used to achieve the agent's intentions; an opportunity analysis process to scan the environment and propose options in response to perceived changes there; a filtering process responsible for determining the subset of means-ends analysis and opportunity analysis proposals that are consistent with existing plans; and a deliberation process that weighs the possibly competing options that survive the filtering process and produces intentions that are incorporated into the agent's plans.

As shown in Figure 3 below, the developed architecture embeds a Beliefs, Desires, Intentions (BDI) unit at the S5 level. This contains three representations:

- Desires – or what the agent wants to do and is taken as a given for the moment.
- Beliefs – or what the agent currently knows and is represented by two structures. A model of the external world and a model of the current internal status of the architecture.
- Intention – or what will actually be done, is determined by a process of deliberation, which interprets desires in the light of current beliefs about both the environment and the 'stance' of the agent. These are passed via the 'central spine' communication channel to System Three for enactment.

S3, using a reasoning process supported by a plan library and the capacity to audit the current status of operational S1 units, structures the intentions into plans, these are then passed to a scheduling process. The scheduling process, in cooperation with a resource bargaining process, responsible for negotiating resource deployment and usage monitoring, schedule the enactment of the plan. The schedule passes to the coordinating S2 channel for dissemination to participating S1 elements. The S2 channel returns schedule-monitoring information to S3.

Environmental change is addressed by S4, which equipped with an Opportunity Analyzer and guided by the S5 desires model, scans the environment for detrimental events or beneficial opportunities. There are two outcomes of this process, the first is the formulation of a view of the outside world which is provided to S5 in the form of the World model. The second outcome is the production of development plans for the future of the agent, either exploiting advantageous opportunities or avoiding detrimental occurrences. To ensure that plans are founded in a realistic appreciation of the current capabilities of the agent, a model, populated by data flowing from S3 is provided. This data is further abstracted and feeds the internal view used in the deliberation process in S5. Plans are then subjected to a filtering process to weigh between competing options and ensure compatibility with the current agent-state. Surviving plans are then passed to the deliberation process to begin the intention forming cycle again. Should a plan in execution fail because of machine breakdown for example, then the alerting channel depicted as a broken line terminating in the "light-bulb" in S5, indicates that re-planning is necessary.

The power of this approach lies in the recursivity of the underlying model. Figure 3 indicates that the entire architecture described above is repeated in the client S1 unit in the next layer. Communications channels serve to bind each recursive layer to the overall agent organization and effect information transfer between layers. Consequently, the intentions channel at one recursion informs the desires model in the next, thus allowing an autonomous response to local conditions at each level while remaining within the purpose of the overall agent organization. Similarly, channels such as the S2 elements permeate the structure and facilitate overall cooperative coordinated activity and alerting channels allow emergency re-planning to be undertaken at the appropriate level.

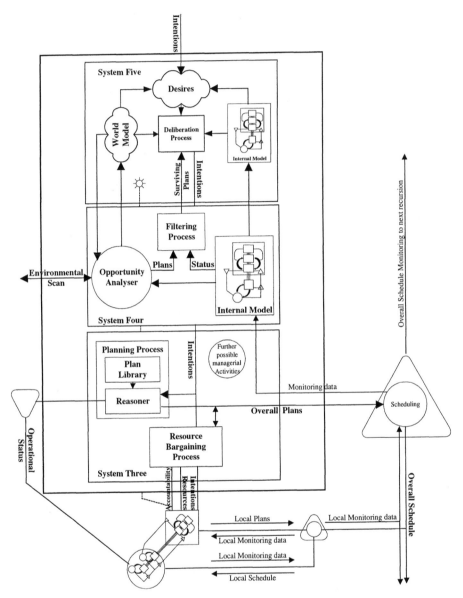

Fig. 3. An Outline Design for a Viable Intelligent Agent Architecture

Furthermore, such recursivity results in a highly scaleable structure as both individual agent architectures and overall system architectures assume the same overall configuration characteristics, although individual agent or system elements will necessarily be implemented differently to reflect the needs of a particular recursive level. In such an approach, each level of S1 units is implemented as a set of intelligent agents of the form proposed above and structured into a coherent whole by the inclusion of the deliberative meta-systems S3, S4 and S5. Coordinating systems such as S2 communication and coordination functions may be provided by Mediating/Facilitating style agents, resulting in a federated architecture of multi-agents. It should be further noted that the agent architecture outlined above represents only the planning and scheduling subset of agent operations, however the scheme is fully extensible allowing further managerial activities such as inventory management and maintenance management to be incorporated into the overall structure.

A Case Study in Intelligent Networked Vehicles

While the conceptual similarity between the cybernetic concepts discussed earlier and the aims of self-adaptive software, in some respects, demonstrate the applicability of these ideas to this area, it remains to provide a means of practical realization of these ideas. To date, an explicitly cybernetic approach to software development, in terms of the earlier discussion, remains unexplored. However, the rapidly developing field of software agents displays some significant conceptual overlap with significant elements of cybernetic thinking. Consequently, software agent technology, already identified as a possible approach to realizing self-adaptive software, provides an immediate and practical means to explore these ideas.

To demonstrate this view, this section presents a case study drawn from our current attempts to move towards a cybernetically-based approach to self-adaptive software through the use of current agent technologies. The study centres on the use of computing and mobile communications technologies in road vehicles and their integration into a coherent organizational system. In-Vehicle Telematics Systems (IVTS) have recently attracted significant attention for their potential to improve the efficiency and effectiveness of vehicular travel, thereby improving the quality of travel experience for the consumer. More particularly, their application appears to be especially appropriate in the provision of emergency services, such as policing, fire and health services.

IVTS are considered as a sub-set of in-vehicle computer-based systems that combine both telecommunications and information technologies and lend support to; driver's information systems, vehicle navigation and tracking and collision avoidance systems. Such systems cover a broad spectrum of systems, ranging from relatively simple Global Positioning Systems (GPS) and security monitoring systems to more complex, network centric systems complete with voice recognition systems used to send and receive e-mail, text messages and internet access. IVTS can combine the use of "smart" devices, such as Palm devices and WAP phones together with small footprint mobile computers, typically running Windows CE. Communications with centralized and other remote mobile systems are reliant on wireless links that may use GSM, Bluetooth or WAP technology.

The success of IVTS depends upon ease-of-use, the ability to adapt in order to accommodate different end-use requirements and the operational demands of a mobile computing environment. IVTS are inherently heterogeneous distributed systems where control and application services may be spread across several processing systems. As such, IVTS pose a need for a software infrastructure that can gather information about the operational context and mobile communications environment and use this information to "auto-configure" systems by adapting behaviour according to context and environment [16].

Middleware has been recognized as a viable means to realize such a software infrastructure, due to its ability to bridge the gap between operating system and application software [6]. The middleware approach has been assisted by the availability of object-oriented middleware technologies such as CORBA, Microsoft's DCOM and Sun Microsystems Java-based Jini [10]. Current object-oriented middleware technologies rely on distributed objects and "stubs" through which objects can communicate via message-passing and remote method invocation. A useful abstraction used in distributed middleware systems is the *service-oriented* view, which regards a distributed middleware systems as a federation of services that communicate in a peer-to-peer like regime.

The service oriented abstraction is used extensively in Jini, which regards a service as a logical concept such as a printer. A Jini system or federation is a collection of service users or service providers that communicate through Jini protocols. Usually a Jini federation consists of applications written in Java, communicating using the Java Remote Method Invocation (RMI) mechanism. However, native code methods can provide "wrappers" around non-Java objects, or even be written in some other language such as CORBA.

In a typical Jini federation, a service provider registers a service with Jini's own lookup service. A service user may then find or "discover" this service and download a service object or stub that is used to communicate with the actual service. The service object is usually implemented as a "proxy", which will communicate back to other objects in the service provider using RMI.

The remainder of the paper provides an overview of the EmergeITS project. The project was to demonstrate the use of IVTS in emergency-related and hazard prevention activities and was developed in collaboration with the Merseyside Fire Service (MFS). The major aim of the project was the development of a service-based architecture to demonstrate the remote management and adaptation of an IVTS through the provision of on-demand application services from centralized systems or from systems residing in other remote locations. The architecture was to be suitable for use over a wireless link and to require minimal user intervention.

From a systems perspective, the architecture was required to integrate the functionality of centralized control computers, corporate database systems, remote in-vehicle computers and smart devices, such as Palm devices and WAP telephones. From a software perspective, the architecture was developed as a Java application, utilizing Jini middleware technology to provide a federated service-based system. The federation of services was based on two main categories of services, namely management services and application specific services.

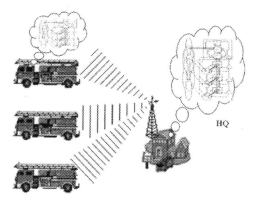

Fig. 4. A Notional View of the Merseyside Fire Service and its Viable Units - comprising a three vehicle example

Management services are responsible for monitoring the operational and communication requirements of the IVTS. The management services gather information relating to the usage context and communication system requirements and adapt and configure the system accordingly to accommodate different modes of operation and communication. Central to the management services is the use of the Java reflection API, Jini/RMI remote event and Jini activation mechanisms. The reflection API is used to provide *structural* information residing in a remote Java virtual machine (JVM). Event listeners, residing on control computers are notified of events generated by the remote in-vehicle computer and smart devices. The events provide *dynamic* information relating to the behaviour of the remote systems. The Jini activation mechanism is used to start or re-start a remote JVM, thereby providing remote management and fault tolerant capabilities.

It is anticipated that future work will provide management services capable of selecting between communication bearer services so that a smart device can be seen to adapt to use the most appropriate bearer service. Selection will be based on the location of the vehicle or user in a similar fashion to the ideas of Dowling & Cahill [11], thereby providing a location dependent management service.

The application services provide domain specific applications to remote systems, which in the context of EmergeITS occur as the provision of vital information resources used by MFS. Typically, application services provide access to information stored on centralized corporate database systems, download/upload services, route-guidance and navigation services. The majority of application services rely on the HTTP protocol for which a management service may be required to initiate a web-server on the serving control computer and provide web-browsing facilities on the remote systems.

To date, the EmergeITS architecture has only been demonstrated using two Pentium laptops, fitted with IEEE 802.11 cards. One laptop was to represent the control system computer while the other represented the in-vehicle machine. Sun Microsystems Java development system (JDK 1.3) was installed on both systems and Jini 1.1 was installed on the control system computer laptop and Sun Microsystems Java

Micro-edition (J2ME), Palm device and WAP phone emulation software were installed on the in-vehicle computer.

Conclusions

In this paper, the authors have outlined the drawbacks apparent in current software design approaches and reviewed the difficulties these present in effectively maintaining a software system in a changing environment. Drawing on work in the software evolution arena has indicated the value of considering software as *"an organism existing in a changing environment"*, and the necessity of maintaining the currency of the software as a model of that changing environment. This in turn, identified the intrinsic feedback loop that is established between the software system, the processes that seek to maintain it and the environment in which it exists. Obviously, the rate and degree of change is dependent both upon the volatility and boundedness of the environment and the completeness of the mapping obtainable between the software and that environment.

A brief overview of the field of self-adaptive software allowed the main aims, goals and current approaches to the area to be rehearsed and served to contextualise the remainder of the paper. The field of cybernetics was then considered with a view to demonstrating both the closeness of concerns between these two fields and that cybernetics appears to represent a ready-made theoretical foundation for work in self-adaptive software. This viewpoint was reinforced by an introduction to the cybernetics-based Viable System Model, which by encapsulating the necessary and sufficient systems required for any purposeful entity to remain viable in a changing environment, appears to offer the conceptual blueprint of a system architecture for such self-managing software. The VSM, as a model-based, reflective structure encompasses the three guiding metaphors, namely; control systems theory, dynamic planning systems and self-aware systems, that have driven work in self-adaptive software to date.

Drawing on a classic design from the field of Artificial Intelligence, an outline design for an intelligent, autonomous adaptive software agent was presented. Integrating and structuring this existing design using the conceptual guidance provided by the VSM, indicated the relative ease by which a mapping between the components required in Bratman *et al*'s IRMA model and the required systems of the VSM was achieved. Although some additional elements were required to satisfy the precepts of the VSM, thus indicating the appropriateness of the VSM as a reference model, this also shows the relative robustness of the original design and demonstrates a degree of commonality in thinking concerning the key elements considered to be necessary to realize such a software entity.

Finally, a modest case study drawn from the EmergeITS project was presented. This sought to demonstrate the use of Jini middleware technology for providing a service-based architecture capable of managing, configuring and providing application services to remote in-vehicle computers and smart devices. Although, much remains to be done to complete the project in terms of the approach suggested in this paper, the project so far has provided some of the required building blocks and promises to demonstrate that such a concept is realizable using existing technology.

References

1. Ashby, W.R., *Design for a Brain*, Chapman & Hall, London, 1954.
2. Ashby, W.R., *An Introduction To Cybernetics*, Chapman & Hall, London, 1956.
3. Ashby, W.R., *Every good regulator of a system must be a model of that system,* International Journal of System Science, Vol. **1**, No. 2, pp. 89-97, 1970.
4. Beer, S., *The Heart of the Enterprise*, John Wiley & Sons, Chichester, 1979.
5. Beer, S., *Brain of the Firm*, 2nd ed, John Wiley & Sons, Chichester, 1981.
6. Blair, G.S., *et al., A Principled Approach to Supporting Adaptation in Distributed Mobile Environments,* in *International Symposium on Software Engineering for Parallel and Distributed Systems (PDSE2000),* Limerick, Ireland, 2000.
7. Bratman, M.E., D.J. Israel, and M.E. Pollack, *Plans and Resource-Bounded Practical Reasoning,* Computational Intelligence, Vol. **4**, No. 4, pp. 349-355, 1988.
8. Brereton, P., *et al., The Future of Software,* Communications of the ACM, Vol. **42**, No. 12, pp. 78-84, 1999.
9. Cannon, W.B., *The Wisdom of the Body*, W. W. Norton & Co., 1932.
10. The Jini Community, http://www.jini.org, 2000.
11. Dowling, J. and V. Cahill, *The K-Component Architecture Meta-Model for Self-Adaptive Software,* in *Proceeding of Reflection 2001,* Kyoto, Japan, 2001.
12. Eracar, Y.A. and M.M. Kokar, *An architecture for software that adapts to changes in requirements,* The Journal of Systems and Software, Vol. **50**, No. 3, 2000.
13. Espejo, R. and R. Harnden, *The Viable Systems Model - Interpretations and Applications of Stafford Beer's VSM*, John Wiley & Sons, Chicester, 1989.
14. Genesereth, M.R. and S.P. Ketchpel, *Software Agents,* Communications of the ACM, Vol. **37**, No. 7, pp. 48-54, 1994.
15. IEEE, *IEEE Standards Collection: Software Engineering,* IEEE Standard 610.12-1990, 1993.
16. Kanter, T., *An Open Service Architecture for Adaptive Personal Mobile Communication,* Special Issue of IEEE Personal Communications - European R & D on Fourth Generation Mobile and Wireless IP Networks, Vol. **8**, No. 6, , 2001.
17. Karsai, G. and J. Sztipanovits, *A Model-Based Approach to Self-Adaptive Software,* IEEE Intelligent Systems & their Applications, Vol. **14**, No. 3, pp. 46-53, 1999.
18. Kokar, M.M., K. Baclawski, and Y.A. Eracar, *Control Theory-Based Foundations of Self-Controlling Software,* IEEE Intelligent Systems & their Applications, Vol. **14**, No. 3, pp. 37-45, 1999.
19. Laddaga, R., *DARPA Broad Agency Announcement on Self-Adaptive Software,* http://www.darpa.mil/ito/Solicitations/PIP_9812.html, 1997.
20. Laddaga, R., *Creating Robust Software through Self-Adaptation,* IEEE Intelligent Systems & their Applications, Vol. **14**, No. 3, pp. 26-29, 1999.
21. Laddaga, R., *Active Software,* in *The First International Workshop on Self-Adaptive Software (IWSAS2000),* Oxford University, U.K., 2000.
22. Laws, A., A. Taleb-Bendiab, and S.J. Wade, *Towards a Viable Reference Architecture for Multi-Agent Supported Holonic Manufacturing Systems,* International Journal of Applied Systems Science, Vol. **1**, No. , 2001.

23. Lehman, M.M., *Programs, Life Cycles, and Laws of Software Evolution,* Proceedings of the IEEE, Vol. **68**, No. 9, pp. 1060-1076, 1980.
24. Lehman, M.M., *Uncertainty in Computer Application and its Control Through the Engineering of Software,* Software Maintenance: Research and Practice, Vol. **1**, No. pp. 3-27, 1989.
25. Lehman, M.M., *Uncertainty in Computer Application,* Communications of the ACM, Vol. **33**, No. 5, pp. 584-586, 1990.
26. Lehman, M.M., *Process Improvement - The Way Forward,* in *Proceedings of the Brazilian Software Engineering Conference,* 1996.
27. Lehman, M.M., *Laws of Software Evolution Revisited,* http://www-dse.doc.ic.ac.uk/~mml/, 1997.
28. Lehman, M.M., *Software's Future: Managing Evolution,* IEEE Software, Vol. **15**, No. 1, pp. 40-44, 1998.
29. Lehman, M.M. and L.A. Belady, *Program Evolution - Processes of Software Change,* Academic Press, San Diego, California, 1985.
30. Lehman, M.M. and J.F. Ramil, *The Impact of Feedback in the Global Software Process,* The Journal of Systems & Software, Vol. , No. 46, pp. 123-134, 1999.
31. Martin, E.A., ed. *Oxford Concise Medical Dictionary.* 4th ed., Oxford University Press, Oxford, 1994.
32. Nauer, P. and B. Randell, *Software Engineering - Report on a Conference sponsored by the NATO Science Committee, Garmisch, 1968,* Scientific Affairs Division, NATO, 1969.
33. Oreizy, P., *et al.*, *An Architecture-Based Approach to Self-Adaptive Software,* IEEE Intelligent Systems & their Applications, May/June, pp. 54-62, 1999.
34. Robertson, P., R. Laddaga, and H.E. Shrobe, eds. *Introduction: The First International Workshop on Self-Adaptive Software.* Self-Adaptive Software, ed. R. Laddaga, P. Robertson, and H.E. Shrobe, Vol, , Springer-Verlag, 2000.
35. Waelchli, F., *The VSM and Ashby's Law as illuminants of historical management thought,* in *The Viable System Model: Interpretations and Applications of Stafford Beer's VSM,* R. Espejo and R. Harnden, Editors, John Wiley & Sons: Chicester. pp. 51-75,1989.

Results of the Second International Workshop on Self-adaptive Software

Robert Laddaga, Paul Robertson, and Howie Shrobe

Massachusetts Institute of Technology
Artificial Intelligence Laboratory
{rladdaga,paulr,hes}@ai.mit.edu

Abstract. The second International Workshop on Self Adaptive Software was held on scenic Lake Balaton, in Hungary during May 17-19, 2001. The workshop was sponsored by the Technical University of Budapest, and organized by Gábor Péceli, Head of the Department of Measurement and Information Systems, assisted by Simon Gyula, Senior Lecturer in the department. This paper reports on the results of three workshop sessions held on the topics of applications, research needed and design patterns, all for self adaptive software.

Keywords: Self-adaptive Software, applications, design, patterns

1 Introduction

We began the workshop with three goals in addition to hearing and commenting on each other's papers. Those goals were to 1. define the category of applications that could best use (or most needed) self adaptive software, 2. point out some useful research directions, and 3. attempt to categorize useful software patterns for self adaptive software. We addressed all three goals partially during three workshop sessions, although more could have been done in each area. In this concluding paper, we will present the findings of these three sessions.

2 Embedded Applications of Self-adaptive Software

The majority of the participants agreed that embedded applications were a good fit for self adaptive software. Embedded systems are systems in which computer processors control physical, chemical, or biological processes or devices. Examples of such systems include cell phones, watches, CD players, cars, airplanes, nuclear reactors, and oil refineries. Many of these use several, hundreds, or even thousands of processors. Even a personal computer is an embedded system with specialized chips that control communication among memory, main processor, and peripherals. Each peripheral (disks, printers, audio cards) are devices with embedded software.

Today, most embedded systems operate with limited memory and use eight-bit processors, yet they are still difficult to program. The trend is toward increasing memory and computational power and significantly increasing functionality.

R. Laddaga, P. Robertson, H. Shrobe (Eds.): IWSAS 2001, LNCS 2614, pp. 281–290, 2003.

With the added functionality and hardware resources comes greatly increased complexity. Each year, the semi-conductor industry produces more processors than there are people on the planet, and the number of processors produced is growing significantly. Almost all these processors are used in embedded applications, rather than the personal computer, workstation, server, or mainframe systems with which users are most familiar.

The real-world processes controlled by embedded systems introduce numerous hard constraints that must be met when programming embedded processors. Among these constraints are

- Real-time requirements, such as latency and jitter
- Signal processing requirements, such as truncation error, quantization noise, and numeric stability
- Fault behavior, such as reliability and fault propagation across physical and computation system boundaries and
- Physical requirements, such as power consumption and size.

Meeting the constraints listed above is hard precisely because they affect embedded systems globally, and because embedded programs contribute globally to these problems.

These real world issues have been with us for as long as we have attempted to control physical processes, and therefore they don't themselves explain the tremendous increase in complexity of embedded software. Two important trends supply some of that impetus: the increasing tendency to utilize embedded software as the main integrator for systems, and the increased dependence on embedded software to supply novel and more intricate functionality. In each case, embedded software is replacing something else. In the first case, the chief integrators of systems were the human users. We are now asking our embedded software to handle some of that integration burden. In the second case we are replacing mechanical and hydraulic linkages with computer controlled electromechanical systems, because only they can meet the new stringent performance requirements that we set for our systems.

The main simplifying technique we have in software development is abstraction in the form of functional, object-oriented, or component-based decomposition. To the extent that we can modularize via these decompositions, we can reduce the effective complexity of the software that we write. Complexity increases whenever such modularity is interfered with, in the sense of needing to take account of the internals of other modules while coding a different module. As such cross cutting concerns multiply, the job of software development, validation, and evolution can become impossible. Real-time requirements, and coordination with physical processes introduces a huge number of such cross cutting concerns, violating modularity with abandon. To deal with these problems, we need software technology in several related areas, including distributed resource management, multiple decomposition dimensions, tolerant and negotiated interfaces, and of course, self-adaptive software.

Self adaptive software is software that monitors its own operation, detects faults and opportunities, and repairs or improves itself in response to faults and changes. It effects the improvement by modifying or re-synthesizing its programs and subsystems, using a feedback control-system like behavior. Non-embedded examples of plausible uses of self-adaptive software are adaptation of numerical codes for optimization, simulation or controlling accuracy time to solution trade-offs, adaptation of resource usage for operating systems. However, it is really the area of embedded software that supplies the most obvious and pertinent applications for self adaptive software. The necessity of monitoring and addressing real world changes makes the case for self monitoring and self optimizing software. This is a theme that we have seen often in the papers of this workshop, where many of the application areas are visual perception, navigation and vehicle control.

Embedded systems always must have some form of reactive behavior that responds to changes in the environment. There is a natural tendency to build such systems in a way that allows the system to have some (possibly rudimentary) abstract notion of the state of the world, and to use that state to choose behavioral responses. However, the structure and content of the programming for the embedded system has not generally been the object of the reactive repertoire. Self adaptive software, in the context of embedded systems, only extends the control system to monitoring and changing the state of the program structure and function as well as the environment.

3   Other Applications of Self-adaptive Software

We also discussed other application areas for self-adaptive software, and agreed that software installation and update were applications where self adaptive software would be useful. We have all experienced cases where an application program quits with an error message saying that some prerequisite software is missing, or that there is a version mismatch between the application being installed, and either the hardware or OS platform. Often the work around or alternative action is very clear, but also it is often not very easy to manually make the changes required, or even to fully comprehend the implications of such changes. Meanwhile the installation software often has had its "fingers on all the appropriate locations", and could easily plan a recovery operation, and execute it at the users direction, after informing the user of the advantages and disadvantages of executing the recovery.

A similar application area is Operating System maintenance, including:

1. Order of installing applications, drivers, and updates
2. DLL maintenance
3. Scheduling optimization
4. User interface dynamic tuning (Sometimes I want the start bar hidden, other times not ...)

All of these OS maintenance items are subject to faults and errors that become manual maintenance nightmares, especially for users who are their own "system staff".

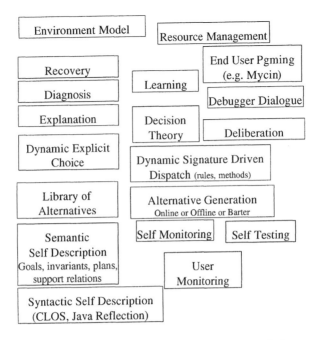

Fig. 1. Component Technologies of Self Adaptive Software.

Other application areas under consideration, along with particular activities that would benefit from self reorganization were:

- Active networks: protocol injection supported by reconfiguration of components
- Information survivability: switch to alternate, uncompromised components at other network nodes upon detection of intrusion and method of attack.
- Mobile computing: adapt choice of compression algorithms to data and desired compression ratio
- Scientific/numeric codes: time dependent PDEs (implicit and explicit methods) systems of linear equations (choice of solvers)
- ELPA (emitter location and position analysis): use of flat or curved earth models, depends on expected distance and accuracy needs

4   Research Directions

As in the first workshop [2, 1], we began with our definitional diagram of the component features of self adaptive software (see Figure 1).

Also as in the first workshop, there was significant emphasis on research into verification and validation technology. There was significant recognition that the very idea of self modifying programs would be unsettling to many people, and that in any case embedded software requires some sort of assurance guarantees.

We discussed the possibility of proving certain bounds on system behavior, even under fault conditions, and where those bounds might be probabilistic rather than deductively proven. Providing assurance in the context of self adaptive software is likely to be rather different than doing so for today's embedded software. Also, the initial idea behind self adaptive software was that robustness had to come from a different source than traditional software testing and validation.

Basically, assurance means that we can put bounds on the divergence of system behavior from system specifications. Ideally, self adaptive software should include explicit representations of the goals (specifications) of the software, and should use the that explicit representation in monitoring the behavior of the software. The place to derive assurance then, is by proving properties of the monitoring, diagnosis and recovery mechanisms, in terms of the specifications. This also suggests that programming language features to support monitoring, diagnosis and recovery in terms of explicit specifications should be constructed so as to make proving crucial behavioral properties easier. This is also suggestive of research into useful patterns for self adaptive software.

A list of some difficult research issues to address in the area of self adaptive assurance is:

- Investigate ways of ensuring stability.
- Investigate ways of ensuring that the high level goals of the system are met – the set point.
- Investigate how to represent models and monitor models for different classes of systems.
- Investigate how to achieve acceptable performance – good enough, soon enough, and quality of service (QoS) metrics.

A second significant research area concerns the box labeled dynamic explicit choice, in Figure 1. By that we mean: choosing, at runtime, and based on current data, what function, module or routine to execute. In self adaptive software, the choice of function to execute implies minimal commitment in most cases, since the result of the execution will be monitored and recovery initiated if there has been some violation of the protocol. An example of dynamic explicit choice is dynamic, signature driven dispatch, where the choice of functions is based on a combination of the function call, and the types of the arguments in the call. One important research question is what (beyond argument types) could inform the choice of function? Most broadly, we can imagine that for normal choice, we would take into account resources, context and preferences. This suggests that some form of decision theoretic mechanism might be useful.

In general, however, choices will be made in the context of some history, and how much of that history might be utilized in making the current choice is an open question. One specific context for choice with history is that of choice during recovery. Recovery is the state we are in when we have determined that the system made an error, we have diagnosed the problem, and are now ready to choose a function to execute the actual recovery. The sorts of information that one would like to use in making a recovery choice are:

- The violated constraint
- The diagnosis
- Recovery oriented structural data:
  - Exception handling
  - Restarts
  - checkpoints
- The expected value of new choice:
  - Preferences
  - Priors
  - Posteriors

A separate research question concerns whether or not there is some decision theoretic meta level within which to choose among various forms of explicit choice.

In the context of our discussion about embedded applications, we also discussed the hard problems that would need to be addressed, particularly for embedded self adaptive systems. These include verification (which we have already discussed in some depth), transient behavior, and timely reasoning.

Whenever one has a state change in a system with transitions, there is a concern about the behavior of the system while the change of state is occurring. This is the issue of transient behavior. For example, in a hybrid control system, where you have distinct, approximately linear control laws operating within distinct modes, you have problems of the transient behavior during mode switches. These problems occur because the system won't have all the appropriate history that the new control law expects. In effect, you are modeling a system with a history by one that has no history, which is often a formula for loss.

Self adaptive software has a similar problem, because the different system configurations can be modeled as modes, and the operation of the system within a mode is something like the behavior induced by a control law. It is then easy to transition to new mode, without having any way to provide the history that the mode expects. We are certainly interested in research that attempts to address this problem.

The subject of timely reasoning is concerned with the amount of reasoning that might be associates with choosing a new configuration for adaptation. Reasoning about new configurations under time constraints could prove to be a daunting task, so we need techniques for reasoning quickly, and delivering an answer quickly with increasing probability of success as more time is devoted to the choice (anytime algorithms). Fast techniques for deductive and non-deductive reasoning would be useful research topics for this issue.

Finally, we have several additional research topics that received a modest amount of consideration:

- Architectures and patterns for self-adaptive software.
- Domain specific programming languages that incorporate support for perception and adaptation.
- Modification of specifications in response to learning of specification problems.

- Generation of new alternatives or adaptations (perhaps by interpolation) in response to learned inadequacies in current alternatives.
- Change coordination for new code (In what sense is an update consistent?)

5   Patterns for Adaptivity

Within the software engineering community there has been a growing recognition of the value in capturing and describing general solutions to frequently occurring problems (itself a common theme in all engineering disciplines). Often these reflect tried and true practices that have withstood the test of time and that have demonstrated their utility across many application domains. The field of self-adaptive software needs to discover, characterize and catalog the patterns that could form the core of the methodology of software adaptivity. Most of these patterns are presumably still waiting to be discovered, but some of them are already clear. We summarize those patterns that we discussed at the workshop in the following subsections.

5.1   Indirect Invocation

Virtually all self-adaptive software involves a decoupling between the invocation of a service and the method for providing that service. This decoupling allows a runtime decision to be made about how best to provide the requested service. In contrast to the standard model of programming where the caller directly invokes the callee by a direct procedure call, all of these indirect invocation techniques allow for a later binding between the caller and callee. We identified several such techniques that have become common practice for self-adaptivity as well as for other disciplines where late-binding is important:

- **Method Dispatch:** This is a technique that forms the core of virtually all object-oriented programming systems. The invoker specifies a call in terms of a method signature, but the actual choice of method is made by examining the data- type of one or more arguments.
- **Pattern-directed Invocation:** This is a technique that is quite common in rule-based programming. Procedures are advertised by a pattern, including variables that also occur in the procedure body. Forward chaining versions monitor a database of assertions, looking for a set of assertions that match the pattern of a rule; when a new assertion completes a set of assertions matching a rule's pattern, the rule's body is invoked. Backward chaining systems invoke all rules that match an invoking pattern.
- **Publish and Subscribe:** In publish and subscribe systems, some components (the publishers) advertise their ability to produce certain types of data while others (the subscribers) advertise their interests. When a publisher produces some data, all subscribers are invoked with the published data.

– **Data Embedded Handles:** This is the most primitive of indirect invocation techniques and therefore it is often used in the implementation of the others. In this approach, a reference to a procedure is stored in a slot of a data structure by one set of components; various other components then fetch the contents of this slot and invoke the procedure found there. Changing the contents of the slot, results in a change in the invoked procedure.

5.2   Decision Theoretic Invocation

This is, in a sense, the generalization of indirect invocation. Here the requestor invokes an abstract parameterized service for which the system has a variety of methods. The requestor may provide values for some or all of the parameters, or these may be left unbound. Each possible method binds the remaining parameters and also specifies the set of resources it will need to carry out the task. These resources are given a cost. At the same time, the requestor of the service provides a set of preferences (or a utility function) that evaluates how well the method meets the callers needs. The system then invokes that method which maximizes the cost-benefit tradeoff.

5.3   Monitoring, Diagnosis and Recovery

Another common pattern of self-adaptive systems is concerned with the management of breakdowns. Typically this involves associating with each computation an abstract "plan-like" description that breaks the computation up into partially ordered units each of which is described by pre- and post- conditions(see Figure 2). Monitors are wrapped around the code units that correspond to each of these plan steps to check that the conditions are in fact satisfied. If not, a diagnostic runtime service is invoked with a description of the condition that failed to be satisfied. The diagnostic service is responsible for determining which component actually failed while the recovery service is responsible for choosing a restart point and restoring the data structures to a state consistent with the chosen restart point.

5.4   Blackboards for Signal Fusion

Many self-adaptive systems function in an embedded context in which a great deal of what they do is respond to and interpret sensor data. Adaptivity involves bringing to bear a variety of different sources of knowledge, ranging from filtering expertise to knowledge of the semantics of the domain to an awareness of context. Blackboards are an extension of the "publish and subscribe" pattern that allows a variety of different knowledge sources at different levels of abstraction to cooperatively solve the problem (see Figure 3). All knowledge sources place data on a multi-level shared database (the blackboard) where each level represents a level of interpretive abstraction; typically, each entry carries some measure of certainty with it Knowledge sources are triggered when blackboard

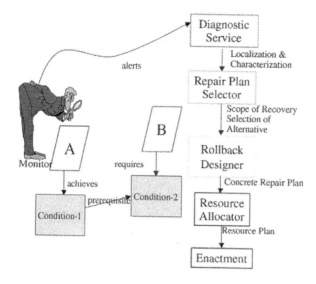

Fig. 2. Monitoring, Diagnosis and Recovery Design Pattern.

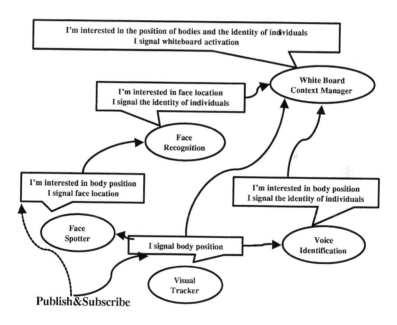

Fig. 3. Blackboards for Signal Fusion and Interpretation.

entries that meet their subscription are created; however, typically knowledge sources that are triggered by entries carrying a higher degree of certainty are scheduled for earlier execution, allowing the interpretation to build out from islands of certainty.

5.5   Other Patterns

Several other patterns were discussed but most of these were either not yet well understood, or they dealt with rather more specific problems. For example, patterns for adaptive access control (for example, dynamic role-based access control) were mentioned, as were a pattern that combined rule-based inference with dynamically constructed Bayesian networks to manage uncertainty. Clearly there is still much work to be done in this area and much of it will depend on gaining further experience in building self-adaptive systems.

References

1. R. Laddaga, P. Robertson, and H. Shrobe. Results of the first international workshop on self-adaptive software. In R. Laddaga P. Robertson and H. Shrobe, editors, *Self-Adaptive Software*, pages 242–247. Springer-Verlag, 2000.
2. P. Robertson, R. Laddaga, and H. Shrobe. *Self-Adaptive Software, Volume 1936 Lecture Notes in Computer Science.* Springer-Verlag, 2000.

Author Index

Lecture Notes in Computer Science

For information about Vols. 1–2506

please contact your bookseller or Springer-Verlag